Working Without A Net

LYNNE
GORDON

Working Without
A Net
My Intimate Memoirs

McClelland and Stewart

McClelland and Stewart Limited
The Canadian Publishers
25 Hollinger Road
Toronto, Ontario
M4B 3G2

Canadian Cataloguing in Publication Data

Gordon, Lynne.
    Working without a net

Includes index.
ISBN 0-7710-3426-1

1. Gordon, Lynne.   2. Consumer education–Canada.
3. Journalists–Canada–Biography.
4. Feminists–Canada–Biography.
    I. Title.

TX335.G67 1986   640.73′092′4   C86-093035-1

Printed and bound in Canada by Gagne Ltd.

CONTENTS

To my Children
Johanna   Evelyn   Frank
Who have contributed so much
to my growth and happiness

Life is a spark between two eternal
darknesses.

—*Unknown*

ACKNOWLEDGEMENTS

In the process of writing these memoirs, I am grateful to a number of men and women. They range from family members through personal friends to professional colleagues. Whether they realized it or not they assisted in the writing. Some of them appear in the pages that follow, but others (for whatever reason) do not. Let me acknowledge them here and now, and thank them for their help. They know who they are. For those people who had a direct influence on my book, I also add my thanks. No author could have had a finer, more understanding publisher than J.G. (Jack) McClelland of McClelland and Stewart. He steadfastly believed in what I had to say and that I could say it well. I am grateful as well to John Robert Colombo, who edited the book with tact and sensitivity.

INTRODUCTION

In my memoirs I describe how I survived three marriages and the death of my fourth partner, how I started three different careers in three different cities (New York; Austin, Texas; Toronto), how I have been through two libel suits that made front-page headlines, and how I raised three children as a single parent. I also tell how I supported one husband for seven years when blacklisting prevented him from working in his field as an entertainer, and when the lawsuit against the blacklisters was finally won, how the marriage of sixteen years and the award money vanished. I later supported a third husband through alcoholism, even though we were separated at the time. Our reconciliation is what brought me to Canada. In a way, I am a woman of the times, shaped by the forces around me. Most of my life, I worked without a net . . . a safety net.

The things that happened to me—not the individual events which, of course, are unique to my life, but the pattern of events, my social history as it were—are still happening to women everywhere. Therefore I have tried with my memoirs to take the reader on a candid journey through my life, to show how a woman living in the twentieth century can come to terms with the need to integrate her personal life with her outside-the-home work life. It's hard to believe that there are today girls and young women who still think that careers are interim experiences between childhood and marriage. They still believe marriage is when "real life" begins.

Every few years I find a burst of new energy and enjoy a host of new experiences. Every so often I have the revelation that I am beginning to take control of my own life. I accept these revelations because few of us grow steadily and in a straight line. We gain an insight, take a step back, regress, and then spurt ahead. That's the process of growth. The conditioning we receive all our lives is so strong that, during vulnerable periods in our lives, insecurities we thought were gone resurface. We may be angry but we usually turn the anger on ourselves. We accept every failure as we would a personal defeat, like a fault or failing.

There were few books to guide women of my generation. Almost every magazine article that was published, every report that was written, and every law that was passed supported "the family." The woman was supposed to do her duty to her man and her marriage, without any suggestion that marriage was a partnership. At the time that the things I describe were happening to me, only a small number of women were living through similar experiences. Now probably the majority of urban women have had, or will have, personal knowledge of a destructive marriage, divorce, widowhood, or single parenting. When I was young, marriage was supposed to be the woman's purpose in life. Being married was so important to my mother that, after she and my father were divorced, she boarded me and my sister out while she searched for a husband and a "father" for us. Children were in the way. The message she presented was that sex was bad but that it could be used to entangle a man who was unquestionably essential to a woman's survival. As was the case with many first-born during the Depression (and even now), I stepped into a mothering role at ten years of age when I was responsible for raising my younger sister, and subconsciously I resented it. Later, because it was a woman's role, I sought fulfillment through being a mother and a "good wife." Mothering was terrific, but the "good wife" part was costly.

My story should interest men as well as women. I hope that males who read about my struggle will understand the struggles of the women they love, whether wives, daughters, mothers, or friends. Obviously, boys and men have to learn that the drawbacks of feminine roles affect them directly. Just as women have been constrained by the nurturing role, so have men been hobbled by the protector's role. Men and women are more varied and complex beings than that. Proof that it is unpleasant to be depended upon is the fact that men have been getting out from under in despicable ways—abandoning families, welching on child support, failing to meet emotional responsibilities toward children . . . .

In 1981, Betty Friedan began to talk about "the second stage" of the women's movement, about accepting all that women had learned and had gained through the first stage, but learning now to ask questions. She suggested that we could eliminate the false polarities so that women could join with men and follow or lead in the new human politics that must emerge beyond reaction. As men begin to question their own lives, their paths will converge with those of questioning women. Walking together they will find a new power and energy for solutions impossible today.

It's not role-reversal that's the answer, with the woman going out to work and the man staying at home. Nor is it the woman moving up the corporate ladder the way the man does. Women want to contribute to a more humane workplace, rather than ape men in their own power games, getting ulcers and heart attacks and missing out on the joy of raising children. They want to be part of a new kind of family when that is desired. The answer is looking forward to partnerships in which women can be nurtured and men can cry. Being autonomous doesn't deny the reality of women's deep personal need for intimacy. Each person, armed with information and the experiences of others, can begin to make more choices.

I felt, in writing my memoirs, that it was vital to be completely honest about my love affairs and marriages. Each relationship represents a period in my life and is described in detail to show why I became involved and, in some cases, why I remained so long with the men in question. For too long, women have been cautious about discussing or revealing what they call their "darker" side. We are used to male authors talking about that all the time, but society has not been as accepting of the disclosures of female authors. When male authors expose their exploits and their *angst,* few readers call that self-serving. A female author runs the risk of having her story so considered. By examining our supposed dark sides we also recognize how hampered we are by the mores of our society, how ashamed we are made to feel and how guilty. It's not just the movie stars and the *femmes fatales* who have steamy romances; the average woman has to come to terms with her own sexuality and her conditioning.

Politically, my life should be a social historian's delight.

Throughout childhood I was buffeted by "isms" from sexism to anti-Semitism; as an adult, I even suffered from anti-communism in the form of witch hunts for the reason that I supported the civil rights movement.

Like countless women around me, I learned the hard way not to depend on a "good husband" for financial security. But financial independence was important from the moment my mother left us. In carving out my various careers, I encountered the employment barriers that prevented women from holding down interesting and well-paid jobs. There was no word like "sexism"; we just lived with the effects. I am of the generation that paid double dues for being a woman and then joined the women's movement to ensure that younger women would not have to do the same.

All through my career I've had to devote unreasonable amounts of energy to be taken seriously—otherwise I would be patronized, taken advantage of financially, given all the work to do and none of the credit. Not only is this unfair, it's demeaning, since it implies you are not as worthy as the next person. For all my independence, my career, my freedom, I was not liberated because earlier I had no understanding of how the world I lived in shaped me, formed what I thought was possible and proper. Liberation for women can come only from understanding, from consciousness-raising, from reading, and from becoming involved. There is no substitute for experience, information, and education.

One of the great and positive gains in my life is the one I could never have predicted in the 1940s or 1950s. This was the emergence of the women's movement. Every woman who has lived through a decade as stifling as the 1950s owes a debt of gratitude to those women who laid the groundwork for understanding the plight of other women through the ages and especially in the contemporary period.

Betty Friedan broke new ground in 1963 with her book *The Feminine Mystique*. Having read it, I began to understand why I had been so angry all my life, and why I had no voice to express my anger and no support system, no network, to approve it. Friedan made this anger acceptable. Since then other feminists have staked out new territory. In fact, the marketplace is bursting with every kind of book that codifies our behavior, catalogues our problems, discusses our "syndromes," and offers possible solutions. We owe much to Gloria Steinem, Germaine Greer, Susan

Brownmiller, Marilyn French, and countless others. If there is one note that is sounded over and over again, it is that women have the right and the need to control their own lives, to have choices. This was the dominant need in my life that sent me crashing against established barriers. One male friend warned me, "Lynne, you will get your head bashed in. You are fighting in a man's world, don't you understand?" I didn't understand then, but nothing would stop me. I understand now, and nothing will stop me.

My memoirs attempt to document that I had to acquire "power-to" as distinct from "power-over." What I wanted but couldn't articulate was "power-to" do what was right for me, to recognize that I, too, had legitimate needs. I used to say I had to get in touch with my center, to respond to a "gut" reaction about decisions. The popular books that are now being published have helped me to understand what I was going through. They have helped me be kinder to myself and have pointed out some possible ways for future dialogue with both men and women. It is important to decide when a personal problem becomes a social issue, so that we no longer feel alone or internalize our fears, but can act in solidarity and through dialogue take collective action. Women have also learned to talk to one another, listen to one another, and trust one another.

This book was written for all who have been through it, who are going through it right now, or who will go through it some day. It's important to know that somebody else has been there and can say, "I'm making it." There is so much more to look forward to.

CHAPTER 1

SUNDAY MOTHER

I was between six and seven years old when my mother finally left my father. For a while it seemed she wanted him back, then she didn't want him back. There would be terrible fights and then violent lovemaking. According to my mother, it was during this period that my sister June was conceived. It was a period of coming and going.

Although I have hazy memories of my earliest childhood, those days are vivid in my mind. Often I remember coming home from school and finding that we were packed and ready to leave again before my father came home from work. So my earliest re-collections are those of loss. I was in a state of panic and tears because I never had a chance to say good-bye to friends or teachers or collect the books that I treasured but had loaned to classmates.

Then there was the time we never went back. My mother said we were going to live with the Ward family in Brooklyn. Mrs. Ward had a big cheerful house next to a farmer's field, and that's where I used to play with her children. I remember the warmth of her kitchen and the smell of baking and the cupcakes she would make for us, and I felt part of a family. Then one day my mother said we had to leave because "Mrs. Ward says you are too hard to handle." I was heartbroken and stricken with guilt. I didn't know what she meant, but I decided it must be because I had been caught with the other kids stealing tomatoes from a farmer's field. I remembered that afternoon. We had all climbed the fence and were picking the tomatoes, biting into them and feeling the juice run down our chins and laughing with pleasure. We couldn't have eaten very many, but suddenly a tall man appeared from nowhere and picked up June. I demanded that he put down my sister, but he carried her screaming to Mrs. Ward. I guess he was the farmer who told her what we had done. It wasn't until years later that I concluded that my mother hadn't come home at night or had come home very late and that probably Mrs. Ward had been tired of the responsibility of caring for us. It was from Mrs. Ward's house that we went to live with Miss Laura Funk.

My mother said that she had found a wonderful housekeeper and we were all going to live together in this apartment in Brooklyn. By this time I was eight years old and my sister was almost five. One cold, wintry afternoon, we took a taxi to Miss Funk's. We arrived at a brownstone that looked to me like a very dreary place. I can see the street to this day . . . rows of similar brownstones lined up like lonely sentinels fronting the sidewalks burdened with snow. We walked up the high stoop as I clung to my mother and held tightly to my sister's hand. We rang a bell and heard a buzzer and walked into a dimly lit hallway and climbed three flights of stairs that smelled of dusty carpet. A door opened and for the first time I saw Miss Funk. To my young eyes, she seemed ancient; she had very short, snow-white hair and a pink, jowled face with watery blue eyes. I wanted to tell my mother we didn't need a housekeeper. I would take care of the house and my sister if she needed to go to work. By this time I was used to taking care of June. But Miss Funk motioned for us to enter.

We came to a large room which Miss Funk used as a bedroom, living room, and dining room. She explained she was a Christian Science practitioner and that there had to be quiet in the house when she prayed. She was an "absent" practitioner who could pray for people even if they weren't present. I watched Miss Funk as she talked, outlining the house rules. While we were listening, my mother excused herself and slipped out of the room . . . to go to the bathroom, I thought.

After a few minutes I began to feel uneasy, and I asked, "Where did my mother go?" Miss Funk said, "She is gone. She'll come back every Sunday to visit you, but you are going to live with me and you are going to learn to obey. I'm taking care of you from now on." I felt sudden terror, a sense of desertion I had never before experienced. I ran screaming down the hallway, burst into the front room, put my head out the window, calling down the street to my mother. I was just in time to see her disappear around the corner. She didn't look back, and to this day I don't know if she heard me or ignored me.

Miss Funk came storming into the room, pulled me away from the window by my hair, smacked me, and said, "You're never to do that again. Your mother said you would be hard to handle, that's why she left you. She needs a life of her own." Then, as a form of relenting, she reminded me, "If you are good, you'll see your mother every Sunday." I kept screaming and kicking, but by this time June started crying. Miss Funk continued, "And, missy, you are never to go into this front room again. It is rented by my gentleman boarder."

Eventually I stopped crying; there was nothing else to do, and we had dinner, one lamb chop, green peas, and mashed potatoes; for desert, half an apple and half a cupcake. I remember it so vividly because over the next four years the menu rarely changed, and the half-apple and half-cupcake or piece of pie were exactly the same. According to Miss Funk, "Children waste food, and it's sinful to give them a whole apple." How I wanted a whole apple! I always felt cheated, as if love were being parcelled out in small portions. While we ate, Miss Funk continued laying down the rules. We were never to bring children upstairs; she needed quiet for her absent treatments; her gentleman boarder must not be disturbed; and we must never bring our father into the house. The last was an order from my mother.

That evening I surreptitiously carved the word "devil" on the leg of her oak table. I don't know if she ever saw it, but it was never mentioned. Then we were sent to bed. I cradled my sister in my arms and fell asleep, with tears running silently down my cheeks. My sister would never know how I felt. I dreamed of my mother and wondered why she had abandoned us.

I thought my mother was so beautiful and wonderful. She was the lovely, mysterious woman whom I worshipped. She had long black hair, big black eyes, and milk-white skin. She and my father, whom she had married when she was nearly fifteen, had been dancing partners and had won many contests. They had run off to be married on a dare, and were so young they had to lie about their ages. When it was all over, she realized what she had done and wanted an annulment, but she said her mother was old-fashioned and rigid and had insisted, "You made your bed, now lie in it." But, in spite of all my mother's talk over the years about being a virgin princess, I always wondered whether the marriage wasn't annulled because she was pregnant. I was born when she was sixteen. They were both such children, but her mother and father put them in business. They gave him a candy store to run. My mother always described my father, whom I hardly remembered, as a playboy. I have a faint image of him as very good-looking, dashing, somewhat like the actor Alan Ladd.

My recollections of my father are blurred and so fragmented I see him in sporadic flashes. There is no continuity. He's like a series of quick snapshots, scattered and unrelated. Whatever memory of him there is lives in my mind alone, because my mother had torn his head off every family photograph. I was supposed to look like him. I had his hazel eyes, his nose, and his blond hair. My sister was cherubic, but had black hair and mischievous black eyes like my mother. I did remember having fun with him, but when I told my mother that, she said, "Oh, yes, but you had fun because he treated you like a toy. You were like a doll he dressed up to show off at baseball games or when he took you out with his friends. But he never supported you. Some day you'll grow up and understand, and you'll never see him again."

Eventually my mother explained to us that part of the reason we were boarded out with Miss Funk was that she was looking for a man to be our father so we could have a home together again. She said we couldn't have a home without a father, and no man would fall in love with her if he knew she had two children. Once a man was in love with her, though, it would be all right for him to know and then we could all live together. It never occurred to me then that she was sending out mixed signals: my father was no good, therefore we didn't have a home; a home wasn't possible without a man, therefore a man was necessary. I accepted her explanations without question. That she hadn't drowned us, that she let us live, that she even came to see us on Sundays was enough, especially since we had caused her and continued to cause her such trouble. I felt I had to appease her continually, tell her how wonderful and beautiful she was, lest she disappear entirely from our lives.

Only as an adult did I realize that my mother, who had inherited money and never in her life had to work, was not a struggling single parent who had to board us to survive. Despite her air of virgin-mother sanctity, it was clear that she kept us apart so she could maintain an active sex life, a sex life that she was constantly denying.

The next morning, the first day of the four years we spent with Miss Funk, I looked outside and saw children playing and sledding down the hill in front of our apartment. I dressed my sister and took her out to play with me. The sled belonged to the six Munro children. Their father was the janitor of the building. Mary Munro was about my age and was the oldest. And all of them, right down the line, had flaming red hair and freckles. My sister and I joined right in and spent the morning sailing down the hill. We had a wonderful time. I suppose at one point they asked me what school I was going to or what church I belonged to. They told me they all went to the Catholic church on the corner. I said we were Jewish and didn't go to church. When they went home for Sunday dinner, they or their parents must have put two and two together. When we came back in the afternoon to play, they turned on us, calling us "dirty Jews," and threw stones. If I knew I was Jewish, it was because I had been told I was Jewish. We had never been religious. My grandmother, whom I adored, had been Orthodox, and there are some memories I have that are very lovely of going to the synagogue with her and during the holidays watching her bake and stuff fish. She died when I was very young.

All I knew was that we had been playing happily with the Munro children all morning and now suddenly they had turned on us and physically attacked us. I didn't know what was happening, but when they started throwing stones, I automatically fought back. I beat up all six of them. I sat on top of Mary Munro, banging her head on the ground and yelling, "Are you gonna stop? Are you gonna stop?" Finally she said yes. I let her up and all my anger left me. I only knew I wanted to be friends and that this girl didn't like me, wouldn't have me for a friend. What was wrong with me? It took me a long time to realize that not everyone had to like me for me to exist. I could become selective only after I had choices.

We didn't play any more that day, but after that there was a sort of street truce. Like most such arrangements, it periodically erupted into open warfare. Sometimes, when the Munro kids couldn't get to me, they attacked my sister. My sister was my charge; she went everywhere with me. I started mothering at a very early age. I hardly remember a childhood of my own. I took care of her. I dressed her. I made sure she behaved. I would play games with her, sometimes sit her on my lap and rock her and sing to her, very close, very protective, and very authoritative. When I heard June crying in the street, I would go charging down those three flights of stairs, coming out like a mad woman, a tiger. I would see her crouched in a corner with others taunting her and hitting her, and I would shout for her to go away, and then I would run into the gang, hitting and punching them in a frenzy. After a while they stopped picking on my sister and knew to leave me alone. But to this day I can't hear a baby cry without my heart quickening and my body tensing.

Later in the week I took on the responsibility of enrolling my sister in kindergarten, and I remember telling the teacher that I would be back to check on her the first day of school and I hoped everything would go well. What did the teacher think of a nine-year-old giving orders? Did they wonder where our mother was, or some grown-up?

Sometimes the Munro children would taunt me about not having a mother or a father. They would say, "You don't have anyone who cares about you. You don't have a mother and a father." They could hardly have hit upon anything that would have wounded me more deeply. I couldn't deal with it, because I couldn't accept how close what they said was to the truth. I'd shriek, "You're a liar, you're a liar! I have a mother and a father and my mother lives with me," and they'd chant, "On, no, she doesn't."

About that time, I started school and at school I found it easy to excel. I was put into what they called a rapid-advance class, two classes in one, and there were rewards for excelling. But there was some concern about how I received A's all the time and didn't seem to be listening because I stared out the window a great deal. They didn't realize school was easy for me. I was bored and lonely, and my only protection from reality was my own fantasy world. Yet later, when I questioned almost everything I was taught, the teacher put a sticker over my mouth to keep me quiet. It was a great humiliation and I had no one to share my thoughts with. My mother had alienated most of her family, and there were long periods when we weren't allowed to see aunts, uncles, or cousins.

I also became active in every extracurricular activity I could join. I was sent around to tell stories to the younger classes. I also discovered the Brooklyn Children's Museum and its library. At that time the museum was housed in an old wooden building, and in my mind it was the home I always yearned for. I'd sit in the big bay window and read every book in the library. I entered every contest, winning prizes for my short stories. I joined all the museum clubs and hungrily learned about archeology, butterflies, and history. I would disappear into the museum till I could forget about the Munro children. Miss Funk, and the aching need to have someone, some child, some adult, be my special friend. Activity was always my way of covering up my loneliness.

Much later I realized that perhaps my loneliness had been partly of my own making. Accepting love and affection from anyone would have been seen as a disloyal act by my mother, and better to have no friends than to risk what my mother might see as a betrayal. So I kept up a pretense that everything was okay; and if it wasn't then in some mysterious way I was at fault.

Besides, there was always Sunday, the magical high point of my week. On Sunday mornings, I would go to church with Miss Funk. The only way I could communicate with her was to let her talk to me about Mary Baker Eddy and Christian Science. If I let her do that, I would be allowed to read the Bible out loud to her, and I liked reading out loud. And when I went to church, I would stand up and testify that I was saved. I loved doing that; it appealed to the ham in me, and on top of that I had lots of approval from the congregation.

Then we would go home and have the same Sunday dinner—one lamb chop, green peas, and mashed potatoes. In a way there was some comfort in the ritual; it was one of the few things that was stable in my life. Right after lunch I would go downstairs and my sister and I would sit patiently on the stoop and wait for our mother. A taxi would pull up and she would step out, wearing a big brown straw hat with a velvet crown, her long black hair circling her shoulders, a beautiful brown velvet jacket, a brown-and-white checked skirt, and her topaz ring. She was surely the most beautiful woman in the world. Sometimes she'd come alone, sometimes with a man, whom we usually called "Uncle." We'd all go to a movie or a play and then have dinner at a Chinese restaurant. That was our Sunday.

Once in a while I'd try to tell my mother some of the things that troubled me. But she always made it clear that she had enough on her mind and she didn't want to hear about my little problems. I remember once I had the mumps and she had to come in the middle of the week to see the doctor. She was furious because it meant she missed her vacation, a cruise. I felt very sorry for her but I was happy to have her for an extra day. Occasionally she took us to her apartment in Tudor City. She was fun to be with. She would bathe us and then wrap us in big towels, pretending we were going to the country, and then pop us into bed. I could smell her perfume as she leaned over to kiss us good night. She seemed very happy and explained that she had a date but she would be back early. I remember her coming home later, standing in the doorway, speaking softly, and kissing this man. Somehow it reminded me of the time when we were living with our father and I had just been bathed and put to bed and my mother was leaving the house. I called out to say good night to my mother and tell her I loved her. I must have awakened my father who was sleeping until his late shift began. He jumped out of bed and demanded to know where she was going and forced her back. It was one of those fights I saw where he seemed to be hitting her and then they made love. I felt so guilty because I had been responsible for waking him, so now I was very quiet and just looked through the slits in my eyes and hoped my sister wouldn't wake up and cause any trouble.

In the four years we lived with Miss Funk, I had no role models, no guidelines on how to behave, no image of a traditional mother. I had no idea that girls were supposed to behave one way and boys another. I know that I began wanting some money of my own, and I noticed that most of the boys on the street made some money delivering newspapers. I wanted a newspaper route like the boys; in fact, I thought it would be even better to have a newsstand of my own. I quickly found out that newsstands were reserved for older people or the disabled, so I decided to sell papers along Eastern Avenue. When I started selling the papers, people were unused to seeing girls hawking papers and I felt them look at me with such pity that I felt defeated from the start. I could never stand anyone feeling sorry for me.

What was curious about the whole thing was that I had no need for money, no conscious use for it. I had food and shelter and plenty of clothes, and it never occurred to me that if I had extra money I could buy my own apples and cupcakes and tell Miss

Funk to go to the devil. I think now it was all part of my constant need to prove that I could handle things; I could manage without parents; I could deal with the kids on the street; I could look after my sister; I could do well in school. The more things I could do, the more I could assure myself that I was independent, confident of my performance, the less I had to acknowledge what I could not do—find the warmth, love, and emotional support I so desperately lacked.

So very early on I established what was to become nearly a life-long pattern: great confidence in what I could do professionally, but confusion and dependency when it came to personal relationships. The conditioning I received early in life confused me about my personal role in life. Even my reading affected my thinking. I used to escape in books, walking to school and back with my eyes glued to their pages, hardly aware of the people around me. No matter how many novels I read, it was the fairy tales that created the myth for my mood. Cinderella was saved from poverty by a prince, Sleeping Beauty was awakened to life by another prince. In fact, no heroine could live without a handsome, rich prince. That seemed to be my life.

At the same time, there was no doubt that I had learned to rely on myself during those four and a half years. I had learned to depend on my own resources. But since I had no emotional support, I was still psychologically dependent. Therefore I acquired my mother's interpretation of life, which was that you had to have a man around to really function. Over the years I had to fight that split in my personality. It was crippling being outwardly independent and inwardly dependent.

It was shortly after we moved to Miss Funk's that my father reappeared. We hadn't seen him for over a year, and it's quite possible he didn't know where to find us because my mother gave him strict orders to stay away from us, on threat of jail if he showed up. This threat she could carry out because he hadn't paid alimony in years. He visited us periodically in his own peculiar way. Saturday was our movie day, a day away from the watchful eyes of Miss Funk. My sister was allowed to come if she promised to be quiet or else she could never come with me again. It was lovely to sit in the comforting darkness and watch a double feature; it was my day of fantasy. Sometimes, perhaps once a month, my father, my prince, would suddenly appear. He would slip into the seat next to me and my heart would jump with joy. I remember him scooping me up in his arms, with June skipping along. He usually took us to Coney Island, our playground—the steeplechase, cotton candy, prizes, presents; and then suddenly it would be over.

There was just time to get back before Miss Funk called the police. There were tearful good-byes, departures, and hugs as we sat in the darkened hallways. He crouched on the staircase as he promised to come back soon. It was more like a good-bye between illicit lovers than a good-bye between a father and his daughters. He told us he loved us and that although he had broken up with my mother it had nothing to do with the way he felt about me and my sister. He understood why we couldn't ask him into the house because he knew Miss Funk had been forbidden to let him in. I never knew how to reach him, and I only assumed he was so secretive because he was afraid my mother would find him. Sometimes months would pass before I would see him again and I remember aching for him, aching to feel his arms around me. One day he stopped coming and I did not see him again until I was twenty-two years old. Nothing seemed to add up; nothing made sense. People just seemed to disappear and come in and out of my life without any explanation.

For four years I watched my mother carry on a desperate search for "that necessary man." Occasionally, when things progressed well with the gentleman concerned, she would bring him along on her Sunday visits. I particularly remember a man named Joe who came with her several times. He seemed young, had sandy hair, and had an easy, rough-and-ready way. He laughed a lot, took us out for our Chinese dinners, and made a little mouse with ears from a pocket handkerchief and made it jump up his arm. I thought Joe was wonderful and asked, "Are you going to marry Joe? Will he be our new father?"

But then Joe disappeared, and another man showed up. He seemed very serious, always wore a hat pulled down over his bushy eyebrows, and rolled a cigar nervously in his mouth. One day he took me to the candy store and I skipped alongside, trying to talk to him, but he just kept rolling his cigar. Later my mother told me that Louis Smith was going to be our father. I asked, "Why didn't you marry Joe instead?" She tried to explain. "Lou is a more solid man. He has his own business. He makes more money and he's more educated than Joe. All Joe has is a garage." I didn't understand. He didn't laugh like Joe. But I was sorry she had to give him up to make sure we had a stable home. Then I realized that my future stepfather had the same first name as my real father—they were both called Lou.

The summer that my mother was to be married she sent my sister to a "family farm" and I was sent to a Girl Scout camp so they would have time to marry, get settled, and have a home for us. I'm not sure why she decided to separate us that summer. My sister was very anxious about leaving me. I looked forward to the camp but found that it was a dreary place, and there were just a few girls who were Jewish. There weren't any fights or name-calling, but somehow every Sunday, while the others went to church, we were placed on kitchen duty, peeling tubs of potatoes. I thought it was punishment for not going to church and was sorely tempted to go, just as I had gone with Miss Funk for so many years. But part way through the summer I got a horrible case of poison ivy that spread all over my bottom. I couldn't sit up but had to lie on my stomach because of the pain. They sent me back to my mother, who at that point was living in a summer cottage in Nyack with my father-to-be. I lay there on my stomach impassive but joyous that she actually had taken me out of camp and into her home. All the neighbors took over my care when my mother and Lou went off to get married. I remember how beautiful and happy my mother looked. Now we were going to be a real family again and live together in a real house. I wasn't going back to Miss Funk, except to pack. The day my sister and I left Miss Funk everything was very polite. I could never really say good-bye to anyone, because I never knew when I would be completely alone. I needed to bank my relationships for the future. I actually kissed her and said good-bye, thanked her for everything, and promised to call her again. And I actually did go back to see her a couple of times to show her how well I was doing.

My stepfather had not known that June and I existed until after he had proposed to my mother; but when he found out about us, he promised her that once they were married he would take us along. My mother, for her part, was adamant that she was not going to raise his son. But once we moved into our first home in East Rockaway, Long Island, Lou insisted that his son was part of the deal. He was not going to leave him with his grandparents. I was really happy when I heard. I had always dreamed of having an older brother, someone who would fight for me, protect me. At that time I was thirteen, June was nine, and Seymour was fourteen. I thought now we were going to have a complete family, a storybook family, two sisters and a brother. But things didn't quite work out that way. What seemed like a doll's house became a house divided.

My stepfather's first marriage had been a disaster, and he was a very angry and suspicious man because his first wife had run around and not taken care of Seymour. He came from a neighborhood where a boy could easily become a gangster or a cop; it didn't matter, it was just the luck of the draw. He had raised Seymour with the help of his mother and father and as a result supported them, too. He had worked hard all his life, believing that a man should stay at one job and work his way up. He had put behind him all his own desires at managing a fighter or a band of musicians or playing baseball, which he loved. Making money was a necessity, and he felt that the job he had as a salesman for a millinery manufacturer would provide him with the steady income he needed as head of a household. He also had it firmly fixed in his head that there were only two kinds of women, good women and bad women, nothing in between. And it was a man's responsibility to keep his wife "good" by keeping her satisfied sexually. To him, and probably to my mother, every woman was quintessentially a sexual creature; every kind of relationship involving a man was sexually charged. I was raised to believe that if a man satisfied his wife, she had a good husband, a real man. If he did that and provided a good home, what more could a woman want? For years, I had no way of deciding what other things were important to a marriage.

My stepfather also had very definite ideas about what made a lady . . . and a man. I was never to use dirty words, and there would be no fooling around with boys. I once said, "I'm so angry, I could spit," and he immediately lashed out at my language. I found out that it was all right to neck, but there were definite boundaries. Hands off breasts, although kissing was fine. A boy standing up and rubbing against me was fine; that was safe. I was terrified at having any boy point me out on the street and say that he had "touched" me or slept with me. I knew very little about the process of having babies; my mother insisted she had told me but I could never recall this occurring.

It was in such an atmosphere that I entered puberty. Lou had great difficulty in dealing with me. He didn't talk to me much, finding it difficult to show any affection. He seemed to think that if he showed me any attention he would be taking it away from his son. Love was something you could subtract. He never thought of it as multiplying. Most of our conversations were short and guarded, and sometimes there were long weeks of silence. I was too close in age to Seymour. But that didn't prevent him from being warm and loving to my sister, who was only nine and still a tomboy. My stepfather knew how to play with boys. In fact, he was so anxious for Seymour to be a man that he would spend long hours in our basement making him put on boxing gloves and teaching him how to defend himself. He didn't mind teaching June about boxing; she had not reached that "womanly" age.

My stepfather was terribly jealous of my mother because she was so beautiful and he couldn't believe that she loved him for his own sake. He still felt conned because she had not mentioned her children in the beginning. He somehow suspected she married him for his position. He was always afraid that as soon as he turned his back she would be off with another man. All the men he knew had mistresses or affairs and his own first wife had men in the house in front of his own son. That was human nature according to my stepfather. He knew about men. So he phoned my mother constantly, watched her, and questioned her every move until she found it easier to stay home, and over the years she began to act like an invalid.

I started to disengage myself from family life. I hated the tension at home, but I didn't dare discuss my problems with anyone. That would be being disloyal. My mother had drilled into me the need for secrecy. "You never talk about your family. You could hurt your father's reputation, and it would affect the way his business colleagues thought about him at work. That could affect his job." In fact, we were warned never to talk about him as our stepfather. People didn't think much of divorced women, and it was none of their business. When I mentioned my own father to my mother and wondered where he was, she scolded me. "You have a father now. If you talk about your first father, you'll hurt Lou . . . and after all, he's supporting you. Let me tell you, if you ever make the mistake of seeing your first father, he'll embarrass you and make a scene. He has no right to see you. He hasn't sent money in years." I didn't tell her that I wasn't concerned about the money but that I missed him terribly.

In the meantime, I joined every club at school. I never came home. By this time we had moved to a larger house in Malverne. I had already been to about six elementary schools. This was a junior high school. I loved the sports. I became a three-letter woman, winning letters for baseball, basketball, and field hockey. I swam, rode horseback, and became president of the drama club. Once in a while, when I brought friends home, I was embarrassed. My stepfather had been reluctant to buy all new furniture for this rented house, since he had no idea how long we would stay. As a result, our living room was still empty of chairs and tables. When it was my turn to have a party, I pretended that all the furniture had been moved out so we could dance.

Then we moved to Brooklyn and our first apartment was in a new building on Kings Highway, only two blocks from a very fine high school, James Madison High. The biggest problem was that there wasn't a separate bedroom for Seymour. My sister and I shared a room, and Seymour slept in the foyer, not a very good arrangement for a growing boy. It was at James Madison High that I started having friends and going out regularly on dates. I was just past fifteen and that's when I got my nickname, Lynne. My name at birth was Evelyn, but the kids shortened it to Lynne. I added the second *n* and the *e* to make it look more feminine. Lynne was a new name; not many children were christened Lynne at that time.

At James Madison I met the Big Six, a group of boys who went around together and had steady girlfriends. Up until this time my dates were short-term, but the Big Six was a serious group of young men who were loyal to each other. I was able to break into the group because one of them had just stopped seeing his "steady." Nat played the violin, was very loving and sensitive, and gave me his athletic letter to wear, which made me his special girlfriend. I got along with the other five boys and their dates and there was a feeling of belonging that I never had before. We went out every Saturday with the boys, but on Fridays the girls wanted to be alone. We were secretive about whose house we were meeting at, but the boys spent hours tracking us down. These girls were my first confidantes. We had endless discussions about what we did with our dates. Did you kiss, did you neck, did you pet, did you let them touch below? We were very concerned about not being called "fast." I think I went steady with Nat for about a year. My parents approved; it was better than running around with a whole bunch of different boys.

But one day, Nat did the unpardonable. We had gone to the roof of my apartment building to look at the stars and hug each other, when I felt his hand slyly slip around my waist and edge up to my breasts. I hardly knew what he was doing, his touch was so light, except that his face had turned beet-red. I think his embarrassment bothered me more than having him touch me because he seemed so uncomfortable and unsure of himself. I decided to break up with him on the spot. I think if he had steamed ahead, and taken over the situation, I might have even enjoyed it. I guess I needed to be "swept away." Had he taken over, I wouldn't have been in the position of having to make the decision. Many years later I read about women who needed to be swept away so they could keep their "good girl" images. If women were swept away, they had no responsibility for the consequences. How much trouble that got me into over the years; although I thought I was in charge I was allowing men to make decisions for me.

I was never without a "steady" for long. My next boyfriend was completely different from Nat. Jerry was more worldly. He had long sideburns and was from a different area of Brooklyn. He came from Manhattan Beach, where working-class people lived. But Jerry was sure of himself and his masculinity and wasn't impressed with our middle-class status. There was a strong physical attraction between us, and Jerry would often take me to the beach to swim. I liked his parents and would change at his house. He necked with me a lot and there was a great deal of standing outside my door and touching and rubbing up against me. I discovered that I loved his attention and I was passionately in love with Jerry.

One day I was swimming with him at the beach when we decided to go to his apartment and get a drink of juice. I went in my bathing suit, and didn't think anything about it. As it happened his parents weren't in. Jerry and I had our drinks, hugged a little, kissed a lot, and went back to the beach. It never entered either of our minds to go any further just because we were alone. It was when I went home and told my mother about my day that I discovered I had done something wrong. According to her, "Nice girls don't go into a man's house in bathing suits with hardly anything on. Only whores act that way." She slapped me and I was sent to my room. I knew I had not done anything wrong, but I was confused about my mother's anger and I hardly knew what a whore was. But I found it difficult to deal with my mother's disapproval. I never knew what my mother would get angry at, and certainly didn't understand that my mother had a lot of unresolved anger against men. My confusion must have entered into my relationship with Jerry. It wasn't long before we broke up. I cried a lot about him, and began to be aware of what we called "torch songs" in those days. The song "As Time Goes By" became one of my favorites.

By the time I was past sixteen, my mother and Lou decided to move to Manhattan. I remember one of my teachers saying, "You're such a sweet girl, I'm afraid you'll be hurt in New York. They have such different values. The girls are so fast and they all wear silver-fox jackets. You're going to have such a hard time." Rather than discouraging me, the picture she painted of New York City sounded so glamorous, so interesting. Our first place was a large apartment on West End Avenue. It was a big limestone building with elaborate stone carvings of lions in the front, which spoke of an earlier elegance. It was the area taken over by middle-class Jewish families.

I was enrolled in Julia Richman High School. It was an all-girls school, which worried me at first. Since there were no boys in the school, that's all the girls talked about, and any male teacher was in danger of his life as adoring students surrounded him. I found the scholastic requirements quite high. Although there were over a thousand students in each grade, divided into many classes, I immediately carved out my own spot. I became literary editor of the magazine *Bluebird* and the editor of *Spotlight,* the news magazine. I was put in a Kings Oak Class, a special English class for writers headed by the most wonderful of all teachers, Mrs. Jones. She became my first mentor, although at that time I didn't know such a person existed. I joined a young people's group at the local temple. I remember, I was asked by the executive if I knew that this group was for Jewish people. They had assumed, since my name was Smith, that I wasn't Jewish. I explained that my name was Smith, but it had probably been given to my grandfather when he came over from Russia and the immigration officers changed names to ones more easily pronounced. They laughed and accepted me on the spot. I felt truly liked by the group and dated many of the young men. We went dancing, did the Big Apple and the Suzy Q. It was the period of the Big Bands. We danced to the music of Tommy and Jimmy Dorsey, Gene Krupa, Sammy Kaye, Woody Herman, Benny Goodman, Cab Calloway in his famous "ice-cream suit," and, of course, Artie Shaw. We swayed back and forth and "dipped" on the dance floors of the large ballrooms of the Taft Hotel, the Waldorf-Astoria, the Astor Hotel, and the Glen Island Casino. It was at the famous Paramount movie theater that I once joined a younger group of women and sat transfixed as the skinny, blue-eyed Frank Sinatra took the stage over, his large Adam's apple bobbing up and down as he sang so sensuously. At the Club International, on another occasion, the orchestra was conducted by Larry Clinton and Bea Wain sang "When the Deep Purple Falls." It was a very romantic time, the scene for romance, love, and marriage.

CHAPTER 2

MY MAN AND I

The next few years were ecstatically happy ones for me. I was enjoying school, enjoying all the activities, hardly home except for dinner. And dinner was the one high point in my memory. Strange that in our family that was the one time all anger and hostility were forgotten. We gathered together to tell the news of the day, and my parents enjoyed all my tales of success, my dates, my involvement in politics. And my mother was a fabulous cook. The dinners were gourmet treats, although she never shared her secrets with us. I never learned to cook and she never tried to teach me. I felt pampered at the time and easily fell into feeling like a Jewish American Princess. It was more exciting to be thought of as completely spoiled instead of the unhappy child I had been. So again, no one, not even I, was in touch with some of the things going on at home that still disturbed me. To the world I was living in a perfect family. By this time, we had moved to a larger apartment, a little farther downtown in a more fashionable neighborhood on West End Avenue, 670 West End. I always had the ability to create and believe in my own dreams—that something good and exciting was going to happen. About this time, I graduated from Julia Richman with high honors, the top third of the class of one thousand.

No one came to my graduation. By this time my mother was having small bouts of illness that incapacitated her. I won a Regent's Scholarship to Cornell, the university I had dreamed about for so many years. I rushed home to tell my parents. But the scholarship was for tuition only; it did not pay for room or board or, of course, clothes or transportation. I was surprised at the reaction of my stepfather; he did not seem pleased at all. He coldly stated, "I'm not going to lay out money for you to go to college. Women don't need a degree to get married. That's what you should be thinking about now." My stepbrother had dropped out of school and my stepfather added, "If I were going to lay out any money for university, it would be for your brother. A man needs an education to get ahead. It can help make him a better breadwinner." My mother tried to calm me by her contribution, "Well, darling, it's not just room and board. You would need the proper clothes to keep up. You would be so embarrassed if you didn't have all the pretty things the other women have."

I didn't go to Cornell. I went to work full-time and enrolled at Columbia University as a night student, with every intention to get a degree. I chose Columbia because it was smack in the middle of New York but still had a campus. It had blocks of grass, tree-lined walks, beautiful old buildings, a magnificent library, and an excellent faculty. I became impatient with all the basic courses I had to take. I was hungry to learn everything fast. I took classes in acting as well as writing workshops, and because a boyfriend suggested advertising (I might find it easier to make a living), I took an advertising course. I was back in my pattern of doing everything at once. The more activity, the less pain. The more activity, the more I learned. The more freedom, the more options open to me in life. I was even involved in politics. I supported the Loyalists in Spain and raised money for the Abraham Lincoln Brigade. I think my early interest in politics came naturally. I was able to deal more directly with other people's problems than with my own. My family encouraged political activity and was sensitive to any issue involving discrimination or loss of freedom.

At eighteen-and-a-half, I was feeling on top of the world. I wore my hair to my shoulders and felt I looked like Katharine Hepburn, who was my idol. Not pretty, but interesting. The drama group at the temple was just casting for a new play and a new friend, Buddy, said there was a good part for me. It turned out that it was a two-character play and he had complete control over the casting . . . and he chose me. I found out that Buddy was the favorite of all the women, each dreaming of getting him for a steady and then a husband. I had so much on my plate that marriage was the furthest thing from my mind, but I liked the attention. I was always getting the affection I needed from the men in my life at that time.

Buddy's full name was Bernard W. Grabois, and he was president of the drama group and was considered a prime catch, for he was as handsome as a movie star, about six feet tall, brown curly hair, long lashes, and big, warm brown eyes. He had just graduated from City College, *cum laude,* and was still trying to find himself. That meant he shifted from one sales job to another, which he hated. He did not have to worry about money. His family was quite comfortable. His father hoped Buddy would eventually join him in the dress-manufacturing business, but Buddy hated the commercial world.

I was in the process of making decisions about a future. Did I want to be an actress, a journalist, a newspaper reporter, or an advertising executive? All these choices were open to me. The world was before me. When I left high school, Mrs. Jones, my English teacher, advised me, "When you are ready to look for work, in whatever you choose to do, send out a hundred résumés. You'll be bound to get one back, and you will have a job. I never forgot that advice because translated it means if you persist the odds are with you. So here I was planning my future, which did not include marriage, and Buddy wanted nothing more than to be alone with me. He had a wonderful collection of classical records and he taught me how to listen, to enjoy them as he did. We loved dancing together; we went out to nightclubs and innocently ordered milk instead of liquor. We both hated drinking and were proud that we didn't feel we had to order any drinks to prove we were grown up. We went to plays, to films, and he wrote poems to me regularly and sent flowers on any pretext. New York before the war was unbelievably exciting. I remember my nineteenth birthday. Buddy planned the evening carefully: a gardenia corsage, tickets to *Philadelphia Story* with Katharine Hepburn, and then to the famous Rainbow Room atop Rockefeller Center for dining and dancing. It was a beautiful evening and was just the way it was in movies . . . a Ginger Rogers and Fred Astaire movie. As we danced, I snuggled into his shoulder. I can still tell any man's height depending on how much I can see over his shoulder. Buddy was tall enough that I could just peer over, but mostly I rested my head on his broad shoulder. We were forever holding hands and kissing, proving to the world we were in love.

We started going steady; I was his girl. We talked about getting engaged some day. First he gave me his fraternity pin; it was all so romantic and fit exactly what I had been brought up to believe was what courting should be. I was sure I loved him. I *assumed* I must love him, since he loved me. And he made it very clear that he adored me; he was attentive, he spoiled me. I enjoyed all the "permitted" sex we had together . . . lots of petting, just about everything but intercourse. It is interesting that the intimacy we had in the form of hugging and foreplay is missing today because a more permissive society permits a complete physical relationship but one lacking in expectation and emotional intimacy. Buddy was very definite that we were not going to sleep together until we got married. We dated steadily for the next two years, and after a while everyone, his parents, my parents, started pressuring us. Since we had been dating for so long, it was time for the engagement ring and then the wedding date should be set.

I don't think I ever thought of marriage. I don't think I even wanted to get married. It was all such a game to me, and we were having such a good time playing. I was going to school at night and loving it. I was acting in off-Broadway plays, I was working part-time. What did that have to do with marriage? I don't think Buddy and I ever discussed how we would live, whether I would continue working, whether we planned to have children. He had no steady job. His mother adored him and would give him anything. I was surprised she liked me so much because I had taken her "escort" away from her. They used to go out together since his father was always so busy with the business. But we got along very well and she particularly felt I should marry Buddy because the war was coming. Buddy could be drafted and get killed just because I hadn't married him. Unmarried men were being called up first and given more dangerous duties. If I was going to marry him, what was I waiting for? My parents thought the longer we dated, the more possibility I might get into "trouble."

So the date was set. How were we going to survive? Well, until Buddy got a job or found out what he wanted to do, our parents would help out. Where would we live? Our parents would find us an apartment. What would we do in our life together? No one thought to ask, least of all ourselves. Marriage was the ultimate goal for all young girls, and there were thousands of kids like us going through the same ritual, children marrying children precisely in order to ward off some dangerous, unimaginable future.

I used up a lot of energy, in the months before our marriage, trying to override my fear and anxiety. I found myself crying a lot and I had no idea why. I came down with a temperature and flu two weeks before the wedding and was almost sure it would have to be called off . . . and I felt some relief at the thought. I got well. Finally I decided to go to a psychiatrist. It was not an easy decision; it was thought that only "crazy people" visited psychiatrists. I walked into the doctor's office and said defensively, "This is the most stupid thing I have ever done. I don't know why I'm here. You shouldn't waste your time with me. I'm sure there are people who need you more than I do. There is absolutely nothing wrong in my life." Then I burst into tears.

He said, mocking me, "Oh, you're very happy; you're fine, and you don't need me. Why are you crying?" That was the beginning of my pouring out all my anger at my mother and stepfather . . . all the anger I didn't know how to handle. I had controlled most of my anger over the years because I found out after each outburst that my mother would withdraw her love and not speak to me for weeks or until I abjectly apologized. So that when I was angry, the anger seemed unreasonable and out of control. I had a nasty temper. It was during those long sessions that I thought my world was going to collapse. If I discovered I really hated my mother, whom would I turn to for love . . . Buddy?

Planning the wedding was a horror. My mother was in charge and there were a few things that bothered her, like my future mother-in-law, Anne. She didn't like her and spent a great deal of time making fun of the way she dressed, how she tried to look so young, her manner. She was also annoyed at the number of people Anne and her husband were asking to the wedding. For another thing, I wanted a white gown and I wanted to be married in the temple and I thought of stained-glass windows and organ music. My mother said that was too expensive. My dream of a white wedding turned into a street-length pink dress made by the local seamstress and a pink bonnet tied with a pink veil. I hated it but I was completely under my mother's thumb, afraid of the scenes and exhausted from the plans.

Throughout all this, Buddy would come up to visit me, soothe me, and remain unbelievably, frustratingly calm. Then the day arrived and the wedding was held at a lovely hotel on Central Park West, the St. Moritz. We were to be married in one of the suites and then have dinner on the roof and dance to a live orchestra. As my stepfather was taking me there in a taxi, I must have been very pale and looked quite frightened because he turned to me and with rare sensitivity and insight said, "Let's turn back. You don't have to get married. I'll call it off." I looked startled and panicked and cried, "That's ridiculous! How can you say that? Everybody's waiting. I love him. I'm probably just frightened." I thought it was natural for a young woman to be frightened on her wedding day, especially for a virgin. It certainly was a time of confusion for me. I was completely happy planning a career, enjoying going steady. I so wanted my mother's approval that I was even getting married for her. Yet even then I couldn't get complete approval; I wasn't marrying the man they would have chosen. They thought Buddy wasn't "man enough" to handle me, not being sports-minded and aggressive.

Just before the ceremony, while I was in the dressing room with my mother, she started complaining about Anne again and her choice of guests. Suddenly I snapped, and instead of weakly accepting her mood, I said, "My God, this is my day, my wedding day. Why are you harassing me like this? Why are you acting so selfish? Just once can't you give me your attention? There is nothing wrong with Buddy's mother. She's been very good to me." As the words left my mouth I knew I had gone too far. Questioning my mother never resulted in any kind of dialogue, just rejection. In this case, she slapped me hard across my face.

I stood there with all sorts of thoughts racing through my mind. I felt humiliated; I was angry. I thought of her as a disagreeable woman and I wanted desperately to be free of her. My stepfather looked on somewhat abashed. Although he never interfered, he once told me when I asked him to help, "Lynne, there's nothing I can do. The only thing I know is that when you aggravate her, she won't sleep with me for days. So do me a favor, try to ignore her when she gets angry." Now that I was about to be married, going away on a honeymoon seemed like a pretty good idea. I wouldn't have to deal with her any more; I would have a husband.

The wedding march was playing. I wiped my tears, stood up straight, and concentrated on the stage that was set for me. Even in the pink dress I looked beautiful and radiant. I had a bouquet of cascading tiny brown and pink orchids . . . so tender, so innocent looking. I don't remember much of the wedding service. I tried to listen to the rabbi, standing in his robes under a bower of green leaves. I tried to feel all the special emotions as I was given to this man in holy wedlock.

Afterward, we all went upstairs to the roof garden to have dinner. Buddy asked me for the first dance and I tried to recreate all the wonderful scenes I had seen in movies and read in books about marrying your prince. I expected to feel differently, but we had been going steady for so long, been intimate for so many years, I could not figure out what extra dimension this legal paper would add to our relationship, except that now we could actually have intercourse. Was that the thing that made marriage so special? I already felt very comfortable with Buddy. Soon after, Buddy suggested we go to our hotel room, since we were planning to take an early train the next morning to go on our honeymoon. As usual, he was most happy when we were completely alone. He was never comfortable with groups of people, even our parents.

As we were getting ready to leave, the bandleader played one last song for us and softly teased, "Don't leave yet . . . stay a while longer. You have a whole night ahead of you . . . in fact forever." I thought for a fleeting moment what it would be like to be with the bandleader. Was he really teasing me or was he flirting with me? I had not looked at another man since I had been going with Buddy. Other men didn't exist. But this was it.

Buddy and I didn't change our routine even that evening. We loved playing pinball machines and we found one in a little store nearby. We played a little game of delay. Then we bought the *New York Times,* as if we were going to read in bed. There was no hurry about being together. Maybe we would wait until we were away. As soon as we went to the room, I put on my honeymoon negligee of soft ivory and Alençon lace. I brushed my long auburn hair, washed my face, brushed my teeth, and quietly slipped in beside Buddy.

I started to pick up the *New York Times* when Buddy enfolded me in his arms. I thought, "My God, I won't be a virgin any more. There'll be blood and pain. But also fireworks, ecstasy." In the lovemaking that Buddy and I had done for years, I'd had lots of orgasms, lots of pleasure, but not a lot of excitement. It was so predictable. I was sure the forbidden act would provide that extra excitement. But I knew Buddy's lovemaking by heart. He was so considerate and so anxious to please me that every move was calculated to give me pleasure; I could almost chart the steps. First he would kiss me lovingly, carefully searching out my mouth with his tongue; then he would hold me tightly and start to stroke my breasts gently, reaching down carefully to kiss them; then, just as slowly, his hands would slide down my body and begin to probe my vagina. I loved his fingers; they explored me so thoroughly, knew every area to touch so that I was soon throbbing with pleasure. He never failed; he was never carried away until he had satisfied me and it wasn't difficult for him to reach a climax when I played with him after mine. Now he was doing all the same things, step one, two, and three . . . but he was not waiting for me to play with his penis, he was mounting me, and I waited, holding my breath for the pain. There was no blood, no pain . . . and no fireworks. All the playing with me beforehand had evidently taken care of my virginity. I was already satisfied and the intercourse was just another step . . . not even necessary, I thought.

As a wedding present we had been given a two-week honeymoon at Green Mansions, one of the more elegant resorts in the White Mountains of Vermont. It was supposed to appeal to young intellectuals. The entertainment consisted of classical music and off-Broadway plays instead of the usual stand-up comics. Buddy's mother took us to the train so she would have some extra time with us, time that my mother found out about and never forgave me for. "If she could come to the train after you were married and on your own, couldn't you call me from the hotel?" I would have to deal with her anger when I came back from the honeymoon, because it took weeks before she forgave me. We started playing house in our honeymoon cottage and enjoyed comments from table-mates who thought we glowed and must be a honeymoon couple. I wanted to glow. I wanted us to be special. I did little wifely things like wash his socks. I had no idea why I did or even why he allowed me to. We played tennis, took long walks, kissed under the moonlight, went to all the hotel shows, and all the time I sat back and watched myself as if I were playing a role on stage . . . and I wasn't sure I knew the lines for the next act.

My idea of our home was to have pink sheets tied up with silk ribbon and pretty china in the cupboard and a tea service on the sideboard. We had none of that. Our married life began in a little furnished apartment on West 84th Street that our parents found for us, an apartment between both their homes. It cost sixty-five dollars a month, and the bedroom was so small that the bed filled it and one of us would have to climb in first before the other could get in. If it was me, it meant climbing over Buddy every time I had to go to the bathroom. A cleaning woman took care of all the apartments and provided linen service, which was a good thing because I had no pink sheets; in fact, since everything was furnished, I had none at all. I also wasn't very good at cooking, but we solved that problem by going to Buddy's parents two nights a week and to mine another two nights. My mother-in-law had her housekeeper do our washing and ironing. We were still playing at being married.

I was still wearing ankle socks (bobby socks in those days) and dressed like a university student in my tailored suits. As a proper married woman, I wasn't working. I was supposed to keep house for my man. I wanted to find a job, but it wasn't encouraged. Since I didn't cook, clean, or do the laundry, I had some trouble filling my days until Buddy would get home from work. I often wondered about the women who proudly talked about ironing fourteen shirts a week, "My husband never goes without a clean shirt." What happened when washing machines and drip-dry became common? According to my sister June, those women began ironing towels and underwear. It was important to feel needed. Sometimes I would meet Buddy's mother for lunch at Schrafft's, the special tea room where young women and mothers-in-law met regularly. It was more like a social club in those days. I even remember ordering lobster roll, a specialty of the house. On the nights that we were home, I would think about what to fix Buddy for dinner. After all, there were three nights that were my responsibility.

Usually he was quite happy with cold cuts and canned corn or a simple roast chicken. I was actually very good at making meat loaf, steaks, almost any grilled food. One of my specialties was a London broil that included a lamb chop, a piece of liver, broiled mushrooms, and a broiled tomato. I would worry what Buddy was going to do with his life, and how I could support him emotionally. He still didn't know what he wanted to do with his life, but in the meantime, his sales job gave us enough to cover the rent and a little extra.

Buddy would come home from his sales job every evening around five-thirty, and he would whistle as he came down the street. I would look out the window and see my husband come home, run down the three flights of stairs into his arms, and welcome him home. Isn't that what wives did? I seemed to be buying the whole package. We didn't talk much about problems. We seemed content to be the perfect couple. I had a husband, he adored me, and according to my stepfather's description of a good husband, he filled the bill. He never failed to "take care of me." If I ever seemed out of sorts or discontented, my stepfather would immediately zero in and ask, "What's the problem? You and Buddy not sleeping together? Isn't he taking care of you?" With those guidelines, I had no idea of what else I should expect from a husband, except, as my stepfather added, "He must make a living." It was a fantasy world, but I believed in it faithfully, and so did countless wives like me.

So it was a shock when I met Marika, a young wife like me but one who had precious little to do with fantasies. Marika lived in our building. She and her husband Jack lived one floor below, in an apartment the same as ours, and we shared the same cleaning woman. The cleaning woman thought Marika had just come over from Germany and could speak very little English. She suggested that I make friends with Marika and teach her how to cook! I was glad at the chance of finding a friend in the building. I went down and knocked on her door one evening and she opened the door a little cautiously. I explained why I was there and she laughed a deep throaty laugh, and said, with hardly a trace of an accent, "I speak perfect English, but I don't know how to cook." I couldn't take my eyes off her; she looked like Marlene Dietrich in spite of a rather large nose, and she slithered rather than walked across a room. Her face was framed with black curly hair fluffed up in the style of the forties. A man was sitting motionless in front of a window, with a glass of liquid in his hands. He turned slightly when she introduced us. "This is my husband, Jack. Don't mind him, he's drunk. He's always drunk." I was shocked at the way she spoke to him and the way she talked about him, but he didn't seem to mind, or even hear her. He stared and went back to drinking. He seemed quite young and handsome. They both seemed to be like me, in their twenties, but Marika was far from a wide-eyed young bride.

Over the next few days we met regularly in the afternoon, when she got off her shift as a waitress at Longchamps, a meeting place for businessmen and radio executives, depending on which area you worked. Longchamps was a chain and each one claimed its own clientele. She told me her story. "I came from Munich, but I managed to escape before Hitler came to power because my parents sent me on vacation out of the country. When I tried to come back, they begged me to go on to America. But no pleading, no begging on my part would make them leave. They somehow thought it would pass over. But they were both killed in the camps."

That was the last time she ever talked about her parents, but I had the idea she came from a middle-class family and had enjoyed a normal life of going to the theater and concerts . . . but it was all gone now. She had no money and she was feeling very bitter about the Germans. "I made my way to Africa where I knew a man who had been a friend of the family. He helped me with money and I began sleeping with him. In fact, I slept with a lot of men until I finally had enough money to get to New York City." She made a vow that, once here, she would never speak with an accent. "I worked night and day to lose my accent. I never wanted anyone to know I was German." It was hard to tell she had an accent but she had a very hard way of talking. She used four-letter words liberally as she described her love affairs, her life in New York, and her unhappy marriage with Jack. "Nothing is going to stop me from getting what I want, and I want it all. I've been cheated out of a home, parents, my life. America is good."

She would take *Cue Magazine,* which listed all the best restaurants and nightclubs, and would methodically mark off every place that she wanted to visit. She wanted money, she wanted pleasure, she wanted the good things, and in the main she saw men as a way to get them. Her waitress job supplied her with some money, but more than that, it gave her a chance to meet wealthy and powerful men, and she had the background to deal with them.

I was fascinated by her. I had never heard the kind of language she used or met anyone who looked at life quite the way she did. She talked openly about her love affairs and I asked her, "What is it like to sleep with so many men? Were they all different?" She said, "Are you pulling my leg? Either you are joking or you are the most naive woman I have ever met." She was finally convinced that I was as naive as I sounded. I told her, "I have never slept with any man but Buddy. I'd been going steady with him for three years and he would never have intercourse with me." She snorted at that but I hastened to add, "We did make love . . . everything but that . . . and he's good to me, so I don't know why I would sleep with anyone else."

She began to educate me about the different qualities of men, the different ways they made love, the ways they showed passion. She liked shocking me and she began to take over my days. I admired her; she had survived her parents' murder and she seemed to know what she wanted. She was tough, sometimes very crude, but I thought she was strong. In later years I realized she was a bully, but I've always had a tendency to confuse these qualities with strength. It took years before I realized that my mother was a bully and manipulative and that I was always being drawn to men who acted the same way.

I had never confided in a woman before. I had been conditioned for so long not to say anything about my family life and also to be careful about trusting a woman. "Never," warned my stepfather, "get too close to another woman, especially a single one. It's dangerous when you have a handsome husband. Make sure you stay close to your man so he doesn't have a chance to run around." This never seemed a problem with Buddy. He hardly left my side and when he wasn't with me I found his little love notes all day long; they were in the mailbox, the teapot, under my pillow, and in between he called regularly or sent flowers.

Marika was so willing to talk about herself, I wanted to confide in her, but it was difficult. I still couldn't tell her that I had a stepfather. I couldn't talk about my mother or allow anyone else to criticize her. I was just beginning to find out about all the hostility I felt during my sessions with my psychiatrist. I certainly couldn't talk about my natural father. Even injected with pentathol, the truth serum, I couldn't remember my life with him except for isolated incidents. I talked glowingly about my love affair with Buddy, only admitting that I had decided to have lovemaking with him only Mondays, Wednesdays, and Fridays. It never occurred to me to analyze what I was saying. It just seemed logical and grown-up to limit the nights to what made me comfortable and take off the pressure of having to make love every night.

Marika laughed and said, "If you really enjoyed sex, you wouldn't be limiting it." I refused to discuss it, so there were always subjects off-limits. For years we never tried to pierce those barriers. She told me about the men in Africa. From her point of view, men were to be used. They were her way of getting needed money. I don't think she ever thought of herself as a prostitute, a call girl. It just seemed that everything she accomplished was through a man. I thought of her as a woman who acted like some men, for whom sex was to be used, and life was something one could manipulate.

It was a curious friendship. Some things we were completely open about, and other subjects we never touched. So in many ways we remained incomprehensible to each other. I thought of her as a mysterious, adventurous woman with no origin, no source. I'm sure she thought I was spoiled, pampered, and without troubles. She was buying the American dream. She believed wholeheartedly in the free enterprise system, hated unions, believed everything was up for grabs and only the strongest survived. She used to make fun of my concern for the poor and the underprivileged. She thought I was soft.

Gradually my life split in two. I had my little apartment, my adoring husband, and my volunteer work. We were experiencing brown-outs in New York at that time and I spent time in an office under tight security plotting the flight paths of airplanes, the point being to detect any enemy planes that might slip through the defenses. Buddy's mother was driving an ambulance for the Red Cross, and his father was standing guard on building tops as an air warden. But the war did not come close to our shores, and I could leave that world, with a sense of daring, and go into Marika's. I could listen to her deride Buddy's blandness, hear tales of her sexual adventures, and listen meekly as she mocked me as soft and naive, unwilling to make legitimate demands on life. I didn't acknowledge, even to myself, that I had the faintest idea of what she was talking about; but I must have been beginning to wonder if my "perfect marriage" was what life was all about. It was the first time I had ever looked at Buddy or our relationship critically. I didn't dare think anything could be wrong. I had sworn when I married it would be forever, and if I had children I would never be a Sunday mother. I protected my relationship with Buddy as fiercely as I protected my feelings about my mother. No one was allowed to criticize anyone I loved, and some of my biggest arguments with Marika were when she broke these rules. She would make comments about my mother's possessiveness and I would refuse to listen, accusing her of being jealous. I know that Buddy seemed more and more disturbed when he saw me spend so much time with Marika. He was uncomfortable about our closeness but couldn't articulate it. Buddy always had a difficult time expressing any negative feelings. I never knew how much he disliked my mother until years later. But for the first time I risked Buddy's displeasure and insisted on seeing Marika whenever I wanted to. Sometimes the two couples got together and we played poker long into the night.

I scuttled back and forth between the two parts of my life, dimly aware that Marika was providing some excitement in my life that I was missing. I titillated myself with endless speculation. Would I some day go out with another man? Would I ever have love affairs? Was this even something I wanted? More to the point, whether I wanted it or not, was my own world real enough to support me if I chose to stay within its safe boundaries? Some afternoons I would be happy to go back to the safety of Buddy's arms, back to my protected enclave. I didn't even know that I was unhappy in it; but I did know that there was an excitement out there that I didn't have at home.

By 1942, married men who did not have children were beginning to be drafted. We had been married a year and strangely never talked about having children. In fact, I dreaded getting pregnant, saying that we were too young and I wasn't ready. Buddy never questioned me. I don't think he had strong feelings about children or anything else, for that matter. He was agreeable, a non-combatant, and anxious to avoid an argument at any cost. He never asked me about going back to the university, which I had left when we married; he never discussed the possibility of my pursuing an acting career and never discussed my writing with me. He seemed to accept our roles without question; he was the breadwinner and I was his wife. But since the draft was coming closer, we decided it would be better if he got training in some area so that at least he could have some say about his assignment and he could volunteer before being drafted. Since he had no skills, just a beautiful *cum laude,* he decided to train as a radio operator. After passing his exams, he decided to join the

Navy. As it turned out, if he hadn't had that training, he might never have been drafted because he was quite myopic. Besides passing his operator's exams, he also went to a great deal of trouble to pass his eye examination, getting his doctor to give him eye drops that helped him see better for a short period of time. At that time, men wanted to join the service for some strange combination of patriotism and a very fuzzy conception of what war was like. Americans of that generation had never fought a war on their own soil. Even my stepfather played with the idea of joining up. He thought it might be a change from the daily grind and pressure of his millinery business. And after all, with his background he would be a colonel, and he could probably make use of his merchandising background. We were carried away with the vision of him in uniform.

The Navy stationed Buddy in Kansas City, Missouri, which is about as far from the ocean as you can get. But the Navy had planes flying in and out of its naval base. There I was, settled in our own apartment in Kansas City. I think Buddy and I needed to be away from our parents and on our own. I thought it would give our marriage the jolt it needed. Buddy's naval run from Kansas City to New York City was a dream assignment. I was away from Marika, and I was glad of that. I wanted to concentrate on Buddy and our life together. Things went on pretty much as they had before; he sent me flowers, and we continued to write love notes to each other. He had started flying and was away for two or three days at a time . . . our first separation.

I loved the excitement of Kansas City. I had never been very far from New York City in my life, so it was hard for me to believe I could enjoy another city so much. But all the things that had been building up inside me—the sense that I was living in a cocoon, the questions that Marika had raised—got mixed up with the wartime feverishness.

I decided to go to work. I had a good excuse since Buddy wasn't home that much, so I didn't have to stay home and play house. He could accept that because working kept me busy. I was hired as an adjustment manager at one of the big department stores and settled in quickly. I met a lot of other women who worked there, mostly service wives, and I would go out with them when Buddy was away. I began to have friends outside my marriage and that was new to me. When we went out in the evening for drinks, we met all the soldiers and sailors on leave. It was wartime and everything was temporary; the men were all on the way to leaving, moving on. Every night was festive, a celebration, as if it was their last night on leave.

There was an early curfew in K.C. and the bars tried to get as much business as possible before customers slipped over to Mary's, the bar over the dividing line in Kansas City, Kansas, where there was no curfew. As a result, things got pretty wild earlier in the evening, and everybody seemed to be operating on a racing clock. Somehow by drinking so early in the evening, my guard was down a little. I was not a good drinker; one or two made me dizzy. The soldiers and sailors came over to where we were sitting and flirted with us, and we rationalized that the men were all going off to war any day and it didn't hurt to be nice to them. We were all lonely and probably had married too young or too fast. We were all nice people who had bought the American dream—marry, have children, live happily ever after. Very few of us had been with many men in our lives. I had only known one and that wasn't until after I was married. I began to make dates to see these men, just to go dancing or have a few drinks.

One night, as I was on my way out to meet the women, Buddy came home unexpectedly from his New York run. I was surprised but wanted to keep my plans. I said, "I'm meeting the women for some drinking and perhaps a movie. I don't want to change plans now. It's too late to tell my friends I won't show up." He was obviously hurt, stunned, but all he said was, "That's your decision and I trust you." I thought, "Why don't you tell me to stop? Why are you letting me do this?" If he had yelled at me, if he had said, "What the hell are you talking about?" or even suggested coming with me, if he even sensed something was wrong and it opened up dialogue, I would have stayed home. But Buddy would never argue, never fight; he would just sit silently while I yelled, argued, berated him for not talking back. I was so disgusted with him and myself. I was angry because he let me go without even articulating his feelings. I was unhappy at myself for going. What I didn't realize then was that I was not familiar with this kind of love. My only knowledge of love had been through my mother, who yelled, fought, pressured. His actions seemed meek and passive.

I went on my evening out; nothing happened. The whole evening was awful and I could hardly wait to get home, but I still couldn't face what was happening to our relationship. Nothing was happening that was bad or obviously bad. Buddy was a lovely human being, a good man. I was a lovely young woman, a good woman. Neither of us meant to hurt the other; neither knew why it wasn't working. Things went on for a while like that, but there was an emptiness. I said, "Buddy, something is wrong. I don't like feeling this way. I don't want to shut you out. I don't like going out with other men. You're a very good lover to me; you are warm and loving. But still something is wrong. Can't we go to a marriage counsellor?" That was a fairly advanced view in the forties. Buddy's answer was brief. "I don't know what you are talking about. I'm perfectly happy." He wouldn't go.

After a while I decided I should have a holiday, take a week off and go home for a vacation. I thought I would sort our problems out and make everything all right. The main problem was that I didn't know what was wrong. I remember the day I packed. I wrote little encouraging notes and left them in strategic spots all over the house. I almost performed it all by reflex. I had always written notes. This was our way of communicating. The notes said, "I love you . . . see you soon." For some reason, I still didn't understand why, I packed everything I owned. Everything. It wasn't till much later that I realized what I had been doing. At the time I wrote those notes in all innocence, without a clue. I certainly wasn't very much in touch with my own feelings when it involved a man, my husband. Buddy put me on the train. I was looking back as the train pulled away, and it started to become clear. I don't want to go back, I don't want to go back . . . the refrain kept in time with the clacking of the wheels. I felt a sense of freedom, but from what I still wasn't sure.

Going home to my parents wasn't the greatest thing in the world. I had been impatient to tell them about my decision. They had never approved that much of Buddy and certainly not of his family. I believed my decision, which was still not clear, would get my mother's approval. She would help me formalize my plans. After all, they had always told me Buddy wasn't the right man for me, and now I was thinking of leaving him. But there is a big difference between not wanting your daughter to marry someone and wanting her to leave once she's been married. It was never easy—in fact, almost impossible—to get my mother's approval about anything. But I kept trying.

I arrived home, and after settling down for supper, I decided to spring the news. "I don't think I want to go back. I'm not happy. And I can't say he's not a good husband. He is." My stepfather jumped in. "I told you so. You should have known. But now that you are married, stay married." I felt a wave of shock when I realized they weren't going to welcome me with open arms, or give me any comfort, or even try to understand what our problems were.

When I told Buddy's mother, she asked, "Did he beat you?" Buddy, the gentlest man in the world! "Of course not." "Did he run around?" "No, not at all." "Well, what do you want, the stars?" I had no answer except to say, "Perhaps. I think I'm too young to settle for less."

When one of Buddy's flights arrived in New York, he came to my mother's house to stay with me. I lay in bed with him, made love to him, and then said I didn't want to go back. He was in a state of shock. He said he had no idea I was so unhappy. He cried, begged me to come back to Kansas City and talk about it. I did go back. I packed a small bag and returned to our apartment in the Club District of Kansas City. Buddy talked to me about his plans for the evening. He thought it would be better for us to go out and have dinner in one of our favorite restaurants, listen to some music, and dance. We both tried to act natural. For the moment, we were together. He talked, but he never was able to reach out and touch me. He seemed strained. We went to the spaghetti house that had been our hangout. The juke box was on and Buddy played "Stormy Weather." We were singing along and crying. Our whole life seemed to be defined by torch songs. The words echoed our feelings, and for a little while we almost felt as if we were back in our courting days. We went home later and stayed up all night talking, hugging, and crying. Buddy couldn't understand why I had never been able to tell him what was wrong. He felt my decision had come out of the blue. My only explanation was to remind him that I had often felt something was wrong, that I had suggested a marriage counsellor, but that he had never taken me seriously. We were also trapped in society's idea of a perfect marriage. We married out of love but knew nothing about love. We married, but knew nothing about marriage. We were fulfilling everybody's dream but our own. It was safe.

I remember Buddy begging me not to divorce him until the war was over, and I said, "Of course I won't." Maybe he needed the comfort of knowing that he still had a wife. If anything happened, I would still be there. I stayed for three or four more days. It was a very painful parting. We went over our life together. I just wanted to run. I felt so sorry for Buddy, but the more he pleaded, the more I wanted to escape.

It wasn't long afterwards that Buddy decided to ask for overseas duty. His explanation was, "It's too painful being in the same country and not being able to be with you." I was furious and frightened. If he got killed in combat because of me, I would never feel free of the guilt. As it turned out, he met a nurse on his new assignment. She was named Anne, his mother's name. She looked just like his mother, dressed like his mother. After the war, he married Anne.

After my talk with Buddy, I decided to go home and make some plans about my future. I thought I might live with my parents until I found a job. I was not prepared for the reaction of my parents. They felt that I had made a failure of my life. Not only did they see me as a shamed woman on the verge of divorce, but they were sure that now I would be a "loose woman" as well. My mother attributed her divorce and problems to her parents and her youth. But she was not so lenient with me. She had no idea of the double standard she was imposing on me. My stepfather lost no time in warning me, "Don't think because you've been married, I'm going to like you running around. I still expect you home at a decent hour." I think he found it difficult to deal with me as an experienced woman, a sexual human being. I was hurt at some of the things they said. I knew that I would have to leave. It wasn't long before I ran into my German friend, Marika. She had just been divorced from her husband and was living alone. How strange that we two should decide to live together . . . two women from completely different worlds with different philosophies. But it seemed to happen at the right time. We were both under the illusion that we were liberated women because we worked, paid our own way when we wanted to, and saw the men we felt like seeing. But we were a long way from liberation. First of all, there was no defined movement, no rhetoric to back us up, and nothing that helped us channel our anger. We acted independently but we were really still angry women, trying to define where we belonged. So we muddled along, angry at men but still trying to define our lives by finding our happiness through them.

CHAPTER 3

INDEPENDENCE

My friend Marika seemed to appear when I needed someone to help me with my transition from re-stricted married woman to free woman. My need for change seemed to come at about the time the world was going through a cultural shift, which started with the war and con-tinued right after. There seemed to be a change in the United States to more sophistication and more Europeanization. And Marika was my link. I was anxious to peek into her lifestyle and find out about the world she had been telling me about all the time I was married to Buddy.

We decided if we lived together we could afford a really nice apartment. The first apartment we found was in a large, old building; we had two bedrooms and a huge living room and kitchen. The man who rented us the apartment reassured us about the amount of money we were spending on the rent. "Most women can save on food. You go out on dates and you ask them home and suggest they buy some chicken or cheese and fruit for a later snack. You cut food bills that way." I silently rejected that advice because I wanted to be independent—I couldn't think of being dependent on a man buying us food and being obli-gated—but this observation pleased Marika.

It was a strange attraction we had for each other. It was heady stuff. We were going to date and I was going to discover the world she had talked about, a world of men, a world without restrictions except those I imposed on myself. I had no idea at the time that Marika would try to impose her way of life on me. I still thought I had choices. After all, we were two free women.

By this time Marika had moved up in the world. Instead of being a waitress, she was now a hostess of Longchamps restaurant. She could now socialize with a different class of men. They were richer and more powerful. Most of the men were executives from broadcasting, advertising, and films. I used to think she was like a warrior putting notches in a belt for so many scalps. The notches marked her successes, which had to do with how many wealthy men she slept with, where they took her, and what they gave her. Her goal was to make sure that she spent none of her own money. Men paid for her food, bought her clothes, and gave her jewelry and cash. To her, being escorted to the best restaurants, the most fashionable clubs, meant she was successful. All this activity helped her wipe out the pain of Munich and the death of her parents. She wanted it all. I think this was her way of getting even for all she had been deprived of.

At the time I was fascinated with her seeming self-confidence, her ability to go after what she wanted, no holds barred. I didn't question her goals. This was a time of no moral judgments, no labels, no categories, no more definitions of "good girls," "bad girls," just two women. So there we were, living together, with her priding herself on the fact that she never had to spend her own money, and my boasting that no one could take care of me. I was still locked into the fact that at least I had a good reputation.

I loved living with Marika. At first she was so colorful, so unpredictable. I began to realize, though, that she was really naive. She had no goals, no motive for the way she was living. She wasn't a fortune-hunter, never deliberately planned to meet a rich man and marry him for his money. She was more of an experience-hunter, a person who needed instant gratification. If she did get some money, she always spent it; it never lasted. It was almost as if she was afraid of really having responsibility for her life. She started to drink a lot on her dates, and that was my first experience with someone who drank. I tended to excuse it as another way Marika had of hiding her true feelings. Whenever she drank, she would get very loud and abusive. She was always asserting how "free" she was. It was a self-destructive thing; she could get a man because she had that mysterious, European quality, but she could never keep one. Besides, she didn't even try. I don't think she liked men; she just liked using them, not realizing how much she was exploited. She was playing games, but only later did she realize that the only game she was playing was with her own heart.

The one thing Marika and I did argue about was my refusal to go out with her on her kind of dates. The men I went out with were ones I met through my association with the theater and fellow actors or through my work. They weren't necessarily rich or powerful, but most of them were interesting. They didn't give me things; in fact, sometimes I was the one who would lend money to the actors who needed to get through another month and didn't have rent money available. I also saw nothing wrong with paying my own way if we went out and they didn't have the money, or even paying for them. Sometimes I would sacrifice seeing a play on Broadway from the beginning because they didn't have the money to get in. We found out that we could get in at intermission time when no one was checking tickets. Although I could afford to pay, I wanted to be part of the group, so I saw a number of plays from the second act on! Afterwards I used to go with them to Sardi's restaurant as they sat at the bar sipping a drink or a beer in the hopes that some producer would notice them. They would also have themselves paged so that their names became familiar to the patrons. It all seemed like child's play to me, but I enjoyed the camaraderie.

I belonged to a strange group of actors called the Genius Club. We were a repertory theater, all working for a so-called producer who insisted that we all help make the club self-supporting. We did everything—performed, wrote plays, swept the floors, ran Saturday night parties to raise money, worked senior citizen homes, had weekend productions in our own theater, and generally tried to stay out of the grasp of the lecherous producer. He was always grabbing someone backstage, but he was never very persistent. After a few minutes of struggle, he would give up and try another young, hopeful starlet. In spite of all that, it was an interesting experience and gave me some guidelines so that I was able to make a decision about the direction of my career later on when I had some decisions to make.

Marika thought my lifestyle was unforgivably stupid. She couldn't understand why I was wasting my time with men who had, she thought, no future. I was amazed that she was making so many judgments about me. I thought if I didn't criticize her, she had no right to criticize me. I had no idea at the time that I had just switched from my mother laying down the rules to Marika setting up the game plan. I've always found it interesting that people who lead what they consider a "swinging" life feel motivated to include everyone else, as if their "church" were the best one. She was trying to convert me. They do the very thing they would resent in others . . . preach. I spent a lot of energy trying to convince her that I wanted to make my own decisions about my life. I did not approve or disapprove of her life and I didn't want her to approve or disapprove of mine. I honestly thought we could enjoy each other for what we were and share experiences. I was certainly fascinated with Marika and somewhat "in love" with her, almost thinking of her as a man. She lived the way some men did who had no need or no ability to be committed to any one relationship.

One evening I was out on a date with one of my young men, and when we came back to the apartment, Marika was there with a current lover, Hernando. We hadn't yet worked out how we would manage things if I came home and found her with one of her dates, so we just sat there and talked. I changed to a hostess gown, a very proper gown with a velvet skirt and a knit top buttoned demurely to my neck. I was bubbling about the evening and found this man she was with very pleasant. He was from South America, in the coffee export business, and was in town for only a few days. Marika had mentioned him to me when she met him and said she was glad he was leaving because she found him boring. I liked his high cheekbones, his obvious Indian heritage, and his swarthy skin. I also noticed his long, slender fingers. He seemed very gentle, something Marika would find weak. She told me he was a millionaire, but he was careful about spending his money. I couldn't decide what age he was, although I felt he was much too old for me.

The next day was Sunday, and Marika was at work at Longchamps. I was relaxing alone in the apartment, enjoying a hot and soothing bath, luxuriating in my privacy. The telephone rang and it was Hernando calling to speak to Marika. I told him she was at work. He said, "I'm alone tonight, too. How about having dinner with me?" I knew Marika wasn't interested in him, and I was titillated by the idea of going out with Marika's sort of man. So I said yes. I was a little nervous because of his age.

It turned out he was about forty, but it was my first experience with an older man. I was just twenty-three and I felt ill at ease. But I loved his accent, and that somehow gave the evening a romantic air. I loved the easy way he took over all the plans. He chose a beautiful restaurant for dinner. He made gentle suggestions about the menu, ordered the wine, and apologized for not ordering any cocktails or highballs. "I don't think we should drink anything that will dull our senses." He talked to me about the night before. "I loved the way your hair fell so simply to your shoulders; your gown was so demure. You seemed so full of life and yet charming and innocent. How rare!" In fact, he said he had thought about me all evening and had planned to call. He said he knew that Marika was working but that he also knew that he and Marika were never going to see each other again. When we kissed good night, I was under the impression he was leaving in a few days, but as things turned out, he decided to stay in New York for another few months. He said it was because of me; he felt he was in love.

I expected Marika to get a charge out of my relationship with Hernando. But over the next few months I realized she was more upset at the time Hernando took—time away from her. We almost broke up because Hernando wanted to rent an apartment just for the two of us. He wanted me to spend every moment of his few months with him. He promised to choose a beautiful apartment where I could do all the things I cared about . . . write, entertain. Marika screamed that I was abandoning her, and I realized that I was still not free of some of my old conditioning, that living with a man might make me vulnerable. Everyone in the building would know I had a lover. Also, I didn't want to leave Marika alone for the few months Hernando would be in town, although it was like a romantic novel and I loved the idea of being a kept woman, a mistress. I erroneously thought it would make Marika feel closer to me. But she didn't want me to have a permanent liaison; she wanted me available to go out with her.

Hernando also suggested I leave my position as section manager in a department store. It wasn't a very rewarding or high-profile job and he felt it wasted my time. I said, "No, no. I want to be independent." It was stupid in a way. I was not making that much and I also knew that I would soon be leaving to look for another job and start a career in a field of my choosing, whether writing, acting, or advertising, the subjects I had studied at Columbia University. I said, "You are going to be leaving soon and where will I be without a job?" I imagine I was somewhat wary of being with him all day. I still needed some semblance of freedom. He said, "I'll pay for the apartment and leave you with money."

At any rate, we compromised. He didn't like the old-fashioned place I lived in and suggested a new apartment. We found one at the Beaux-Arts on Second Avenue and 44th Street. It was a new complex, twin buildings. At first he was going to move there with me, and then when he left Marika would move in. But Marika didn't think that was going to work, in spite of the fact that he offered to pay for her apartment while she was waiting. In the end we took the Beaux-Arts apartment. He paid my share of the rent but didn't move in. He stayed at the magnificent Waldorf-Astoria on Park Avenue. That's where I spent most of my evenings.

I had a lovely three months with Hernando. It was a complete escape from reality. I knew I wasn't in love with him, but I loved the entire fantasy, the idea of being a "mistress," of being cared for by an older man who treated me like a precious child. I also enjoyed showing Marika that I could have a rich man in love with me. I enjoyed having him buy me things because I knew I didn't need them; it was like being an actress in a play. I almost felt part of me was on the sidelines watching a wonderful Hollywood film. Doesn't every young woman need the experience of a rich, older, handsome man in her life?

I believed for a long time that every woman deserved that type of experience. Certainly I was intoxicated with my new life. I was "swept away" but I was also conscious that I was testing new roles to play in life. Now the relationship of the older man with the younger woman may be one of the oldest relationships in history, but it was new to me and I enjoyed playing my part to the hilt, as I am sure Hernando appreciated the opportunity to play his part, too. Looking back, I can say that, with Hernando, I was able to establish, at least for some months, a sane relationship with a man. Today it goes without saying that men and women are free to test new roles without shame or disapproval. Older women are finding satisfying the company of younger men, and vice versa. At the time I did not feel like a "kept woman" but like a person experiencing life for the first time.

Even the way our rooms were set up created another secret life for me, away from my own world. The Waldorf-Astoria had a special floor set up for all the visiting South Americans. A receptionist was on this floor and screened everyone coming through; complete privacy was guaranteed. Once I was introduced I had unlimited freedom to come and go. Hernando planned our every moment, as if each day was the most important of our lives. In the beginning I was somewhat anxious. I had never been with an older man; in fact, I had not had a relationship since I had left Buddy. So lovemaking with Hernando was a very important step. I really had no idea what to expect or what he needed from me. Hernando seemed to sense my concern and I think that also intrigued him. It was almost as if he were dealing with a virgin and that excited him.

He would set the scene carefully, never rushing me into bed. I was treated like a spoiled princess. The first evening he drew a warm bath for me, filled with bubbles. While I soaked, he came to rub my back and stroked me gently. He liked pinning my long hair on top of my head. Then he would carefully towel me off, carry me to the bed, and then slowly and passionately start to explore my body. He lingered over my breasts, stroked my thighs, and hungrily kissed me all over before he wanted me to do anything to him. I could sense that he was completely lost in making love to me, and I began to feel myself respond almost wildly. I forgot my self-consciousness. I found his body lean and taut, his skin alive. His passion for me carried me into his world, so that I surprised myself when I found I was finally begging him to enter me. It had been so long since I felt such complete abandonment, such release. I relaxed happily in his arms and enjoyed his stroking and petting after we both lay there exhausted but laughing with joy. He was like a child himself, in the way he expressed his glee. He tried to explain his feelings, but he found English still too difficult for the kind of things he wanted to say to me. He also kept murmuring words of love in Spanish. He was a magnificent lover.

Later, he planned a night at the theater and then late supper, everything that I enjoyed. He became my guide, my teacher as well as my lover. Although I had always gone to plays, the world he showed me was new. I had recently bought a whole wardrobe of new clothes, which included a brown skirt and a checked taffeta blouse, as well as a simple black dress with pink sequin-studded cuffs and collar. But he found my clothes too unsophisticated. He was a little sensitive about my age. I looked even younger than twenty-three, with my long hair and bangs. There was a popular song in those years that said "They are either too young or too old." So many of the young men were still away at the war or beginning to return. Hernando took me on a shopping spree and chose some clothes for me to try on, while he sat comfortably in the lovely salons of Saks Fifth Avenue and Bergdorf-Goodman, the two finest stores in New York City. He chose a lovely soft gray coat of the finest wool lined with fur. Then he bought me some lovely black dresses, including a velvet dress with black lace outlining the square neck and cascading from the wrists over my hands. He bought me shoes, perfume, and hats to finish off the shopping. He loved my hands and insisted that I take care of them and let my nails grow long. He drove me to a manicurist twice a week. He insisted I wear my hair pinned and curled on top of my head, so that I would look a little older. He arranged to have me photographed wearing the black velvet dress, my new hair style, and my fur coat trailing at my side.

There wasn't an evening when we didn't go to a play, to dinner, to dance. I loved dancing and considered myself an excellent dancer. But Hernando was a master at the rhumba and most of the other Latin dances, so popular then. He insisted I take small steps and make sure that my shoulders were held very still. It was a very sensual dance, as if at any moment uncontrolled passion would be released. It was more of a promise than a show. He stood so tall, so erect, so sure of himself as he led me around the floor. Usually dinners were at places like the Stork Club or the El Morocco. But, as exclusive as these clubs were, he still knew about the separate rooms reserved for the inner circle. The main room at the El Morocco attracted many socialites and movie stars. The zebra-striped seats and the Latin band were a draw for many years and often used as a background in films. A small group knew about and were admitted to the private dining room, where I went with Hernando. There we were treated to strolling violinists and privacy, venturing out to the main room to dance when we felt like it. That's when I also learned about the proper wines to order for each meal, the most unusual liqueurs, and the best champagne. Hernando introduced me to Chartreuse. I had a choice of gold or green and Hernando always ordered the gold, which was for the more sophisticated drinker. I followed and loved the bite of the Chartreuse on my tongue and the warm, euphoric feeling that would suffuse me. To this day, I can order Chartreuse and summon back those few months in a moment.

Other times we danced in the Waldorf-Astoria Ballroom. Many of his friends were in town at the same time on buying trips. Bandleader Xavier Cugat was playing at the Waldorf, and many times we would all be invited back to "Cugie's" apartment for drinks. He still had his wife Abby Lane fronting for him, long before Charro. In the privacy of his suite, he was quite a vulgar man; he loved to tell dirty jokes and show off his cartoons. He was quite talented, but I found him rather unpleasant in manner. Hernando sensed that and also seemed offended by his vulgarities. I felt protected by Hernando.

Hernando was quite aristocratic in his bearing and was brought up in a very rigid class system, which I didn't fully understand. One evening we were having dinner when a waiter happened to mention that I had beautiful hands. I was wearing the black velvet dress and the black lace fluttered around my wrists. I was pleased and acknowledged his compliment by thanking him. Hernando was in a rage. "He had no right to be so personal with you, and you should have known better than to thank a servant for a compliment." I thought Hernando was joking at first, but I soon realized he was very serious. I didn't know then whether it was because of his training or because he was unbelievably possessive and jealous. I always kept a part of me locked away, knowing that I could never have a permanent liaison with Hernando because of what he would expect if I were married to him or even lived with him. I also knew that Hernando had a voracious appetite for young girls — young girls who were pliant and wide-eyed. I also knew that if you married that kind of man, you would soon be relegated to the role of "wife" and it would be expected that he could have time to himself. But marriage wasn't on my mind.

It was rather surprising to me that it was on Hernando's mind. I pointed out to him that he was still married and that I wouldn't be free until the war was over. I also asked how he could divorce if he was a practicing Catholic. He assured me that there were ways. But in the meantime he begged me to come to South America and he would set me up in an apartment in the small town of Cali near his home in Colombia. He would make all the arrangements when he returned to South America. He promised that he would then make plans for our future. I didn't believe him, but I toyed with the idea of going to Cali for a while.

The day he left, I felt pangs of withdrawal. I would go out to a restaurant and moodily sip on my Chartreuse, remembering how beautiful our romance had been, how unique and how impossible. Soon after I received a hundred tiny orchids from Hernando, all kept alive by having their stems inserted in balloons filled with water. He sent me a lovely emerald from Colombia and money for my passage. He called one evening when I was out with some friends. He called back later that night and complained, "You are dancing on my grave. How could you go out so soon after I left?" I assured him that I was just out with Marika, and I still thought of our time together; I had checked about a passport and had begun to make arrangements to come to South America but there were two stumbling blocks. One was that all my friends were afraid that I would be murdered if his friends found I was living in Cali. I was, after all, a foreigner and he had a wife. But more important, the American government said servicemen's wives could not leave the country without permission from their husbands, and I did not feel I could ask Buddy to let me leave when he was off somewhere in battle.

Hernando was furious. He had counted on my coming down; he loved me; he wanted to marry me. I began to feel pressured, and without him next to me the dream faded and the fairy tale ended. But I never forgot Hernando, never stopped appreciating all the wonderful things he showed me in my own city of New York. It was years later that I stupidly saw Hernando again when he came back to New York. By this time I was more experienced, had a career, had thoroughly explored New York with many other men. I was not the wide-eyed young girl he had been in love with. I had grown too old for Hernando, too impatient . . . and as we sipped our Chartreuse together and tried to recreate some of the magic, I noticed his eyes wandering to the young Spanish singer on the stage, and I said good-bye forever to Hernando.

CHAPTER 4

CAREER CHOICES

After Hernando left, things were a little better between Marika and me. She seemed relieved that he was gone and I was able to be with her a little more. I did go out with her after that, but still didn't like the men she dated any better. I also found her drinking embarrassing, for it gave her an excuse to say angry, bitter things. There was a lot of anger in Marika that she hadn't learned to confront as yet.

It was time to think seriously of a career and use the talents that I had. It seemed I knew what I wanted to do since I was ten years old. Later I began taking acting, writing, and advertising courses. My first career decision was to join Walter Lowen, an excellent personnel agency for people in the communications field. I was immediately put on their roster as a client. I had a good academic background, I dressed well with the mandatory hat and gloves, and I had an outgoing personality, a by-product of my acting days. All my interests were reflected in the activities I had engaged in all through high school and university. All the subjects I had taken provided me with an excellent background and a good starting point. After I joined the agency, I also did some searching on my own; I covered all the newspapers for writing jobs, crashed producers' offices for acting parts, and answered Walter Lowen's call for an advertising position.

Then one day I found I had a choice of three jobs, each in a separate field. I had to make a choice, and that decision would point me in the direction I might want to concentrate on. I was offered a position as rewrite woman at the *Daily News;* an acting part with Theron Bamberger, the king of summer stock; and the job of fashion editor for a buying office. I decided to put aside the job at the *Daily News* for the moment because it was on the "lobster shift" (12:00 midnight to 4:00 a.m.) and paid eighteen dollars a week. My biggest decision was between acting and fashion editing, two completely different worlds.

I had burst into the office of Theron Bamberger, convincing him that it was vital that I speak to him. He decided to listen to me and then asked me the question I knew I would have to answer honestly. "Why do you want to be an actress?" I couldn't summon up all my energy to reply convincingly, "That's all I have ever wanted to do in life, nothing else matters." A lot of other things did matter. Acting was exciting, acting was wonderful, but acting also meant dependency, dependency on producers, directors, fellow performers, as well as having talent. It depended on luck, on timing. I hesitated and he added, "You know, you'll never be an ingénue, you are not pretty enough. You are more of a character type." I retorted, annoyed, "I never wanted to be an ingénue. I know I look like a character actress. I'm only interested in that kind of role." I reeled off the kinds of parts I liked. To me Katharine Hepburn was a character actress, and I felt I looked a little like Hepburn or her type. I had a strong sense of the parts I could play and the parts I did well. I also knew I was good at comedy, at heavy drama, and at drunk and bitchy women. He seemed to enjoy my outburst and my confidence and then gave me orders. "If you are really interested in acting, come back next week. I have a role in mind for you. But wear a simple black dress, pull your hair back off your face, and let me see you again." I walked out of his office, feeling triumphant that I had had an audience with him, but feeling somber and concerned about the future. I liked more control of my own life than was possible in the area of acting.

I walked over to my next appointment with the head of the advertising department for the buying office of Felix Lilienthal. A tall, slightly balding man with a warm grin asked me into his office. Milton Green was about thirty-five years old and had a nice, calm manner. He explained that a buying office did exactly what it sounded like; it did the central buying for stores all over the country that were its clients. They had a large fashion department and were responsible for putting out a newsletter that gave the stores and their own buyers an idea of what was going on in the marketplace. It was like a fashion magazine, but on a smaller scale for their clients. I would also be responsible for sending out "flashes" on the hottest fashions to the stores. It meant being on top of everything in the fashion world. I would have to do the writing, but I would have a small staff of artists in my department. My title would be editor and my pay would be thirty-five dollars a week to start. He took me around to meet the people I would be supervising and I was delighted with the welcome I received from the three women artists with whom I would work, all about my age and very pleasant looking. He asked if I would mind writing one column on the spot, to give him an idea of my writing style. I did and he liked it. I made the choice to stay.

I liked the idea of having a salary immediately. I liked the surroundings and the easy schedule. I could make my own time, and from that day on that was a prerequisite for any job that I took. It must have flexibility. I never wanted to be tied to a desk or to rigid hours; I must have a variety of jobs to do within the umbrella of my job; I must have freedom to change the format of the job either by adding to it or by creating a new form. Within certain limits, I had all that freedom at Felix Lilienthal. And the young women I worked with acted as a great team. We were not in competition because I had skills they knew nothing about, and they had their own specialties.

It never occurred to me that I was making any choice that was etched in stone. I had too many options. I have always believed that everything I did added up as valuable experience for anything I wanted to tackle. I still intended to keep up acting as a hobby. I still intended to keep on taking writing workshops in the hopes I would write that great novel some day. But for the moment I had some structure, some money, and I had freedom.

When I told my stepfather about my new position, his reaction was that he paid his porter more just to sweep up his factory. I was hurt at his response, but I reminded him that my job was just a start. "In my business the jumps in salary can be astronomical, while your porter might get a few small raises with little hope for any advancement." I was disappointed that he wasn't as excited as I was about the beginning of my career.

I worked at Felix Lilienthal for the next nine months. I really loved it. As the head of my department, I had lots of responsibility and contact with the buyers, who were pleased with my fashion letter. I took time to explore the garment district, meet the manufacturers, and learn about the fashion business. I dressed well and set my own style.

I was still registered with the Lowen personnel agency. I didn't realize that if you were a valuable client they would keep upgrading you if you had the talent in spite of the fact they had already placed you. So when a bigger job came along, they called me to see if I was interested. I had not thought of leaving the buying office at that time. I was still learning a lot and enjoying the job. The money was adequate and I was very relaxed. I also had a strong sense of loyalty. I felt a little uncomfortable about even talking about another job. If I wanted to change, I would have talked with my boss, Milton Green, to let him know I was discontent because the money wasn't good enough or I felt the need for a more challenging position. But neither condition had emerged as yet. And now I was being offered a job as fashion editor for a new teen magazine published by the giant firm that also published *Parents' Magazine*. I was convinced by Walter Lowen at least to go for the interview. "You owe it to yourself to examine all opportunities." So I did go, somewhat uncomfortable about the appointment.

I met the publisher of the *Parents' Magazine* empire, George Hecht. He was a bit of a tyrant and he had very little patience with anyone who didn't jump at his offers. He was used to getting what he wanted, fast. He looked powerful. He was sturdily built and had a shock of steel-gray hair and dark beetling eyebrows. He seemed to size the situation up instantly, liked my résumé, and offered me the chance to be editor of this brand-new magazine, *Polly Pigtails*. I would control the fashion pages, hire the photographers, and write the copy, again using all the skills I had honed at the buying office as well as in my courses at Columbia University.

I asked him about the profile of the job and what he expected. It was different from the established high-fashion magazines. I would also be responsible for merchandising and marketing: *Polly Pigtails* needed to be distributed and sold; readership needed to be built. I was concerned that I wasn't quite ready for that much responsibility. I also asked him why Betty Green, the long-time editor of his other magazine, *Calling All Girls*, wasn't handling the launching of this new one. He said he wasn't interested in one person having that much power and that each magazine had its own profile and needed a different approach. I sensed trouble, one woman pitted against another woman. To get off the hook, I made the mistake of lying about my salary. I doubled the salary I was getting, sure that he wouldn't want to meet it. If I didn't want the job, I should have flatly refused. He didn't bat an eye. No problem. I insisted that I would still have to think about it. I extracted a promise that he would not call my boss at Felix Lilienthal, who did not know I was looking for another job, and if I decided to join the *Parents' Magazine* group I wanted to be the one to break the news to him. On top of that, I would have to give at least a month's notice.

But by the time I got back to my office, Hecht had already called Milton Green. He called me into his office and I could feel my heart pound. I always dreaded being called to a meeting when I was unsure of what was going to take place; I still get nervous around police officers, principals, teachers, and customs officers. I don't know why authority still frightens me when I don't know what to expect. It's different if I arrange the meeting; nothing worries me. I still have the sneaking feeling that I must have done something wrong, that I will be punished.

When I walked into Green's office, he pounced. "Why would you look for another job without telling me. I had no idea you were unhappy. I thought we had a good working relationship." I was shocked that he knew, and I told him the truth. "I wasn't looking for another job; I am happy here. Walter Lowen told me this was an excellent opportunity and I should at least examine it, but since I had no desire to leave, I felt it was useless to raise the issue. I didn't think it would hurt to see what was in the mar- ketplace. I might want to leave some day. I assure you that I would certainly have talked to you if I was actively searching. I'm sure if an applicant came to you for a position, whether you had one open or not, you would certainly feel obligated to interview a good prospect, even if it was only for the future. Why are you so angry?" I then added, "I think Hecht acted in bad faith. I had him promise not to call you until I had a chance to think about the change, even though he offered me double what I'm making here."

It seemed George Hecht told Milton Green that he offered me double and that Green should not stand in my way. What Hecht had not told Green was the amount, and I didn't tell Green that I had lied and had quoted a figure that had doubled my salary and in fact I was being offered almost four times as much as I was now making. But in spite of the jump in salary, I wasn't ready emotionally to leave my present place. I was angry at Hecht, but also angry that Green had pounced on me. Green softened and then said he would match Hecht's offer.

Now I felt boxed in. The magic for me had been destroyed and I knew that it would just be a matter of time before I would have to make the decision to leave. I hated leaving this comfortable relationship, but I felt I had no choice, it was too late. I felt that our trusting relationship was damaged. I still was acting emotionally rather than learning to negotiate. So I took the editorship of the new magazine, *Polly Pigtails,* and at first it was hell. As I suspected, Betty Green wasn't happy about an outsider getting a piece of her empire and she wasn't about to help. Once George Hecht accomplished his mission, he could not be involved in day-to-day problems. I spent a few months of absolute anguish learning the ropes. There was no problem writing the copy, hiring the photographers, planning the pages, and choosing the fashions. But the merchandising and marketing were different matters. These areas were completely new to me, except for the little bit I had learned in my advertising course. I did find that everything I had studied came to my rescue at one time or another. George Hecht arranged a beautiful launching party for me, where I was introduced to the industry as well as to the rest of the empire. I dressed in a black satin, two-piece suit designed by the couturière Adele Simpson. It was simply tailored with jet buttons and a heavily encrusted gold ascot. I gave a proper speech, planned a mini-fashion show, and was propelled into the business world of fashion, a top executive at twenty-four years of age.

I discovered the work of the now-famous photographer, Richard Avedon, and was anxious to sign him up for the covers of my magazine. He was just beginning to make his mark on the high-fashion world, one of the first photographers to break away from the typical, stilted photographs of the day where every wrinkle, every crease, had to be retouched out. I loved the way his models jumped through the air, the clothes following the line of their bodies, giving an impression of great style rather than an exact picture. He was a young man, quite accessible then, with black-rimmed, oversized glasses. I loved talking to him and convinced him that he could do the same thing for *Polly Pigtails.* I promised, if we could make a deal financially, that he would have complete freedom in shooting the child models, an unheard-of promise. But I felt very confident that I would be breaking new ground. We finally agreed he would do the covers in color for the very low price of two hundred dollars a cover, if I could promise him a year's contract, twelve covers.

I went back to the magazine and talked to my art director about my coup. I was so excited at the prospect of working with Avedon that it almost made me forget the nights of anxiety, the feelings of rejection from Betty Green, and the long hours I put in at the office checking every release, every merchandising and marketing plan, and all the ideas for contests to boost distribution. This magazine was a no-nonsense business and had little of the glamor associated with working for *Vogue* or *Harper's Bazaar*. I knew they had a different department for each function I was handling. I didn't appreciate it then but I was learning a lot about the industry. I became a top-notch generalist.

I wasn't expecting the negative response I received about Avedon. My art director told me, "There is no way you are going to get the money for him . . . that's a hundred dollars more a cover than we are budgeted for. Besides, I doubt whether Hecht will go for that free approach. When Avedon takes a photograph, the fashion seems secondary." I assured him that the clothes would make more of an impact if they were seen on live, active models rather than on straight, robot-looking children. He retorted, "The manufacturers will never buy that. They want every seam to show, every button, and they don't want to see creases." I was so frustrated I decided to talk to George Hecht. He saw me, was patient but completely disinterested in setting any new directions: "Forget it; we are a nuts-and-bolts operation. You are doing fine; don't get diverted."

That experience only convinced me that *Polly Pigtails* was not going to provide me with enough pleasure to make the long hours worthwhile. I made the magazine a success but there was very little pleasure in the accomplishment. I had too many ideas that were shot down. I wanted to include more stories that related to social issues, feeling that even young children should be exposed to ideas and thoughts. I decided I was the square peg in the round hole. I could do the job, but that was never enough for me. I had to feel that I was making a contribution, especially a creative one, or it was like the law of diminishing returns: the amount of reward didn't warrant the effort. I made a conscious effort to leave *Polly Pigtails,* the entire *Parents' Magazine* corporation, and George Hecht.

This time I called Walter Lowen and told them I was interested in a change. The agency was delighted. They can make easy money with a seasoned client. It was easier to move a successful one around than discover new candidates. In a few weeks I was sent to Sterling Advertising Agency, one of the largest fashion agencies in the business. Women were funneled to fashion houses; the doors were still pretty much closed to women account executives in the other advertising agencies that handled hard goods. I went down to be interviewed by Frances Rafferty, a large-boned, imposing woman who sat behind her desk wearing a huge, wide-brimmed hat. (Women executives wore hats so no one would confuse them with secretaries.) She was a vice-president of Sterling Advertising and head of the copy department. She asked me about my background and why I was interested in leaving *Polly Pigtails.* I told her that I was beginning to feel stifled. I had tackled the job, enjoyed what I had learned to do, but was not very excited at the prospects. She said that there was an opening in her department for a good copywriter. The agency concentrated on fashion accounts and they had the best. I would have every opportunity to write many different kinds of copy for the heavy amount of work that came through her department. The salary, of course, included a substantial increase over my last job.

She showed me around the copy department, and I noticed about four other copywriters all working busily at their desks in this huge room. I liked Frances Rafferty; she seemed down-to-earth, an older woman who had no problems about competition. But I had that terrible feeling of being chained to a desk. I would be doing nothing but writing copy all day long. I would be punching in at nine and leaving at five. At least, as editor of *Polly Pigtails,* I had a variety of jobs to do, and I had complete freedom to come and go as I wished and was expected to cover the marketplace. I liked that part very much. As much as I wanted to work for Sterling Advertising, I realized the change was not the right one. At least in my old job I was responsible for all the elements—copy, make-up, photography, and so on. As a copywriter in Sterling, I'd only be responsible for one piece of one small job. I would also miss the contact with other people. So I said, "I don't want to work as a copywriter. I like writing copy, but I want to do it for my own accounts."

In those days there were no—or certainly very few—women as account executives. Women could make the media purchases, they could write copy, but they could not be account executives. Mrs. Rafferty was taken aback but she said, "Well, there is an account executive here who is swamped with work. He really has too many accounts to handle by himself. Perhaps we could create a new position. There isn't one in the agency for an assistant account executive. But you could handle all his overflow accounts on your own. You would be under his supervision, but would have complete responsibility for dealing with the clients, writing the copy, planning the campaigns, and working with the art director. You seemed to have that responsibility at *Polly Pigtails,* so let's go down and meet Ray Hanna and see how the two of you hit it off."

Ray Hanna and I liked each other immediately. He was a big burly Irishman with a shock of red hair and a twinkle in his eyes. He evidently liked his liquid lunches, but he had a tight grip on his accounts. He learned my maiden name was Smith—I had been adopted by my stepfather—and he immediately started bellowing, "Smitty, you think you can handle it? I'll give you about twelve department-store accounts. You'll have a secretary, and they are all yours. Just don't make any mistakes!"

I felt excited at the prospect of my own little kingdom in a world that seemed to have more potential for the future. I was going to crack the advertising world, and I still marveled at how that one little bit of advice I had taken so many years ago—"Take advertising, you may want to eat some day"—had been so responsible for my moving ahead so fast. I had no regrets about my choice of advertising over newspapers, although many people felt that in advertising you were selling your soul to a commercial devil as opposed to the "pure" world of journalism in the news business. I had no problems with this, loving it all and deciding that everything you liked and gave your best to was worthwhile. At any rate, I never felt I couldn't change careers in the future, since I had training in so many areas. If there was anything positive about society's attitude toward women in the work force in those days, it was the freedom women had to leave jobs for more enriching ones, or to change careers midstream, something denied men who were brought up to believe that a solid, stable man stayed at one job throughout his life, climbing the ladder to the top. Since women weren't taken seriously in the work force, they also weren't condemned for what might be considered "flighty" in a man. It's only in recent years that men have had a chance to drop out and drop in to other careers or try alternative lifestyles. I always felt so sorry for my stepfather, who told me stories about his youth, managing a band, a fighter, a baseball team as hobbies. He never considered them as careers because he had so many obligations: old parents to support and then a family. He was also very rigid about his view of men and their responsibilities. I felt, if he had not been burdened, as most men have with prime responsibility for others, he could have realized his dreams and probably made enough, if not more than enough money, along the way.

Hanna turned over his ten top department-store accounts so I had to deal with the client and plan the individual image of the store through the selection of layout, models, typography, and copy. They all dealt with fashion. In fact, that was the main area that women were allowed to touch in those days. Fashion was considered a legitimate woman's area as opposed to the knowledge of technology that was needed in the "hard" accounts like appliances, watches, automobiles, and corporate advertising. It was only later, when the element of fashion was introduced in these fields, that women began to crack those barriers. For example, instead of discussing performance in refrigerators or even cars, copywriters were concerned with appearances. Merchandise was becoming color co-ordinated. That was fashion. Therefore a woman's expertise was needed, as if a man didn't have any fashion or color sense!

I hired the top models of the day and recall feeling somewhat uncomfortable when they were sent on a cattle call to my office so that I could choose the right type for my client. At that time the leading models, like Eileen Ford, were making top dollar of $200 an hour or more. But they still came to my office and paraded before me as I checked their measurements, their weight, and their "look." They were also treated like furniture by the photographers. I used the best photographers, such as Irving Penn and the Elliott brothers, Michael and Steve. They yelled, taunted, and pushed the models to make them move faster, change poses more easily, get a certain look. I became involved in every area, even areas I'm sure I wasn't welcome in. I insisted on looking into the camera before the shots were taken to check the composition and the last details of the merchandise. I worked closely with the art director. I went upstairs to the printing plant to understand and learn about the different methods used for reproduction. Today that would be appreciated, but there weren't many women executives in those days to do these things. I always seemed to be a little out of step with the times, almost always without back-up except for the few imaginative and secure men who admired my spunk.

It was fun and I loved working for Sterling Advertising, one of the biggest fashion houses in the forties. But I had to learn to be a teamworker. I had been given responsibility and I grabbed it. I felt, too, that if there were any problems with my accounts I should handle them and I would correct them. One day Ray Hanna called me into his office, shouting and pounding his fists on the desk. "Smitty, goddamn it, why didn't you tell me you had a problem with a late ad for Joske's?" I was startled but assured him that the ad finally made the magazine in time. He snorted, "That's great, but when the client called I didn't even know what he was talking about. What I felt like was a fool. I don't like feeling like a fool. They are my accounts. I'm the account executive. I'm the boss. You must tell me what you are up to!" I learned a valuable lesson that day. Most men learned about teamwork through their experience in sports, a form of training denied most women, who were not encouraged to be athletic. But my own past involvement in the competitive world of sports stood me in good stead.

CHAPTER 5
SHATTERED

My year at Sterling Advertising was a productive one, I was doing everything I enjoyed. I managed my own time and I had the status of having a secretary, someone who kept me informed and protected, and the admiration of my boss, who was one of the first men to treat me as an equal. Then one day my secretary, Naomi, told me that there was a man asking for me at the reception desk who wouldn't give his name or explain why he was there. She suggested that I let her handle the man and try to find out what he wanted. Without understanding why, I began to feel a strange flutter in my heart. There was a hard knot in my stomach as I said, "No, that's all right. I'll see what he wants." I walked out slowly and saw the man standing there, somewhat middle-aged, a little faded looking. He was wearing a coat down past his knees, like the camel-hair coat usually worn at that time by singer Perry Como. It was the style. His face seemed almost blurred, without any strong features; his hair was thinning. Although my heart was beating wildly, I calmly asked, "I understand you wanted to see me. What can I do for you?" He stood there, very passively, his arms hanging limply at his sides. But his questions exploded in my ears. He asked quietly, "Don't you know who I am? Look at my eyes; they are your eyes. Look at my nose; it's your nose. I'm your father."

Without missing a beat, I retorted, "You're not my father. I have a father." All I could think of was my mother's warning, "If you ever see him, ever talk to him, he'll make a scene. You'll be embarrassed." In the ten years away, I had missed him so much that I had blocked out all memories of him, and besides, I knew that if I acknowledged him my mother would consider it a prime act of disloyalty. She had impressed me with the fact that she had raised us without any financial help from him. And now, she had reminded me, my stepfather had assumed responsibility for me, and I owed him. I felt trapped and was frightened of losing my mother. My father might disappear again. No matter what, she was still the only one I had contact with all my life.

It seemed like ages that we both stood there. Then he tried again. "You know you have a cousin who has the same first name as you do. She would love to see you. Won't you just come downstairs and have a cup of coffee with me so we can talk about it?"

I said, with my heart thumping, "Why, in all these years, has no one ever written to me? There is nothing to talk about. I think you should leave now."

He didn't make a scene. He didn't reach out. Somehow I wished he had been more forceful. If he had only given me a card with his address or telephone number, I might have had time to think, to call him. I walked him to the elevator. We said nothing to each other. The elevator door closed and I felt a horrible emptiness. As I stood there in shock, the elevator man came back and asked, "Wasn't that your father? He looked like you." I shook my head and went back to my office to call my mother. Subconsciously, I needed her approval, some recognition of what sacrifice I had made. Her response was instant and matter of fact. "Of course you sent him away. He hasn't been a father to you. He probably came up for money." Not a word of comfort, no understanding of how that experience might have affected me. I felt shattered. I felt so alone. That was the last time I ever saw my father.

Years later I started a search for him. I never quite forgave myself for not talking to him, even if it was just to find out why he had deserted June and me all those years. Sometime later I tried to excuse his behavior when I found out that my mother had threatened him with jail because of back alimony if he ever came to see us. I didn't know about that then. But if a parent wants to see a child, there is always a way.

When the war was over, I finally made preparations to end my marriage to Buddy. My mother was so concerned that a divorce would mark me as damaged property that she offered to arrange an annulment so the slate would be wiped clean, as if I had never slept with the man. I agreed to the annulment because I was convinced it would be easier on everyone, cheaper, and less traumatic. At that time, it was easier to get an annulment if you could prove fraud—that someone lied about the finances or swindled a partner or promised to have children and then refused to. I chose the latter, and it was decided that Buddy would say he had changed his mind about having children although I wanted them. How ironic that we put the burden on Buddy. He didn't want the separation, I did. He always wanted children, I didn't. But since I didn't want any financial compensation from Buddy, he agreed. I never believed that an able-bodied woman should expect a man to support her if she had other means of taking care of herself. It was only when a woman stayed home, out of the workplace for years, that she needed support until she had more experience supporting herself. Support for children was a different matter. It was a very civilized parting. The "ideal" American marriage was over. We had been so much like the movie couples, Janet Gaynor and Charles Farrell, Fred Astaire and Ginger Rogers. We had met, fallen head-over-heels in love, and courted. I wore his fraternity pin, accepted his engagement ring, and then pleased our parents by marrying. I had the nagging feeling that I had failed.

The end of my marriage to Buddy, the actual legal parting, left me feeling empty and I began to feel old. I had closed off one portion of my life. But even the party life I was living was beginning to lose its glamor. I had unwittingly honed the art of flirting, catering to men, which gave me immediate acceptance but no lasting approval. There was no problem gaining approval in the office because I had always been successful there. But in my personal life there were problems. I decided to go west, to California, for a vacation. Aside from my period in Kansas City, I had never traveled outside New York. I loved it so, it was my world.

Planning to go to California was my way of getting off a treadmill. But although I had told my parents that I was only going for a vacation, I prepared for any eventuality. I had to leave Sterling Advertising, which by this time was suffering budget cuts. The fashion business and the advertising industry were experiencing a mild recession. It seemed a perfect time for me to examine what I wanted out of my life. I asked Ray Hanna for some letters of recommendation just in case I wanted to explore the job market there. He gave me the letters and the names of some excellent contacts. I didn't tell my parents of my plans because they weren't that clear even to me. This was typical of the way I approached life. I always made sure I had something to fall back on if the bottom dropped out of my plans, and at that moment I didn't know what was waiting for me if I did return to New York City. It didn't hurt to have alternative plans. It was a strategy that stood me in good stead most of my life, helping me to survive many a crisis.

I was still going to a psychiatrist once a week on an off-and-on basis and had to tell him of my plans to go to California. He suspected that I might be running away and was concerned with some of my supposedly off-hand plans to check out the work available. He felt we were just getting closer to some of the things that made me cry, although I kept protesting I was happy. But I was angry with my mother for the lack of support she gave me whenever I turned to her for help, and this was the topic of most of my visits. I was finding it difficult to handle my anger. I had suppressed it for so many years. I was in a state of shock when my psychiatrist said one day, "Perhaps you would have been better off if you were an orphan. At least then you would know you had no mother. You can't seem to accept the fact that you will never have a mother, certainly not a mother who will give you the approval you need, not a mother who is even capable of showing you the love you dream about."

I was terrified at what he was saying. I had so much vested in loving my mother. Even though I fought her over the years, I usually ended up by apologizing for my behavior, always anxious to get my mother's approval. Since I had vested her with so much power to give or withdraw her love, I was not strong enough to let go, to get free. I was so afraid that my world was going to crumble that I was unable to articulate my feelings clearly or even to be in touch with them. When it was suggested that my mother was incapable of loving me because she wasn't able to love herself, it was as if a dam broke, and I shouted, "I hate her! I hate her!" My anger spewed out.

It was a breakthrough, but I was not yet in the clear. I had tried being a "good" daughter; I had tried keeping house; I had tried to bury myself in work and in after-hours night life, but I still had my anger. Now I would try to run away to California and put three thousand miles between my mother and me. I told my analyst, "I am going only for a vacation. I need time to think about what's happened. I can't pretend any more that I have a loving family. I don't know what I can do to change things." He suggested that perhaps I was repeating the same patterns all over again, and that all my plans pointed to putting my feelings on hold. Perhaps he was right. I ended up staying in California almost a year.

Yet how difficult it was to leave Manhattan! I loved working in the city and I especially loved the late-night jazz scene. There was so much to choose from—the clubs that are almost legendary now, the Copacabana, where I saw Frank Sinatra and Sammy Davis, Jr.; the Versailles Supper Club, where Edith Piaf and Perry Como appeared; La Vie en Rose, where I marveled at a young Pearl Bailey. There were the Café Society Uptown and Café Society Downtown, Theodore's—Teddy's to the regulars—Blue Angel, the Stork Club, the El Morocco, Eddie Condon's . . . the list was endless. The plays were plentiful and exciting: Tallulah Bankhead in *The Skin of Our Teeth*, Robert Morley in *Edward, My Son*, Laurence Olivier in *Oedipus Rex*, Lee J. Cobb in *Death of a Salesman* . . . all part of an average evening. I still get goose bumps at those magnificent performances, the staging, the writers. Sometimes the experiences were so heady, the evenings so full, that I must say I longed to go home early and just savor the play, the concert, or the dinner. I have a sneaking feeling that part of my reason for marrying again was to have the luxury of going home early, going to bed with someone warm and loving on a regular basis, rather than dating new men all the time. That may sound flippant, but it is the way I felt. I loved being with the musicians and entertainers. It was my secret world. At that time you could go to the clubs and spend the evening talking with the performers. It was an intimate experience. It was a far cry from the tribal experience of today's rock concerts where thousands flock together but are never close enough to the stage to see the performers' faces or the expressions in their eyes, never close enough to experience direct contact.

At that time the "street" was filled with little clubs, some no bigger than a living room, dark little caves, where for the price of a drink you could find the Duke (the incomparable Duke Ellington) at The Famous Door, pianist Art Tatum at the Three Deuces, the magnificent stylist Mabel Mercer at Tony's restaurant. There were strip joints and the famous hangout for the rich, the Twenty-One Club . . . all located on Fifty-second Street, "the street that never sleeps."

Billie Holiday was singing at her peak. A few years later she got busted. I remember the boxer dog at her feet, the white gardenia in her hair, and a blue spotlight bathing her face, her husband in the background playing heartbreaking blues. There were rumors that she was Thelma Carpenter's girlfriend, but Billie seemed inaccessible. There was something so moody and remote about her as she sang, but what a stylist she was, what pain came from her lips! The jazz violinist, Stuff Smith, was fiddling his heart out and writing songs for a skinny, hard-drinking little girl named Sarah Vaughn. I became friendly with Stuff, who introduced me to the very private and secret jam sessions in Harlem.

At the time I never understood why we had to arrive at the apartment where the sessions were held by going through back-yards and climbing fire escapes. Later a union man told me that they weren't supposed to be jamming and the musicians wanted to cover their tracks. Somehow I think it was more than that. By going through the yards it was hard to find the place again, and they weren't taking too many chances of being discovered by strangers or "white" women who might talk.

Usually it was a railroad flat, long halls and lots of rooms, the kind of place used as a whore house as well as a place to light up or do whatever else one wanted in the bedrooms and kitchens. I was taken to the front parlor where there was an old beat-up honky-tonk piano, and that's where the sessions took place. I blended into the background, hiding in the shadows, and for hours heard the most wonderful, honest music I ever heard. I guess I feel the "rush" from hearing music that some people get from alcohol or drugs. The music would almost drive me mad, making me forget all my problems, getting me in touch with the most primitive side of me. At twenty-three I was living Life with a capital "L" and feeling accepted. But in that world you could also stay anonymous if you wanted to. Around seven in the morning, the musicians would begin to wind down or disappear into the rooms to make love to their women. They would send out for spare ribs, and that would be my breakfast, until I left around eight o'clock to go home, shower, and go straight to my job, feeling completely refreshed.

CHAPTER 6

CALIFORNIA AND BACK

When I left for Los Angeles, I decided to go by train. At that time the Chief and Super Chief were like luxury commuting trains for Hollywood stars and business people who made regular trips from coast to coast. The club cars and the dining cars were truly elegant. I went on the Chief and wasn't prepared for such an exciting time. There is something marvelous about life on a train or a ship. You feel cut off from all responsibility. There is nothing you can do while you are captive on the train. I had a comfortable roomette and intended to read and relax and think about my future. Instead, I met some interesting women and men on the train and we partied all day and on into the evening. We laughed, dined, and played cards. No one seemed to notice or mind that I didn't drink along, although most of the men I was with on this trip seemed to be heavy drinkers. They were in their late thirties and forties. They loved hosting and they spent money freely.

The trip to California took four days and three nights, and as we were near our destination, the men suggested to another woman and me that we take a weekend off and see Las Vegas before we settled into our vacation. I hesitated, concerned about taking off with strangers who would be footing the bill, but we had spent three days on the train and they had behaved like gentlemen. I had their business cards and they said they had business in Las Vegas. My woman friend and I would have plenty of time to sightsee and relax while they worked and, they added, there were no strings attached. We consulted with each other and decided it would be an interesting adventure. It was naive and could have been dangerous but rootlessness was in the air and I felt safe with a female companion along.

I registered at the Roosevelt Hotel in Hollywood, where I had made reservations for two weeks. I dropped off my luggage and packed a weekend bag. And then our group was off to Las Vegas by car at a hundred miles an hour through the desert. We arrived at the Flamingo Hotel, the most lavish complex I have ever seen. I was a little surprised at the look of the people in the lobby and around the pool. I remarked, "Why do the men look like gangsters and the women like gun molls?" They certainly looked like characters from all the gangster movies I had ever seen. My friend laughed and said, "They are. The gangster Bugsy Siegel was killed just a few weeks ago, and gangsters have come from all over the world to protect their investments. Bugsy Siegel built the magnificent Flamingo Hotel and there is a lot of money in the hotel and the casino. In fact, that's why we are here. We have some debts owed us to clear up." Then it dawned on me that these free spenders might be involved in some way with the underworld. One of the men could sense my withdrawal and assured me, "Honey, don't worry, no one is going to hurt you. You're a nice girl. Just keep your nose clean and you'll enjoy yourself." After that I treated him almost like a father. I was both frightened and intrigued by his companionship.

One day he joined me around the pool and lightly suggested that I come to live with him. "Why do you have to work? I'll take care of you. You can expect $2,000 a month to do anything you want, so long as you are my woman. You can buy all the clothes and jewelry you want." I remembered what my stepfather had told me. "Gangsters are usually gentlemen with women, so long as they are not involved with them. They will treat you like a lady, if you don't cross them. But if you do get involved, you'd better toe the line." My sense of survival told me I had better not fool around or even suggest that I was interested. I told him that I appreciated his offer, thought he was a wonderful man, and said he had showed me a great time. I would never forget it, but I did have to get home to my mother and father after my two-week vacation. They would be looking for me. After that he never raised the subject again, was somewhat reserved for the rest of the time, and drove me back to Los Angeles and my hotel. That was the last time I saw him.

In retrospect, I realize that going off with him was a stupid thing to do. It's understandable to me how women get caught up in this life, especially if they have no roots. Luckily, I escaped without a traumatic experience. Yet in spite of a marriage and an affair with an older man, I was still very romantically minded and somewhat out of touch with reality. I was not an innocent but I was naive.

The Roosevelt Hotel in Hollywood was a great choice. At that time there was a tennis club across the street and that's where I made some friends easily. I played tennis every day and began dating some of my partners. The easiest way to break into a strange environment is to do it through some sport you enjoy. At least you have common interests with the people you meet, and that is much more rewarding than sitting in bars.

While I was sightseeing, dating, and thoroughly enjoying swimming and sports, I managed to make a few appointments with my contacts to talk business. One recommendation was to Hugo Scheibner, the owner of a small advertising agency who agreed to see me, warning me that things were as slow in California as in New York. I explained that I was not really looking for anything right now, just interested in exploring the market for the future.

My supposedly casual visit to the Scheibner Advertising Agency turned into a three-hour job interview. He was so impressed with my credentials and the work I had done that he felt he could afford to hire me. He said, "We have just fired three account executives, but with your background you could handle all those accounts easily yourself. Besides, the fact that you are a generalist and can handle copy as well as clients and studio work takes the pressure off my other departments."

At first I protested, insisting that I was here on an exploratory basis. That seemed to make him more eager to keep me in his circle. I remember thinking that he looked unlike any agency head I had known, completely opposite the powerful, burly Ray Hanna. He was short, rotund, about forty, and enjoyed hand-kissing. "Part of my Hungarian background," he explained. I think I suspected that he was flirting with me and that the job offer was secondary. But after talking some more, I realized he was serious; he wanted to hire me and was willing to meet my salary demands! He told me, "I will be willing to pay for your transportation here and your two-week vacation, if you will stay." I made my decision after he added, "I would also want to groom you to take over the San Francisco office. You'll make regular trips there until it's time to move permanently. You see, there is a constant battle between L.A. people and those living in San Francisco. But New Yorkers are welcomed with open arms. So I have many reasons for thinking you will be valuable to me."

Everything seemed to fall into place. I had a strange sense of relief that I didn't have to go home just yet. I wouldn't have to call my mother every day and deal with my feelings about her and my stepfather. I could buy time. I was also very lucky because Scheibner introduced me to a client, a young woman who had her own small house in Beverly Hills. She was glad to have me as a roommate. So within two weeks I had a new job, a new roommate, and the same rush of pleasure I always got when I thought I had a chance to start a new life. As long as I kept busy, I didn't have to probe too deeply into my feelings.

I threw myself into my work. It wasn't long before I was commuting to San Francisco to service the accounts we already had and to make new client calls. I loved going up on the train, the Lark, which was a regular commuter for businessmen. It was an overnight train, and there were more weekend affairs started and continued on that train than most people knew. It was a traveling Peyton Place. I began to be a regular and partied with most of the gang. Then I went to stay at the Palace Hotel, one of San Francisco's oldest and most elegant hotels, with a huge enclosed courtyard that used to be for horses and carriages and was now converted into a turn-of-the-century dining room.

San Francisco suited me emotionally more than L.A. I loved the fog, the tiny sparkling city, the steep hills, and the cable cars. It had Chinatown and the harbor, and for a ferry ride you could be transported to Sausalito, a residential community with lovely boutiques and excellent restaurants. I used to hate going back to L.A. because of the long distances to drive to work and appointments. I thought L.A. was ugly, like one big used-car lot. At that time it was called a city that grew topsy-turvy. There were certainly beautiful homes in selected areas, and there were some wonderful nightclubs on the Strip, but for people who could afford it, it was just a jumping-off point for Palm Springs, Las Vegas, or for skiing up north. I missed the theater and concerts, the easy access to lectures and museums. I felt Los Angeles was a wasteland culturally and a stifling place, although I studiously avoided talking about this to any of my colleagues. Nothing is more repulsive than a visitor to a strange place who constantly raves about what he or she left behind.

No matter how much I worked, I always found time to be involved in the important issues of the day. There were fund-raising campaigns for the Progressive Party, which we all called "the third party," and benefits for the film writers who suffered from the blacklist even before the McCarthy period. The Hollywood Ten were unable to work in the motion-picture industry, except under assumed names, and there were threats of possible violence wherever they made appearances. At these meetings, women were always seated by the aisles, so that if fighting broke out we would be in a position to trip the goons running down the aisles toward the stage. I also did a lot of standing on street corners collecting names on petitions for the third party.

As for my work, I felt happy and successful, and there was very little pressure. Somehow the song is right: "If you can make it in New York, you can make it anywhere." New York City teaches you to handle competition and to have a lot of drive. No one is laid back in New York and they like it that way. So, with my energy, I could handle the work with very little effort. My politics brought me into contact with some wonderful young men, but I wasn't ready for any more relationships. I needed to be unattached. When it came time for Hugo Scheibner to send me to San Francisco, permanently, I suddenly balked. I began to miss the East and had a strong desire to go home. The work was easy here, but not challenging. I reasoned that if I went to San Francisco, I would be committing myself to a long stay; I would feel an obligation to the clients who would be my full responsibility. Everyone tried to convince me to stay. I even went to an astrologer for a reading on my future and was told that I should prepare for a long trip at the end of which I would find romance! I decided it was time to go back to New York City.

By this time I had been away almost twelve months. I felt I was ready to handle my relationships at home. I had survived completely on my own for a year, made friends, held down a job, and still managed to be involved in world problems. I felt very much together. No one was around to criticize me or question my decisions. So I decided I would go home and spend some time with my parents until I could decide what I wanted to do next. It never occurred to me to prepare myself emotionally for my return. Now I was stronger and I could handle anything, I thought. I thought I needed to live with my parents for a short time because I had spent every penny I earned. I didn't know whether I wanted to stay in advertising, write, act, or become professionally involved in politics. I wanted to do something that was more challenging.

My mother wanted me back at home because she was having problems with June, my younger sister. June had just separated from her first husband and her life seemed to be floundering. My mother thought I could give her some support and also motivate her to get a job and be self-sufficient. June had wanted to be an artist all her life and had studied at the Art Students' League after she dropped out of high school. Her first marriage was to another artist, and neither of them had much money to live on. They managed between some financial help from my parents and some commercial art work her husband was able to get. June had no money, no business experience, and no desire to get any. Her idea of death was to have a nine-to-five job that would take time away from her painting. My mother felt it was unhealthy for her to stay home and paint, and they didn't want to subsidize her. So I jumped right in, sure I could straighten everything out, naturally taking on a mothering role yet again.

I returned to a fairly pleasant atmosphere for a while. My mother and father were happy to see me home, but we all knew that my stay with them would be temporary. New York City welcomed me with open arms. It's there I felt most alive; I felt I owned the city and knew every nook and cranny of it. I'd been involved in politics since I was sixteen; in California I had fought for the blacklisted Hollywood Ten, and I did so again. That's where the most exciting things were happening. There was a big push on to get the Progressive Party on the ballot and run Henry Wallace for President. It was such an idealistic, exciting time. If that period could be labeled, it could be called the Period of the True Believers. We had hope. We thought we were really in touch with a new world in the making and we could change it for the better. We worried a little about Henry Wallace. He had been a gentle vice-president, he had led the New Deal farm program, but he was somewhat of a dreamer. He was also a farmer who raised a very successful strain of hybrid corn. We made him our hero. I don't know that he ever wanted that but he agreed to stand as the Progressive Party's presidential candidate in 1948.

We weren't the official version of the middle class; we weren't suburbanites paying off mortgages. We thought we were part of a new grassroots movement. We really believed we were in touch with the working class. We were from New York; we were in the arts; we were romantic. We were raising money for the third party . . . and I became involved in the fund-raising. In fact, I joined the advertising branch of the Wallace-for-President movement. I had so many contacts from my previous activities in the advertising area, and the advertising group seemed the most practical and the most organized. Some of the members included wealthy, socially conscious people like Horace Titus, the nephew of Helena Rubinstein. We had hootenannies because folk music spoke for the people and New York was going crazy over country and folk music. There were Pete Seeger and The Weavers, and they could stir up thousands to sing-a-long. Our arts council rounded up the talent to perform for Wallace in small cabarets around the city. I organized a series of special parties in the homes of millionaire sponsors who found they could safely relate to this cause. For each party we would approach a select group of about one hundred, invite them to some beautiful mansion for tea and entertainment. We would have celebrities appear and sing, dance, do monologues, or just host. Those people who accepted the invitations were asked to pledge an advance donation, usually around $1,000 each. It never occurred to me that, while we were talking about a grassroots movement, we were actually tapping the middle class and the rich for help. We saw no paradox in that except that we really began to lose a sense of what the average person was thinking.

I began to meet all the entertainers and it was an exciting time for me. The talk was also going around about a new talent in town, John Henry Faulk. The story was that he had been brought up from Texas to be groomed as a new Will Rogers. He was a raconteur who also did monologues that took sharp pokes at the foibles of society. This was then a fresh approach to all our concerns—racism, poverty, unemployment, atomic war. He was evidently in heavy demand but he was willing to give his time. I had never before met a Texan, knew nothing about Southerners or "good ol' country boys," but I was anxious to meet him and see why he was creating so much excitement.

I planned a party that would bring together the Broadway actor and singer Alfred Drake, playwright Paddy Chayefsky, and John Henry Faulk. Although Paddy was a writer, I understood he had also developed some monologues around his own material. His approach was influenced by his New York street background. All three accepted when I told them who was sponsoring the party, how we were raising funds, and that we had a financial commitment before the date. I was very excited about pulling this party off. It sounded as if it would be a perfect balance of performers. Actually, Alfred Drake, the best known, was successfully appearing on Broadway in *Kiss Me Kate*. The night before the party, John Henry Faulk called to say he would have to cancel. At first I was stunned, and also taken off balance by his strange-sounding, thick southern accent. It was really like a foreign accent to me. But it's what he said that completely confused me. I was sure he was spaced out on drugs. He sounded very friendly, although we had never met. "Lynne," he said, somehow stretching my name into three syllables. "Lynne, honey, I'm not goin' to be able to come tomorrow. Mama is sick and I have to fly to Texas to see her."

I murmured, "I'm sorry. It must be serious if you're going home."

He chuckled, "Oh, don't worry your little sweet head about it. Mama will never die; she'll just turn into an old gray mule. I'm sorry about the party. It sure sounds as if everyone is goin' to eat high off the hog." I didn't understand so I just said, "Oh, no problem, some other time. I understand. Thank you for calling. Good-bye."

The night of the party, Paddy came and so did Alfred Drake, and it was a very successful fund-raising event. Paddy turned out to be a very down-to-earth man who was delightful doing his monologues. But he was an intense, dedicated writer who worked very hard at his craft and didn't seem to have much time for playing or laughing or being spontaneous. I think the night I met him he was at his most relaxed, and he became very interested in me. He looked slightly taller than I, round, and rather cute with a droll sense of humor. We were both the same age, in our late twenties, but somehow, in spite of his serious attitude, I felt I was older. Perhaps it was his short, rotund appearance, his almost boyish, cherubic face. But he was so intelligent, so bright, and so comfortable to be with that I began to date him.

He had recently broken up with a woman he was later to marry. But at that time he was unattached and I think somewhat hurt and lonely. I felt more like a good friend, or even like part of his family, rather than a potential lover. But Paddy was patient and tried talking to me somewhat seriously about the future. He shared his dreams about his writing, said it was his number-one priority, but felt very close to me. He was the kind of man who nurtured his family ties, took his obligations seriously, and had a small circle of loving friends. Most of our time was spent visiting these friends and getting into stimulating conversations about the state of the world and the arts. They all seemed to accept me as Paddy's fiancée. I had the feeling they were happy that someone turned up to take his mind off his recent breakup with a woman he had been seeing for a few years.

Paddy was becoming recognized for his writing, which in later years included the scripts of *Marty* and *Network*. We celebrated the acceptance of a major story by *Cosmopolitan Magazine*, which paid him $25,000 for the work. He was so practical that even at his age he carefully put it into the bank, after paying off all his debts, and had the balance put into "income averaging," which meant spreading the money over five years, giving himself about $5,000 a year to live on. I respected him for that, although I was sure that I would never have been so careful. (Of course, $5,000 a year in 1947 was probably the equivalent of $15,000 now.) We kept on seeing each other, but he was adamant about weekends. He needed these for uninterrupted writing, which left me free to date. He was not happy about this, but I had not made any commitment. He never pressured me to sleep with him, and evidently that was not a very strong issue between us, but it also meant I slipped more and more into being a friend and put the thought of marriage out of my mind. I don't think sex was a high priority for him. He liked companionship, hated big parties, and never splurged on too many material things. He had very simple desires, something that I understand never changed, even when he became a successful film and stage writer and a millionaire. We shared a lot of interests. Sometimes I think if he had been a little more aggressive sexually, I might have been more interested. I seemed to need that chase, that courtship.

I'm not too sure that sex or lovemaking wasn't some sort of addiction for me. I didn't drink much, never smoked, but I could get lost in lovemaking. That seemed to mask any pain I felt. I had a great hunger to be loved, to collect people, to be sure I would never be abandoned and left alone as I had been in my childhood.

One night he took me back to the club called Cabaret for Wallace to watch him do his monologues for another fund-raising event. For years after I never went to a party without half-expecting it to be a fund-raising event. John Henry Faulk was also performing that night. It was the first time I had seen him or heard him since the telephone call. I was surprised to see a man older than I expected. He seemed to be in his mid-thirties, slightly balding, with a small paunch. He certainly didn't fit the image of the tall, lanky Texan I had envisioned, since he was not only pudgy but also not very tall. But I was mesmerized by his performance. When he finished his turn, he joined a woman he was sitting with, whom he kept calling the Countess. She had a small child at the table with her. My first thought was that he was married, but while I sat there, he kept smiling at me, leaning over toward my table and whispering remarks about me being such a pretty woman. His companion had taken the little boy to the washroom during Paddy's performance. I smiled but tried to pay attention to Paddy's act. John Henry was acting outrageously and explained that he was going to wring the neck of that child, who was kicking him under the table. "If he doesn't watch out, I'm goin' to kick his butt until he barks like a dog fox." I was sure that he was pulling my leg, but he was refreshing and different. He saw his date returning and quickly asked me, "Can I call you some-time?" I just had time to smile and shrug my shoulders.

When Paddy finished his routine and came back to the table, he asked what Faulk had wanted. He said that name as if he had bitten into something sour. "That man is talented, but be smart and stay away from him. He hasn't been in this town very long, but he's made the rounds. He's a womanizer." I don't know how many women really know what that word means. I just assumed it meant that he slept around a lot, but only because he hadn't met the right woman. Then Paddy told me that he had an assignment in Hollywood to work on some scripts. He would be gone for six weeks but hoped I would wait for him. He asked, "Please don't let anything happen to you. I do want to talk to you seriously when I get back." I had no reason not to promise. Six weeks wasn't such a long time. So I promised.

CHAPTER 7

JOHN HENRY

After Paddy left for California, I was involved in yet another fund-raising party. As I walked in I noticed John Henry Faulk surrounded by a group of admiring women. I had done some checking on him, and no matter to whom I spoke I got somewhat the same story. He was a terrifically talented man, a man who swept into town and charmed the women as well as the men. He had the kind of charisma that you could find in some leaders or demagogues or even evangelists. But the message was always the same to me. "Don't get emotionally involved until you see the whites of his eyes. He's had a bad marriage and a lot of problems around custody of a daughter. He'll never settle down." I must admit that everything I was warned about intrigued me, and on top of that I felt protective toward him. Any man going through a traumatic divorce and having problems with his child touched me. Surely a man like that was only running around because he had been hurt so badly. I was staring at him when he looked up and caught my eye. I felt myself blush, averted my eyes, and immediately went to another room where I pretended to become engrossed in the paintings on the wall.

While I was lost in thought, he startled me by tapping me on the shoulder. "Why are you running away from me?" I felt awkward and mumbled, "Oh, I saw you were surrounded; I knew you were busy." He patted me on the arm and reminded me that he had asked to see me again. I looked at him and completely forgot his physical appearance. He seemed so sure of himself, so mature, and so interested in everything that I couldn't help but be attracted to him. And there was a certain delight in being sought

90

out by one of the most talked-about personalities in New York at the moment.

John Henry looked at me approvingly, sucked on the pipe he was smoking, and said calmly, "Are you rich?" I was absolutely disconcerted. Who talks so openly about money and asks such personal questions of a stranger? In his tweedy suit, smoking his pipe, he looked somewhat professorial, and there was a feeling that he was in control. Here I was, a sophisticated New Yorker (I thought), completely baffled and thrown off balance by a Texan (a country boy, he told me). In a strange way, he made me feel wide-eyed and young, a rare experience for me.

He laughed when I didn't answer his question about money and explained, "Look, honey, the only reason I want to know if you are rich is because I don't have much at all, and I'd like you to come to my apartment where we can talk. So if you have money, how about you buying the eggs and we'll have breakfast?" That seemed logical to me and I thought very honest. He wanted to tell me about his CBS experience and what happened to him when he was thrown on a full-network broadcast without any preparation. He also felt we had a lot to say about "the way the world wags."

We left the party and took a taxi to his apartment. The building was on 52nd Street near the East River and close to one of the most exclusive apartment buildings in New York City, River House. But his apartment was in the basement, and I don't mean it was a basement apartment. It was the basement; there had been coal bins there, and heavy water-pipes still covered the ceiling.

But as he showed me through the place, all I could summon up was, "Oh, so much room! You are lucky, so many apartments are tiny boxes that feel like small cages." He laughed at my attempt to be polite and didn't seem at all bothered by his quarters. He explained that most of his furniture had come from adoring fans. He spoke frankly about his tough times on the country-music radio show he hosted from five in the morning to nine, and had a very personal relationship with his listeners, who would send him things. He said they were all fans who had also come from the country and missed it. He had five old leather couches spread throughout the big space he used as a living room. His silverware came from Schrafft's; a waitress had filched it for him because she had what they call Down South "totin'" privileges. If people felt underpaid, it was understood they would make it up with whatever they could "tote," and that certainly sounded better than stealing. The walls were a light canary yellow in an attempt to provide some light to the almost windowless basement. Part of the ceiling was painted with stars. It was all sort of whimsical and imaginative. We stood under "the stars" talking a bit about his problems with CBS. He explained that some big executives had met him at a party in Austin. He was doing his usual off-the-cuff performing at his friends' house, and the top brass became very excited at this new, fresh talent. It was the nearest thing to the kind of humor Will Rogers had used to captivate a nation still able to laugh at itself. John Henry said he was in fine form that night and didn't know who they were. He mostly made his living as a college English teacher. But they didn't take any time to convince him that he belonged in New York. His kind of humor would fit in with the country-music craze that was sweeping the country.

So he packed his bag of monologues that he had honed over the years at parties. There was the one about the little boy who had no shoes that began, "Mister, shoes ain't so important, 'less you ain't got none." The routine about the Republicans noted that "they should be put on reservations, 'cos they walk backwards all the time, and they could hurt themselves . . . we want to preserve them for our children." There was the garden-club lady who said, "You know how good it was to find that good ol' darky to take care of my dahlias . . . when you have someone in your bed who knows just what to do it's heaven . . . and then old Jim just went up and died on me." There was the Southern Congressman who was filibustering in Congress one day and was told, "Tom, you remind me of a baby mockin'bird, a whole lot of mouth and very little bird." He had monologues that could make you cry . . . the young black farmer who had his prize watermelons slashed by marauding white boys . . . a preacher who transported you into the hearts of his congregation . . . John Henry had the rhythm down pat, something he had learned from listening carefully to the preachers in the churches. He got his Master's degree with a collection of songs and sermons. He could tell heartbreaking stories about blacks in chain gangs. He filled that evening with me with magic. I became one of his most adoring fans. He was stimulating, outrageous, and almost completely off-the-wall. He was an educated man but he could use the idiom of the sharecropper.

We finally ate the eggs I had bought and cooked. Afterwards we sat on one of the leather couches and I stretched out and put my head on his lap, as he told me why he was now doing a country-music show on station WOV instead of full network on CBS. It seems they thought he was not yet ready to do a five-day-a-week show. He didn't have enough material and his talent was still a little raw for that medium. He had not been trained, he was not given enough time to prepare. They weren't ready to spend a lot of money on him as an investment. He said he didn't have the discipline to turn out as much material as the show needed, and he insisted most of his regular material came out of years of ad-libbing. That was to be a bone of contention with us for years, as John Henry kept insisting that he was best at ad-libbing, and I reminded him the audience didn't care whether he worked one minute on his sketches or one year, just so long as they sounded fresh. Even Will Rogers would work for hours on a three-minute piece to make it sound spontaneous.

At any rate, he was fired from CBS, and after a difficult few months he did get his own show on WOV as a disc jockey who spun a line of country patter between the records. He had plenty of time to ramble on that show, and he liked it. The problem was there was very little money. He seemed to be pouring out his whole life to me that night, as if in a panic to include me in all phases of his life. I was fascinated as he leapt from topic to topic. He talked about the South and the problems the blacks still had, the poverty and the ghettos. He told me about his childhood and his feeling of being a loner. He cried, I cried, and we formed, I thought, a wonderful friendship. Throughout the evening, he hadn't tried to kiss me or in any way make love. He just stroked my hair in a most comforting way. I felt so privileged because I thought he had let me see his most vulnerable side and had shared so many of his feelings about the world.

I enjoyed his boyish enthusiasm, although to me he was an older man, more mature and authoritative than anyone I had known before. He certainly was the opposite of Buddy, I thought. Where Buddy was passive, gentle, and unable to express his deepest feelings, John Henry was active, articulate, able to cry, and in charge. He was also a foreigner, as far as I was concerned. I was charmed by his accent, his colloquialisms, and his strong feelings on every subject. His honesty about his family was completely alien to me, since I had been brought up never to discuss the private lives of family members. At one point he looked down at me, stared into my eyes, and said, quite out of context, "Do you have a handicap?" I didn't know what he was talking about, but he pointed to my eyes and said, "Your eyes squiggle, they move back and forth." I laughed and said, "It would be just like you to call it a handicap. Most men when they see my eyes move call them 'dancing eyes,' or they think I'm moving them on purpose to flirt." I explained to him that I suffered from a congenital eye complaint called nystagmus, which is characterized by rapid but tiny eye movements. I can't feel it or see it in the mirror but people have said it draws their attention to my gaze.

About this time the dawn was breaking and the city would soon be bathed in daylight. The evening had been enchanting and I hated to break the spell. But I thought I had better get home before my parents would awaken and worry. I was still a little concerned that my stepfather would get upset about my being out all night. John Henry called a cab, handed me a package of promotional material about himself, and said, "Read the material. Show it to your parents and they'll see what kind of man I am, and then save tomorrow night for me. I'll come and meet them." He put me in the taxi, and as it drew away I watched him do a little jig in the street. He was irrepressible.

I showed my mother and father all the material on John Henry. They were impressed by the description of his talent, his involvement in political and social issues, and his future potential. The promotional material prepared them for their meeting with him, although they were somewhat stunned by his thick Southern accent. I was not prepared for John Henry settling down for the evening with my mother and father, comfortably talking about himself. I thought we were going out to dinner. But he seemed to enjoy sharing his problems and his feelings with them and they were dazzled. My stepfather's usual distrust of Wasps seemed to fade as he listened to John Henry talk about loving matzo-ball soup and black-eyed peas. He also talked about how wonderful the Jewish community had been to him. They welcomed him with open arms, had him lecture at their fund-raising parties, and were surprised by his knowledge of Jewish culture. My mother insisted that he have some dinner; it would be easy to warm up a plate of stew she had made. He accepted, and praised her wonderful cooking. I looked on in wonder as he held them in the palm of his hand. Their approval and the whirlwind courtship that followed gave me little time to check all the danger signals along the way.

After he finished eating, he turned to me and said, "Let's go. I promised to take you out and it's still early." I was not prepared for what followed. Instead of going dancing or to a movie or even a party, we went straight back to his apartment. I wasn't concerned because I looked forward to another evening of conversation. I had not yet realized that most of the conversation centred on him and I should have been warned when he commented, "I enjoy a woman who can enter a conversation, who makes a contribution." I hadn't opened my mouth, I had been so awed by his repertoire, his force of energy. It should have made me aware that his idea of a conversationalist was someone who listened. It might have prepared me for the future.

We were no sooner in his apartment than he turned to me and said, "Come on, honey, take off your clothes. We're going to bed." I must have looked shocked. I was certainly not ready for this kind of aggression. He looked at me and chuckled, "Honey, what's botherin' you? Something has clicked between us. When things are right, you don't have to play games. You know I'm in love with you." For me those were the magic words. Why, he loved me even before he got me into bed! He didn't like playing games, and he had proved it by opening himself up, not only to me but also to my parents. I even felt I was making a mature choice because it was not the same high I had in the early days with Buddy, nor the feeling of abandonment I had felt with my Latin lover, Hernando. John Henry was older, more mature, and not at all like a dashing, handsome Romeo. He had already seduced me with his mind. I found myself doing just what he wanted, but not quite sure how I was going to feel in bed with a man who so coolly told me to get undressed. But when he started making love, it was a different matter. He was an excellent lover, almost a technical genius, completely absorbed in doing everything possible to arouse me. I completely surrendered. His poetic vision of life had touched me, and now he was also able to satisfy me physically as well.

The next few weeks we were together all the time. He wanted me to meet all his friends, and he had a wide circle of people he had met in his short time in New York. He was still friends with

CBS executives, all of whom still enjoyed having him at parties. They were relieved that John Henry was a survivor and that they had not destroyed his life by enticing him up here as the new Will Rogers and them dumping him without warning after only a short time on air. He introduced me to his political friends. I was impressed with Alan Lomax, a huge, burly man who had made his reputation collecting folksongs and sponsoring some of the best folksingers of the day. I met the activist Corliss Lamont and the gentle but opinionated Southerner, Clark Foreman, who headed Emergency Civil Liberties, a spin-off from the more conservative but now-established Civil Liberties group. These men had a special camaraderie, a closeness I had not seen in men before. They were not afraid to hug, hold hands, and generally exchange the most intimate feelings. They were all involved in the rights of the disenfranchised, and most particularly in getting Henry Wallace elected.

John Henry introduced me as the woman he was going to marry, although we had not even discussed the matter at that point. He told them his father had said, "Marry a Jewish woman and you'll be assured of success in the business world." He teased me about that but assured me that I was a kind of talisman for him. It's interesting, we never went dancing, we never went out for intimate dinners, and we were always surrounded by his friends, all of whom seemed intelligent, unique, and articulate. It was unusual for me to be so quiet; I was used to holding forth, claiming part of the spotlight, but it was different with John Henry. With him, I was willing to be his mirror, to provide admiration, to make him feel good. I certainly had had enough experience doing it for my mother. He was certainly being generous about including me in his life. He seemed to focus all his attention on me. He made me feel that he had found the right woman.

When we had known each other for about a month, he told me he wanted to speak to my parents about our relationship. I cannot believe how docile I had become with him. He told me to wait in another room so he could speak to them privately. He was going to ask for my hand in marriage. I felt I was the star of a dramatic play. So, like a "good girl," I played out my role. I sat on the floor eavesdropping. I heard him tell them he wasn't earning much yet, but he expected that some day he would make it to the top. He loved me very much and wanted to give me everything, including New York, which he expected to take by storm. (I felt I had already "captured" New York.) He recognized the fact that we had known each other for a short time, but he professed to know me well and he hoped I knew as much about him as if we had been "courting" for years. In any case, he had long since won over my parents and while they suggested we wait before we set a marriage date, they seemed completely happy with a man who seemed so sure of his own destiny, who had the gumption to stick to his goals in spite of disappointment.

During those few weeks he also introduced me to his bank manager, secure in the knowledge that my presence and my background would make it easier for him to obtain a loan. He thought the bank manager would accept him as stable now that he was planning to marry again and take on responsibilities. I also met his former wife and her new husband and was able to convince them that their daughter shouldn't be used as a pawn.

Then one evening Clark Foreman told John Henry he was concerned about our rushed wedding plans. "John Henry, how much do you really know about each other? I haven't heard much about Lynne except that she is Jewish. I wonder if you are treating her like some exotic flower rather than a real person. You seem more impressed by her Jewish background than by any accomplishments. Is it because you have never dated a Jewish woman?" I was shocked but Clark seemed genuinely concerned about both of us, and I had a sneaking feeling that he was right; John Henry didn't know that much about my emotional problems, my feelings of insecurity, my home life, and I was disturbed about his constant need to mention my Jewish background. In fact, I was uncomfortable about his repeated statement that Jews were so much better, so much more sensitive, so much more cultured than other people. I suggested that his feelings were based on a reverse anti-Semitism. I reminded him that Jews are people, and as human beings they are entitled to all the faults of other human beings.

That night, after we left Clark's house, we had our first real argument. It was the first time I had ever challenged him and he saw that as disloyalty, as if I was turning against him. He demanded absolute approval. I was amazed at some of the stirrings of relief I felt at our discussion and used the opportunity to suggest that we take a little more time to get to know each other. I suggested that we stop seeing each other over the summer and I would spend time at my parents' summer home in Nyack County.

The moment I said that I unwittingly set up a challenge for him, and evidently fueled his determination to get married. My father seemed happy, my mother seemed happy, and I thought I must be happy if everyone was so pleased. At last I was doing something right. I must have been marrying for all the right reasons. How typical of that era that we never discussed what we wanted out of the marriage. I never talked about my goals. We never talked about children, except that he told me it was difficult for him to have children; his sperm count was low.

John Henry decided he didn't want to wait; he didn't want all the fuss of a planned wedding. He asked, "Why don't we just go down to City Hall and get married?" I did insist that we have something more formal than City Hall and asked for us to be married at Ethical Culture, a humanist organization that welcomed people of every religious denomination. I had been to some meetings and was stimulated by the leader, Dr. Algernon Black. Ethical Culture fit in with my ideology and my feelings about the world, without having to deal with religious teachings. The leader was out of town, but we were able to engage his assistant, Dr. Nathanson, to act immediately. I think Nathanson was charmed by John Henry and made some concessions and rearranged his schedule to accommodate our new wedding date. We were going to have a small ceremony in his study and invite a few friends, including Elizabeth and Alan Lomax. They were probably the worst possible people to have at a wedding. Their own marriage was in deep trouble and they were in the destructive stage of fighting and acting out at every opportunity. But they were long-time friends of John Henry. I just prayed they wouldn't say anything obstreperous at the ceremony, because they had so little respect for the exchange of vows.

The morning of our wedding day, John Henry and I planned to meet our friends at the Ethical Culture building. We were spending the night at my mother's apartment since my parents were staying at their cottage in the country. The Ethical Culture building was about twenty blocks from the apartment. It was a hot June day and I so wanted this day to be beautiful. I was glad my mother wasn't around to interfere, and I thought we only had to worry about ourselves. But we almost didn't "make it to the church on time." As we walked along I realized that I didn't have any flowers and asked John Henry to stop and choose some for a small bridal bouquet, with a *boutonnière* for himself. He balked, saying, "Honey, this is the hottest damn day! The flowers won't live that long. It will be a waste of money." I argued that, if we took a taxicab, we would be there in a few minutes. He refused, arguing that he wasn't going to take a taxi for a few blocks. I found myself standing in the middle of 57th Street and 6th Avenue, screaming at John Henry for the first time in our courtship. "I don't know why I am marrying you. I don't know that we have that much in common except our politics. You don't like intimate dinners for two. We are always surrounded by a mob of people. You don't like flowers. Why can't you be more romantic? Why in the hell are we getting married."

Two friends, Steve and Mike Elliott, wandered by and stopped to ask if anything was wrong. I sheepishly introduced John Henry and said, "We are on our way to get married." They duly congratulated us, and when they left we broke down in laughter at the ludicrous sight we must have presented. But, oh, how I should have listened to that inner voice! I was willing to believe that John Henry's actions were part of his eccentric nature, just his way of being outlandish. I did get the flowers; we didn't take a taxi; we did get married; and Elizabeth and Alan Lomax emitted only one grunt when we used the words "honor and obey."

CHAPTER 8

LOVE AND MARRIAGE

When I think about it, I realize that from all my actions during dating, John Henry had every right to expect me to be his alter ego. I rarely questioned him, admired him unconditionally, made only a few demands on him, and never broached the subject of my needs. I'm not so sure I knew what they were. And at that time I wasn't working because I was reassessing my future, so I had all the time in the world to spend with him, happy to allow him to make all the arrangements.

While I was fascinated with his Southern background, I was also unprepared for the unbelievable differences between us, not just Judeo-Christian but also Easterner-Southerner. There was a strong tradition in the South that expected women to be soft, gentle, and acquiescent. They learned to ask for things in very roundabout ways. "Now, honey, if you don't mind, if it isn't too much trouble, will you take tacky little me to go shopping?" Believe me, this wasn't an exaggeration, but I didn't have any idea such manipulation existed. When I wanted something, I usually went straight to the point, and that was the worst way to handle a Southern man. You needed a strong fist in a velvet glove. But then I hadn't even opened my mouth too much in the beginning, so all hell broke loose when I did. I had completely confused his political views with his views about the role of women. I was not at all prepared for his traditional views on marriage—the man as head of the household, the breadwinner; the woman, the mother and back-up for her man. Even if I accepted that, I was not ready to accept that men had a need for "peccadilloes," as he described the actions of men. Straying apparently had nothing to do with marriage. Our first encounter with that started the night of our marriage.

We had all returned to the apartment for a small reception. During the evening, I felt isolated when John Henry spent most of the time speaking to a woman friend, gently stroking her arm as he talked. That evening I complained about his attention to her on our wedding night. He immediately chastised me, "Don't be a child. You are behaving in a very neurotic way. I liked the woman. It has nothing to do with our relationship. Don't be possessive." Of course, I felt he was right. I knew that my stomach churning and my feelings of abandonment were all related to my childhood, and I had no right to impose my feelings of jealousy and inadequacy on him. He added, "You know, Lynne, I have been told by a mother and three sisters what to do all my life. No woman is ever going to tell me what to do again." I asked him if his problems with his family were going to be visited on our relationship. I didn't think I was telling him what to do, just trying to keep open communication about some problems that seemed to need airing.

But for a few weeks everything seemed to be going relatively smoothly. We went to the country to spend two weeks with my parents. We swam, played tennis, and made love. He seemed to get along well with my parents, until he began to invite his visiting Texas friends without checking with my mother. He assumed he had the same rights as I did. They were a wild bunch and when my mother complained about them overrunning the place, he warned me that my family wasn't going to run him either. "Don't think because they have money they have the upper hand." I was shocked. "I don't know what you are talking about. What kind of money are you talking about? You talk as if we are millionaires rather than a comfortable, middle-class family."

We finally went back to our basement apartment on 52nd Street to take up married life in earnest. Now he decided that since he had to rise every morning at four to get to his radio show for the 5:00 a.m. to 9:00 a.m. stint, my role as a wife was to get up and make breakfast and send him on his way. I thought it odd, as all he wanted was a bowl of cold cereal. I might have understood (oh, that conditioning) if he had wanted a hot breakfast and we could have shared some conversation before he started for work. But it seemed important to him. I did want to please him, and I did want to "grow up" and act like a wife.

Since I was getting up every morning, I decided to go to the show and keep him company. I wasn't prepared for the people who wandered into his studio every morning. At first I thought they were country people; they were a different group than I had ever come in contact with. They seemed shy, poor, and they only came alive when they saw John Henry, their hero. He played the kinds of songs they could relate to, and often cry to. It was a combination of hillbilly music, western, and country. I always remember lyrics like "It's no use to bother to talk of mother now, would only hurt father" or lyrics about sharing a bed with six other siblings and sharing "one cold potato and bed." In fact, most of the people came off the streets; they were the whores, the pimps, and some shift-workers going home. What they all had in common was that somewhere in their lives they had been on a farm, and John Henry's program on wov made them remember their beginnings, and some of them had a lot to cry about. At different times John Henry would invite a drifter, a cowboy called "Slim Jim," to come and chat with him. Their off-the-cuff conversation was wonderful, but it could only happen on a small station at five in the morning. They chatted about the old times, what happened in their childhood, and about the experiences "Slim Jim" was having drifting around the U.S. For a while he seemed to have found his "stompin' ground," the city. Even here, John Henry was surrounded by a coterie of adoring fans.

That's how I started to appear on the show with John Henry. I was there and he would sometimes ask me to sit in with him. I never pretended to be anything but his adoring New York wife. I would make lots of unintentional mistakes when I tried to express myself in their terms, and the audience would laugh sympathetically. That came across to the radio audience and they began to take me to their hearts. After all, I was just what they admired, a young wife who was willing to get up and share the chores with her husband. They never thought of me as a radio personality. The show began to take on a different sound and become more interesting to a wider spectrum. John Henry saw this as an opportunity for me to begin appearing regularly so I could take it over when he went on his lecture tours, which would last about a week at a time. That's when he did his monologues and was able to supplement his small salary at wov. Before that he would have to pay another disc jockey to take on his schedule and it cut into his income. Now he saw that I could do it and he wouldn't have to pay me. I didn't mind because I was so delighted to be working and making a contribution and sharing this part of his life with him. The station managers apparently approved because Johnny didn't get any flack about having a woman take over.

I did not know that they were very interested in the way I handled the show or that they were listening and monitoring me every morning. What happened was that we had a spirited conversation going every morning about our views on life and the world, including thoughts on married couples. I realized that I was talking too much when John Henry would kick me under the table and motion for me to shut up. But there was a fire, a tension going between us that caught the imagination of the listeners. I'm not sure John Henry was prepared for my outspoken opinions, and he didn't always seem comfortable at my taking over the reins. I wasn't even aware that there was any jealousy between us, or that he might see my aggressiveness as competitive. We were right for the times; there was a rise of Mr. and Mrs. Shows like the "Tex and Jinx" show with Tex McCrary and Jinx Falkenburg and "Breakfast with Dorothy Kilgallen" and her husband. Audiences liked peeking behind the scenes in a marriage and being accepted in the family. We would argue a little more at home because I thought the show would profit from more planning. I wanted a loose index of some of the topics we would discuss, so we could choose important issues of the day as well as focus on some philosophical problems surrounding relationships. He balked at that, again stating that his greatest successes came from ad-libbing. So I prepared and tried gently to guide the show so it wouldn't ramble too much. I gave him free rein from five until seven, but from seven to nine, I structured it a little more, because I felt we could draw in a wider audience. Then I began doing the show alone when he went off on lectures.

I did the commercials while Johnny was away, commercials that he as a personality resented doing. I loved doing them. My old advertising background made me understand the work that went into them. I changed them to make them stronger. I wrote some myself for the station's advertisers and the top brass loved it all. Those first few months were wonderful. I felt so close and so much a partner, and I was getting such satisfaction out of being on the air and being successful.

Our life seemed to be divided between the radio show and partying most of the night. Since we had to get up at four in the morning to do the show, it rarely made sense to go to sleep. It was a perfect schedule for us; it gave us lots of time to see all of his friends, catch the round of events, do our show, and even come home in the morning and feel refreshed enough to make love, knowing that we could sleep all day. It was on weekends when we had no show to do that I realized that our sleep was being disturbed by friends from the past, gypsies (chorus girls) who had keys to his apartment and used it to crash in or start a party. We had to change the locks and finally tell them he was married and his single days were over. We didn't have to deal with reality very much at first. It was so much fun living this unstructured life.

After a while, management came to me while John Henry was away on one of his trips and offered me my own radio show. They thought I had a good rapport with the audience, they liked my range of topics, and they thought I handled the commercials beautifully. Since I had taken over the commercials, their sales had jumped. I was breathless and said I would love to discuss the show with them and they set up an appointment with me to go over contracts. I was going to get paid and still be able to do the Mr. and Mrs. Show with my husband. Surely this would make him happy.

There was no discussion possible. He told me it was impossible; I could not be tied down to a paying job. At least on his show I could take off when necessary. Not only did John Henry say no, but my parents reinforced him. It was one thing to help out but to compete with my husband was dangerous to our marriage, they said. I was heartbroken at the lack of support I received for wanting a career along with my marriage. I tried to explain that it would only be a few hours a day, not like working nine to five. But John Henry was unyielding, and about this time he decided to talk to me about having children, which would add fuel to his argument that I was needed at home. Up until that time we had not even discussed a family. He said that we were going to splurge, go to a restaurant, and talk about this. I was pleased that he was going to spend some time with me alone and discuss something that important. I grabbed at any incident that seemed as if we were making mutual decisions. I always felt off balance with him, and just when I felt most frustrated he would turn around and do something that set things straight. Now he was going to discuss our future. Perhaps what we talked about would make it easier for me to delay a career in radio or even advertising.

That evening over dinner and with candlelight, John Henry explained, "Look, we've been married six months now. I think it's time we discussed having a family." He laughed and said, "You know, Southerners believe in keeping their wives barefoot and pregnant." (What they really meant was that to keep your wife pregnant was to keep her out of the way.) He added, "I always wanted a whole passel of children." He would always lapse into colloquialisms when he was entertaining, nervous, or trying to make a point. I had never given much thought to having or not having a family before that. I imagine it was because I had raised my sister from such a young age that I had already been a "mother." But when he told me he wanted a family, all the romantic ideas of bonding, having the baby with the man you love, the closeness of a family, the ties that make a relationship stronger . . . all came rushing to my mind. Here was more proof that John Henry was indeed settling down. And, of course, if I had children, I didn't want to work for the first few years. That certainly settled the decision about the radio show. I had sworn that if I ever had children I would not be a "Sunday mother." I would always be available for my children. And I wanted children with the man with whom I was going to share the rest of my life.

I became pregnant almost immediately. We wanted this baby. We had planned for this baby. I was doing something I really wanted to do. I assumed he wanted to be a father, too, a father like the one I had never had. Surely if a man wants babies, he intends to be involved in their care—feeding, diapering, cuddling, disciplining, loving. I wrote the whole scenario. I never for a moment thought realistically about John Henry's background. I didn't recall that he told me that "havin' children is just like shellin' black-eyed peas." I didn't realize that for a lot of men from the country having children was just a way of life, part of the assets of a family. It had nothing to do with the day-to-day care; that was "woman's work." I found out the hard way. But I created a whole fantasy about being pregnant. For me, it was going to be the most beautiful time of life. It was my spotlight. I was going to be pampered. I spread the news to anyone who would listen—

my family, my hairdresser, waiters in a restaurant. I am pregnant; I am unusual. No one in the world has ever been *this* pregnant.

We chose a doctor whom John Henry met at a party. He turned out to be a wonderful obstetrician. I think John Henry liked him at first because he was a Southerner from Kentucky. He was a Southern gentleman and he understood the role of women. But to me he was more than that. He was gentle and most concerned about me as a prospective mother. All my plans to glow throughout my pregnancy were thwarted for a while as I succumbed to hideous, twenty-four-hour morning sickness. I couldn't stand the smell of any food without getting sick. I found that staying up all night partying was too demanding. I was tired and wanted to rest. John Henry saw that as an act of sabotage. I was interfering with his party-going and I was demanding too much attention. He was accusing. "Your really don't want this baby. Your sickness is psychosomatic." I cried, "My God, of course I want the baby. That's all I've been thinking about."

"Well, why are you sick? You better look into yourself, and if you are too tired to go out, stay home. You don't have to go out with me all the time."

For a moment that struck a note of terror in my heart. Why did he want to leave me at home alone? This was his baby, too. And my stepfather's words came back to haunt me. "Always go everywhere with your husband. Don't leave him alone, or he might end up with another woman."

My mother wasn't very excited about becoming a grandmother, and she also worried about where the baby was going to sleep. Certainly the basement apartment was no place for a newborn. She pointed out that the basement was damp and there were no windows. I cheerfully answered, "Why, there is a window in the back, in the kitchen area. I'll arrange the bassinet there, and I'll fix the backyard up for her outings." There is no doubt that I lived in a dream world, but I felt love conquered all. As it turned out, we didn't have to live in the basement apartment when the baby was born because some exciting new prospects developed.

John Henry had been approached by a management group who were creating programs across the country for a fictitious figure called Pat the Rancher, and they wanted John Henry for that show. The format would be what he was used to, music and talk, but he would have to become part of the community as Pat the Rancher. This was a name they had syndicated. It also meant moving to Paterson, New Jersey. Going across the bridge and leaving my New York City was like pulling up roots and going to a foreign country. But it did mean better pay and more exposure. I fell in with the plans. I met the men involved and was instinctively concerned about their tough negotiating and the antiquated method they had of dealing with talent. I thought they were rough with John Henry, but he seemed oblivious to it and put it down to the suspicious nature of a native New Yorker. He wanted that show. Since plans were still in the embryonic stage, and they didn't expect things to materialize until September, John Henry decided he wanted to go home to Texas to visit Mama and "get his creative juices to flowin' again" before he tackled a new job and we tackled moving. He was elated at the thought, and this became a pattern over the years. Whenever he was in trouble, John Henry would go home again.

Now that he had the promise of a new job, he asked if we could take the money we had received for our wedding present and buy a new car to travel to Texas. He wanted to drive down so we could stop along the way and visit all his friends in the South—the Tennessee gentlemen farmer who raised walking horses, the young preachers from Kentucky who had been "carnies" (carnival men) before they had found the truth. We would visit the prison farms where he had collected prison songs, the black churches where he had gathered material for his sermons, the material he used on the lecture platform. He made me feel that the trip would be the most wonderful adventure, and then at last I would meet his family, his mother, his three sisters, and his "crazy" brother. There were also grandchildren and assorted cousins and nieces and nephews. I was somewhat concerned about taking all the money we had received as wedding presents out of the bank. My parents had given us this money to buy furniture when we had a proper apartment. And since they had already been supplementing our income with generous gifts, I wasn't sure they would approve. But, as usual, John Henry convinced me it was the best thing to do, and the right time. "Look, darlin', this may be the last time in a long time we can do this. We are startin' a new family of young 'uns, I'm startin' a new job, and I want you to share all my past with me and know about my childhood."

After a warning from my doctor that we shouldn't drive more than a couple of hundred miles a day, since I was just approaching my third month, we took off to conquer the South. John Henry left his job at wov, we had taken all our money out of the bank, and we were expecting a baby in six months and nothing but the promise of a new job to come back to. It was in the heat of the summer and the only air-conditioning units we had on the car were the old bullet type that fastened on the outside of the window.

The trip seemed to come at a time when our friends had lost some of their idealism. We had believed so firmly in Henry Wallace for President that we were sure he was going to win by a landslide. In fact, he lost by a landslide and we were still shaking our heads wondering how we could be so wrong. Did we really think we had the pulse of the grassroots movement, or had we in fact been preaching only to the converted? In a way, I rationalized this as a trip that would let me see the real grassroots, give me an insight into the rest of the country. I had led a very protected life as a New Yorker. I began to look forward to the trip and John Henry seemed so happy. I thought I could stand a few weeks or months away from my mother and stepfather, the pressures of politics, and the worry over money. All that was on the back burner.

CHAPTER 9

THE REAL SOUTH

It was a fascinating trip, interspersed with arguments, morning sickness, and, despite my doctor's warning, drives of about five hundred miles a day. The air conditioner broke down and I kept cool by patting the dripping water from the conditioner on my face. But we kept to the schedule John Henry had set, and the contrast in our visits was amazing. First we spent a few days with his friend who had Tennessee walking horses, and it was a genteel, quiet time. We were put up in an old-fashioned bedroom with a four-poster bed and lovely patchwork comforters. There were parties planned and we had a chance to meet the neighbors and enjoy a bit of the "old South."

Then we traveled on to another part of the country and another society that was in stark contrast to the mannered world we had just left. We arrived in "Bloody" Harlan County, in Kentucky, to stay with the young preachers who had set up their own religion after repenting of their lives of crime. The women were not allowed to wear make-up or take any role in the church. They very clearly had full responsibility for raising the children and feeding the men and obeying their masters, their husbands. The women were colorless, withdrawn, and moved like ghosts throughout the wooden frame house. We were invited to services the next morning and John Henry agreed. We were separated in the church and the men sat on one side, the women on the other. No one seemed concerned about my pregnancy and I joined the women on the long hard benches that had no backs. I was not prepared for the four-hour sermon, which included violent throwing down of the Bible to the floor to illustrate points and angry, bullying calls to come to God. They stomped, shouted, and moaned. I was almost afraid I would faint from the heat and exhaustion. John Henry seemed to enjoy it all. That was the amazing thing about him: he could feel equally comfortable in this environment or in the aristocratic environment of the Tennessee gentlemen farmers. I just wanted to die and go on our way.

After "Bloody" Harlan County, which got its name from the violent race riots that had flared up around that time, we went on to visit some of the prisons. That's where John Henry had done most of his research for "the easiest Master's degree ever received . . . nothin' to do but collect ten songs and they handed me this piece of paper." He was part of a rebel group of Southerners who chose to be contemptuous of higher education. He felt that a Ph.D. demanded nothing more than moving one pile of bones from one spot to another. He used his own experience as an English teacher. "All I had to do was tell stories and give A's, and the students and me got through with no trouble. Why, I was the most popular teacher in the university."

We were welcomed by the governor of Tennessee and given a courtesy tour of the prison and then brought back to a large auditorium. The administration had prepared some entertainment for us with the prisoners performing. We certainly didn't get to see some of the terrible conditions and violence and fear that John Henry had showed me through the songs of prisoners who had no way out. There were black people who had been incarcerated for some small offense and then forgotten about, the key thrown away. I marveled at John Henry's camaraderie with the prison officials. Evidently they were not worried about the songs he had collected. He was a Southerner just like them but excused as being "one of the bleedin'-heart liberals." I was uncomfortable watching the show but touched by a prisoner who sang a song, "Just Walkin' in the Rain," with such pathos and longing. It was a song he had written about his walk from his cell to the laundry room where he worked, and it referred to passing through the outside courtyard, feeling the rain and seeing the sky and dreaming of freedom. Later, Johnny Ray took it and made it popular, treating it like a love song, without anyone really understanding its origin. How unfair. I asked John Henry if there wasn't any way we could help this man get his freedom. To my unpracticed eye, he seemed to be so sensitive and evidently a model prisoner or he would not have been included in this theater company. We were allowed to talk to the prisoner. We said we were going to try and do something for him, and after almost a year of trying we did secure his parole.

After that visit we stopped along the way to see some of the tourist sights, to sample Southern cooking, to marvel at the great muddy Mississippi. I ate catfish, cornbread, and black-eyed peas. I enjoyed the slow pace of the people, the friendliness of the wait-resses, and the colorful characters we met along the way. But it hardly prepared me for meeting the Faulk family. We were finally on our way to Austin, the capital of Texas, and the home of the University of Texas. John Henry had talked so much about his sharecropper roots that I think I half-expected to see characters who looked like those I had read about in *Tobacco Road*. The moment we arrived in Austin, John Henry began to get excited, pointing out landmarks all along the way. And then he turned up a dirt road and parked. He pointed to a huge ante-bellum house down the pathway and said, "Honey, we're home!"

That was the longest path I had ever traveled. This was no sharecropper's house; it looked like a mansion to me. As we walked up the path to Green Pastures, I could discern an army of rocking chairs rocking furiously. All eyes were watching to see this pregnant Jewish woman from New York whom John Henry had married. In spite of the confusion and the sudden chaos as relatives jumped out of their chairs to greet us, I realized that John Henry had described his family accurately. I could almost pick them out.

There was Botchie, who was short and somewhat dumpy. She was so named because she seemed to "botch" everything up, yet it was Botchie who invested her schoolteacher's salary in real estate and made more money than the rest of the family put together, loaning it out at responsible rates of interest to encourage fiscal responsibility. Then there was Texanna, named after two states, Texas and Arkansas, who was noisy in voicing her rigid opinions on everything under the sun. She was a pietistic churchgoer who seemed to have very little tolerance for the foibles of others. She believed that "if you are a drinker you should stand in the middle of the road and get kilt." Hamilton, the oldest brother, was affec-tionately called Hamtoon because down South everybody has a nickname. He had been in and out of hospitals and was diag-nosed as a manic depressive but was as much a victim of the state hospital system as anyone I had ever met. When he wasn't on a tear, he was gentle and rational, with twinkling eyes and a warm sense of humor, and he later married the "widder woman" Bernice.

Then they brought me over to Mama, who was patiently waiting and rocking in her chair. She was a strong, feisty woman, and she grasped my hand so warmly that I immediately felt welcomed. I remembered hearing stories of her strong disciplinary action, and how she would threaten to give her son to "the niggers" if he didn't behave, but I saw in her the mother figure that I had never had. She was in charge of the family and was evidently adored in spite of her strong hold. Then I heard a loud voice call from inside the house, "Welcome to Green Pastures," and I saw a tall, cheerful figure emerge. This was Mary, who had moved into the house with her husband Chester, who was a Catholic. Mary had converted to Catholicism from Methodism. I don't know whether that conversion caused the family more grief than John Henry's mixed marriage to a Jewish girl. Actually, being a Catholic was worse than being a Jew because, as I was told, Jewish women had reputations for being great housekeepers and money managers. Neither was true in my case. Mary raised six children and turned the wonderful house, with its white columns and sweeping staircase and large rooms, into a fine restaurant called, inevitably, Green Pastures. That way Mary could make some money and enjoy a lifestyle she couldn't afford and still keep the family home intact. She knew how to manage and even made use of her Catholic connections by occasionally borrowing funds from the Catholic nuns who had money to dispose of for "charitable" purposes. Consequently, Green Pastures was always filled with nuns and priests who were hosted at wonderful lunches and dinner parties.

While I was meeting the family, I could feel they were sizing me up. One aunt summed it up by saying laconically, "Well, she ain't pretty, but she ain't ugly." I was glad I was already pregnant because I thought that would give me some extra points with the family and they would have to accept me. I wanted to like them. I wanted to extend my family. I had led such a lonely life, with few cousins and aunts, that I was glad to join this family, if they would have me. They teased John Henry a lot about being big time and leaving Texas to "eat high off the hog." He was the only one that had left; all the others lived a stone's throw from Mama. The next few weeks we were on a round of parties, dinners, breakfasts, and coffees. It seems that every few hours Texans break for something to eat, any excuse to socialize.

It was Mama I liked the most. We had long talks and she told me a lot more about her late husband and her relationship with him, the quiet understanding they had, the long hours of reading together, the easy sharing of duties. She admitted that he lived in his own world and she was concerned that the children never had a chance to really get close to their father. She said she had learned a lot from him. She had always been tolerant of "the nigras" but learned to call them "coloreds" instead. She warned me about John Henry always needing his way and softly said, "Be firm with him or he'll run you to the ground." She picked up my hands and smiled, "These hands are such soft hands, not spankin' hands. You'll have to learn to be tougher." She ruled the family with such a firm hand and I was amused to find that John Henry changed completely in front of her. Although he "cussed" freely at home, told shockingly obscene stories to shake an audience, and revealed more than he should about his family, he was a model son in front of Mama. He stopped smoking and using bad language, resisted telling stories, and was sure to address her as Ma'am. But there was no doubt that she doted on him in spite of all of her warnings about his behavior. She wanted to make sure he didn't get his head turned too easily by the big time.

Then he took me to meet two of his long-time friends. Roy Bedichek and J. Frank Dobie, who were much older than John Henry, had been his mentors and teachers. Roy Bedichek was tall and lanky, charming and gentle, and spent his life as a naturalist observing birds, especially the whooping cranes. J. Frank Dobie was the storybook picture of a Texan. He looked somewhat shorter than Bedichek, with more meat on his bones, a shock of startlingly white hair, clear, twinkling blue eyes, and the perennial Texas sombrero. He loved to tell stories and I sat at his knee and listened. He rarely asked for opinions and rarely interrupted his stories to allow anyone to interject, but then no one wanted to. He gave John Henry credit for opening his eyes to "the problem of the niggers." Both men seemed to know a lot about John Henry, teased him about his braggart ways. The two men were legends not only in the South but also throughout the United States.

Dobie had been on an exchange program to England, where the British found him exciting and stimulating. Dobie was married to a shy, upper-middle-class woman who never failed to be appropriately dressed with white gloves and a hat. She shuddered at foul language but was well-bred enough to pretend she hadn't heard it. She took excellent care of Dobie, making sure he always had the time for writing, preparing his meals, and keeping away visitors who were unwanted interruptions—a role John Henry tried to get me to play when we returned to New York.

Later I met Cactus Pryor, the popular radio personality who worked on KTBC, Lyndon Johnson's television station. And we went to Johnson's ranch for a fish-fry and met his wife Ladybird and their two daughters. I was in awe of the tight community and the closeness of the family to most of the state's political figures. Lyndon Johnson came for a small dinner party of twelve at Mary's house. I was amazed at how he treated this intimate gathering as if it were a huge rally. He didn't miss an opportunity to get up at the end of the dinner and start a speech with "Ma Friends . . . " and then launch into an account of his goals as Congressman. He was quite sure that every word he uttered was making an impact. I will never forget his eyes, which could be cold as ice even as he was being most warm in his greetings. It would be years later that I would look directly into those eyes as he asked me, "What can I do for you, honey?" That would be the start of a lawsuit and a confrontation with the man from the South who was at one time the great hope of the liberals. But for now he was just country folk and a friend of the family. And so was Ladybird, who was adoring, quiet, and approving. Rumors even then were that he had a stable of women and that most of the money for his communications empire came from her side of the family.

It was like being thrust into a time warp to meet the staff at Green Pastures . . . all the servants who worked for the family had grown up on the land in shacks that were still standing. Amy was one of my favorites. If you talked to her when most of the family was gone, you would be treated to her singular impressions of the members of the white household. There was a lot of laughing behind our backs, but also a lot of loyalty from most of the blacks who had been treated "right" by members of each generation.

It was soon time for us to go back to New York City, to find out about work and a place to live and to prepare for our new baby. By this time, I was feeling quite fit, and as my doctor had promised, my morning sickness was over. I was well into the fourth month and beginning to feel the baby kick. A wonderful feeling of well-being suffused me. The night before we left, the whole family got together. There were impromptu speeches and a little song sung to the tinkling of glasses. A tradition was to welcome and cheer guests on the way by tapping spoons against glasses and singing songs. How I loved all the rituals, the close family ties, the teasing. I envied the size of the family and thought of my lonely child-hood, raising my little sister with no help from aunts or uncles or cousins. John Henry seemed more real there and I felt very close to him, and I suppose safe from his encounters with other women. The trip home was fast. We didn't stop much along the way to visit. It was important to get back and see what was waiting for us. We had no idea at that time that we would be returning to live in Austin ten years later.

CHAPTER 10

RAISING A FAMILY

Shortly after we returned to New York City, John Henry was able to negotiate the contract for the new job as Pat the Rancher. The contract with station WPAT came just as we were down to our last penny and expecting the arrival of our baby in a few months. After he signed the contract, we started looking for a new apartment in Paterson. Going to New Jersey terrified me, for it meant that we were preparing for a more structured life, more responsibility in a "country" that was foreign to me. I suppose it meant growing up. On the plus side, I was looking forward to a strengthening of our family. Having children, I thought, would keep John Henry and me closer together and would tighten the reins on his wanderings. We would have a traditional apartment in a traditional neighborhood. There were plans for John Henry to do interviews with the popular country-western stars of the day, make regular appearances at events, hoedowns, and rodeos. His employers were into heavy merchandising of Pat the Rancher because they hoped to syndicate the show across the country with different personalities. It also meant that John Henry would have to be very active in the community, going to press functions, cutting ribbons, and addressing service clubs.

I was also happy at the thought we wouldn't have to take any more money from my parents. I had resisted as much as possible because I felt there were strings attached that could strangle me. My father had slipped money to John Henry, sometimes over my objections. But he insisted, "John Henry is an artist. He'll make it big some day and it's no problem giving him a little subsidy. And, most important, it makes life a little easier for you." Now I wanted it all stopped, although John Henry saw nothing wrong with the help. He believed he should be subsidized. He figured he was owed. Society owed him. The rich owed him. After all, wasn't he making a contribution to the betterment of society? Wasn't he giving his time and talent raising money for a better world?

John Henry started to ask me questions about my family and especially about my father, my real father, and what happened to him. I told him how I had sent him away, and how desolate and empty I had felt after that. John Henry was outraged that my mother had been responsible for keeping my father from me and insisted that I begin to track him down. His questioning opened up all my wounds, and I found that I was sobbing uncontrollably as I started talking about my natural father. I started to look for him, to get the adoption papers opened to find his last address. I called every Levinson in the telephone directories in the area. I tried to find him through our mutual relatives. Short of hiring detectives, I did everything to find him, anxious to find out more about my past, but my search yielded no new facts. Over the years I tried to track down new leads.

There were other anxieties. John Henry was beginning to come home late from long business meetings. Plans were being formulated for the new show and he spent a great deal of time with the packagers and an executive assistant who also happened to be the mistress of the boss. He would show up at odd hours, and when I questioned him he would become quite irate and tell me to grow up. He said, "Don't be so possessive. A one-night stand has nothing to do with my love for you." I was horrified at the thought. All my fears of abandonment were stirred up by the thought of infidelity. I couldn't conceive of sleeping with anyone else while married, even with the consent of my husband.

We found a nice apartment in a lovely complex of townhouses in Paterson, N.J. Our downstairs apartment in the duplex had two sunny, large bedrooms, a separate dining room, a large living room, and a complete kitchen. It also had a backyard. I was happy that I had a neighbor upstairs who would later become my friend and supporter. We were also just a few blocks from all the shopping, so that I didn't need to learn how to drive. I had never needed a car in New York and never thought it was necessary to drive, as long as I could walk to shopping or use taxis. Although we had spent all of our money on the car and the trip to Texas,

John Henry convinced my parents they should "loan" us another two thousand dollars to put a down payment on furniture.

No sooner was the apartment in order than my waters broke. I was anxious to get to Doctor's Hospital, which was an elegant institution set up like a hotel. One wing was set aside for rich and famous people to come and dry out. I fantasized, as usual, that John Henry would spend long hours with me in my huge hospital room, sharing the intimate dinners I had always wanted. This was one of the few hospitals that had room service for guests. I also thought I would be a terrible patient. I was afraid of illness. I hated hospitals. But having a baby was different. It was a positive experience. I had spoken to the doctor about natural childbirth, but although he encouraged me to learn about it, he asked me to let him make the final decision about medication. Because it was my first pregnancy, it took six hours before I went into the labor room. I remember noticing a huge clock on the wall and every now and then I would watch its hands move, almost as if I were watching a television show and the clock symbolized time passing. I also remember being told to push and I was so anxious to co-operate that I evidently almost sat up straight. But the doctor pushed me back and said, "Don't sit up. Don't be so eager to follow commands. Just lie down and push." Today doctors realize that it is normal for women to squat in labor, but then doctors wanted as much control as possible, and a supine woman was easier to manage. I wanted more responsibility but there were no institutional mechanisms to support individual requests in those days. Yet I did trust my doctor, and that was important. He had certainly tried to listen to my needs as much as his generation could.

I was amazed at how hard the pains were, but I was not frightened. Push. I pushed. I kept remembering why I was having the pain, and that made it easier. At one point I thought I was going to explode. I felt there was a rocket inside me, going to tear me apart. But I didn't explode. A most beautiful peace came after that last pain. My baby was born. I kept thinking of pink clouds and sunbursts. I felt so successful. I couldn't wait to call home.

I awakened John Henry, burbling ecstatically. "We have a baby, a baby girl. Oh, Johnny, it was wonderful. I feel wonderful. The whole world is bathed in pink. I can hardly wait for you to see her." I sensed he was drifting back to sleep, and I hung up thinking ahead to the future. We hadn't yet named our baby. And he wanted me to nurse. I wasn't anxious to breast-feed, but I wanted to please him, thinking that this was evidence of his concern about our child. It would be healthier, he said. I immediately romanticized it and secretly thought it would keep him at home more, sitting adoringly at my feet. I bought the entire picture of contented nursing mother and baby.

My doctor didn't approve. "You lead such an active life. Nursing is best when mothers are content to stay at home and can maintain peaceful surroundings. Your home sounds too active." But I sincerely wanted to try, not having any idea of how painful it is to stop before your milk dries up at home without expert nursing help.

That morning they brought my baby to me for her first feeding. I was impatient because I was on the same floor as the nursery and I was sure that every cry belonged to my child. I ached to hold her. She was considered a good size—seven and a half pounds. I was now down to 105 pounds, looking somewhat gaunt. I thought she looked beautiful, round rosy cheeks, a tuft of honey blond hair, and the most startlingly blue eyes. I could not believe that she had been inside of me just a few hours ago. It was a miracle.

Nursing isn't quite as natural as they make out. The baby doesn't automatically find the nipple and doesn't automatically keep on sucking. Sometimes she would fall asleep and a nurse would flick the bottom of her feet to awaken her. I hated that and felt she was being cruel. I didn't feel any great sensations in nursing. I just liked the idea of holding my baby so soon after birth.

I waited for John Henry to show up, putting on lipstick and combing my hair so that I would look appealing to him. I actually felt quite sexy and sensual, which evidently made John Henry feel uncomfortable. "How can you want to have sex? You just had a baby." I said, "It's not sex, I just want you to hold me. I need you close. It's such a beautiful time." We ordered our first dinner from the extensive menu and added a small bottle of wine. We talked about naming baby Faulk. Since he wanted the first baby named after him, if it was a boy, we compromised. We looked through books of names and found Johanna, which is a Dutch feminine version of John. He decided that would be her name, although it is frowned upon in the Jewish religion to name a child after a living relative. My mother had hoped we would name her after her mother, Rachel.

Finally it was time to go home and I was happy to leave the hospital and be able to be with Johanna more. My parents had paid for me to have a baby nurse for two weeks, but this turned out to be a mistake. The nurse was an old-fashioned type who insisted that she was in charge and that I must allow her to train our child. I must never pick her up just because she was crying. She was a firm believer in the four-hour feeding method popular at that time. You feed a baby every four hours, not sooner. You must let them cry until they learn that they are not to be picked up every time they wail. But I didn't believe in the wisdom of the four-hour schedule. I had heard about demand feeding, and it felt right to me. This would allow me to use my judgment and feed my baby whenever she expressed the need to feed.

I decided to fire the nurse and take over the running of my own home. What I wasn't prepared for was the lack of help I would get from John Henry. I began to realize that he liked the idea of nursing because it did away with washing dirty bottles and sterilizing them. It also meant he had no responsibility in any of the feedings. But instead of having him around more, I found he used the nightly feedings as a time to go out and visit. He made it clear, "Raising the baby is your job. You have all the time in the world." I began to feel incredibly lonely when he was away. I decided to stop breast-feeding. It was difficult and painful to stop. But I wanted to be with the baby and John Henry. Off breast-feeding, I found it easier to take her with us. I could hear her cry almost before she opened her mouth. I doted on her.

I tried to make the meals on time and take care of John Henry when he returned from the radio station. He would be annoyed if I was tied up with Johanna, but refused to take over her feeding or bathing when he wanted his dinner. He felt I was going to spoil her but was determined not to get involved in my job. I called a psychiatrist friend of ours for advice. I was frightened at my depression so soon after returning from the hospital. The psychiatrist explained that John Henry couldn't help. "He does have a problem with competition for his attention. You have to help yourself. Whether you beg, borrow, or steal, hire some help." I called my mother and asked her to help me find someone. I suggested she call the agencies, since most of them were in New

York. She said, "Absolutely not. I don't feel well enough to spend all that time on the telephone. Make your husband do it. It's your baby. You made your bed, now lie in it."

One night John Henry came home, quite disturbed. He said he had a confession to make and needed my help. It seemed that he was having an affair with his boss's mistress and was found out. It got quite ugly and he was almost fired. Instead, the solution was to remove the mistress from the scene. I was in a state of shock because I had bought his accusation that I was possessive and neurotic. He told me that he had been trying to break it off but he wanted to be completely honest with me. He was concerned that someone else would tell me, and he didn't want me to be hurt. For a moment I felt a sense of relief that I was not completely crazy and that what I had suspected was true. I couldn't understand how he could take such a chance with his career. We had a huge fight that night and in frustration he went to strike me. I was furious and hit him back and swore that if he ever hit me again I would kill him. But the focus was taken off the origin of the argument, and when he reached out to hold me, he began making love to me passionately. I had been so hungry for his arms, I was ready to forgive him anything. I felt he had suffered enough and accepted his promise that it wouldn't happen again. It also seemed to establish a pattern that our best lovemaking came after a violent fight. It was as if he had to create some disturbance if things became too calm. He would goad me until I fought back and then we would make love. If I refused to make love because I was so upset, he would accuse me of withholding sex to control him. Having sex was a wife's duty. When I felt most angry, he would calm me by making love. He would point to my anger as "overreaction." By the time I would analyze my feelings and try to understand what he meant by accusing me of overreacting, he was in charge. It never occurred to me to brush aside his complaint by replying, "Maybe I'm overreacting, but that doesn't mean we have to brush aside my legitimate concerns."

Things at station WPAT had calmed down and we were making appearances at rodeos and press conferences and hoedowns. John Henry started to dress the part, cowboy hat, boots, the whole costume. I still played it straight as his New York wife. We met all the country and western stars of the day and they were a lot of fun. I began making some appearances at the station, and this time the station asked me to work with John Henry on a regular basis. I tried to show him how I could be home by ten in the morning and have the entire day with Johanna. It wasn't like taking a nine-to-five job where I had to be away. I could do all my writing and research for the show at home. But it was still no go.

When Johanna was seven months old I became pregnant again. We had talked about having another baby close to Johanna so she would have a sibling. Again, I didn't know I would get pregnant so fast. My mother wanted to disown me completely. She had reconciled herself to the fact that I had one child and now adored her first grandchild. How did I dare bring another child into the world to usurp Johanna's place? She wanted no part of it and handled the problem by not speaking to me for a few months. She reminded me that her doctor had told her she must protect herself from stress.

About that time John Henry saw an ad in the paper for an "executive mansion" for rent, high in the hills. It turned out to be a huge stone house set on about six acres of woodland, with a running stream and deer that roamed freely. John Henry loved it and promised he would spend more time at home if we took that place. He said he would have more room for a study and be able to do some writing. And since we were having another baby, we would have to get a larger place at any rate. I didn't want to move. I agreed it was beautiful, but it was miles from any store or public transportation. He finally convinced me that he would be much happier there. It was the nearest thing to the kind of upbringing he was used to. I wanted to believe it would be best. I agreed.

For a while, John Henry did come home regularly. But he filled the house with people. It was great for entertaining. We had four bedrooms, sun porches, dining room, living room, and acres of ground for hiking and outdoor cooking. By this time I had a full-time housekeeper. Sometimes I think these women were more necessary as surrogate mothers than as help. I always took care of my child; they were responsible for the house and cooking. John Henry was never very happy about having full-time help. He felt that if I was a "real" woman I would enjoy cooking, keeping house, and raising the children. I told him that I couldn't do it all and keep up the entertaining he liked. I wanted to take care of the children; the rest wasn't high on my priority list. I began to question what he meant by a real woman. My stepfather had said a "good wife" has a hot meal on the table at six o'clock and is constantly at the side of her man. Now I was told be be "real."

We were so isolated at Gionti Place in the Haledon Hills of New Jersey that I turned to my daughter Johanna for a great deal of my comfort. Johanna was about a year old. We played together, did housework together, and spent long hours reading together. I'm sure that I put a lot of responsibility on Johanna over the years because of her quiet, thoughtful nature. She seemed so independent, I was sorry that there were no other children for her to play with. Not only were we in a secluded area, but the community was mostly made up of older German families who had settled that area years ago.

John Henry was making a great many appearances for charity for the station but he was also getting tired of parading under the name of Pat the Rancher and felt it was really beneath his dignity to always be a cowboy. He was beginning to look for work back in New York City, and I was hopeful. Then the day came that I began to go into labor with our second child and John Henry rushed me to my mother's to wait out my time. He had an appointment in the city and left me for a few hours. My mother wasn't happy about having that responsibility and urged him to get back soon.

At about ten in the morning I called my doctor to tell him about the pains. He thought I had another few hours to go. He expected this birth would be faster than the first, so he told me to keep in constant touch. About twenty minutes later, the pains started harder and faster than ever. I called the doctor again, and he barked, "What are you waiting for? Get over here. It seems as if the baby is about to arrive!" This left me dependent on my mother to get a cab and come with me to the hospital. We couldn't find John Henry anywhere but left a message where he could find me. By the time I got to the hospital, the pains were so close together that they rushed me into delivery without even prepping me, and a half-hour later Evelyn was born. It happened so fast that I almost refused to get off the delivery table when they were removing me to my room. "Why are you taking me off? I want my baby; where is my baby?" The nurse said, "You just had a beautiful baby girl." I started laughing, and was laughing as they wheeled me back to my room. They had found John Henry by this time, and I startled him by suddenly appearing only minutes after he arrived. He couldn't believe that I had had the baby so fast and was up and talking and laughing. Evelyn was over eight pounds, with black intense eyes, and lots of black hair. We named this baby Evelyn at John Henry's insistence, after me. He said he loved the name Evelyn.

I came home from the hospital a few days earlier than planned and this complicated John Henry's plans for the evening. He had been invited to the opera, by the opera star herself, and was anxious to go. He had bought a new tuxedo and had been looking forward to the evening, sure that I was safely ensconced in the hospital. I was shocked that he didn't intend to change his plans. Throughout our marriage I had been told that either I over-reacted or I didn't articulate my feelings clearly enough. I decided that I would try to be as calm as possible but tell him how much it meant to me to have him home on our first evening with Evelyn. I was nervous about being alone on the hill. I tried to appeal to him but he felt that I was safe at home.

A large chunk of me was chipped away that night. I had always believed if I could be rational with him I would be able to reach him. Wasn't it rational to want him to change his plans for my arrival home? Was it silly to disappoint his friends, when I was a grown woman and could manage for a few hours without him? Why was I making such a big deal taking care of "young 'uns?" Unaccountably, Evelyn had a fever that night and I had to call a doctor. John Henry returned home to blazing lights and an annoyed doctor who was angry at him for leaving me alone, and I felt as guilty as if I had staged this crisis.

That summer we enjoyed the beautiful grounds, picked ber-ries, and picnicked. There was also the promise that we might be moving back to New York City in the fall. Things between us would be better when we got there. John Henry would have a better job. WCBS, the local radio station, was negotiating with him for a disc-jockey show, four hours to play music and talk, again the perfect unstructured format for him. Surely our home life would be better. He would feel more successful as John Henry instead of as a fictitious figure. He was also interested in tele-vision.

I wouldn't feel so isolated and so lonely back in New York City. Perhaps I wouldn't be making demands he couldn't meet. I would also be able to get around without asking John Henry to drive me. It wasn't that I didn't try to learn how to drive, but some people, despite all beliefs to the contrary, are not good drivers, and I am one of them.

Then the contract for WCBS was signed and we were ready to move to New York. We had the biggest party ever at Gionti Place, and as my daughter has said to me thousands of times, "Mother, you are future-oriented. No matter how bad things are, you really believe it's always going to be better." I wanted things to be better.

CHAPTER 11

HIGH LIVING

As soon as John Henry signed his contract, I started looking for an apartment in New York. It was difficult but not impossible. There were some rent-controlled buildings but there were also long waiting lists. I spent days walking the areas we were interested in, meeting every superintendent, every janitor. They knew who was planning to move out and could be receptive to a little "key" money. Since we didn't have that much money to open doors, I depended a great deal on becoming friendly with these people, coming back day in and day out, until finally an apartment was available. The first place we found was in an old building right on Riverside Drive and 97th Street. Our friends Clark and Mairi Foreman lived there and helped us to get the apartment. It was wonderful, with a living room overlooking the Hudson River, long halls, three bedrooms, and high ceilings. They had two children who became our ever-ready baby sitters. I felt such a sense of freedom being back in a neighborhood with friends. It can be so alienating to raise children alone in a city, a long cry from the extended families of yesterday with grandparents and even aunts, uncles, and cousins taking over some of the caretaking. My sister had her own children and husband to care for and we didn't see each other very much during those years from 1950 to 1957. John Henry didn't encourage them to visit too much, and her husband was having a rough time finding enough work as a musician.

My job before I left for the park each morning to let the children play was to monitor John Henry's radio show and tell him what I thought. I became involved in the business end of his career, although I had refused to become his official business manager. I agreed to sit in on business meetings, to go to special events with him, but I was concerned about the image of a tough wife behind the scenes. So I settled for doing the work informally. In the meantime, I had plenty of time to be with Johanna and Evelyn and I loved it.

John Henry seemed to be happy again with his work. He began to appear at benefits and reactivate his old contacts. I was feeling fulfilled with my children and our family life seemed to be stable. He was also being offered spots on such television shows as *We Take Your Word* and *What's My Line*. He was very good as a panelist because the responsibility of the show didn't fall on his shoulders. He was good at cracking jokes, but some of the "ad libs" were planned in advance. The producers, Mark Goodson and Jerry Todman, enjoyed John Henry's seemingly honest, country-boy approach. They were sophisticated and tough game-show inventors. We began to make more money and I unwisely began to buy John Henry more sophisticated clothes. I had no idea that this professorial country-philosopher would respond so fast to his new image. He would come home with stacks of shirts in every color with the then fashionable white collars. He began sporting homburgs. He loved spending money on clothes, but he wasn't that generous about spending money on the children. Then he would fall back on his country ways, referring to sharecropper times. "Young 'uns don't need much. I had one pair of good coveralls and was glad of that. You're spoilin' 'em."

About this time I became pregnant again. It looked as if I was really fulfilling John Henry's prophecy that he was going to keep me barefoot and pregnant, which meant he was going to keep me housebound. But I didn't mind, because I felt a certain sense of peace taking care of our children. The only thing that marred my happiness at the time was John Henry telling me about some of the women he had slept with. "You see her?" he would say at a party. "I slept with her . . . but it's all over."

I could feel my stomach get so hard and my breath so fast that I could hardly talk. "Why, why are you telling me if it's all over? You are going to kill me."

"Honey, I never spend any money on them, I just want to make sure there are no lies between us. I love you. I'll never leave you. No one will ever understand you the way I do. Don't you know that?" Then he would act reflective. "Maybe I just want to prove to you that I'm a man. Maybe I'm insecure."

I would cry, "Oh, I'd rather know you did spend some money on them, that you cared. It sounds so rotten, so cold. Why do you feel you have to prove yourself to me? I love you. We have two wonderful children. You have a good job." Then he would hold me and things would calm down for a while. I would finally say to him, "If you have to sleep with other women to prove you are a man, don't tell me about it. Women aren't the issue. I don't think you even like women. What I don't need is an absentee husband. What's important is that you're home more with me and the children. I need your time and your affection."

There were times when everything seemed to be going all right. I tried not to demand too much affection from him. I knew he couldn't show any unless we were alone. I was enjoying being home with the children so much I didn't nag him about becoming involved. Having full-time help was a relief. I just accepted that certain fathers weren't demonstrative, although I ached for him to hold his children or get up with them in the middle of the night just once or enjoy feeding them. I wanted them to have a father like the one I never had.

One morning as I was getting Johanna ready to go to nursery school, I knew that my pains were starting to come, and I knew that they would be coming much faster than the last time. I took Johanna downstairs to wait for her school bus and explained that I was going to be in the hospital to have another baby and that when she got home from school her daddy would tell her whether she had a new sister or brother. As I waited for the bus a neighbor looked at me and said, "You look like you are ready to pop. Shouldn't you be in the hospital?" I smiled weakly and said, "Just as soon as the school bus comes, I'm going." When Johanna left, I went upstairs to speak to John Henry, who had just returned from his stint at the station. He showed a great deal of emotion. He could see I was having my pains very close together and he ran down the street frantically trying to flag a taxi and then we were on our way.

Hours later I had my third child, a baby boy. There is something wonderful about completing a family with children of both sexes. This time I didn't stay in the hospital more than a few days.

They were getting mothers on their feet almost the next day and sending them home. In a way, I'm sorry some mothers don't have the luxury of a two-week stay because they will never have so much time for themselves again. Something must be planted in every mother, something like a time capsule, that keeps sending out little bursts of responsibility. She never, never stops worrying about her children, even after they are married.

For the first few months after Frank was born, I would spend as much time as possible lying beside his crib on a bed next to it. Those were magnificent, stolen moments. I would talk to him and tell him how wonderful it was to have a son. I talked about his sisters and how he had a family that loved him. Even at a very early age, Frank Dobie Faulk was shy. (J. Frank Dobie's last names became Frank's first names.) He seemed to be most like Johanna, quiet and thoughtful-looking, but with some of Evelyn's energy. If I held him, he would curl into my body, nestling his head into my neck.

By that time we had decided we needed a larger apartment. Someone at CBS had some connections in a newer building on 79th Street behind the Museum of Natural History and a block away from Central Park. It was a rent-controlled building, and for the magnificent monthly sum of two hundred dollars we were able to move to 118 West 79th Street. When people ask how we raised our children in an apartment, I point out that those apartments were built for the very wealthy. We had four bedrooms, three large ones and a small room for the housekeeper. There was a full dining room, a large living room, three baths with double sinks in the butler's pantry, and a walk-in closet for canned goods. The rooms were separated by a long hall down which I'm embarrassed to say my children rode their tricycles. (The buildings were so solidly constructed that no one ever had reason to complain.)

I was so proud of our new home. But I didn't realize how differently people from different cultures see things. John Henry's mother had finally come up for a visit. I was so happy to have that large apartment for her to see because I wanted to share my New York with her. I wanted her to approve of my children, her grandchildren. I stood in the middle of the living room and pointed out the view. "Look, you can almost see down to the river. No buildings to block our view."

Instead of looking out, she looked down into the street and said, "Honey, all I see are some dirty old rooftops." She stayed only two weeks. "People are happy to have you come the first week, happy to know you stayed the second, and glad to know you'll be gone by the third." She didn't believe in overstaying her welcome.

I felt I was fulfilling an important role for John Henry, advising him on business deals, playing hostess to his many acquaintances, throwing huge parties for all the people who became his friends through his activities at benefits and in politics. But I found myself taking a backseat role without realizing it, the role that most of his male friends seemed to expect. I wasn't aware of it at the time. There was a dichotomy in the way we lived and in what we supposedly believed. On one hand, we thought of ourselves as liberal, political, free-thinkers. On the other, men of that generation still wanted traditional wives, although I don't think they ever realized that's what they clearly wanted. They wanted freedom, but needed us for their base. And because we were proud of their politics, we also assumed we were proud of them. It was years later that Pete Seeger, an inspiring singer and activist, admitted to the press that he had been a chauvinist in those days, that while he sang of freedom for oppressed minorities, he was practicing oppression at home. But no one was talking about chauvinism and women's liberation in those days. Many of us were confused about the roles assigned to us and I for one was angry about being relegated to the sidelines at times. But I was also willing to feel guilty about my anger. Friends never could see what made me so angry, and I could never discuss the deep hurts I had suffered in our relationship.

All through these years in which my private life was in such upheaval, there was a parallel upheaval in society around us. Those were the years of Senator Joseph R. McCarthy's influence, and no American who lived through those years was untouched by the experience. What John Henry and I didn't know at the time was how closely intertwined our personal lives were to become with the political turmoil.

Joe McCarthy was an obscure senator from Wisconsin until he got hold of the Joint Committee on Un-American Activities in the 1950s. He then used the tactics that later came to be identified with McCarthyism—innuendo, the waving of "documentary evidence" that was never tabled or disclosed, character assassination, guilt by association, intimidation—to create a wave of hysterical anti-communism that for a time eroded the bases of democracy in the United States—the free press, academic freedom, artistic freedom, freedom of discussion, the presumption of innocence. I am still terrified when I think that, were it not for the mistake he made when he attacked the U.S. Army, McCarthy might very well have parlayed the hysteria he created into a successful bid for the presidency. There was a fear in the land . . . and those people who were not yet touched were afraid to talk about anything controversial, even in the sanctity of their own homes. McCarthyism had effectively stilled any dissent or sent it underground.

Feelings ran high, and we banded together in our fury as we watched such people as Larry Parks, Abe Burrows, Elia Kazan, Sterling Hayden, and Jerome Robbins desperately try to save careers and reputations by first confessing "sins" and then having to "name names" as proof that they were real Americans. There were others—Lillian Hellman, Arthur Miller, Paul Robeson—who, knowing that there was no possibility of dealing with the committee unless they named other people, pleaded the Fifth Amendment and refused to co-operate. Some suffered loss of work and some even committed suicide. Many who were blacklisted improved their positions by fake repentances. The tragedy is that people were forced to take extreme positions when the committee's concern was not with rooting out Communists but with the control of liberal thought. Justice William Douglas most beautifully described that period when he wrote: "The struggle is always between the individual and his right to express himself on the one hand, and on the other hand the power structure that seeks conformity, suppression, and obedience. At some desperate moment in history a great effort is made once more for the renewal of human dignity."

Those days the air was charged with strong, intellectual conversation. Our home was a meeting place for entertainers, artists, political figures, and screen stars. It was not unusual for John Henry to call from a benefit he was doing and tell me that he had invited all the performers home. One night the entire Roberto Iglesias dance troupe showed up at midnight. Before they came, I had shopped for all the ingredients for a paella: lobster, shrimp, mussels, clams, rice, everything they had asked for in order to make a paella in true Spanish fashion. They would cook, we would eat. Then they decided to dance. They danced until dawn, singing, stomping, and making the most complicated turns in our living room. I am surprised that no neighbor complained. John Henry attracted people like bees to honey. As I look back, I realize that most of our friends were actually his friends or acquaintances first. I didn't think in those days of forming my own network. In fact, that was usually discouraged by John Henry. Any time I invited a particular friend of mine, he felt it was an intrusion. All my activities were centered on our children and John Henry and his needs.

Composer-songwriter Yip Harburg was a close friend of John Henry. The composer of "Over the Rainbow," "Happiness is a Thing Called Joe," and "Brother, Can You Spare A Dime?" was one in a long line of older men who seemed glad to be his mentors. It was easy for John Henry to be openly affectionate with these male friends. They would hug, with arms flung across shoulders, all outward signs of affection he otherwise found so difficult to show me. If his children or I tried to hug him in public, he would stiffen and retreat.

Our political activities brought us in close contact with Harry Belafonte, Martin Ritt, Sidney Poitier, Ruby Dee, Pete Seeger, Woody Guthrie, Ossie Davis, and the Weavers. Our home was a meeting place for anyone connected with the civil rights movement. We were strong supporters at that time of the National Association for the Advancement of Colored People.

At one of the benefits John Henry was asked to introduce Tallulah Bankhead. When she learned who was her introducer, she grew incensed, maintaining that a bigger name would be more appropriate. When we met in the Green Room, she persisted in addressing him as Canada Lee, a well-known black writer. Tallulah, without her glasses, was almost blind, but she could certainly tell the difference between a white man and a black man. She had a vicious sense of humor and was usually surrounded by an adoring group of gay men who danced attendance on her every wish. She was a devourer of both men and women, and as the daughter of a Southern governor who embraced liberal causes, she was something of a wonderful anomaly.

After addressing John Henry as Canada Lee for the second time, she took out her long cigarette holder and waved it in the air, calling out to no one in particular, "Cigarette, anyone?" John Henry whipped out his pack and offered her one. She turned away and said, "Dahling, not you. You can kiss my ass." Without missing the beat, he answered, "Honey, I'm a Southern gentleman. Ladies first. Turnabout is fair play." She blinked for a moment, then laughed uproariously, as she threw herself into his arms. "Wonderful, dahling," she enthused. "What did you say your name was?"

About this time, his activity with other women started up again. I began to be suspicious when he received a great many telephone calls from "bluebonnet belles," as most Southern girls were called. One day, I heard one of these Texan girls say, "You are just like my daddy. I sure do appreciate all the help you are givin' me." I accused John Henry of sleeping with the girl and wanted to know what all the daddy nonsense was about. I could feel that hideous tightening of my stomach and I started to shiver. He was angry. "What the hell were you doin' listenin' on the telephone? It serves you right, hearing something you shouldn't. Don't tell me now you are jealous of a little ol' baby. I'm just trying to get her started. Her mommy and daddy are great friends of mine. You know, you need to have a little fun on your own. Why don't you go find yourself a nice man to have an affair with? It wouldn't bother me one bit, and maybe you'd stop fretting about nothin'."

This was the first time in years he had suggested I go out. I felt icy cold and began again to think of ways to leave. I looked around our home, watched my children playing, thought of our life and how much we had accomplished, and I couldn't understand what John Henry wanted, what made him need to flirt or sleep with other women. What was I doing wrong? Was I too strong? Was I too demanding, as he suggested? Was I too needy? Perhaps he was going through some identity crisis. Were things rougher at the station than he told me? I cried a long time that night, and began slowly to withdraw from John Henry.

I began to see him more as a bully and a tyrant than as the strong, powerful man I had believed him to be. I also think I was experiencing some of the things physically battered women feel. Although I was not hit, I felt emotionally battered. I didn't realize then how little self-esteem I felt as a woman, because I had all the outward signs of someone in control. I didn't hesitate to argue, to fight back, but I always folded when he accused me of being too emotional, insecure, and competitive. People saw me as strong because I rarely confided in anyone. But underneath it all was stark terror that I would be left alone. After all, it had happened to me before.

I had a great deal invested in making this relationship work. My three children were probably the purest form of love I had ever felt. I had no doubt they loved and needed me. We did have a lovely home. They had a father figure, in spite of the fact he spent so little time with them. When people asked me years later why I stayed with him so long, I replied that when you are living with a problem, so close to it, the solution, whatever it may be, is not always that clear. Our relationship seemed to do best when it was in the middle of a crisis, real or imagined. I once accused him of creating problems, since every time we seemed to be getting along and everything was smooth and quiet, I felt he drummed up an argument. The public image of John Henry was warm, easy-going, and talented, and I'm sure most people agreed with him that I was intense, defiant, and difficult to deal with. I didn't even have one close woman friend to confide in, even if I had been in touch enough with my feelings to articulate my sadness. I realize that we never had a chance in hell of communicating. It would not be until years later that I appreciated the fact that there was one standard for men and another standard for women when it came to marital infidelity, and that the double standard ran deep in social mores and human nature.

By this time we agreed that we needed a business manager who in some way could control our spending. I was immediately put on an allowance, although the entire reason for getting a manager was because John Henry was spending money thoughtlessly on parties, his clothes, and outside entertaining. I was rather adept at getting the money I needed, by making sure my charge accounts were active. The poor Japanese grocer became my banker. Whenever I needed money, I would borrow about a hundred dollars and ask him to charge it to my grocery bill. In fact, my children were introduced to charge accounts when I allowed them to charge at Jimmy's. It wasn't until Jimmy told me that they were buying twinkies for all their playmates that I realized I should explain that someone had to pay real money for these charges. There was a time when my children were so used to charging, when I didn't have any ready cash, that they would go into a restaurant and ask for a glass of water and say, "Please charge it to my mother." I was amazed at the deals many women made with their butchers and cleaners. I was buying sides of beef for our freezer when the butcher suggested he pad the bill and give me the extra money. "All the women do it. That's how they get their extra spending money." I was self-righteous then and replied, "Why, that's like stealing from myself." What I didn't realize is that most women didn't have their own savings accounts or money of their own. It is still a sore point in most households today, although the women's liberation and the consumer movements point to the necessity of women having their own money.

It was about this time that Edward R. Murrow, the celebrated broadcaster, took on the frightening task of interviewing Joseph McCarthy. Murrow was not a radical, but a very rational, small-l liberal who was concerned about the world. He had every intention of interviewing McCarthy in the same manner he had used in interviewing all his other subjects, whether they were politicians or celebrities. Did he know how dangerous it was to ask McCarthy questions on the air and insist on answers? We were afraid that Murrow would end up doing a puff-piece or laying his job on the line. And we were afraid that the CBS network would buckle under pressure, so that McCarthy would be treated with kid gloves.

We held our breath the evening of the show. We were stunned with the clarity, the reasoning, and the care that Murrow used in questioning McCarthy. We stared in disbelief as we saw McCarthy for the first time squirm as he answered the carefully put, carefully researched questions. McCarthy was exposed for the irrational, angry, and bitter demagogue that we all knew he was. And as Murrow puffed on his cigarette calmly and as the smoke lazily spiraled upward, we saw McCarthy symbolically go up in smoke. We fully expected the next morning to learn that Murrow had been fired. It didn't happen. McCarthy had finally run into bedrock. It was the beginning of the country's turn-around. Suddenly people found they could speak freely again at parties and openly espouse liberal causes. For the time being, at least.

CHAPTER 12

SIDESTEP

In the mid-1950s, Senator Lyndon Johnson was grooming himself for the presidency of the United States. He was "a good ol' boy" who had been a protégé of President Franklin Delano Roosevelt. Many of us hoped he would follow in FDR's footsteps, but we were concerned that when he had absolute power he might be corrupted absolutely. He was known to brook no dissension. He demanded absolute, unquestioning loyalty from his minions.

Lyndon Johnson had been a friend of the Faulk family in Austin for many years. The Faulks had been quite political, working hard for their candidates, including Lyndon Johnson and Congressmen Homer Thornberry and Tom Conway. One day we got a message that Lyndon Johnson's people were coming to New York and wanted to talk to John Henry about joining their team. The plan was that he would relocate in Austin and host a television show with his friend Cactus Pryor. The hidden agenda was to groom John Henry to go on the campaign trail for Lyndon when he spread his news that he was going to throw his hat in the ring for the presidency.

The Johnson team hoped that John Henry would be able to mobilize not only the Southern vote (because of his strong family ties) but also the Eastern vote because of his high profile as an entertainer on WCBS. They felt he would have the ear of the people, and the offer seemed to fire John Henry's imagination. I couldn't believe he was serious about accepting the offer. It meant giving up everything he had been working for in New York City. I thought he was well on his way to becoming a permanent fixture; he had carved out a special place for himself. There was a certain rhythm to our lives that had become comfortable. There seemed to be some structure. Besides WCBS and television panel shows, John Henry was the voice of Daniel Boone on a syndicated radio program. He had hosted game shows and rodeos, and he was beginning to do commercials like Manischewitz wine ("You don't have to be Jewish to like Manischewitz"). Yet he was ready to chuck it all for a place in Lyndon Johnson's team. John Henry felt secure with another Southerner; he had surrounded himself with them even in New York. I'm sure he expected Lyndon to be loyal, protective, and grateful for any service he provided. Besides front-running for Lyndon, I think John Henry hoped there would be a position in politics for him. He had toyed with the idea of running for Congress. At first I resisted. I had always enjoyed political activity, but I dreaded the idea of being trapped within the political system. I began to understand that New York really frightened John Henry; he ran back to Texas, familiar ground, each time he felt under pressure. It never occurred to me that I had a vote in the matter. Everyone expected that I would do what my husband wanted; and if it was good for his career, there was no room for argument.

A month before we were to leave for Texas, we were invited to Washington to be the house guests of Lyndon and Ladybird. It was to be a chance for us to get briefed by Lyndon, and for John Henry to test one of his monologues at the Democratic Convention being held that year. It was all part of the grooming process. John Henry acted as if he had a new lease on life; he was thrilled at the invitation. I began to be caught up in his excitement. I so wanted him to be happy, I began to believe that this might be the right move.

As soon as we arrived at Lyndon's home, we were whisked to our room and advised to rest because we had a heavy weekend ahead of us. His home was lovely, comfortable, and unpretentious. But there was the feeling of old money. The antique sideboards, the heavy silver, the mahogany dining table, and lovely large couches all reinforced this feeling. At dinner that night, I watched Lyndon Johnson with fascination. He could be quite charming and solicitous, but I couldn't get over his cold eyes, which belied everything he said. He was an imposing figure of a man, over six feet tall, with larger-than-life features and an unsettling Texas drawl. I half-expected him to speak like a gangster, in brusque, staccato speech.

Ladybird was a true Southern matron: carefully coiffed black hair, soft-spoken, with a pronounced drawl. Her sharp, piercing black eyes took in everything, darting around constantly and yet lingering lovingly on Lyndon's face whenever he spoke. She adored him despite the fact that he seemed to almost snap when she asked a question or made a request. She never seemed ruffled, but handled it all with grace. Their daughters Luci and Lynda Bird joined us for dinner.

Our schedule was tightly packed for the next day and a half. We were to rest that night and then on the Saturday I was going to a luncheon with Ladybird to honor the wives of former presidents. Later in the afternoon we were to go to the White House and be taken on a tour by Lyndon himself. That night was the big night, a private reception with top-level Democrats, and then the Convention, with John Henry performing and Lyndon giving a speech.

We went to sleep on Friday night with high hopes and a great sense of anticipation. The next morning Lyndon was up at dawn, working on his speech and planning his tightly packed day. He was a complete workaholic, watching over every bit of his empire pire from managing his political career to managing the television station KTBC. Although everyone knew it was Ladybird's money that bought these things for Lyndon, he was going to make sure that everyone knew that success depended solely on his control. We had breakfast together and then John Henry was to follow Lyndon around, while I went with Ladybird to the luncheon. I had the strange feeling I was walking through history, meeting the wives of former presidents. I felt as if a wax museum had come to life. I sensed that the main goal was not money but power, and that everything and everybody was secondary to that goal. There could be no satisfying anyone who had that vision. I could see in these women's eyes the control they had learned, the knowledge that words had to be guarded, that no slip of the tongue was ever excused. Empires could be toppled, candidates eliminated, and careers destroyed. These women must have learned their lessons well. They were gracious, they inquired carefully about my background, and they murmured innocuous compliments to each other. I began to feel as if I were smothering and wanted to escape. I wondered if we could ever fit into this society.

After a discreet time, Ladybird decided we should go on to the Congress where we were to meet Lyndon in his office as majority whip. On the way there I confided, cautiously, to Ladybird some of my reactions to the women. She smiled sadly and said, "That is the price you pay as the wife of a man in politics. The higher up he goes, the more vulnerable he is, so the more discreet the family has to be." I was amazed at her openness because, at first, she, too, seemed so closed, so robot-like in her duties. But she went on to disclose more about her feelings, as if we were now part of the family. "I worry a great deal about my children, especially Luci. I don't think I've given them enough time, and of course Lyndon is so rarely home when they are awake. And when he is home, I focus all my attention on him. I hope it's all worth it. But Lyndon is a good man." This last she said almost wistfully, and I felt a closeness to her for the words, both spoken and unspoken.

We arrived at Lyndon's office and he was waiting to give me a personal tour. His enthusiasm almost turned him into a young boy, a personality trait of his that often left enemies off guard. He suggested I sit in his chair, a chair of power. He handed me a simple pen with an old-fashioned nib, but his name was engraved on the holder. He gave it to me with the same flourish one would give a precious diamond. I realized that I was supposed to be impressed; one of the most powerful men in Congress, a possible future president, was allowing me to sit in his place, was giving me a personal memento. I tried to show the proper respect and awe. He then took me on a walking tour and reminded me that I would meet some very important men at the reception. He would have the honor of introducing me. I thanked him profusely, and then was whisked away by Ladybird to go home and prepare for the big evening.

John Henry was bubbling with excitement at his day. He said it was unbelievable to follow Lyndon around. He never stopped wheeling and dealing and no issue was too minor for him to attend to. John Henry told me he was preparing to do his Southern Congressman monologue, which ribbed people like Tom Conway. I asked him if he thought that was the most politic one to do as his introduction. Perhaps the black preacher would be more acceptable. John Henry dismissed my suggestion and said he had been working all day on perfecting the Congressman and didn't want to switch.

We were soon dressed and ready to go. Joining us in the limousine was Jessie Kellam, Lyndon's hatchet man at KTBC. Jessie was right out of the ante-bellum South. He was a slight man with beautifully groomed, almost silver hair, a face that seemed set in granite. He had handsome features, but when he smiled nothing else lighted up. His eyes would stay almost dead and cold. He sported a gold-tipped cane and spoke very sparingly. Ladybird's brother, a large, affable man, was also in the limousine. He was ostensibly Lyndon's right-hand man, but if he became too effusive, Lyndon didn't hesitate to shut him up. He grew silent when addressed by Lyndon. He had made his decision to accept all the strings that were attached to the plum, well-paying job as Lyndon's lieutenant. That was the strange group that started out together and would finish the evening together gathered around the fire in Lyndon's living room at midnight.

John Henry was the only one who seemed at ease, telling stories and making extravagant statements about Lyndon's future. He was almost "out-countrying" Lyndon with his country-boy phrases. Johnson felt that he could get the nation in the palm of his hand by talking to them as if they were just "down-home" folks. He thought that meetings should be treated like barbecues or fish-fries, and he sometimes used the same manner whether addressing twelve people or thousands. That's what he was banking on tonight—John Henry's monologue and his own "down-home" humor. He thought he could shrink the world into one big backyard.

As promised, Lyndon escorted me around the reception and introduced me to the other guests, including Dean Acheson. I appreciated his personal attention but was a little amused by the way he treated me like some country cousin. He assumed that I would never have the chance to meet these important figures face to face on my own. I listened quietly and nodded approvingly as any young woman should. I don't remember him asking me one personal question or being interested in any of my own opinions. Women were decorations in his life.

For a while John Henry disappeared as he prepared his monologue. I sat at a special table with Ladybird and a seat was saved for John Henry after he finished his turn. Soon he was introduced and I heard him doing the Southern preacher. I was surprised but pleased that he had changed his mind about doing the

Congressman takeoff. But when he came to our table, I could see he was disturbed. I assured him that he was excellent, but nothing would calm him down. I had never seen him so distraught after a performance. It was only when we were alone that he confided that just before he was to go on Lyndon asked him what he was doing. When he explained, he was given orders to change the content. Because he had to make a change at the last minute, and didn't have time to brush up on his other material, he felt shaky about his performance. When he came off the stage, he was surrounded by members of the press who asked him about his choice of monologues. Feeling somewhat unnerved, he wasn't thinking too clearly and told the press that he had prepared a much more political monologue "which would have taken the hide off the politicians, but Lyndon didn't think this was the right time to do it, so I had to change in midstream. Hope it sounded all right to you. . . ." That's all the press needed. They converged on Lyndon and demanded to know why he was censoring his own performer. Lyndon was shocked and said there was no intent to censor; it was just a discussion about which piece to do. But John Henry knew he had made a mistake in talking to the press without clearance.

He sat through the rest of the evening, strangely quiet. Then we listened to Lyndon speak, and his familiar, "good-old-friends" approach just wasn't washing. He never did grab that large, so-phisticated audience. His approach had misfired. On the way home, crowded into the limousine, the failure was the topic of conversation. Lyndon turned to Ladybird and asked her opinion of the evening. She confirmed that he had played it too laid back. He needed to save that approach for the smaller fish-fries. They discussed every aspect of the speech. Lyndon listened closely. John Henry and I kept quiet and nothing was said about his conversation with the press.

When we finally arrived at the house, we were all invited to the living room for a good-night drink and tea. But Lyndon wasted no time in small talk. The next topic of conversation was the daily receipts from KTBC. This involved Jessie Kellam and the brother-in-law. I sat in amazement as he gave the same intense attention to the amount of money collected that day as he had given to speaking at the Convention. He was furious when told that a woman evangelist had cancelled her program, for this meant a loss of something like fifty cents a minute for her commercial time. Then it was time to go to bed.

John Henry asked me what to do about the problem of the press, and I said it might be important for him to speak to Lyndon and explain what happened. But the next morning Lyndon was gone by the time we awakened . . . and we thanked Ladybird, said good-bye to the family, and flew back to New York City. A few days later Jessie Kellam called and said Lyndon was going to be in town and had some very important matters to clear up. We were going out to a dinner party that evening, but arranged to meet with Lyndon and his entourage early in the evening. I don't think they expected me to show up for this meeting. Women rarely came to business meetings unless expressly invited. But John Henry explained that we were going out right after. I was dressed in a black linen dress with a scoop neckline and a large-brimmed hat. I almost looked like the stereotype of the Southern lady. I resolved not to open my mouth and left all the talking to the men. Anyway, you didn't speak to Lyndon unless he addressed you first.

The brother-in-law was sitting on the radiator of the hotel room, Jessie was sitting in a chair, and we were motioned to the bed, where we poised on the edge. Lyndon was due later. We were welcomed warmly and then Jessie started speaking quietly in his monotone voice. "Now, John Henry, we've been doing a heap of talkin' and we realize we haven't been fair to you. You are family and we have to level with you. Ladybird is waiting by the phone in Washington, just as soon as we finish talking. She knows that we're going to release you from your obligation to come to Texas. We can't ask you to give up your lucrative career in New York for the piddlin' salary you'll be getting at KTBC. It just won't be fair, as much as we love you. So John Henry, you just pick up that telephone and tell Ladybird you are not comin' to Texas and she'll understand."

I listened in disbelief. Something was wrong. I felt in my heart they were trying to dump him, perhaps because they thought he would make too many blunders with the press. He didn't act like a team player. Ladybird was nominally running the station. But John Henry just turned white. I could see he was visibly shaken and completely confused. "But I made a big decision to give up my career. I knew it wouldn't pay as much as New York, but I wanted to be with Lyndon Johnson, and there are freelance things, like the Daniel Boone radio I can do to supplement my salary."

Jessie Kellam shot back, "No, that's impossible. If you work for Lyndon, you cannot do anything else."

John Henry stammered, "Well, that's all right. We'll manage."

I couldn't resist interrupting, "Mr. Kellam, what are you trying to tell John Henry? It sounds as if you are trying to break a contract with him. Then be kind, tell him why. What's changed? You know that we both made emotional decisions to leave New York. John Henry felt he wanted to work for Lyndon. We have given notice to WCBS, to our landlord. What are you talking about?"

At that point John Henry turned on me angrily. "Lynne, why are you so rude? Don't you know these are my friends? They are just concerned about us."

I couldn't believe he was so naive or that he would scold me in front of them. Jessie picked up on this and said, "That's true, Lynne. We wouldn't be able to look you in the eye if we allowed him to throw away his career. We were not thinking when we asked him. Ladybird will understand. Just pick up the phone and call her."

I tried once again. "All right, John Henry. If you think they are thinking of you, just do me one favor. Let's go to the dinner, talk it over, and then come back with our decision."

"That's fine," said Jessie. "Lyndon will be able to join us then. And you can give him your answer." We got up and left, promising to return about ten o'clock. As we left, John Henry asked, "Why did you turn on them? They mean well."

I looked at him incredulously. "All right, John Henry. Let's say they mean well. The point is that you have made the decision to go. You are willing to take that risk with your career. When we go back, don't argue with them, just insist you want to go. You want to be part of the team. Money isn't everything. You stick to that, John Henry, and promise me that under no circumstances will you get them off the hook by resigning."

He laughed a little nervously. "Of course, I promise. That makes sense. I do want the job. I do want to go back to Texas.

You'll see, when they understand, there won't be any problems. You just don't understand Southerners. They are not tough like New Yorkers or devious. They mean what they say."

We returned from our dinner party and they were waiting for us. Lyndon had arrived and was stretched out on the bed, waiting. "Well, welcome, son! Have you made up your mind? As much as we'll miss you, that's the best thing for you to do. We don't want your career on our conscience."

John Henry took a deep breath and carried on the way we planned. "I've thought about it, Sir, and nothin' will shake me loose from my determination to help make you the next president." John Henry warmed up to the task and became more flowery and more Southern than Lyndon. Instead of crossing swords, they were using their Southern accents as weapons.

I sat quietly in the armchair given to me by Jessie Kellam. He had relinquished his seat of authority when Lyndon appeared. Lyndon chose to stretch out on one twin bed; Kellam took the other. There was something surreal about seeing one of the most powerful men in America negotiating from a supine position. I stared out at him from under my big black hat, fixing my gaze on his eyes. I waited, knowing that John Henry now had the bit in his teeth. Lyndon looked at John Henry and said in a flat, emotionless voice, "Well, son, there just ain't no job for you."

For a moment it looked as if John Henry had been struck a blow to the head, the way he jerked and shook as if to clear his thoughts. Then he understood the message. "You mean all along there hasn't been a job and yet you've been trying to get me to quit?"

I bit my tongue and said, "It's obvious, if you quit, they wouldn't have any more responsibility toward you."

Lyndon sat bolt upright, swung his legs over the side of the bed, and pushed his face an inch away from mine. He snapped, "Now, honey, what did you expect me to do? If there is no job, there is no job. I was just trying to let him down easily. I didn't want to hurt his feelings. How would you handle it, honey?"

I sat back and without moving smiled. "Why, Sir, I would expect you would handle it in the fairest way possible. I would expect you would want to talk about breaking his contract, Sir. I would expect you would want to give him some remuneration, Sir. I would expect you would want to see what you could do about getting him his old job back, our apartment, Sir." I smiled, but my eyes were just as cold as his.

I felt ill at the intrigue and deceit that had gone on. I couldn't believe that Lyndon would play the oldest game in the world. His smile froze on his face. He hadn't expected me to answer him or criticize him. "I have no responsibility. I have no control over the fact the job doesn't exist."

At this point John Henry jumped up, obviously shaken at this revelation, and furious that he had almost been duped by one of his own people, his friends. He became eloquent. "Sir, I have heard that you love power and that power corrupts. I had no idea you would sink so low. The next time you hear from me, Sir"—and this time when he said "Sir" it came out "Suuuh"—"it will be from my lawyer." He grabbed my hand and I followed him out of the hotel room, proud that he had taken a stand.

As we started toward the elevator, Lyndon ran down after us, brandishing his fist and shouting, "How dare you talk to a senator that way. Just wait until I bring your name up in the Senate. I'll blacken your name. I'll tear you from limb to limb." He was talking about the immunity senators had in the Senate, implying that he could say anything he wanted. I had a strong suspicion he was talking about John Henry's political views. Probably his run-in with the press didn't help when he implicated Lyndon in the issue of censorship. So John Henry had made a fatal mistake in Johnson's eyes. But there was no excuse for cutting him adrift in such a callous manner. After all, an entire family was affected.

As we rode down the elevator, I reached out for his hand. "I'm so sorry that you were treated so badly. I'm so sorry that all your plans have burst." He looked hurt, and I could feel myself responding to his need again, wanting to soothe him. If I could have taken him in my arms and rocked him, I would have then and there. We went home and talked long into the night about our strategy. We had to see about getting the radio job back and inform the landlord we wouldn't be leaving. I prayed there was still time. Although I was very angry and saddened by what we had been put through, part of me was happy that we could now stay in New York.

I called the landlord and, luckily, he was glad to have us stay on. But getting back the radio job looked almost impossible. They said it was not available any more. John Henry went to Gerald Dickler, our lawyer and business manager, and they mapped out the lawsuit. Lyndon was not supposed to play any active role in the television business. As a senator, he wasn't even supposed to be involved with KTBC. Ostensibly this was his wife's business. But everyone knew that Lyndon Johnson ran up and down Madison Avenue making deals. In fact, we heard through the grapevine that Lyndon had already been to a senior executive at CBS to tell him about our threat to sue. Johnson evidently told him to pull the plug. Our lawyer thought it might be a good idea if I had a meeting with the executive, to suggest that trouble was brewing and that CBS might be implicated because of his "unethical" conversation with Johnson about John Henry. He did see me and, surprisingly, seemed to understand what I was saying. He paled at the thought of trouble with the regulatory agency and, while he didn't admit to having any discussions with Johnson, he said he would try to do everything he could for us. He knew that we were in a very sensitive position, especially as John Henry had a family to support.

I left the meeting and reported to Dickler, who was pleased with the outcome of the meeting. Then he served papers on Lyndon, advising him that we were suing, and we waited for the explosion. Instead, one Sunday we received an unexpected call from Washington. I answered the phone and it was Lyndon asking if he could speak to John Henry. I shook my head in disbelief and said, "Your friend Lyndon is on the phone. He wants to talk to you. Do you think you should, since it's in the hands of lawyers?"

John Henry nodded and went to the telephone. After about ten minutes he hung up the receiver, clapped his hands, and did a war-whoop. "You won't believe it . . . but we won, we won! Without firin' a shot."

"What are you talking about?"

Then he described the conversation. "The first thing he said was, 'Johnny, what's this I hear about some dang-foolish lawsuit? I just got served some papers. Why would you do that to family? We can settle our differences without any dang lawyer. Just tell me what it is you want, but just keep in mind that right now Ladybird and I are having tight times. We just puttin' all our ready money into building a new porch on our house. But what do you think is fair?' 'Well, Senator, I don't want your money, I just want my old job back. I need to make a livin' for my children, and the folks at CBS say there ain't any job.' And then, Lynne, what do you think that ol' rascal said? He said, 'Just give me a few days and I'll see what Ladybird can do.' Why, he's still playing the game that it's all Ladybird's influence."

"So what did you decide?" I questioned him. "Why didn't you ask for money, too?"

"Hell, if I just get the job back I'll be happy." And, somehow, like magic, not only did he get his old radio job back but there was an opening as host for the summer on the *Today* television show. So we were better off than ever. We were quite excited at the chance for his own television show. That was his biggest chance yet.

John Henry was having a wonderful time with his new television show, bringing a more bucolic look to the show, which had used more sophisticated hosts. He milked a cow on the show and even brought on a little Mexican goat that he named Katy Gonzales.

I spent the summer with the children on Fire Island, a long, narrow strip of beach, easily reached by ferry, at the end of Long Island. Fire Island itself was at this time divided into distinctly different and separate communities. Ocean Beach attracted models, performers, producers, advertising people, and writers. Seaview appealed to more suburban types. The Pines was frequented by writers who enjoyed quiet and seclusion. Bohemians enjoyed Bayview, and Cherry Beach, at the extreme end of the island, was a protected area for the rich and flamboyant homosexual community.

There were no cars and the only way to get around was by walking or taking the beach taxis. We stayed at Ocean Beach, which had all the little restaurants and night spots and the community center. It was an easy place to look after children and mix with friends. We became friendly with Carl Reiner, Mel Brooks, Norman Lear, Charles Collingwood, the political writer Izzy Stone, the performer and comedian Jack Gilford and his actress wife Madeleine Lee, Lionel Stander, and club owner Max Gordon. We spent a good deal of time in each others' homes. At most of the parties the wives were the audiences for the men, who practiced their newest monologues, sit-com plots, and comedy routines. I listened with fascination as Mel Brooks and Reiner ad-libbed their two-thousand-year-old-man routine until it was finely honed for television.

  But it was on Fire Island that the plan to become active in the performer's union started. It grew out of our discussions on the beach during which we decried the terrible things that were happening in the union under its "right-wing" executive. What it needed was not a "left-wing" executive, but some "middle-of-the-roaders" who would work on behalf of the full membership.

Weekends were always exciting. If I was now a weekend wife, I had plenty of company. I used to be very critical of weekend wives, thinking how deprived and lonely the men were all alone in the city. At least that's what I thought. I found that most of the women loved the peace and quiet we had when the men were away. We became great friends and began to make small dinners for each other and visit and compare notes. I found that a lot of the women were dealing with neglect, boredom, and infidelity. It was my first experience with forming a group of friends that had nothing to do with John Henry. I still wasn't able to confide in them about my problems. I felt so disloyal if I ever said anything against him and felt that I had to protect him because he was a public figure. I was beginning to think more about what I wanted from the marriage. I wanted so much to grow up, to stop feeling so insecure. I knew I was emotionally dependent, but I wanted to break away from that. I wanted to be able to make decisions rationally, not in the heat of emotion. I tried to understand what was making me so unhappy in the middle of a supposedly exciting life. Strangely enough, I felt very lonely in spite of being surrounded by people. There was very little sharing of emotions, problems, or goals with John Henry's friends.

Near the end of the summer, two traumatic things happened. First, John Henry was notified that his contract wouldn't be renewed for the television show. We wondered if it had just been a bone thrown to him because Lyndon had asked for it or whether his kind of country humor just didn't make it on national television. It was quite a blow to Johnny because he enjoyed doing the television show. He had plenty of back-up support: researchers, story editors, directors, producers. I reassured him that we still had the radio show and that, after all, it was a summer replacement. It probably had nothing to do with his performance.

Then a more devastating thing happened. One day I noticed a large lump, almost the size of an orange, on the back of his neck. It felt as hard as a rock. I insisted he visit the doctor the very next morning. He finally agreed, and it saved his life. The doctor said a week later it might have been too far gone. A biopsy was taken and it was found to be malignant. When I visited him in the hospital, I found him joking with the nurses. He was suffering lymphatic cancer and the doctors were debating the best way to treat him so his voice wouldn't be affected and his career ruined. They decided on radiation and carefully aimed the machine as much past the larynx as possible so he would be able to speak normally. Even in the hospital we had little time for ourselves. He was usually surrounded by adoring nurses and admiring doctors. He kept them laughing.

The summer was drawing to a close and I took long walks on the beach wondering whether my husband would survive the treatments. I wondered if I would be a widow. I was horrified to realize deep down that if he died I would not have to make any decision about leaving him. John Henry didn't die. In fact, he came through with flying colors. He never seemed to have any ill effects from radiation. If he was concerned about dying, he never shared his nightmares with me. Whenever he talked about death, he made light of it. I had always an inordinate fear of dying—or rather not living—and he found it hard to understand how a mature person could be afraid of death.

CHAPTER 13

THE LIBEL SUIT

W e thought we were seeing the end of the McCarthy era in the years 1955 and 1956. He had been discredited. Edward R. Murrow's interview had helped to turn the tide. But there was a seedy little group of people who, under the banner of Aware Inc., formed a business for the "clearance" of radio and television personnel. This world, even more than show business, was vulnerable to McCarthy-style tactics. Actors, directors, writers, and other high-profile people were good copy for the press, and attacks on them made headlines. More important, they depended for employment on a network at the center of which was the American form of artistic patronage—advertising sponsorship. That group threatened to ruin any sponsor who supported any production that employed any artist who had been accused (not charged) with having any connection with a "front" organization.

What most people to this day hardly understand is that Aware Inc. worked like a protection racket. They were interested in power and money. The strategy was to go to a producer and suggest that a particular talent or group of performers might need "clearance" before they were used. In other words, whether it was a single production or a series, the idea was to do research on those performers before the production was completed and a fortune spent on its distribution. The Aware group, headed by Vincent Hartnett, a veteran of the McCarthy days, would charge so much a head to do the research, anywhere from five dollars for a minor part to thousands for a high-profile personality. If one refused the services of Aware, the assumption was that the person was willing to promote communism.

It's hard to believe that a shabby group like that could almost throttle an entire industry, but supporters were lined up in key posts. McCarthy's followers held positions of power and backed its demands. Others believed there was a Red menace. Still others had no commitment to any belief whatsoever and just wanted no trouble. Sponsors were known to pull out if there was any negative reaction from the audience. Their main concern was dollars. A book was published called *Red Channels,* which listed many of the most talented performers in radio and television and smeared them with innuendo. It was such an imposing list of names that if you were left out you almost felt overlooked. The terrible thing is that Aware Inc. was a small group of vigilantes who had set themselves up as a security force. They were not interested in the regular police—the FBI, for instance, or the government's security agencies. Aware Inc. accused them, too, of being "soft" on communism. If there was any reason to worry about infiltration, the cure wouldn't come from the hands of a business set up to bleed people who were afraid of dissension or were willing to throw others to the wolves if there was even a hint, true or not, of any association with communism. Aware Inc. took the law in its own hands.

It had been organized in 1953, and it called itself an organization to combat the Communist conspiracy in the entertainment-communications industry. It issued bulletins from time to time, accusing performers in television and radio of Communist or pro-Communist activities. Most performers it attacked were automatically blacklisted throughout the industry. They didn't even have a chance to defend themselves because the bulletins were secretly distributed and if a performer was fired, he or she was never given the real reason. No one wanted to be involved in a court case, so usually they were told that ratings were low, the job wasn't performed satisfactorily, or another person had been chosen for the role. It left many performers feeling as if they were in limbo. It was Kafkaesque.

It turned out that Aware was also a powerful influence in the affairs of AFTRA. The American Federation of Television and Radio Artists was a national union with strong locals in New York, Chicago, and Hollywood, and the directors made anti-communism a big issue. In fact, a number of them, including the president of the New York local in 1955, Vinton Hayworth, were actually officers of Aware Inc. Many of the members who had voted to condemn the interference of Aware Inc. in the union were subpoenaed by the ailing House Un-American Activities Committee.

The union executive, taken over by a group of Red-baiters, spent more time kicking people out of the union for alleged Communist connections than they did working on contracts. They had hired a producer as their lawyer, a man named Henry Jaffe who was in a conflict-of-interest situation. In the thirties, Jaffe was a left-winger, but he had cleared himself during the McCarthy era by testifying against his wife, actress Jean Muir. It was a scandal and Jaffe had become a bitter man. Although the membership in 1955 voted overwhelmingly to condemn Aware, the AFTRA board of directors remained in office stoutly defending Aware. It served notice that anyone who ran in opposition to an Aware-supported slate of officers had better think twice.

We decided to run our own slate against the entrenched board of directors. John Henry thought it should be called the middle-of-the-road slate in the hope that it would attract all independent-minded people. That summer, on Fire Island, we talked about nothing else with our friends. We met with Charles Collingwood, a news commentator at CBS who had a summer home nearby. Like us, Charles had not been very active in union affairs. Sadly, most performers who worked with contracts far above scale tended not to attend meetings since they felt unaffected by most decisions. But it was this kind of apathy that had allowed the union to distintegrate. He agreed to run with us, and his wife, actress Louise Albritton, joined us. They were so respected that we began to feel enthusiastic about the kind of solid support we would get. We began to feel better about our chances of stopping Aware's blacklisting. It was Charles who suggested that if he and Louise and John Henry were going to run, they might as well try to get a whole slate of members and go for a complete sweep. At that time I was not an AFTRA member so I could not join the slate, but I helped in rounding up the slate, hammering out the plat-form, and hosting all the meetings at our home. John Henry and Charles convinced Garry Moore, Faye Emerson, Orson Bean, Janice Rule, Tony Randall, Cliff Norton, Dick Stark, and other well-known performers to join. Later, some of the others left at the first sign of trouble. We didn't have any idea of the dangerous game we were playing. At first we were carried along with the camaraderie, the idealism, and the enthusiasm.

At one point John Henry suggested that we be our own censors, that once we decided on the slate we make sure that there was nothing in any individual's background that could be called into question, and that the slate must be squeaky clean. I was indignant at the thought and pointed out, "You are forgetting something very elementary. You don't have to have anything in your background to be attacked. Once you oppose them or threaten their power, they will find something to smear you, counting on fear to make you run away."

The announcement that there was a middle-of-the-road slate opposed to the blacklist caused quite a stir among the membership in New York. At election time the middle-of-the-road slate swept into office and won twenty-seven of the thirty-five seats on the board. Charles Collingwood was elected president, Orson Bean first vice-president, and John Henry second vice-president of the local. They took office in January, 1956. Euphoria didn't last long. Although the middle-of-the-road slate was in power, they were up against some of the strongest and most experienced members who had been re-elected to the board, among them Clayton (Bud) Collyer, Alan Bunce, Rex Marshall, and Conrad Nagel. They offered unyielding opposition to everything the middle-of-the-roaders tried to do. The new directors decided that the legal counsel, Henry Jaffe, must be fired. Fearing reprisals from his support group, they decided to allow him to resign instead of firing him, but this resignation set off a storm of protest.

Just a few weeks after the election, the House Un-American Activities Committee, in its annual report, let go with a blast at the middle-of-the-road administration of AFTRA. It declared that the issue of blacklisting was being used by the Communists to reinfiltrate the union. The report was released to all the papers and was widely publicized. The crowning blow came one morning, on February 12, 1956, right after I had taken our three children to Central Park for our daily outing. When I came back home, I found that John Henry was visibly upset and shaken. He told me that he had just received a call from Val Adams, a radio and television columnist for the *New York Times*. He wanted to know if we had seen the bulletin that Aware Inc. had just issued attacking three officers of the slate for pro-Communist activities. According to Val, it had five pages of rhetorical questions about the patriotism of Orson Bean, Charles Collingwood, and John Henry. It also alleged some pro-Communist affiliations. The Aware bunch were pros. They were very careful not to call anyone a Communist. That would mean they would have to plead the truth in a libel suit. This way they could be just as effective in destroying a person's career, by innuendo, putting the burden on the accused. Bulletin 16, as it was called, zeroed in on John Henry, who was the most articulate and politically involved member of the slate. Aware Inc. thought if they could get John Henry to resign, then the whole slate would crumble. I'm sure that was all they had on their minds at the time—eliminate John Henry.

One paragraph of Bulletin 16 pointed out that "John Henry Faulk was further quoted as saying that 'all [middlers] were chosen for their opposition to Communism as well as their opposition to Aware.' In most cases this may well be true. But how about Faulk himself? What is his public record?" Seven allegations were listed, not one of which was proved or explained. In other words, the bulletin listed allegations later found out to be either false or inaccurate. They had nothing to do with communism. They imputed guilt by association. For instance, they claimed John Henry was a scheduled entertainer on a program, dated April 25, 1946, with a well-known Communist, and two non-Communists, held under the auspices of the Independent Citizens' Committee of the Arts, Sciences and Professions (officially designated a Communist front and predecessor of the Progressive Citizens of America). In fact, this later turned out to be a celebration for the first anniversary of the United Nations, and it had some prestigious names from the government on the dais. Just linking the name of a non-Communist with a supposed Communist automatically made the non-Communist suspect, even if they had no knowledge of each other and had no part in the planning of the program. Many supposed "front organizations" were found to be innocent and had been irresponsibly labeled so by the witch-hunters. But once named, few people had access to any platform for protest except through costly and time-consuming litigation. Another ploy was to link a name with an article published in the Communist paper, *The Daily Worker*. "According to the *Daily Worker* of April 5, 1948, Johnny Faulk was to appear as an entertainer at the opening of 'Headline Cabaret' sponsored by Stage for Action (officially designated a Communist Front). The late Philip Loeb was billed as emcee." There they cast doubt on John Henry by quoting a known fact from a Communist newspaper, even though the event was covered by other newspapers.

The accusers acted as judge, jury, and executioner. They left performers in the position of fighting a blacklist that did not officially exist. Rarely would anyone admit the existence of the blacklist or the fact that one's name on the list was the reason he or she was fired or let go. Contracts were just not picked up. Many people could never prove that the firing or cancellation of·contracts was directly related to the rumors that were spread through these bulletins. It was the reason many people, like Philip Loeb, committed suicide; they were caught in such a net and watched their careers go down the drain. In order to be cleared without going through a long, costly, and difficult trial was the sickening choice of admitting some wrongdoing. "I once belonged but now see the error of my ways . . . I must have been a dupe of a Communist Front, I knew nothing about it . . . I never belonged and to prove how clean I am and how opposed I am to communism, I will name others." Those who were squeamish about giving names were allowed to choose from a list of names of Communists already punished and could just put another nail in their coffins. "After all," Aware reasoned, "you are just showing your distaste for the party, and you don't even have to bring in original names." Anyone who did that may not have hurt the socalled Communists they vilified, but they certainly hurt themselves. What a black mark on history that well-meaning people had to make such a decision in a democratic society! Just as tragic as the lives of those named were the lives of people who played this nightmarish game and succumbed to save their own careers: José Ferrer, Abe Burrows, Larry Parks, and Elia Kazan.

The bulletin had its effect among the executive almost immediately, and some of the middlers began separating themselves from the slate. Nelson Case, a prominent and successful announcer, called John Henry and asked for a letter stating that he was not a member of the middle-of-the-road slate and had never been one. It seems his mistake was congratulating the slate on winning such a victory. A couple of days later, Orson Bean called to say that he had just been told by his agent that the bulletin had got him in trouble with Ed Sullivan, and he could not be used on his show again until he had done something about the allegations. John Henry said it seemed like a clear case of blacklisting and it would be the perfect opportunity to institute a lawsuit. But Bean's agent refused, and some time later Orson Bean withdrew from the slate. Henry Jaffe tried to get John Henry to clear himself by bringing charges against others in the union who were suspected of having Communist ties. Then Jaffe would get some informers to testify against them. What was even more revolting was the fact that some very decent middlers even thought it was okay, and felt Jaffe was making an honest effort to help John Henry clear himself by showing he was anti-Communist. They didn't understand John Henry when he said he could not protect his career or his reputation by ruining another person's career or reputation.

This was all happening at a time when John Henry's career was in high gear. He was making many appearances on television as well as receiving a hefty salary for his radio work. Mark Goodson and Jerry Todman were starting to build an empire with all their game shows, and John Henry was a favorite guest on *We Take Your Word, What's My Line,* and others. He could have made an excellent living just doing game shows. Money was not a problem but we were concerned about the effect of the bulletin on John Henry's career. Our business manager, Gerry Dickler, was also concerned. He knew about the power of the blacklist and the influence of supermarket king Laurence Johnson, Vince Hartnett's friend, who shared the political philosophy of Senator McCarthy. As soon as a name appeared in the bulletin, Johnson went to the sponsors who advertised on radio and television and sold their products through his stores. He demanded the artist's dismissal or threatened to remove the products from the shelves. Johnson was greatly feared, and a lot of credence was given to his demands because he was thought of as very powerful and very rich.

Gerald Dickler tried to be rational about the entire situation. He suggested we round up support from the union and, barring that, forget the union and figure out a way to save our own skin, even to kissing and making up with Aware. It was not a suggestion that either John Henry or I liked, and we put it down to nervousness on Gerry's part as well as a sincere concern for a client.

We surely felt that Sam Slate, the program director of WCBS and John Henry's immediate superior, would stand by him. Sam had become a close personal friend, as only two Southerners can, except Sam hailed from Columbus, Georgia. He had approved of our involvement in the union because McCarthyism had made such inroads in the union. Gerry advised us to get in touch with Sam immediately, and at first Slate said, "Ignore it. You are no more Red than I am. I personally don't think anyone pays any attention to these fools." But he did suggest John Henry take it to Carl Ward, his superior. We still didn't realize how much damage these blacklisters were prepared to do. It dawned on us that damage was being done when Carl Ward told John Henry that Laurence Johnson was in New York going up and down Madison Avenue seeing sponsors and demanding that they withdraw from his show. Libby's Frozen Foods cancelled immediately. Then Carl Ward dumped the whole problem back in our lap. He suggested an affidavit might help to answer all the allegations.

John Henry came home that evening, frightened, angry, and momentarily confused about his next course of action. We called a few friends in for a brainstorming session, and I was most adamant that an affidavit must not take the form of a statement of John Henry's patriotism. Nor must it be a loyalty oath. He must not bow down to this pressure. It was very clear to me that no compromise could be expected. First, we had already seen that just admitting any personal wrongdoing was never the answer. The next step was always to involve others, to name names. This was totally unacceptable. There was nothing to do but stand firm. We had made the choice to fight that battle in the union. We believed firmly we were fighting a home-grown battle. And because of the fear in the land, we also knew there would be serious consequences.

I felt we had to handle one day at a time. Never in my wildest dream did I think that we had embarked on what would seem in retrospect like a lifetime crusade. For me, making the decision to fight the blacklisters seemed like a simple decision. I knew we had no choice, or at least the choice for us was unacceptable.

The evening our friends came we agonized together over the affidavit and decided it would be a positive statement of John Henry's principles, not a defense of his actions or a response to the allegations. In a careful checking of the bulletin, we realized that there was not one quote by John Henry, not one instance of a single word or thought, on radio or television, that could be pointed to as being Communist-inspired. It was ridiculous to give any credence to the allegations.

That night he hammered out an affidavit that was a positive statement of all his accomplishments, his work record, and his many citations for speeches he gave before civic, business, and religious groups. He pointed out that when he started work at WCBS he was required (sadly), with other employees, to sign a statement that he was not then nor at any time a member of the Communist Party or of any Communist-Front organization nor of any of a long list of organizations whose names were imprinted on that CBS form. It always made me ill to think Americans were required to sign that kind of statement. It seemed to me to be an invasion of privacy and an indignity that one had to profess innocence when there were no charges at all. But in spite of the affidavit, John Henry found a cloak of silence had already been tightly drawn. Carl Ward didn't seem to want to discuss the affidavit, Johnson, or his campaign. No one else at CBS wanted to talk about the blacklisting or the loss of sponsors. It seemed the legal department had called for a clampdown.

We began to feel that there might be real reason to worry about John Henry losing his radio show. There was no way of proving that sponsors left because of pressure or normal attrition, at least not until we received a most amazing and unexpected call from a man named Tom Murray at Grey Advertising. He explained that he had received a call from Johnson and then Johnson's letter viciously attacking John Henry. Johnson said unless Murray removed the Hoffman Beverage account from John Henry's radio show, he would boycott Hoffman's products in his supermarket and send the American Legion post in Syracuse after the agency. That made Murray so mad he told Johnson to go to hell. It offended his sense of justice and his belief in the American way. A letter did come from the American Legion post and Tom Murray brought it over for John Henry to see. For the first time a performer had the evidence and had been allowed to see the charges. That help came from a complete stranger, a decent man who put his own job and reputation on the line.

John Henry also had a meeting with Sydney Davis, then a young lawyer from Louis Nizer's office, who had set up the meeting because John Henry was looking for counsel to replace Henry Jaffe at the union. Now it seemed irrelevant, but John Henry wanted to meet him and talk about his recent problems with Aware Inc. and WCBS. They talked about the possibility of Louis Nizer taking the case if it ever became necessary to start a lawsuit. John Henry told him he was going to fight for his livelihood. Sydney Davis said he would talk to Nizer, who had an international reputation and had handled the controversial Westbrook Pegler lawsuit.

Our break came when Louis Nizer agreed to meet with John Henry. Nizer and his partner Paul Martinson questioned him in considerable detail during the visit in order to prepare a formal complaint. They asked him to remember everything. Had he ever been jailed, belonged to any subversive organizations, issued bad checks, incurred debts, been in any trouble of any kind. Nizer explained that we might all be in for a hard time, the court case might be lengthy, it might take several years to bring it to trial, and that we would feel not only economic pressure but also subtle emotional pressures. He told John that his wife and children would suffer the most and before he made any decision he wanted to talk to me.

I don't know what I was prepared for when I met Louis Nizer, but I had heard that he was a million-dollar lawyer who represented some of the biggest corporations in America and was considered one of the finest trial lawyers in the land. In fact, he had a reputation for handling some of the most notorious divorce cases in the country, one of the most exciting being an Elizabeth Taylor divorce. There was also the rumor that Louis Nizer was thinking about running for Congress and was interested in more cases with social issues. But Louis Nizer wasn't about to take on a case he couldn't win, and he would leave no stone unturned to uncover any information he needed. In the past, cases like ours had been handled by civil liberties lawyers, but there usually wasn't enough money for them to fight long, hard cases. The opposition usually had so much money they could play the game of delay until money ran out. It was unusual for a prestigious law firm to defend unpopular causes. But Louis Nizer had been impressed by John Henry's Southern humor, his Methodist background, his folksy approach to life, his disarming boyishness, and his fighting spirit.

The firm of Philips, Nizer, Benjamin, and Krim had offices taking up a whole floor of the Paramount Building, high above Times Square in Manhattan. In addition, they had offices on other floors of the building. After waiting a few moments in the reception room, we were ushered into Louis Nizer's private office. As I stood at the door, I saw Louis Nizer at the other end of a large room. His desk was between two windows that overlooked the Hudson River and across to New Jersey. The desk was on a platform and Nizer was seated on a chair with a tall back. Framing his chair on each side was a battery of telephones in easy reach. I felt awkward as I started to make my way to his desk. Sensing that, he immediately left his chair and came around to the front of the desk to greet me. I was shocked at his height. He was so much shorter than I had realized. He welcomed me warmly and pointed to two big, comfortable chairs in front of his desk, and we sat down. I couldn't help but steal a look at the surroundings. There were Persian rugs on the floor, large comfortable couches, and walls lined with bookshelves. He took time to explain all the problems that we might face if we started this libel suit. He painted a bleak picture and said it would be difficult to win, and even if we won we might not see any money. We would just have the satisfaction of having cut out a cancer on society. He went on gently as he said, "You have three children to worry about, their schooling, their lives. You and the children will probably suffer the most. You have to be prepared for losing friends who will be afraid of being linked with you. Libel suits are the most difficult ones to win. You may not have the money to continue your lifestyle, if they try to starve you out. Can you handle the pressure? Are you willing to go through this?"

I asked, "Do you want to take the case?"

"I'm interested in it. I assure you if I take it we will win. I just don't know how long it will take to bring it to court. They can try all kinds of delaying tactics. But, yes, I am interested in the case. I just want to do some more checking."

"Well, Mr. Nizer, if you are willing to take the case, I can handle it. I don't see any choice. I don't think Aware will ever let up on John Henry unless he capitulates and becomes a tool for them to spread their propaganda. They will never let him alone unless he proves he is on their side. We cannot do that. I could not do that. I think what they are doing is sleazy and rotten and cruel and they are no better than the cheapest hoods."

John Henry smiled, reached over, and patted my hand approvingly. provingly. "I told you she was a fighter. She will be behind me one hundred per cent!" I looked straight into Nizer's eyes, and he was also smiling approvingly. I could feel the strength coming from that man and I felt safe. Although he was short in height and had tightly curled, close-cropped hair, and a rather commonplace but comfortable-looking face, I could sense his power through his control of situations. It was such a relief to have him in our corner.

A few weeks later we received a letter from Nizer. I will never forget that moment as we opened the envelope. The message was simple but as exciting as if we had already won the case. It said that, after careful investigation, the firm had decided that our cause was meritorious and they were prepared to take our case. John Henry and I hugged each other, almost feeling that this was our biggest hurdle. We had been accepted by a man to be feared in the courtroom. For the first time in months, we felt optimistic about the future. Some of our friends cautioned us to find out what Louis Nizer would charge before we went overboard. He was one of the most expensive lawyers in the country, and they were sure he would need a minimum retainer of $100,000. We looked startled. We had assumed he was taking the case because he believed in the cause and that he would be paid if we won. Our friends reminded us that often you came out of lawsuits like this winning a moral victory but losing money. Someone had to have the money for you to collect. They wagered that the seedy Aware group might have more power than money, and even if they had money they probably had ways of hiding it. Our concerns didn't last long because Louis Nizer assured us at our next meeting that while his firm ordinarily required a large retainer, in this instance all his firm needed was enough to cover out-of-pocket expenses. There would be no retainer, but expenses were estimated to be $20,000. John Henry came home somewhat relieved but still worried about raising even that small amount. The case was being carried on contingency, which meant that the firm would collect one-third of any amount awarded. One-third of nothing would be nothing, of course, so the firm was gambling on winning.

In spite of the success of the radio show in the last few years, we had only managed to save a few thousand dollars. After all the years of living on a small salary, we had just begun to have enough discretionary income to begin saving money and think about investing. We decided to take out all our savings, but we still had to find the rest. John Henry wouldn't listen to my suggestion that I get a job and help with my salary. He remembered that Charles Collingwood had promised to help him raise the money. The executives at CBS were not generally happy about the possibility of a lawsuit. Carl Ward thought it would only call the public's attention to the troubles with Aware. He thought, if left alone, the whole thing might blow over. Sam Slate was excited at Nizer taking the case against Aware and figured that he would knock Aware out. Our business manager, Gerry Dickler, was concerned about John Henry's career and felt that, after the suit was filed, the defendants would probably step up their pressure to get him fired. It would be a rough fight, with their backs against the wall. We argued, "There never is a good time to fight. You always have to put something on the line."

In the meantime, money was being raised for the retainer for Louis Nizer. Some wealthy friends, Anne and Herb Steinman, had a huge fund-raising party in their beautiful brownstone home in the East Eighties. The party list included such wonderful people as Eleanor Roosevelt, Myrna Loy, David and Evelyn Susskind, and many others. I didn't go to the party that night, feeling somewhat embarrassed at its purpose to raise money for us. I also felt it was John Henry's night, automatically taking the back seat without even realizing what I was doing. I didn't stop to think that this was my lawsuit as well.

John Henry came home that evening with glowing reports of the party. A letter came from Eleanor Roosevelt praising him for his brave stand. A large sum had been raised that night, but we were still $7,500 short. In the meantime, Paul Martinson called and said that he was filing the suit. The evidence indicated that there was a conspiracy among Aware, Vincent Hartnett, and Laurence Johnson to carry out the blacklisting. The addition of Johnson's name was an inspiration because, if the lawsuit was won, there was the hope that money could be collected from Johnson. He was supposed to be a multimillionaire. The lawsuit was filed on June 26, 1956, in the New York State Supreme Court, and the following day all the New York papers carried the story of Faulk v. Aware, Laurence Johnson, and Vincent Hartnett. It shook up Madison Avenue and was the subject of conversation at lunch and dinner meetings as well as meetings behind closed doors. John Henry was still concerned about the $7,500 and told me he was too embarrassed to go to Nizer and admit we didn't have any more money.

After the news hit, Edward R. Murrow called John Henry upstairs to his office to congratulate him on his fight. When he found out that he still needed money, he told him the money would be in his hands the next day. When Johnny protested that he didn't know if he could ever return the loan, he replied, "I'm not making a personal loan to you of this money. I am investing this money in America. Louis Nizer must try this case." We found out later that Murrow had mortgaged his farm to back up his beliefs. Although he had been a friend for years, since a meeting through a mutual friend, J. Frank Dobie, Murrow had kept up contact mostly through meetings at CBS. But he said he agreed with Carl Sandburg, who had written to him, "Whatever the matter with America, Johnny ain't." So our immediate financial difficulties were over.

CHAPTER 14

THE LULL

In the next few months we were involved in all the preparation for the trial. We became part of Nizer's "family," being invited to his home for dinner, getting to know Mildred, his second wife, learning something about Nizer the man. He liked to be thought of as a fine artist. He spent much of his leisure time and his summer months painting at his retreat in Ocho Rios, West Indies. He liked to talk about some of his most exciting cases and the people he knew and enjoyed. He professed to be a "simple" man, but he was an absolute tyrant when it came to work. His brilliance in court was largely the result of the hours of painstaking work he did covering and uncovering every detail beforehand. No detail was too small to escape his notice, and sometimes he would stay awake till dawn working on a brief. Later, John Henry found he was expected to do the same.

For the while, the Nizers were entertained by John Henry's monologues and delighted in having him spout forth at every opportunity. John Henry, Wasp, Southern, at times vulgar and indiscreet, made a strange partner to Louis Nizer, Jewish, mild-mannered, genteel, and sophisticated. I sometimes cringed at John Henry's raunchy stories and explosive way of expressing himself on every subject, including politics, but Nizer seemed to enjoy the contrast and had a soft spot for flamboyant personalities. Although he spoke like a moralist, he was able to absolve his client Elizabeth Taylor of any supposed transgression because "she is so beautiful . . . she is like an angel." She could do no wrong. I think he could excuse John Henry some of his behavior because he admired his talent so much.

I usually felt like a little girl when visiting the Nizers, as someone who was liked and allowed to come to the party. But I was quite aware that my role, as Nizer saw it, was to provide the strength in the background. The relationship was between client and lawyer, and in Nizer's mind John Henry was the client. I didn't realize then how destructive that would be to me later on. I wasn't even aware of the implications. I never thought to ask that my name be joined in the lawsuit or that a separate suit be filed for me, when it became evident that I was going to be blacklisted or at least affected by the case when I had to find work.

Things quieted down. In December, 1956, WCBS renewed John Henry's contract. Sam Slate was appointed to the job of general manager in May, 1957. Carl Ward was moved to a position in the television network. We were delighted because we felt Sam would now be in a stronger position to be a real ally. Sam assured us that the show retained most of the sponsors and everything seemed on an even keel.

We made plans for a much-needed rest at Ocho Rios in Jamaica, West Indies. I realized that for one-third the price of a cottage on Fire Island we could rent a villa with a private pool, fully staffed, for only $300 a month. My hidden agenda was that we would be too far away for the hangers-on and that would mean a decrease in the parties. Some friends thought I was mad to take three young children to that "unknown" island, concerned that there would be no refrigeration, no milk, and nothing for them to do. I felt as if we were going to discover paradise. John Henry was excited at the thought of the scuba diving and snorkeling. I rented a suitable villa for under a thousand dollars for three months.

Two events happened before we were to take off. John Henry was offered the role of Jeeter Lester, the lead in *Tobacco Road,* by a friend, Buff Cobb, then the wife of Mike Wallace. She had a summer theater in Lake Hopatcong, New Jersey, and she thought John Henry would be perfect as the sharecropper. It was going to run for only two weeks, but it didn't interfere with John Henry because he was going to meet me in Ocho Rios a little later at any rate. Then Buff Cobb asked me to read for the other lead, Ma Lester. I was ecstatic. I had so missed acting. I accepted, although it meant delaying my trip for two weeks.

It was one of the few times that we were thrown together in such close quarters and dependent on each other's company. At first John Henry had a rough time with the part. He was not used to the stage and was awkward in moving around. There were a few young, experienced performers in minor parts, and they weren't too enthused about John Henry taking the lead with no experience. They used every trick to upstage him and leave him shuffling in the background. I spent hours with him in our dressing room, coaching him and giving him directions on how to move on the stage so he could command attention when he was supposed to be in the spotlight. Since I played opposite him, I played counterpoint to his role and gave him all the support he needed, and we managed some nice chemistry between us.

After our successful two-week run with the play, I thought it would be a good idea to have a going-away party before I left for Jamaica with the children. It would make sense for all the people who were concerned and involved in our recent decision to meet. Actually, it was a party to introduce Louis Nizer to some of our friends. We decided to have forty people and I wanted a catered, sit-down dinner. It was going to be elegant. Louis and Mildred came to meet the Susskinds, Yip Harburg, Clark and Mairi Foreman, Myrna Loy, the Steinmans, Sam Slate and his wife, Gerry Dickler and his wife, and others. Yip played the piano and sang songs from his upcoming musical, *Finian's Rainbow*. There were speeches and assurances from Sam that Johnny's job was secure. I was wished a happy vacation, and all in all it was a beautiful evening. I did not know that that was the last time we would ever be able to have such a lavish party. I had no premonition of the trouble to come.

In the middle of June, I left for Jamaica and John Henry was arranging his schedule with the CBS star singer Lanny Ross to take over his shift. He would come down the first week in July and stay for a month. John Henry had always managed to be away whenever any moves had been made, even from one apartment to another.

Ocho Rios was still unspoiled. Our villa was a small cottage with two bedrooms on either side of the large living room, which had the entire side open to the trade winds. Our staff was expecting us and immediately made us feel comfortable. High tea was waiting, our bags were unpacked, and the children were helped into bathing suits. They ran squealing with joy into the pool, splashing and laughing, my heart bounding with joy as I watched them play. The sky was cloudless and intensely blue, and I began to feel the tension slowly melt away. I had found paradise.

That night, after the children were put to bed, I found Duncan, the cook, waiting to talk to me. He stayed only long enough to mention quietly that he had dreams of moving to the United States some day and he hoped I would think about taking him back with me. It was my first indication that Jamaica wasn't a paradise for the majority, the blacks. I told him that I would be in Jamaica for three months and we would talk about that some more, when I became more familiar with the problems there.

The next morning I was awakened by a strange babble of noises in the backyard. It was the usual early-morning trading. Vendors would come to the back of the tourist homes and sell fresh fruit and vegetables to the cooks in charge. I tried listening to the conversation, but although it was English, the Jamaicans spoke a patois, and when they spoke to each other it was almost incomprehensible to strangers. But they spoke with such a lilt it was like music to my ears.

After breakfast we made plans to spend the day at the Tower Isle Hotel. We arranged for a taxicab to take us the three miles down the road. The hotel was a huge, rambling low-rise that got its name from a small tower on an island a short distance from the private protected cove right at the door of the hotel. The children had the choice of the Caribbean or the large pool. Banana stalks hung from trees overlooking the pool, available to anyone who could reach up and take one. I was settled in a lounge, while drinks and slices of coconut were passed around by willing waiters. A small band played music for dancing.

I was surveying the scene when the lifeguard, Barry, was introduced to me. He was an Olympic champion, a beautiful man with a magnificent physique. He also gave swimming lessons, and all three children became his devoted admirers as he taught them diving and swimming, taking them out to the tower island on his back and spending time with them alone, away from prying eyes and a concerned mother.

I found there was a small community of white people who, for a variety of reasons, made their home in Jamaica. Most of them came from England. I met some of the local bachelors who were available for dancing or whatever else pleased the women tourists who were along. I soon found out that although this was a black island, it was strictly run by the white people in power. I sometimes felt conflicting emotions about the carefree time. I was trying to decide how much involvement I could have in local customs and politics. At first I was certain I could never accept the strict orders I had to stay out of the kitchen and to please clap my hands when I wanted something done, even if it was only moving a chair. I rebelled but then saw that I was creating a problem for the staff, who were trained to perform that way; my interfering made them feel like failures. How soon it became second nature! I realized how easily one can be seduced by a culture. I tried to assuage some of my guilt by insisting on doubling their meager salaries, but that created problems with other whites who pointed out that I would make it difficult for others to maintain any kind of order after I left the island. I also realized that, although the island was abundantly rich with fruit and vegetables grown locally, the beaches were forbidden to the blacks and most of the fruit trees were considered the property of the whites, and there were problems of hunger in spite of the productive land.

I began to dream of John Henry coming down to be with us and fantasized how romantic it would be. I would have him alone and be able to offer him all these delights. I had already checked out the scuba diving, which was unparalleled, and I knew John Henry would enjoy that. I began to think this might be the honeymoon we never had, a chance to be close again without anything to mar our vacation. It was a wonderful way for a family to be together without strain.

At the airport in Montego Bay, I was excited at the thought of meeting him and was bursting with information. When he came down the steps of the plane, I waved furiously and ran to throw myself headlong into his arms. I forgot how much he resisted public demonstrations of affection. He pecked my cheek dutifully and gave me a fast bear hug. The moment we arrived at the villa, the children surrounded their daddy and insisted he go into the pool with them. He put on his bathing trunks and dived into the water and his vacation began. There was hardly a moment that he wasn't under water, either snorkeling, swimming, or scuba diving. It was difficult to get him to plan excursions with us, he was obsessed with scuba diving and spending time with Barry.

He seemed to forget the lawsuit and all the problems back home.

It wasn't long before we were accepted into the small community. They were on a constant round of cocktail parties and polo playing. The group included some of the wealthy black Jamaicans and professionals as well as the wealthy members of the British community who were there as trade representatives or vacationers or refugees from the supposed "fast" life in England. We were invited to everything, and I almost despaired of ever being alone with John Henry, even in that supposed outpost. All in all, it was the best month we had ever spent together. I tried not to be too jealous of the time he spent away and the attention he paid to the women in our group. He was adored, protected, and teased. When we did dance together, I resorted to old-fashioned flirting, softly stroking the back of his neck as he held me, resting my head gently on his shoulder.

Now it was August and time for John Henry to go back, but he had had such a beautiful time in Jamaica that he promised he would make arrangements to come back in a few weeks and spend the rest of our holiday together. August 16th was my birthday, and a dinner and party were planned to help celebrate. There was a glorious night of dancing and late-night swimming. I looked up at the stars and thought, "I don't want to go home again ever. I don't think I can face my marriage in New York, the frantic activity, the tremendous pressures, the constant arranging of parties, and juggling family and John Henry." It was so much easier here. The dark, velvet night blanketed me and I closed my eyes and felt tears running down my cheeks.

John Henry had seemed happier in Ocho Rios than I had seen him for a long time. I looked forward to returning with him from time to time. But it wasn't to be. After my birthday I received a terse telegram from John Henry. "I lost my job. Come home." No letter, no explanation, no preparation, just an order. I felt cheated. I wanted to talk to him about our life while we still had a chance to make decisions.

The decision to return then and there was taken out of my hands when Evelyn came down with a fever and we were quarantined and unable to leave the island until they found out if it was the highly contagious Hong Kong flu that was invading the country. I called John Henry and told him what had happened but assured him I would be home soon and we could make plans of how to survive. "Think about packing it all in and taking off for Mexico or renting a thatched-roof cottage in England." I was casting around for any solution that would give us a chance to change our lifestyle and an opportunity to work on our marriage. I cheerfully suggested, "You can write that book you always wanted to write and I could make a living writing advertising copy and doing freelance articles." John Henry didn't seem to respond to any of my suggestions.

Then the doctor discovered that Evelyn did not have the Hong Kong flu but he could not determine what was causing the fever. I immediately made plans to fly home, anxious to get Evelyn to a doctor and find the trouble. As we were leaving, the rainy season started and the sunny island of Jamaica became windswept and rain-soaked. I wondered if that was prophetic of my life in the future. I felt sad and apprehensive as I left Jamaica.

CHAPTER 15

THE FALLEN STAR

By the time I returned with the family, the story had hit the headlines. John Henry Faulk had been fired by WCBS and he was suing for half-a-million dollars. That was the amount until Louis Nizer decided to crank the claim up to three million dollars. John Henry seemed like a different man. He appeared anxious and frightened by the fact that he was now out of work. But even more surprising to me, he seemed to miss the "star" attention, the adoration of fans, the recognition of fellow workers, and the acceptance of the WCBS family.

I didn't realize at the time that there was a gnawing feeling in his stomach that in a way his stand in the lawsuit wasn't as "noble" as some political activists would have liked. They felt he had compromised by allowing Nizer to pursue the case by defending John Henry as the great American instead of by having him take the Fifth Amendment. They felt taking the Fifth showed contempt for the witch-hunters and their attempt to muzzle dissenters. A lawsuit to defend John Henry as a great American and prove that he was clean seemed to them to be playing right into the hands of the attackers. If they had you on the defensive, it gave credence to their attacks. There were people like Louis Nizer who believed that John Henry's lawsuit could be a landmark case, and that he was a hero for risking all to take the stand. I think that conflict gnawed at John Henry for years and was probably responsible for some of his self-hatred. I think he felt he had been handed a hero's mantle that could be taken back at any time, leaving him naked.

I was protective of him, but I didn't know where to go for counseling. I was brought up to believe that you never discussed any weaknesses a husband might have. It might affect his stature in the community and his earning power. And now that he was a martyr, I certainly could not confide in anyone the difficulties we were having as a family, or the pain I was going through personally. If I had known that hundreds of other women were going through the same conflicts, it would have helped to have that support at the time. It was years later I found an ally in actress and producer Lee Grant, who said she had gone through a similar experience with her husband, Arnold Manoff, a blacklisted writer. Not only had the blacklisting affected her career but she couldn't discuss their marriage with anyone because he, too, was considered a saint and a martyr.

It was important to make some decisions about our lives and our lifestyle. I urged John Henry to begin thinking productively. Were we going to stay in our apartment? Was John Henry going to find other work? Could he consider going back to teaching? Was I going to get a job (something I secretly desired)? If so, would I be able to support our present lifestyle? These questions stayed suspended in air for a few months as we tried different alternatives. We considered moving to an artists' colony in Mexico until we discovered how expensive it was, even there. Although our business manager warned us about spending money needlessly, he seemed delighted when I told him I wanted to attend a gourmet cooking class. He came up with the tuition willingly, glad that my interests were turning to more domestic areas. This was more normal in his estimation than my continued fight to have a career of my own.

John Henry turned down any suggestion that he look for work outside his field. He felt that these were his most productive years and he was afraid to lose too much time away from his profession. All talk of the writing he wanted to do went by the wayside. I felt sympathetic to his feelings and realized how difficult it was for him to have to deal with someone else making decisions about his life. The lawsuit had cut his career down: he had not made the choice. I refused to push him into any other decision. He had to make his own decision about the possibility of changing his career goals, but I had no problem going back to work. I desperately wanted to, but I was not prepared for his anger and negative reaction at this time. I could not believe the rhetoric that spewed out of his mouth. "You are not a real woman. If you were, you'd rather stay home and scrub the floors and take care of your children."

I answered, shaken, "It's not just staying home. Where is the money going to come from to pay the rent, buy some food? We have to have some cash coming in."

He snapped, "You'll never make enough money to keep us living the way we are. Most of your salary will go just to pay the housekeeper, Rhodelle."

I thought for a moment and agreed. "It's true, I probably can't make enough money immediately to support us, and we may have to move eventually, but if I go back to my former career in advertising, make some contacts, soon I will be able to get back to my top earning power. My kind of job doesn't progress slowly. Once I'm established again, I can make leaps in my salary demands. And there comes a point we can't keep taking money from our friends just to live. It was all very well to accept help in the beginning. If we can hang on with my working, maybe the case will be wrapped up within six months or a year." We had been warned that it would take time but didn't believe it would take six years. We were not at all prepared for the half-dozen years that it finally did take because of the strange way our justice system works.

I felt guilty about going back to work because of John Henry's accusations. I also felt some disapproval from friends, who hinted that I was "emasculating" John Henry by wanting to take over the breadwinner role. I remember discussing that with a psychiatrist who remarked, "What do they suggest? Should you stay home and manipulate John Henry back to work? You are not taking anything away from him. He has the choice to pursue his career, make other career choices, or nurse his wounds. Whether you go back to work or stay home, he still has to make the choice. At any rate, no one person can emasculate a man. He can only do it to himself." I tried to keep that thought in mind but it wasn't easy.

I made the decision to go back to work and try to manage both the job and home. I had discussed the possibility of John Henry helping more around the house and with the children, but he refused to take responsibility for what he unequivocally felt was "woman's work." He also felt he would be too busy exploring opportunities for the future to be tied to the house. I could never quite understand what he meant by "woman's work," but he meant what he said. I could never equate the progressive, political liberal with that conservative stance about a "woman's role." But there were not many other women who agreed with me at the time.

My parents felt I was hurting John Henry by going to work, but the issue with them was John Henry. Why wasn't he, the man, going out to support his family, even if he had to drive a cab? I tried to defend him by saying that it was more important for him to be accessible and available for interviews than to be making a meager salary driving a cab. My neighbors weren't very sympathetic and were insistent that if I worked I couldn't expect them to baby-sit my children. I pointed out to them that we always had a full-time housekeeper and that, in fact, it was our flat that was usually filled with children playing. My children were allowed to bring their friends home and they had a great deal of freedom under the wonderful supervision of Rhodelle. I had been paying Rhodelle sixty dollars a week, an excellent salary that also included housing and food. She was willing to take a cut in salary because of our situation and because she loved being part of the family, but I refused to cut her salary, feeling strongly that I could not go out to work at her expense. Besides, she would now have more responsibility.

It was a strange experience entering the marketplace again after almost ten years at home. I went to see the personnel agencies that specialized in placing advertising and public relations executives. I was angered at some of the questions put to me by counselors now almost half my age. "Where have you been for the last ten years? Have you been working?"

I replied with fury, "What do you mean, I haven't been working? In ten years I've raised three vibrant children, supported a husband in his radio and television career, performed as co-host for our own show, never stopped reading, managing, organizing, and budgeting. What the hell do you mean, what have I been doing? Do you think I disappeared from the face of the earth? Do you think I haven't kept up with current events? Do you think I forgot everything I ever knew about my profession?" The young counselor retreated under my barrage and then admitted that I had not left the planet. I registered with the agency, left my résumé, and went home, expecting a call.

In the meantime I heard that there was an opening on the show *Name That Tune* for a researcher and program organizer. I applied for the job and was welcomed warmly. The producers knew of my professional work with John Henry and my background in advertising and marketing as well as research. They seemed pleased to have me aboard and began outlining my duties. They said there would be a great deal of traveling around the United States because they liked the promotion that went with producing on location. I would be responsible for screening the contestants and the follow-up publicity and promotion in each city. It seemed a snap to me and I was ready to talk salary when the producer excused himself in order to make a telephone call. As I waited I read all the previous releases to get a feel for what had already been done. He arrived back in the room, strangely pale and uptight. "I'm sorry. I'm so sorry, but there is no job." I could feel my head beginning to spin as it dawned on me that the industry blacklist extended to me.

I was stunned and said quietly, "You don't have to put me on the payroll as Lynne Faulk. My maiden name is Smith."

He looked pained and just kept shaking his head. "There is no job, there is no job." I walked out feeling confused. I had not expected that reaction. I walked, dazed, over to a friend who had a public relations office and asked if he could help. I told him that it seemed that, as the wife of a blacklisted man, I, too, was considered undesirable in the industry. He tried to be helpful and advised me to drop the suit. "Things are shut down against Johnny. Why are you both acting like martyrs? You have three children to support. Settle this thing and I'll help you get the blacklisters off your backs. I'm friends with Larry Johnson. I can pick up the phone and in a minute . . ."

I looked at him incredulously. "You just don't understand. No one wants to be a martyr. But there is no way of settling with these men. The decision is very clear-cut. If we back down now, that would not satisfy them. They would want us to make some statement to show that we were 'pro' their philosophy. Or we would have to prove our sincerity by providing them with names of other people who still buck them. Too many people have tried to cooperate and had to sell their souls."

He shook his head and said, "Then I cannot help you." For the first time, after I left his office, I felt defeated. I felt I wanted to run away to sea, the way men under pressure did. No one seemed to understand what the fight was all about. I couldn't run away to sea, but I did the next best thing. I decided to scrub out my personality, to become anonymous, to take the least likely job I was suited for . . . to become a waitress. I had read an advertisement for coffee waitresses at Schrafft's, the well-known chain of tea rooms. I would be in a different milieu. I wouldn't have to deal with people who knew anything about me and who probably cared less. It was also a morning job so I could be home in the afternoon to take care of my children. I applied and found that I was hardly able to concentrate on the simple test, which had me adding up sales slips for food. I was terrified that my addition would be wrong and I would fail to get the job. They asked for references and I gave Louis Nizer's name. I couldn't think of anyone else who wouldn't react to my decision with concern.

I was hired and the next few days I kept my job secret, while I went for training. I learned how to balance a tray and take orders. After three days of training, I was allowed to go on the floor and wait on tables. I was going to be the best damn waitress there was! I was never going to hassle people who liked to linger. I had a difficult time remembering my first order, trying to write it down quickly. I dashed through the swinging doors, bumped into a waitress getting ready to enter the dining room, picked up my order, and then, just as it has been shown in cartoons, almost spilled the entire tray on my customers. I had learned how to unload a tray but in my hurry had forgotten and unbalanced it. I caught it in time and apologized. I then proceeded to give my customers excellent service, filling their coffee cups many times. When they finally left, I picked up a ten-cent tip, took off my apron, walked off the floor, and quit. I realized I could not hide.

The next day I returned to the personnel agency and was directed to my first job interview. It was with the owner of a very exclusive bathroom shop that supplied gold fixtures and other accessories to mansions and yachts. They needed a public relations person. I was working again. After a few months, I decided to take another job as public relations director for a dress firm called Kay Windsor. It involved going into department stores across the country with a line of dresses and setting up fashion shows. I had to do the commentary and train the sales people at morning meetings on how to sell the new line. I enjoyed working again and the salary was good. It certainly paid Rhodelle, took care of the food, and had the potential for much more if I could concentrate on getting ahead.

So, in 1958, in my mid-thirties, I actually thought I was starting over again in my profession, or at least in one of them. I tried desperately not to act tired when I got home. If I showed any sign of fatigue, John Henry would pounce on me and say, "No one is asking you to work." I made sure there was time to sit with the children at dinner and time for bathing and tucking them into bed. In the meantime, John Henry was considering his options.

There had been a few offers of jobs that had miraculously appeared and then mysteriously disappeared. The experiences had rocked us both. One day, in the middle of feeling desperate about work, John Henry had an air-mail letter from a former colleague, Bill Schwarz, who had become program director for wcco, a big station in Minneapolis. Bill had been a director on one of John Henry's shows a few years earlier so he knew his work well. He said they would like to groom him to take over for a well-known local personality, Cedric Adams, in case he was ready to leave or retire. John Henry was excited and agreed to bring me to look over the station and check into available housing. At the same time he advised Bill about his lawsuit and mentioned that the offer came at precisely the right time.

Just before we were ready to go, John Henry was offered a small but excellent part in a Broadway play called *Fair Game*. He was to play a Dallas buyer, leering and gauche, but humorous. The only hitch with the play was the time limit. The producer needed to know within a few weeks, or they couldn't hold the part open. I was anxious for John Henry to accept the part. The legitimate stage wasn't affected by blacklisting since there were no sponsors to be pressured. It also meant we would stay in New York. But the Minneapolis bunch was so excited about John Henry coming, they made the offer sound very tempting. So off we went to Minneapolis. Suspicious me, I began to worry when we were kept waiting in Bill's office for about an hour. "Stars are not treated like this, John Henry. In fact, future employees are not treated like this. They pushed you to come out, arranged contests around your coming, and set up interviews with their top personalities. Yet why hasn't anyone greeted us?" Bill did show up, apologized for his lateness, and invited us into his office. John Henry gave me a withering look, as if to say, "You're always cynical."

The interview went well. John Henry took part in the promotions, but the station never got around to discussing contracts.

They were displaying him as their own but nothing had been settled. They finally had to admit there was no job; the blacklist had followed him to Minneapolis. I called the producer of the play to tell him that I had a feeling John Henry would be available and asked him to extend the deadline just a few more days. But it was too late. They had already cast the show.

The rest of the year we both went through assorted bizarre experiences. John Henry kept trying to find a spot on radio or television, hoping the blacklist wasn't air-tight. He made an appearance on the *Jack Paar Show* and while I watched, praying that he would be sparkling and clever, he crumbled in front of the television audience as he tried to make light of the blacklist and the experience of standing in an unemployment line. The result was grim. Jack Paar summoned Henny Youngman, the next guest, who never let John Henry get in another word.

Our friend Herb Steinman loaned us some money to help us through some tight spots. Then one day I discovered that some jewelry I had was missing. I did not have much but what I had was valuable. A bracelet that had been made from my grandfather's watch chain was among the missing pieces. Somehow I felt the loss was symbolic. I felt betrayed and vulnerable. It was just the forerunner of other strange occurrences.

After John Henry's humiliating experience on the *Jack Paar Show,* he was offered a weekly show on WBAI-FM by Louis Schweitzer, who was happy to give John Henry an hour of time. It was a very loose arrangement, allowing him to do any kind of show he wanted and also allowing him to keep the advertising revenue he attracted in addition to his salary. Shortly after starting on WBAI, John Henry received a letter from Wendell B. Campbell, an old friend, who offered him a job in San Francisco. It was to be a daily show from three to four hours in duration for KFRC. We were both excited about the offer and loved the idea of going west to San Francisco. At the same time, Campbell called Sam Slate at WCBS and let him know that he was very interested in employing John Henry, as he assumed the lawsuit had been dropped. Then, strangely, a letter arrived from him suggesting that John Henry cut an audition tape and do it at WOR with Robert Leder, whom we did not know. All expenses would be paid. But as if by divine providence, another letter arrived in an envelope identical to the one John Henry had just opened. That letter should have gone to Leder advising him that John Henry would be calling, and it added that John Henry seemed to be victorious over Aware and if it was true he was free of controversy "then we will definitely be interested in having John Henry Faulk out here." We couldn't believe that letter had been sent by mistake. We almost wanted to believe that some guardian angel wanted us to have concrete evidence that Aware was a factor in John Henry's unemployability. The affair smacked of "the carrot and the stick"—offer a wonderful job and hold a stick over the offer. The stick was "drop the lawsuit."

It was a time of emotional turmoil and confusion. In a startling turn of events, the lawyer for Aware, Godfrey Schmidt, withdrew, and the new attorney turned out to be Roy Cohn, the lawyer who was so close to Joseph McCarthy in his investigation days. The battle lines were drawn between two giants . . . Roy Cohn against Louis Nizer. What a show!

John Henry could hardly wait to see Roy Cohn in action bucking Louis Nizer and felt exhilarated by the new development. But Roy Cohn lost no time in postponing the examinations before trial for about four months.

Our money problems grew worse. I was working and for a period of time John Henry sold mutual funds. But our lifestyle was too costly. We discussed alternative ways of living and cutting down on our expenses. One thing was certain; we had to get out of my beloved apartment, but where could we go for much less rent? For Johnny it was simple—he wanted to go back to Texas. He felt he had contacts in Texas, and in fact thought he could work out an arrangement with the manager of a small station, KNOW, to pre-sell a program through his contacts before we finally moved down there. John Henry convinced me that we would be able to afford a house in Austin, through the good graces of a buddy and builder, A.D. Stenger. For a small down payment and reasonable monthly payments, we would be settled in a nice community. We would live near Barton Springs, the beautiful three-mile, freshwater spring that runs right through the town and provides a place for concerts, barbecues, and picnics. I could feel my heart palpitating again at the possibility of the move to Texas, but I began to rationalize, as I always did, that perhaps it was the best move for us. I began to add up the pluses. We'd have an extended family for the first time; the children would have cousins, aunts, uncles; they would have a new "country" to explore; their father would spend more time with them swimming, hunting, and camping. I dreamed a lot. Anything to still the terror in my heart at leaving New York City and again leaving "my career."

About the time we were all packed, good-byes had been said, furniture had been sent, and the day for departure was upon us, John Henry received an air-mail letter from that small, insignificant station in Austin, saying the station had program plans that made it impossible to include John Henry as one of its personalities. They had to forget the whole thing. The blacklist had even reached KNOW and Austin. But there was no turning back. We had said our good-byes to our friends. Our apartment was empty. I had again said good-bye to my parents, who felt this was a necessary move. In a way I was glad to get away from my family and hoped we would have a fresh start both financially and emotionally in Texas.

It was on Saturday, March 14, that we pulled away from our home, passed by my parents' apartment on East 41st Street, and looked up at them leaning out over the balcony as they waved good-bye. When I saw the skyline, I wiped away some runaway tears, and then turned to the children and said, "We are off to a wonderful new adventure." Our miniature Schnauzer, Major Whiskers, or Whiskey as we called him, snuggled on the floor of the car and settled down for a long ride. Then the Faulk clan was off to Texas, a strange and foreign land.

CHAPTER 16

TEXAS LIVING

The trip to Texas started out well. It had been a long time since we had spent so much private time together. The children enjoyed the drive because we had planned the hours carefully. They had plenty of toys and games to keep them busy during the time on the road, but we always made sure to make plenty of stops for breakfast, lunch, and dinner. They loved eating out in restaurants, and in the evening we stopped during daylight hours so they could get familiar with the hotel, order dinner in their rooms, and watch television. They were quite happy to stay in the hotel or motel rooms alone, while John Henry and I took advantage of the time to have dinner in the restaurant by ourselves. In all the years that we were married, that was the only time I remember actually having intimate dinners with John Henry.

I was always the romantic. John Henry seemed to be in better spirits at the thought of going home. He loved Austin and spent hours retelling me about his father, who had been raised a share-cropper but later became a lawyer and a judge who read Emerson, Jefferson, and Thoreau. His mother had been a pious Methodist who became somewhat concerned when his father became involved with civil rights and social justice, but she backed him all the way. He was "the head of the family." John Henry had been the rebel, starting to use profanity at an early age and spewing out the facts of life whenever he wanted attention. His friends became the other outcasts, the Negro children. And when John Henry felt ostracized by his friends, he would ride a donkey up to the schoolhouse, pull its tail, and cause it to emit a loud fart. Judge Faulk hoped John Henry would follow in his footsteps and study law, but in the university his chief interest had become literature. J. Frank Dobie, Roy Bedichek, and historian Walter P. Webb became his mentors.

Soon we were in Texas and then driving up to Green Pastures on West Live Oak Street where we were going to stay for a few days until our furniture arrived. The entire Faulk family—sisters, brothers, cousins, grandchildren—were waiting on the front porch of the old home place to greet us. The children had made welcome-home signs, and banners were posted up all over the house greeting John Henry and the New York cousins. There was a great deal of jubilation and celebrating around the huge round dining table that had an immense revolving lazy Susan attached. The lazy Susan kept spinning as we all sat around, ate, and talked about our future in Austin. The neighbors had already been told that John Henry had made enough money to "semi-retire" and he wanted to bring his family back home to enjoy Austin and have them grow up in natural surroundings.

That night the children doubled up with their cousins and spent the evening laughing and whispering in bed, while we sat up and talked halfway to morning, making plans about our future. I loved talking with Mary. She was my favorite in-law. She was flamboyant and colorful and the most accepting of the family, being somewhat of an outcast because she had left the Methodist fold for Catholicism. She was envied for the lifestyle she managed. She used her catering business and the beautiful old home as a backdrop for all her own social obligations. Of all the relatives, she was least threatened by my emotions and outspoken opinions.

After a few days we were able to move into our new house on Airole Way, a two-storey stucco house that overlooked the hills and a deep, undeveloped valley. I was terrified of rattlers, but John Henry assured me that they were strictly a myth put out by New Yorkers. But the day we moved in, I saw a snake coiled up on our front lawn and screamed. John Henry came running and shouted for all to hear, "It's a rattler, stay away." The next-door neighbor came out with a gun; another neighbor, a vacuum-cleaner salesman, ran to get one of his metal hoses; and we waited, hypnotized by the rattler slowly beginning to uncoil. John Henry grabbed the gun, looked down its barrel to see if it was loaded, realized the stupid thing he was doing, and aimed and with one shot tore off the rattler's head just as it began its deadly rattle.

I wanted to go home, back to New York. "What do you mean, there are no rattlers? The valley must be filled with them."

"Hell," said John Henry, "they don't want to bother you. Just never run when you see one. Stand completely still. They'll get out of your way. If the children go into the valley, just make sure they wear high boots, so the rattler can't strike flesh."

That was just the beginning of my getting acquainted with Texas and the world of nature. The stone walls of our home provided a perfect breeding place for scorpions, which hid between the crevices, and black widow spiders, which crossed our driveway daily, completely unafraid. That week we were invited to a potluck supper by the neighbors, and everyone brought a dish. I brought my favorite salad, which uses three or four different greens, tomatoes, scallions, crumbled blue cheese, and my own mixture of oil, vinegar, garlic, oregano, and a pinch of sugar. We were now accepted.

While John Henry was looking for some way to make money, I decided to run a little business out of my home. I felt I could combine work with being a mother, and in that way John Henry wouldn't feel so threatened. My first attempt was at selling handbags. I had an idea that I would have a one-price policy. My stepfather agreed to be my New York contact and buyer. He was going to send me a shipment of purses, one price, $3.50. It was a great way to start because he paid for the first shipment and there was no outlay of money on my part. The bags were a good buy and there was a wide assortment of sizes. But big or small, I would only charge $3.50. Then I had to think of a way to publicize my new "store." All the neighborhood women had helped me put up shelves in our huge living room. I covered the shelves with mint green, satin-finished paper. I prepared huge quarts of green tea, synchronized my color scheme with cookies with green icing, and added green paper plates and napkins. Then I had the bright idea for a television show that might appeal to our friend Cactus Pryor. If he liked it, I might get on his television show and have a chance to really push my new venture. I told him that I had purses of every shape, but the problem was that most women traditionally bought small purses if they were short or large ones if they were tall. I wanted them to break out of that mold and be more imaginative. In fact, I felt that the way they dressed reflected their personalities and their secret dreams. I pointed out to Cactus that although I was only five feet three inches, I always carried huge handbags and wore large hats and over-size chunky jewelry. Everyone who bought a bag from me would get a "purse analysis." Cactus loved the idea; it tickled his funny bone, and I was booked for a half-hour to talk about my "pursanalysis." That gave me the chance to bring ten bags to the show to talk about. Cactus said at the end that this was the longest commercial he had ever run. But the show and the idea caught fire, and people from all over Travis County beat a path to my door for an analysis and a purse "for only $3.50."

I was so successful that I began to think of ways of expanding. The newspapers ran stories of me surrounded by my bags and business boomed. I thought of taking my bags on the road, but then realized that I would have to buy new stock for each season and I would have to start making a substantial outlay for the new stock. I couldn't depend on my stepfather to keep supplying me with merchandise. In the meantime, John Henry had been called by a friend, newspaper editor Buck Hood, to help direct a film for the Salvation Army. I became very friendly with Buck Hood, who was an effective publicist. He listened to me quite intently as I described my advertising and public relations background. I told him I admired his ability to get newspaper coverage for his charities in such a productive way.

It was about this time that Teddy Berenson, an owner-developer of large shopping centers from Boston, was in Austin trying to get some publicity for Capital Plaza Shopping Center, which was in the process of being built. There seemed to be a freeze on any mention of this expensive venture, mainly because Berenson was an "outsider" and local business groups were concerned about the competition. In every community that Berenson had built before, radio, television, and newspapers welcomed him with open arms, aware of the business and jobs he was generating. But Austin was a one-newspaper town, and that newspaper was not co-operating. Berenson needed public awareness to get the project off the ground, not only to attract stores to his complex but also to promise heavy traffic through the center.

Buck Hood suggested we set up a meeting with Teddy Berenson and see about handling his account. I began to understand from Buck Hood's encouragement that I would at least have his co-operation at the newspaper if I did land the account and could successfully break the blackout that existed on mentioning Capital Plaza. I did some fast checking on how the advertising agencies worked in Austin and was shocked at the "bush" way they handled their accounts. Most agencies in New York got their commission from placing expensive space: but most Austin agencies, which had limited commissionable space to deal with, counted on kickbacks from printers and photographers, a petty way of making a living. I realized that I would have to charge a rather hefty retainer from any client so that I could plan a campaign that would be best for the client without being worried where the commission was going to come from. I also knew that any service I could perform for big, out-of-town accounts would be very valuable, because cracking the Austin market was tougher than other markets where you could deal with a variety of media and a number of newspapers competing for your client's advertising dollar. I knew that if I set up an advertising agency, I would only be interested in the big accounts. I certainly was not anxious to go scrambling for the local accounts that the few agencies in Austin were tightly guarding.

From my first meeting with Teddy Berenson, I felt completely at ease with him. He was a big, burly, tough-talking man who discussed openly his problems with the press. He wanted to know our credentials and what we could deliver. I liked straight-talking tough businessmen. I understood them better than politicians. I suggested that he drive us out to look at his property, so that I would know what we were talking about. While we were riding around I would be able to tell him more about my background and what I thought we could handle. Since John Henry had no background in advertising, and had no idea what we were talking about, he came along to provide the local color and to impress Berenson with his family connections and the Faulk clan and their political contacts. After a few hours of driving and talking, I began to understand that the work needed a number of things: a pre-publicity campaign that would raise the consciousness of the community to this positive business; discussions about future publicity and advertising campaigns with prospective stores that were signing up; an opening celebration and heavy newspaper advertising with ads and editorial copy supplied by my agency; even preliminary discussions with the individual stores about handling future advertising for them. It was a huge but exciting undertaking, and I felt that all my experience would be invaluable in doing the best job possible for the group. But I also knew that I had to be paid properly or I could not perform at peak level.

Very little of the work would be able to return enough of a commission to compensate me and whatever staff I needed. I always make decisions from a very trustworthy "gut" reaction, so when we went back to the office to discuss contracts, I had made up my mind that we needed a $2,000 monthly retainer, which was a lot at that time, plus expenses and whatever 15 per cent we were able to collect legitimately. From my point of view, kickbacks were not only tacky but also unethical. When Berenson first heard my terms he jumped up and roared, "I don't pay my agencies in Houston and Dallas that kind of money! Who the hell are you?" I patiently explained that a problem existed with commissions, that Austin was a tough market to break, and that I had already figured out the campaign he needed. If we couldn't get together on a price, he didn't need me. I suggested the other agencies in town. We needed the account, we needed the money, but I have never been able to work under conditions that were unfair. I also felt it was important to establish a respectful working relationship from the beginning, and I wanted him to be aware that there was a great deal of work to get his project off the ground and I was prepared to dedicate my energies to it. I then suggested he think about it and we would return in a few hours for his answer. A few hours later we met again, and Berenson was ready to talk business. I was excited at the prospect and knew that my agency was off the ground.

With our first check, I found a small office, interviewed an art director, and hired a secretary. We crowded into a small space, with my secretary fielding visitors, while I sat behind her, turning my back to the door when I wasn't "available." The artist and I prepared a slick brochure for the new firm to use to get other business. I was unbelievably happy. I felt important. I decided to call the firm John Henry Faulk Associates. This gave some status to my husband and it also made good use of the Faulk name, which was important in the community. There was also a problem at that time with women in business. I was presumably not allowed to own a business or to get any loans without my husband's written permission. He would have to co-sign any loans. The only reason I escaped that indignity was because the bankers did know the Faulk clan and neglected to enforce the rules. I was furious at the legislation, but since no one bothered me about it, I didn't create a fuss. I also had too much on my plate to make waves in that direction.

I was invited by the few advertising men in town to join the advertising club, which met monthly for lunch. I accepted and was treated to a solicitous lecture by the four or five men who appeared. I'll never forget their advice. "Now, Lynne, we know you come from New York, and everybody worries about money. Let us give you some advice. We don't care about money down here. We like to go huntin' and fishin' and enjoy life. If you have any business meetings, don't talk money at first. Wait until you have had a nice long lunch, and then quietly bring up business. Don't be pushy." This was all told to me in the most syrupy Southern accent. I told them I appreciated their advice. "But you have to realize that my temperament is different from a Texan's. I operate in a much faster way, and I can't change. Besides, I don't have the time you have. I have to get out and hustle. But I promise you one thing. I will never, never go after one of your accounts." I knew that the only accounts I could land with my large retainer would be accounts coming in from Chicago, New York, Boston, and other big cities. I spoke their language and I knew how to deal with Easterners. I was aware that my colleagues didn't promise me the same courtesy.

When Berenson heard that I opened an office immediately after he signed us as his agency, he seemed annoyed at first. "I hear that you started your agency with my money." I retorted at once, "You forget that it was my money, not yours. We earned it, and I presume I can do anything I want with my money. If I thought your account could be serviced more efficiently out of an office rather than my home, then that was my decision."

While I was working on the Capital Plaza Shopping Center, I decided to look for more business while our name was being bandied around in the community. We had caused quite a stir landing such a plum account, especially since it meant we had first crack at all the stores that were part of the Plaza Shopping

Center, including the two or three giants who usually took most of the space. I learned how to run the business meetings for Berenson and talk frontage and advertising budget. I had a strong sense about getting everyone involved in the community as soon as possible and began to arrange projects where people would be photographed making charitable donations and lending support to local clubs.

By that time we were asked to promote the very conservative Austin Savings and Loan Association. I impressed the crusty old president, Earl Howell, with the research I did, making sure I made no mistake in the terms used to describe a savings and loan association, which is completely different from a bank. I thought that most financial institutions sounded the same, cold and unfriendly. My idea was to take their board of directors and make them visible and human. I reasoned that if you know the board of directors you can count on its integrity. It was a delicate operation to convince them that I could profile each one of them in a tightly produced, one-minute commercial. The one minute would start with them in their own place of business, fade into a meeting of their favorite charity, show them enjoying individual hobbies, and then depict them at home with their families. "After all," I said, "what makes one trust company different from another trust company? The board of directors. Do you trust the people behind your trust company?" Although the board of directors was nervous about this kind of commercial exposure, it was done so well that they gave me a round of applause at the presentation. Interestingly enough, most people thought of the commercials as non-commercial television appearances and would greet them by saying, "I saw you on television the other night. I didn't know you were interested in that charity or had such a hobby or so many children." It worked well and we tied it up with a newspaper advertisement juxtaposing pictures of the Austin Savings and Loan building and the state capitol building in Austin with the headline, "Symbols of Stability."

After getting the account, I moved my office into the Savings and Loan Building. That made good economic sense to me, as not only was I more tightly involved with my account but Earl gave me an excellent deal on the rent. I expanded into two large offices only a few months after John Henry Faulk Associates went into business. I had them decorated with huge black-and-white squares of linoleum and ordered some comfortable furniture, including a large tea wagon and bone china, and a large electric "gold" coffee pot. I designed a huge, pumpkin-color round arborite table for my desk, so it could be used as a conference table and allow John Henry to have a space if he wanted to make an appearance.

He was fascinated with the office, enjoyed coming in to dictate letters and then leaving to go fishing. He admitted that he had a terrible time discussing advertising and hated being on the other side of the fence wooing clients instead of being wooed. My secretary confided to me that she was just as happy when he didn't show up because he kept her busy with personal letters. She became very protective of me. I tried to explain that he was having a difficult time changing careers, but that I loved the work. Now that I was working and creating a business, I didn't have much time to worry about our personal relationship, and in fact began to sublimate all my anxieties about our personal life. It also freed me from becoming too involved with my neighbors, as I always had the excuse that I had to be at the office.

About that time I was offered the Driskill Hotel as an account. The hotel was one of the oldest and finest in Austin, but they felt that it was an honor to be offered the account and weren't willing to give us a retainer. I thought about it a long time but decided I could not do the job they needed without being paid properly, and besides it would eliminate any chance we might have of getting any of the larger and newer hotels beginning to open in Austin. The manager was quite shocked when I refused the account and felt I was short-sighted. Again, I listened to my "gut" reaction and stood my ground.

I had to expand my staff to handle the accounts that were beginning to come to us. We were getting a reputation as experts in opening shopping centers and the workload was too heavy for a freelance artist. I hired a young man for the job as art director, but the rest of my staff were women. There were very few good men available for work. If they were good and in Austin, they were employed. If they were out of work, there was usually a problem. But I had a choice of some sensational professional women who had moved to Austin with their husbands and also women who needed part-time jobs while raising their families.

About that time the Villa Capri Motel opened on the highway

and launched a new, glittering supper club called The Caravan, the first for Austin. We approached the owners, convinced them we could handle the advertising and the public relations and help book the talent. I used the adjoining office so that my public relations staff would appear separate from my advertising staff. Now it meant that I was working all day, going home in the evening to be with the children at supper, bathtime, and bedtime. Then, about nine o'clock, I would leave for the club, make sure the media were covering an opening act, and then stay until closing to entertain the performers, taking them out to breakfast at 4:00 a.m. For about a year I would end up at home just in time to get a few hours' sleep before rising in time to get the children off to school and start again at the agency.

Now that I had some solid accounts, I wanted something that would also guarantee me regular income that wouldn't be dependent simply on the whim of a client. The problem with many agencies is that they lean heavily on their big accounts and can suffer a great deal if they lose one. I hated being dependent on anyone. I realized that Austin needed a magazine, and none was available. The large national magazines were folding because they were too expensive for the advertisers. The large publications charged advertisers for a huge market when only a specific segment was needed. In came the small, controlled-circulation magazines that could deliver a specific market much more cheaply. No one had tapped the Austin market, which had a university and was the state capital. There were lots of small restaurants, night spots, a large undeveloped lake area, and lots of celebrities and high-profile lecturers brought in by the university and the politicians. It was the home of Lyndon B. Johnson. I thought a magazine called *Austin on the Go* could work and then be franchised, expanding to *Dallas on the Go, Houston on the Go,* etc.

The possibilities were endless, but not so the enthusiasm of the bankers. At first my banker tried to convince me I should start cautiously with a mimeographed sheet. I rejected the advice. "I don't relate to mimeographed sheets. There is room here for a slick magazine." After winning that point, I asked a friend who had magazine experience to help me set up the pages. I had no idea how to begin. He was strangely brusque with me. "Don't be silly. You can't make money in this town with a magazine. Forget it." He refused to help. I then spread out a dummy on the floor with my young art director and we figured out the folds, the size, and how to predict where the color pages would fall. I then sat down and worked out the format, making the decision to combine a calendar of events with local profiles and stories, vowing never to buy any canned or syndicated material. That magazine had to be alive. I created titles for all the special sections and then created pages of editorials to fit with the advertising. Some of my inspiration came from *Cue* magazine and *The New Yorker*. I adapted that format to Austin. It would be the most complete entertainment guide available, sprinkled with good local stories and special monthly themes. I realized that the only way to sell that magazine was to print the first issue exactly as it was supposed to look so that potential advertisers would have a concrete idea of what they were buying.

I had no financial cushion to put out the magazine so I started bartering. I asked a printer if he would invest in the first sample issue, and if it went to press he would have my business in the future. A local artist did a cover on speculation, with the promise that he would be paid if the magazine was printed. I researched and wrote all the stories and editorial content. The only things not in the magazine were the actual ads. We provided different sizes of blank ads, so that prospective advertisers could see where their ads would go. I spent the next month going non-stop from advertiser to advertiser—restaurants, night spots, fashion stores, retail outlets, fishing camps, hotels, concert halls, real-estate developers—and I sold non-stop. I made up six-month contracts, knowing full well I couldn't legally keep anyone to the contract but wanting to instill a sense of obligation. Once their signatures were on the contracts, they felt locked in. I not only sold the ads, I offered my agency to small advertisers who had no agencies to prepare their copy. This was done as a courtesy. The magazine sold out and was ready to go in time to use all the material that was already written.

I surprised my banker, who had tried to discourage me by suggesting I start out slowly with a mimeographed sheet. "It's impossible for me to think that way. This is a slick magazine. Austin deserves the best, and it will be the best. I'll see to it." All I knew was that I was prepared to spend twenty-four hours a day working on the magazine. My banker threw up his hands, insisted

I was crazy, but agreed to lend me the money to publish the first issue.

The magazine was a roaring success. My first hurdle was to get the only newspaper in town to give me coverage, in spite of the fact it was concerned that I was cutting into its advertising pie. I convinced them that what I had done was to enlarge the pie, motivating more people to think about advertising. I got the coverage, and then I was able to have my magazine placed in strategic places that had been off-bounds to other publications. It was allowed on Bergstrom Airfield, which reached families coming to live there, the University of Texas, at border points, at tourist offices, on airplanes, and so on. Every advertiser was allowed to distribute a certain number of copies from his place of business, depending on the advertising dollars spent. Even the Chamber of Commerce blessed the magazine and used it to attract tourists and investments. People planning to buy homes to settle in Austin or planning to attend the university used the magazine to discover available real estate, clubs to join, a lifestyle to appreciate. We increased our circulation, joined the Prestige Group, a New York-based association of small magazines that met certain criteria and were entitled to receive national advertising. The idea was that an agency had to prepare only one ad for these magazines and then buy the exact market wanted. I became so excited about the magazine that I began to dream wall-to-wall magazines, filling my station wagon with copies so that I could always stop to sell an ad along the way. I hired a terrific space saleswoman and added a woman editor stolen from the newspaper. We had regular pep-talk meetings. We became a tight little family.

John Henry, during this time, turned to the Swedenborgian religion and spent long afternoons discussing this philosophy with friends. I was busy morning and night running between the advertising clients, the magazine, and my public relations job for the Villa Capri at night. I escaped into a world I understood, a world I could control. I was running my home, running my business, and forgetting my pain. Some people turn to alcohol; work was my addiction and my safety valve.

CHAPTER 17

THE FIVE-YEAR PLAN

More than five years would pass before the lawsuit would come to trial. In those years our children tried to adjust to a completely new way of life in a place where they were considered outsiders, "Yankee" children. They were teased about their accents, their way of dressing, and their unfamiliarity with country living.

My son Frank made a good adjustment, learning to hunt and going off with the boys to explore the ravine and swim in the Camel's Hole. I watched him establish himself by beating up the two or three neighbor boys who jumped him at once. I remember looking out of the window, watching them hide behind some garbage cans, waiting for him as he rode his bicycle home. I was furious at this ganging up and started to run out the door to chase them and warn Frank that they were waiting to ambush him, when John Henry grabbed my arm and said, "He has to fight his own battles. You can't do it for him." I was furious as he restrained me, but watched as my son jumped off his bike and flailed his fists at the attackers. It was over soon and they walked off to play. It was a problem for me most of their growing-up life to keep from interfering. I wanted the world to be fair for them, and I wanted to leap in to help make everything right, whether with teachers, neighbors, or other children. I had lots of advice from all my Texas relatives who didn't understand my complete involvement with my children.

I started early over-compensating for the lack of attention from their father. One of the things John Henry did that was most destructive was to compare them to other children. They were constantly trying to get his approval. It was reminiscent to me of my constant need for approval from my mother, approval that rarely came. It was particularly difficult for Johanna and Evelyn because their parents were considered "different." I worked away from the home and John Henry used profane language during parties at our house, language that rang out over the valley. We lived next door to a very religious family, the Bowmans, and they would sometimes forbid their daughters to play with mine "because your father uses dirty words." I tried discussing this with my neighbors and tried to restrain John Henry, but only time could take care of those problems.

John Henry's family had to get used to what they called my "flamboyant ways and my dramatic language." They thought I was very emotional and I found that my intense expressions of momentary anger or pleasure confused them. I remember that I was kept waiting at the hairdresser's. Annoyed at this disruption in my tight schedule, I expressed displeasure, but by the time the family heard about it, word came down that "Lynne sure had a temper tantrum at Elsie's beauty shop." It reminded me of all my arguments with John Henry. All he had to do when I was upset with him was to look at me and say, "Aren't you overreacting? You are so emotional." This ploy successfully turned me away from dealing with the problem instead of dismissing his charge by saying, "Perhaps I am overreacting, but that doesn't negate the issue. Let's discuss the problem, not my overreaction."

Those five years were a strange mixture of working, dealing with my new extended family, and integrating into a new community. What I didn't realize was that while I was juggling all the parts of my life, my children were feeling the tension between John Henry and me. I closed my eyes to the problems that kept cropping up—his constant involvement with other women, his predictable confessions, his moments of self-analysis, and his promises to change. I wasn't even aware of how many explosive arguments we had in front of the children. I tried spending more time with the children.

We also moved into a larger new house down the street, built to our specifications. I had resisted the move because of the expense, but John Henry was excited about the extra room, the huge suspended wooden deck, and the extra backyard space for barbecuing. He also tempted me with the fact that there would now be a separate bedroom for each child as well as room for his "study." The move to the new house was fairly painless. I was making enough money to support that lifestyle, but it still meant monthly negotiations with the bank. It was nip and tuck but we were growing steadily and I was becoming a fixture in the business community and being asked to speak at business functions more regularly. I was also the guest of honor at a party to honor the work I did in opening up the lake area by encouraging the fishing camps and small motels to open year-round. The advertising in the magazine had begun to focus attention on this neglected area.

I enjoyed the family outings, loved the long weekend breakfasts at Green Pastures, and saved my sanity with other weekends on our new houseboat. When I went on board and we chugged away from land, I felt some moments of peace. I had fixed up the houseboat with red-and-white striped curtains and berth covers. The boat was painted a soft gray. Early in the morning John Henry would awaken Frank Dobie and they would spend a few hours fishing from the side of the boat, which usually ended up with freshly caught fish fried lightly in butter and served with John Henry's special corn-bread muffins. Later in the day, other friends would join up with us, speeding to our destination in motorboats. And while parents sat on our deck sipping wine or sour mash, others would be water-skiing behind the motorboats. I usually cooked up huge batches of shrimp curry. The only problem was that our houseboat became a pleasure boat instead of a sanctuary, as I had hoped at first. Because it had an upper deck, from two to twenty people could get sleeping bags and spend the night, still leaving the four bunks and a berth below for the family.

There were many guests but the people I did enjoy the most were John Henry's wonderful old friends, J. Frank Dobie and Roy Bedichek. I was allowed to join the sacred circle and would meet with them early in the mornings at Barton Springs where they had gone for their regular swim for the past fifty years. After swimming we sat on a rock under a tree, and in the tradition of the ancient philosophers we sat and talked. Bedichek said he always wondered how "a rare flower" like me could bloom in the "concrete jungle" of New York. It was sad the day Bedichek died. But he did it so quietly, while eating lunch—he put down his fork and his head slowly sank down on the table, no clatter, no fuss. I felt I had lost a strong supporter and friend. J. Frank Dobie continued to invite us to his ranch where only John Henry and I would have dinner with him and we would talk for hours about the "way the world wags." He was very pleased that we had named our son after him, since none of his family ever named a child Frank Dobie. He showed his appreciation by sending Frank all his books, appropriately autographed to his namesake.

Another close friend, Cactus Pryor, who had a regular television program on KTBC, had a droll sense of humor. But I had little time for my own personal friends, partly because John Henry rarely extended himself for anyone I would bring home and partly because I was so busy with my business. I became close to Alma Jean and Fred Ward, who had a home at the very end of our dead-end street. Alma Jean was giving my children piano lessons and I learned she had come from the East. I knew she had a lot of problems to solve with Fred, but she was a lusty, open-faced woman. I loved looking at her and hearing her laugh, and sometimes I felt I could confide in her, as she told me things about her life. I was never sure that she wasn't handling some of her problems by drinking, but that seemed to be prevalent in the neighborhood.

It didn't strike me then that this paradise John Henry had always yearned for covered up so much anguish, that green grass, soft breezes, and starlit nights didn't necessarily provide an emotional security blanket for its residents. In fact, the hard reality of concrete streets and hordes of people in New York City sometimes nurtured strong personalities.

The Faulk family entertained Lyndon B. Johnson and Ladybird at Mary's house or went to fish-fries at the LBJ Ranch. Johnson could never quite forget that he wasn't "politicking." There were twelve of us one night for dinner, and Lyndon was called upon to say a few words. He struck his familiar pose, outstretched his arms to embrace the entire table, and started off, "Mah friends . . . " It was difficult for him to behave like an ordinary guest, and the evening took on the atmosphere of a meeting hall.

I kept hiding from myself the fact that I was praying for the trial to be heard, so that there would be some hope of going back to New York City. I missed it so much. I knew my daughters missed it, too, but Frank was settled in. I knew there would be a problem uprooting him. And John Henry never stopped talking about getting back to his career. We didn't communicate with each other and unfortunately didn't communicate with our children. I was so intent on creating the image of a happy family that I still hadn't been able to confront the problems we were having. But then I was never clear on what was happening to me since I was always so busy just surviving. We had to survive the lawsuit and then things would be different, I thought, I believed. I spent so much time assuring my children, "When the lawsuit is over you can have your ponies; when the lawsuit is over we will spend more time together; when the lawsuit is over your father will be home more; when the lawsuit is over I won't work so hard."

Then finally one day we heard the news. I will never forget that day. I was doing my rounds, still selling ads for my magazine. I had called in to my office to get my messages, when my secretary told me that Louis Nizer had called to say that the trial date was set. I wanted to run, to shout. The trial was coming at last; there was light at the end of the long, dark tunnel.

Nizer invited us to come up to New York to discuss the case and how he wanted to handle the next few months. We sat in Nizer's home talking excitedly about the lawsuit. I began to feel alive again. Then Nizer said he wanted John Henry to come to New York a few weeks before the trial was to start. He wanted to go over every step of the case, to grill him, to groom him. He warned him not to make any plans for partying in the evenings. Nizer's strongest suit was his unbelievable attention to the smallest detail. Nothing was ever left to chance. He would be working with him every night until dawn, and the earlier nights John Henry must get to bed and get sleep so that he would be completely clear and fit for the next day. Nizer was only insisting on a schedule that he was prepared to follow. He demanded top performance from everyone, including himself.

As for me, I was sent back to Texas to "mind the store." Nizer expected a long trial and he assured me that the first few weeks wouldn't be very interesting. He would call for me in the last part of the trial when he would cross-examine and address the jury. He assumed I would have no other interest in the proceedings. He metaphorically patted me on the head and told me to be a good wife and stay with the children back home. I felt so left out. I wanted to be there, wanted to be included. I had waited so long for that trial, but it never occurred to me to insist on being there. I immediately fell into the role assigned to me, the role laid out by Nizer as supportive wife in the background.

I went back to Austin to run our business, but now my heart wasn't in it. Everything seemed so temporary. I felt disoriented and alone. Letters were coming back from John Henry about his delight at New York. He talked about staying up till all hours with Nizer. He had never worked so hard in his life. The most important trial of our life together was going on without me. I had worked for five years supporting the family emotionally and financially in Texas. My dreams had been focused on that day. I had suppressed my pain and anguish at our personal relationship. I had put my life somewhat on hold until the day of reckoning. I had made no waves, rocked no boats, made no demands, and now I felt empty and apprehensive. That was when I met Alfredo Castaneda.

CHAPTER 18

LOVE IN THE AFTERNOON

When news of the trial became known in Texas, people began asking a lot of questions. Will you be staying in Texas if you win? Will you be going back to New York? What will happen to your business? I said I didn't know what was going to happen. We might not win, and even if we did win, there might not be any money. John Henry and I hadn't discussed our future, since we had no idea what our future was going to be. I tried to be as vague as possible because I knew I had to keep the accounts comfortable. I didn't want to lose my agency because the business community thought I was going to leave. If we were going to leave Austin, I wanted to be able to sell my business, and I knew that was only possible if it stayed healthy. So I was in the position of juggling answers, fielding questions, and facing the community alone.

About that time I had a phone call from Alfredo Castaneda, a professor at the University of Texas, asking if I would host a group of Mexican students at the Villa Capri. The students were part of an exchange program and Castaneda thought they would enjoy an evening of American entertainment at the Caravan Club, which at the time was featuring a group that played the dance called the Twist, made famous by Chubby Checker. I told him that I would check and call him back as soon as possible. I did some research on Castaneda and found out that he was a highly respected and internationally known child psychologist who was involved in valuable research. He had a coterie of graduate students who adored him, but they warned me not to try to get him to talk about being Mexican or to speak Spanish. "He has shut that part of his life out and spends a lot of time being hip and using hip jargon." I couldn't understand why he would turn his back on such a rich heritage, but I was told that Mexicans were treated worse than black people in Texas, and he might be sensitive to the discrimination. I was curious about the man.

I decided to arrange a party for his Mexican students and called him to ask if they would mind being televised for the news that night. I didn't want to invade their privacy but it would be helpful to the club if I could get some coverage for the club as host of that exchange program. It would also give the exchange program some good publicity. Castaneda said he would trust my judgment, as he had heard that I was a very imaginative entrepreneur. The night arrived and I reserved a number of tables but asked Castaneda if he would sit at my regular table. I was interested in speaking to him and finding out how a Mexican, involved in Mexican affairs, could ignore his heritage.

When they arrived that night, I was amazed to see that Alfredo Castaneda almost looked like one of his graduate students. Although he had silver-white hair, contrasted with his dark skin and long, angular face, he still looked younger than his almost forty years. I was introduced to his students and he graciously accompanied me to my special table, where we could talk uninterrupted. His huge brown eyes canvassed my face and I could feel myself the object of a man's attention for the first time in years. There had been some aborted flirtations, but they had been almost hostile incidents in the hopes of easing some of my loneliness. I had also heard that Castaneda was quite shy, but that evening, above the blare of the music, we talked incessantly about the program, his concern about the treatment of Mexicans, his love of jazz, his San Francisco family, his love of writing poetry, and his background as an Olympic swimmer. He complimented me on my ability to handle the Villa Capri and the party. We enjoyed watching the students dance and the television cameras added a note of gaiety. It was an evening full of fun and stimulation. He asked where my husband was and I explained briefly about the lawsuit and his stay in New York to prepare for the trial. He seemed to be sensitive to the fact that I was left behind. "You have done so much, you should be handled tenderly and with love." He spoke so romantically I felt transported into another world, a world completely foreign to the world in which I had operated for the last few years.

Soon the evening was over and I said good night to Alfredo as he went to join his students. I gathered some of the entertainers and the musicians and we went to have our usual late-night breakfast. While I was sitting there recounting the evening, I noticed that Alfredo walked in with some of his group. After they were seated he came over, kissed my hand, and thanked me again for the evening. I felt giddy, and we both laughed as the rest of the evening was spent sending sidelong glances in each other's direction. I made light of the situation with my colleagues, attributing the courtly behavior to his Latin background.

I suddenly realized that I had grown heavier over the years, and I had a meager wardrobe. It was a form of self-punishment, something I seemed to do when I was unhappy without being that self-aware. My rationale had always been to spend money on the children, but not to fight John Henry for money for me. I wished I looked more glamorous now, and I thought that was the end of my encounter with Alfredo Castaneda, but I soon received a note from him thanking me for my hospitality and asking me for lunch. He suggested I come to his office at the University of Texas and look over his department and then we would go to some small place and take time to eat and talk.

As I sat in his office, going over his published articles and discussing his work, he pulled open a drawer and took out a pint of whiskey and asked me if I wanted a drink. I thought it rather odd, especially since he said he had to be careful because, as he told me, drinking on campus was forbidden. He took a fast nip and I joined him to be sociable. I had no idea at the time that that was an important signal that he might have a drinking problem. I knew that he was considered very shy and that seemed to relax him. Over lunch he asked me more questions about the lawsuit and the blacklisting and again expressed the opinion that I was being ignored. I began to talk to him more openly about my fears, my loneliness, and my marital problems. Alfredo was going through a divorce at the time and I was able to comfort him about his separation from his two children, a little girl and boy. I found him very sympathetic and began to think of ways to talk to him about his background.

I thought of a way to involve Alfredo in my world. I would convince an advertiser, Monroe Lopez, to take a full-page ad in my magazine. He was the owner of a string of very popular

Mexican restaurants who didn't need to spend any money on advertising. His restaurants were always full and he was considered a millionaire in his own right. I thought that it would make sense for him to use some of his money to help his people. I created a campaign to promote Mexican heritage. The format would be a monthly page devoted to a high-profile Mexican who was making a contribution to Texas—a scientist, a musician, a writer. The headline would be "Salute to Mexican Heritage" and the logo at the bottom of the page would be that of the Mexican restaurants with the slogan repeated. The first person I approached was Alfredo. "Would you be willing to be my first subject? I'll take a picture of you in front of your blackboard as you write equations about your research. I'll go over all the copy with you. I think it's time Texas recognized the contribution of their Mexicans, citizens as well as visitors." He agreed easily, much to my surprise. His co-operation didn't compute with the information I had about his reticence to talk about his past. I then sold the idea to Monroe Lopez and promised that he would have framed photographs of all my subjects to hang on the walls of his restaurants.

I met Alfredo, took his photograph, wrote the copy, and then went back for his approval. It was then that he seemed to find fault and kept asking for corrections before he would initial the ad and give the go-ahead for printing. I suddenly realized he was stalling and I angrily pulled back the layout and copy and said, "Forget it. I think you do have a problem coming out of the closet, and I don't want the responsibility. There are plenty of other Mexicans who aren't afraid to talk about their heritage. I think you are holding up your signature because you'd like to kill the ad." He looked startled, pulled back the layout, and hurriedly scribbled his initials. "Go ahead, print the ad. Now let's go out and celebrate." I laughed happily, felt good about his decision, not only for myself but also because I felt it was an important move for him.

It was late afternoon by now, and we decided to go to a little tavern near the campus where there was a juke box. We ordered some tavern food, a couple of glasses of beer, put some money in the juke box, and started dancing slowly to the music in the dim light of the afternoon. Dancing in the middle of the day made me feel somewhat wicked, and I liked the feeling of cutting myself off from my other responsibilities. We laughed a great deal and then he asked me back to his apartment for one more drink. I was feeling relaxed and it had been so long since I had had any romantic feelings that I didn't think I would recognize them should they happen. He had an apartment in a large complex, a rambling, two-storey building, all with balconies surrounding the huge pool that was "mandatory" in Texas. It was still light out and the pool was filled with tenants splashing and laughing happily in the late afternoon.

I sat on a couch by the window overlooking the pool and Alfredo brought a drink and sat down beside me. As we talked, he mimicked me gently, insisting that I had a charming lisp. I began to feel like a child, changing roles from an aggressive businesswoman trying to wrap up a project to a shy, vulnerable woman being teased by a confident professor. He saw me blush and gently leaned over to slip my silk dress off one of my shoulders. He leaned forward very quietly and kissed my bare shoulder, very softly. He held me carefully, as if afraid I might bolt or fly away. I felt my heart flutter like a bird might that was being cupped gently in a rescuer's hands. It all seemed so unreal . . . the late afternoon sun, the sound of laughter, soft music from his hi-fi, a half-finished drink, and his arms around me. We began kissing hungrily, and then he slowly undressed me and gently carried me to his bed where he patiently and sweetly spent hours kissing my body all over, caressing my breasts and thighs, whispering the most wonderful love words in Spanish. It was as if he reached down into his past, and he was ready to expose himself to me, to be vulnerable and accessible. I heard the Spanish words and I felt as if I had entered his most secret place. We made love for hours, holding each other, moaning and crying and laughing triumphantly. I felt some of the pressure of the last few weeks lift. I had found a refuge, a place to wait out the last few months of the trial.

We began to meet fairly regularly, but mostly late at night after I finished with my work at the Club Caravan. They were a few hours of stolen time. Alfredo would wait for me, have some dinner waiting, and we would dine by candlelight, dancing to Mexican music. By now he was so thoroughly out of the closet that he became consciously Mexican, just as he had tried, before, to leave his heritage behind. The reaction of the community to the ad and his biography had been so positive that he had reaped extra benefits from the university. He enjoyed his new celebrity status. Now he was making special Mexican dishes, playing only Mexican music, and suddenly his conversation was filled with Spanish phrases, almost as if the language had come to him miraculously overnight.

Our life at night was so far removed from reality that I didn't even have the time to be concerned about his drinking, which I noticed was considerable. At first it didn't bother me because his slight tipsiness and extravagant lovemaking only added to the romantic evenings. He was so passionate and full of endearing terms that I was swept away with his ardor. I recognized that I wasn't in love with Alfredo but I reminded myself that John Henry had always said that I should go out with other men, that I should stop being so old-fashioned. I didn't feel any guilt at this time. I intended to keep it our secret and never intended to talk about it to John Henry. I had warned him that if I ever did have an affair I would not tell him about it because I saw no point in it. In fact, I hated hearing about his affairs and didn't accept that this was honesty. I rather thought of it as very punishing and destructive to talk about it, never mind indulging in it.

That affair came at a very low point in my life, and I also knew it would be a short-term thing because each of us had other obligations. He had to be careful about scandal because of his university position and because he was still in the process of divorce. I was in the middle of waiting out a very important trial that ideally would end up with our family back in New York. Alfredo began to write me the most overblown love letters, full of poetic descriptions of my body being touched by moonlight and of love that belonged in another era. He saw me clothed in floating chiffon walking the sands of Israel. His letters talked about love but never actually described the process. He was too poetic for that. I stashed the letters away. I suppose I still needed evidence that I was lovable.

During the weeks that John Henry was in New York preparing for the trial, he would call the house at unexpected times looking for me. He didn't seem satisfied with my answer that I was working at the club or out entertaining one of our performers. I was confused about his questioning, but my mother called one day and said John Henry was asking them a lot of questions about whether I was seeing someone. I was furious at his questions and told my mother that it didn't make sense. "Why would John Henry check on me? My God, you know how he has behaved over the years, how he feels about affairs! Why would he suddenly become so moralistic about me? I think you must be imagining it." I confronted John Henry and asked why he was involving my parents. "You don't really care about what I do. You have said that for years. What is behind your questioning?" He denied that he was checking but asked me if I was seeing anyone. I didn't deny it but I said, "I told you that I would never tell you. That isn't the issue. Our home life is the issue." I refused to answer directly, but I had no qualms about him knowing. It all seemed so academic at that point because I knew that I would have to stop seeing Alfredo soon anyway. I would be going to New York to sit in on the last few weeks of the trial.

What I wasn't aware of until later was that most men lie. They may say they want their wives to go out because it assuages their guilt. They may say it doesn't matter. But a man's masculinity is threatened when his wife finally has a relationship apart from the marriage. Even today I hear men say, "Of course my wife can go out with other men if she wants to, but I know my wife, she would never do it." There is still the feeling that men have physical needs not shared by women. Men assume also that marriage is too important to women for them to fool around. A man's affairs are inconsequential, but women can't separate emotion from just having a good lay, they seem to believe. For a while there was a testing of the "open-marriage" concept, in which women and men openly arranged lives apart from their partners. This, too, failed. Now people are beginning to examine, all over again, the entire concept of fidelity, truthfulness, and commitment. It's ironic that now that we are looking at choice and consent, choice has almost been taken away because of the fear of diseases like herpes and AIDS.

Nizer said John Henry only had "peccadilloes." My affair broke his heart. I never could understand what he meant. Was it a peccadillo when I spent hours crying alone at night, waiting for him to come home? Was it a peccadillo when a young woman came and confessed that he had been sneaking out at night to meet her? Was it innocent when he goaded me into arguments so he could storm out of the house or a party and meet some new woman? John Henry had always excused his affairs by saying they had nothing to do with our marriage, that he never spent money on women, and that they were all short-term affairs. He could handle it if I had one-night stands, but any time I had a relationship it seemed to be a love affair and that was threatening to our marriage. How could I explain that I would have had more respect for him if he had spent money on the women he saw? There was always the danger of falling in love if you were open to affairs, short-term or not. Most important of all, our home life was not good. I did not feel loved when he was with me, and I didn't feel he spent enough time with his children, all promises he had repeatedly made whenever I threatened to leave him. I told John Henry how difficult it was for me not knowing what was going on in New York, not being with all our friends, and not sharing in the excitement. I explained that I felt in limbo, torn between Texas and New York, not knowing where I belonged, where I would end up. He at least had Louis Nizer and all our friends to bolster him through those months.

John Henry was locked away with Louis Nizer, preparing the case and tracking down witnesses who were willing to stick their necks out in his defense. It wasn't as easy as he thought it would be. There were many people who had unpleasant and frightening experiences with Aware, and they didn't want to reopen wounds. John Henry was calling regularly, keeping me in touch with what was happening and describing the grueling days and nights with a relentless Nizer. Finally witnesses began to line up: David Susskind, Tony Randall, Garry Moore, Mark Goodson, Kenneth Roberts, Walter Cronkite, Charles Collingwood. Nizer also felt it was important to get the testimony of the actress Kim Hunter, who had been given a hard time by Vincent Hartnett.

It was about that time that I came up for a brief visit and went along with John Henry and Paul Martinson to Kim's home to ask if she would participate in the trial. Kim Hunter had such a grim experience with Vincent Hartnett and Aware that she still found it hard to discuss it without tears coming to her eyes. I think the most crushing blow had come when she was attacked, and the price of her clearance included sending a congratulatory letter to AFTRA and the old board of directors for the fine work they were doing in clearing out Communists and Communist sympathizers from the union. She had suffered two years of unemployment before her "clearance" and now she wanted to forget the past. She also reminded us that her husband, Bob Emmett, was a promising playwright, and she didn't want to hurt his career. As Paul Martinson tried to convince Kim, her public relations man, and her attorney that there would be a sweeping victory and that she would benefit from the case, Kim walked over to the window and stood alone for a long time looking out. I felt as if I wanted to go over to her and hug her. I knew that it was a very important decision for her to make and only she could make it. While the rest talked furiously, she suddenly turned and said, "Enough, I've made the decision. I want to help. I want to rub out the nightmare I've been having all these years because I allowed myself to be frightened into co-operating. This will help me sleep again. But I'm not doing it only for you and myself. I'm doing it on behalf of my children and my profession and my country." For the first time her face seemed to light up and she smiled.

I met her years later when I was doing an interview show on radio and cautiously reminded her of that day. Once again I saw a very serious, reserved woman break out in uncustomary smiles as she began to talk openly about that period. The tape was running but she was completely unconcerned about being recorded again. She had certainly freed herself from fear, and we hugged each other warmly, having shared the same experience.

I went back to Austin, still operating the business as if we never intended to leave, but knowing that our whole future would be weighed in the balance, and that everything we believed in was finally being put to the test. John Henry said he felt better knowing that if everything failed he would still have a healthy business to go back to. I prayed that we would have the victory Nizer believed was so possible. Like Kim Hunter, I wanted it not just for ourselves but also for our children and our country. Even at that time I had to keep most of my feelings to myself because of the strange circumstances of running a business while one part of me was planning and hoping to leave. As I look back, I am rather surprised that I didn't realize that, once again, I would be pulling up roots and leaving another career in midstream, at its most successful point. Again the future beckoned to me, holding out even more hope, more challenges, more excitement.

I began to look around for possible baby sitters to stay in the house with Johanna, Evelyn, and Frank, who were fourteen, eleven, and nine years of age. It seemed as if so much of their lives had been affected by the lawsuit. They were excited by the news that Daddy was finally going to court to fight the blacklisters and that by now we were suing for three million dollars. The amount of money seemed unreal, beyond their comprehension, and I warned them that although that was the amount of the suit, we might win and be victorious in principle but not be able to collect any money. "But winning in principle is the most important," I assured them. And whatever the outcome, I promised that at least our life would be free of the lawsuit and we could begin to make plans about our future without the added caution: "Just wait until the lawsuit is over."

I began to feel myself withdrawing from my relationship with Alfredo. My mind, thoughts, and emotions were now so completely absorbed by the lawsuit that I had little left over to give anyone else. Alfredo sensed that and began to be more demanding, talking about the possibility of our marrying when the case was over. "You'll be free then of all your obligations. You have stayed at your husband's side all these years. You have put your own life on hold. You admit that your marriage has been shaky. I love you and want you to be my wife." I felt my heart constrict as I tried to tell him that no matter what went on in the past, I had high hopes that when John Henry was vindicated and back at the top of his profession, we might have a chance to make our marriage work. I wanted a marriage. I wanted my children to have a home with a father and a mother. I had lived through a painful divorce when my mother and father separated. And now, after all John Henry and I had been through, perhaps we would have a stronger marriage. At any rate I would try for it.

He argued that I was a dreamer, that I had been trying for years, using each new situation, a new crisis, to bolster the marriage, and nothing had changed. "Even now," he pointed out, "he hasn't stopped seeing other women. Oh, he cries about it, apologizes, but it's the same pattern over and over again." I tried to reason with Alfredo. "But, my darling, you, too, have a problem. I am worried about your drinking. It was none of my business while we were having a clandestine affair, but it seems to be getting worse. I could never live with a man who drinks so much. You have to get your own life in order before we could ever talk about a serious relationship. Please take care of yourself. Find out what to do about your drinking. And, for my sake, understand I still love my husband, or at least I need him and want him to be part of my family. I think we must say good-bye."

For a while Alfredo seemed to accept what I said and only asked that I not cut off seeing him entirely. He would find it too painful. In the meantime he wanted to be at my side through the difficult period. In fact, he was very helpful in finding a family to agree to move into our house when I was called to New York City to participate in the final weeks of the trial.

Then I heard the jury had been chosen. Tom Bolan of Roy Cohn's office was to try the case, a lucky break for us. On April 22, Louis Nizer was to make his opening speech and the trial was to begin. I had word that news of Nizer's opening speech brought out all the reporters and a number of our friends. It was a standing-room-only crowd. John Henry confided in me his terror at sitting in court the first day and realizing that twelve jurors held his life in their hands. He could not get any feeling about their thoughts from their completely deadpan faces. In fact, not until the end of the trial did any of them move so much as a muscle or indicate in any way that they knew where John Henry was sitting or that his friends and supporters crowded the first few rows. For a few weeks I had to be content with reports in the newspapers, which covered the trial extensively. John Sibley of the *New York Times* had been assigned to cover the case. Then, late in May, I was asked to come up for the final weeks of the trial.

CHAPTER 19

THE TRIAL

When Louis Nizer heard that I was coming to New York to attend the trial, he spoke to Ben Bodne, who owned the Algonquin Hotel. Nizer usually held court at the Round Table there, as many of the literati had done years earlier. Ben offered to host us for the duration of the trial so that we would have our privacy and be centrally located. I was delighted at the prospect of staying at the Algonquin, a wonderful old and dignified hotel with a great tradition. It had housed many legends in the theater and was a meeting place for writers, playwrights, producers, and performers. The after-theater buffet was legendary. I left Texas promising to keep my children in touch with what was happening. John Henry and I spent the first evening at Louis Nizer's home, surrounded by his paintings, classical music in the background. Mildred brought me up to date on all that had happened. Nizer seemed confident of the outcome; John Henry was filled with self-doubts.

When I first walked into the courtroom, I felt strange, but our friends soon made room for me in the center of the front bench. I was somewhat self-conscious because so much time had passed since I had seen most of them and I had no idea how much of our life in Texas they knew about. The night before, Nizer had given me an assignment. There was some background material he needed from the library. I knew that any one of his clerks could have researched the subject, but I felt, as I always had with Nizer, like a little girl he had to keep busy, while the men got on with the job of handling the big problems. I hated being away from the courtroom even for a moment.

210

The courtroom proceedings that followed were spine-tingling. I sat listening intently to every word, knowing that each statement was recording a part of our lives and that our future hung in the balance. As I listened, I also felt as if I were on trial. Watching Nizer maneuver in court was a stunning experience. He was ruthless in his attention to detail, and his eyes never stopped exploring every face in the crowd. Once, standing in the hall during recess, he spotted an unfamiliar man's face and immediately asked me to find out who he was and track down the reason for his appearance. Standing before a jury, he at first seemed almost nondescript, but when he started talking, energy shot through his body; his questioning was relentlessly cold and deadly. He would speak in a low voice, almost deceptively conversational in tone, and then he would swoop in unexpectedly on his victim, raising his voice suddenly to emphasize a point. And then his anger would fill the courtroom. It was common knowledge that although he was in his sixties, he could work all night preparing the next day's notes, shower, and come back to court refreshed. John Henry felt Nizer was like a machine, but it was this machine that was eventually to win us the largest libel suit in history.

I watched as our witnesses came to the stand. I knew them all. They talked about John Henry, his fine character, his interesting and profitable show, the damage that had been done to his career. Most of the witnesses were putting their reputations on the line. If we lost, they lost. But win or lose, they felt an obligation to stand up in court and help stem the tide of blacklisting, which smacked more of gangsterism and the protection racket than it did of honest political beliefs. Nizer used the testimony to explode the defense's claim that John Henry's ratings had slipped, punching holes in the ratings service known as Pulse that controlled the industry. He brought to light the hundreds of other performers and artists who had been damaged by Aware by being refused clearance—people like Oscar Hammerstein, Richard Rogers, Moss Hart, and Jerome Robbins. When actors were rejected, orders were given to the employer seeking clearance not to inform any rejectee why he or she had been rejected. David Susskind described the long lists of names he was instructed to supply for clearance before he could cast a television show. Once he had submitted the name of a child, eight years old. When her name came back rejected, Susskind demanded to know how an eight-year-old could be political. He was told it was because the child's father was suspect.

The lurid stories went on day after day, with audible, horrified gasps from the audience. Nizer was able to produce evidence that Vincent Hartnett and his agency made thousands of dollars doing research on names entered for clearance. Once he even cleared the name Santa Claus! Murray Kempton of the *New York Times* went so far as to say in his first article, "There is a sense that when this is over, Aware will never be able to hurt anyone again." It was a heartening statement. Sadly, what he didn't realize was that Aware itself might be crushed but blacklisting could still surface in other guises. But this trial certainly was the first to illustrate so clearly the methods of the blacklisters and their dishonesty and greed.

Louis Nizer and Tom Bolan provided the pyrotechnics as they battled each other in court. Nizer's opening points were to show that Aware Inc. was not an organization that had any authority from the United States government. It was a private organization that had as much standing as a private citizen, and no more. He also pointed out that Laurence Johnson had not been designated a Communist-hunter: he was self-appointed and self-annointed. He had no authority from any governmental agency to pass judgment on the lives of American citizens, economically, patriotically, or in any other way.

David Susskind was an excellent witness, telling how he resented submitting names to the advertising agencies that sponsored his shows, who in turn submitted them to this self-appointed vigilante group that not only could reject names for money but also could clear names for the right price.

At lunch at Nizer's favorite restaurant in Foley Square, I listened with fascination as the jurors were discussed one by one, their facial expressions recalled when Nizer had been addressing them. That way the lawyers could assess what interested the jurors, when they seemed to be deeply interested or when they seemed indifferent. Each day John Henry and I would assess the interest of the spectators by the number of people who came back. Evidently the court was crowded whenever Nizer was to speak. Tom Bolan drew few spectators, but there were always the court afficionados who came to everything. In the evening we sometimes took time to have dinner with some of our friends and go over the day's proceedings.

The distinguished newsman Charles Collingwood was a strong witness, as he described his part in forming the middle-of-the-road slate for the New York local of AFTRA. As president and director of the union, he was able to discuss the fear that was rampant then, and how difficult it was to get a slate together. Over Bolan's objections, he discussed the practices of the industry, when rumors or accusations brought a performer's patriotism into question. He then testified to John Henry's reputation for loyalty, patriotism, and integrity, and described some of the sponsors, networks, and local stations as gutless. Advertising executive Tom Murray of the Grey Agency, who had first alerted us to Aware's bulletin, was a strong witness. The *New York Post's* columnist wrote a pithy, colorful column about Murray's stand. "He exists as proof that no one can draw an indictment against an entire profession. He is a short, pleasant man, but there are refreshing traces on his person and his voice of a capacity for indignation unadjusted to the rules of his calling." The *Post* columnist went on to say, "Yesterday he stood up in court and testified against a blacklister, and one brave man per profession is not so far below the national average."

Murray's testimony was particularly important in establishing that Laurence Johnson, "the millionaire grocer" from Syracuse, was involved in the blacklisting. Murray told how he had received a call from Johnson in March, 1956, and then a series of calls afterwards. He said Johnson had said it was a disgrace that Grey Advertising was using Faulk to advertise their products, Hoffman Beverages and Coca-Cola. Murray testified that he had no such knowledge of Faulk and he was told, "Well, you better get in line because a lot of people along Madison Avenue are getting in line . . . and the display case which the Pabst Brewing Company has in the stores that I either own or control is what is called hard-won space."

Murray objected to that kind of pressure and insisted he didn't intend to drop a first-rate salesman for the product, especially as the threat had just been made by telephone. He said he felt there were legal ways of establishing whether or not Faulk, or anyone else for that matter, was a Communist. Then Johnson said, "How would you like it if your client was to receive a letter from an

American Legion post up here?" Murray went on to testify that he was a veteran himself and could not believe that the American Legion would lend itself to what he considered an obvious blackmail attempt. He was told, "Well, you will find out." And it did happen.

And so the days went, more exciting than any film on intrigue and spying and espionage that I had seen. The newspaper accounts were stirring up widespread interest in the case, and Nizer began to receive calls from people volunteering information, many anxious to appear as witnesses. Mark Goodson of Goodson and Todman explained why so many agencies complied with the blacklisting. He testified that a sponsor is in business to sell goods. He has no interest in being involved in causes. He does not want controversy. Given a choice between a controversial and a non-controversial performer, the instinct is to use the non-controversial one. Goodson said a favorite saying on Madison Avenue is: "There are a lot of other actors, a lot of other performers. Why bother with this one? Why buy this headache?" He showed clearly how callous the industry could be, how little worth a human being had in the market place. He noted that "over the years I have found that same indifference, inability to care about a fellow human being exists on every level . . . in the groves of academe, in small towns among 'good' people, in show business . . . as well as in the business world."

As the trial approached its final days, two very exciting events happened that proved to be turning points. Quite unexpectedly I had to make a brief trip back to Texas. Our son, Frank Dobie, had to be hospitalized for an emergency appendectomy. I wanted to be with him and decided to risk taking a few days off, hoping I would be back in time for the wrap-up. No one but our close group knew I had to leave, but until that point the reporters were very aware that I was sitting in the front row, following the testimony in an almost hypnotic trance. That was the day that Nizer noticed that Hartnett was scribbling furiously some notes on a pad, even as he was being cross-examined. Nizer had established that Hartnett was taking down the names of people entering the courtroom.

When Nizer was finished with Hartnett and Bolan began to reexamine his witness, he was anxious to repair some harm done through a confused redirect examination. Then Bolan made a big mistake. He thought it would be to the defendant's advantage if he asked Hartnett to tell the court whose names were being written down. Hartnett immediately replied that he noted the names of those actors who came into court "like Eliot Sullivan, who was sitting next to Mrs. Faulk; John Randolph; Alan Manson; Jack Gilford." The point he was making was guilt by association. Some of the actors had refused to answer questions before HUAC; some were considered Communists or Communist sympathizers. I had sat next to them, and according to Hartnett's testimony that proved yet again my husband's sympathies. This was the opening Nizer seized upon. He knew that I was in Texas with my son. In his re-cross-examination of Hartnett, he backed off across the room and his voice was tinged with sarcasm as he asked Hartnett a question. "You have testified that Eliot Sullivan sat down next to Mrs. Faulk. Do you see Mrs. Faulk in the courtroom now?" Everyone—jury, spectators, judge, reporters—leaned forward expectantly as Hartnett scanned the rows of spectators. Finally he pointed to a lady and said, "I believe she is the lady over here. I am not sure."

Nizer turned to the lady and asked, "What is your name, please?" She stood up and said, "My name is Helen Soffer. S-O-F-F-E-R."

The courtroom was in an uproar. The lady who stood up was a redhead and a long-time admirer of Louis Nizer. She had been in court every day. Hartnett insisted that John Sibley of the *New York Times* had identified her as Mrs. Faulk. Judge Abraham Geller could not escape the emotional impact of wrongly identifying the wife of the man on trial. Nizer waited dramatically and then, in a cold, accusing voice, said, "Sir, is that an example of the accuracy with which you have identified your victims for the past ten years?"

I read accounts of the dramatic turn of events in Murray Kempton's column while I was on the plane to Texas. It brought to mind just how sloppy and indifferent our accusers were, how little they knew about the persons they were vilifying, and how sometimes they didn't even recognize them. During the trial, Bolan had used McCarthy tactics by sending an investigator to Austin, Texas. Although it was rumored that Roy Cohn was going to slip down to Austin to do some fast investigation and see if he could dredge up a real Communist as a witness, it turned out that someone else from his office went. I was still in Austin waiting for my summons to come to New York when Nizer phoned to tell me of the news. He told me to keep an eye open for a Mr. Lang from Roy Cohn's office and to try to find out what he was doing. He even suggested I hire a detective to follow Lang and give us a report. It was an exciting few days. I hired a woman detective who set herself up in a hotel room and went about the business of surveillance or counter-surveillance. I understood they were looking for me but didn't know how to find me. Strange actions from an investigator who couldn't track down a Mrs. Faulk even when her agency was called John Henry Faulk Associates! We found out later that Lang returned empty-handed, without even a description of me.

After visiting with my son and helping him get through his appendicitis operation, I made the trip back to New York to take my place on the front bench again, expecting the trial to wind up in a few days, when a tragedy occurred that almost caused a mistrial. Nizer had been trying to get Laurence Johnson to the stand, and Bolan had maintained that Johnson was too ill. Nizer wanted him submitted to a medical examination by a specialist of his choosing. The judge explained to the jury the importance of the question. If a party to a suit fails to appear in a trial without valid excuse, the jury is entitled to draw the strongest inference against him. They then have the right to infer that he would not have been able to refute the evidence against him or substantiate charges made on his behalf. In spite of evidence by a noted physician that he felt Johnson could appear, Johnson did not make an appearance. It was soon thereafter that Nizer said the welcome words, "The plaintiff rests."

Just before the summation began on June 26, Judge Geller asked the two lawyers to draw together the various lines of evidence and to argue and try to convince the jury to arrive at conclusions which each lawyer advanced. First was Bolan. John Henry recoiled from the viciousness of Bolan's summation, which caused Nizer to say, "Don't listen. Let it go in one ear and out the other. It will cost him dearly." The *New York Times* carried the full attack, but the next morning there were hundreds of people waiting to hear the summation on which Nizer had worked all night. At last our personal trial, as well as our lawsuit, was coming to an end. As he spoke, the brilliance of the man shone through. He touched every point, starting out by putting down the defendants for spilling so much malice and hate. He went on to show this was not an issue of communism but of private vigilantism. The issue wasn't whether an employer had a right to refuse a man a job, but whether Hartnett or anyone else could threaten economic boycotts, whether anyone at all could take the law into his own hands, especially as there were government agencies to deal with security risks. During his summation, he turned his attention to John Henry, speaking glowingly about his character, his wartime service, and then his career in radio and television and how he had been fired. While John Henry had wanted to hide the day before because of Bolan's attack, now he wanted to hide because he was embarrassed by the unqualified reports given out by Nizer that made him feel as if he were being painted a saint.

It was during his summation that I began to feel uncomfortable. He talked about Faulk's bravery in not knuckling under. He said that there were days we didn't have food to eat, that our so-called advertising agency couldn't support us. Why did he feel it necessary to downplay my contribution? The truth was that my advertising agency had completely supported the Faulks in a very comfortable lifestyle. I had earlier challenged Nizer on this approach and asked why it wouldn't be more truthful and more dignified to take the tactic that the lawsuit had forced me to take full responsibility for our livelihood, that John Henry had been completely unemployable in his profession, and that the blacklisting had not only damaged John Henry's ability as a provider but also had affected his emotional health as well as his own self-image. Was there something wrong in saying that a wife had stepped forward and kept the family together? Was the only way to win the case to distort the role of the wife to bolster the image of the man?

Nizer had not understood or appreciated my concern. I wondered if I was, in his eyes, a "loose cannon," someone who had to be tightly controlled, safely pushed into the stereotype of the acquiescent housewife. Our manager, Gerald Dickler, had tried that with me, constantly trying to reinforce John Henry's wish that I stay home and do all the housework. He always used his own situation to say, "My wife manages to stay home, take care of our children, and save on household help." I used to laugh at Dickler then, trying to explain that women had different needs and that no doubt his home situation was completely different from mine.

I had a husband who liked to entertain lavishly, go out constantly, and have me by his side through all his business negotiations, besides having me take care of the house and the children. The children were my priority. I couldn't care less about the house! The rest of my energy was devoted to John Henry, his concerns, his career, as his hostess.

Nizer's closing remarks shook me out of my reverie. He quoted Robert Frost: "The people I am most scared of are the people who are scared." Then Nizer shook his head as he ascribed malice and deliberate deception to the defendants in their attempt to destroy an artist's career. Then without warning, Judge Geller called a short recess.

We had no idea that the whole case was now in jeopardy, and if it wasn't for the fast thinking of the judge, a mistrial might have been called, a godsend for Bolan. A reporter dropped the bombshell that Laurence Johnson had just died. Nizer came over and said a body had been found in a seedy Bronx motel and it might be Johnson's. My mind was a jumble of thoughts, the important one being what that meant to our case. Would it result in a mistrial?

By that time the jury had returned, unaware of what had happened. Nizer was ordered to finish his summation as if nothing had happened. Before the recess he had told the members of the jury that they had a chance to give a clarion call to the world on this historic case, to make an award of punitive damages of several million dollars and of compensatory damages of over a million dollars. It didn't matter whether the awards could be collected or not. "Let the word get out that this kind of thing must stop. Give, by your verdict, a clear answer to the kind of un-Americanism which this case represents."

He finished with a flourish by saying, "I will not go on with the rest of this terrible story of this man's ordeal, but now I place his life in your hands. I place his wife's life and his three children's lives in your hands, very literally, because this man's reputation is either going to be restored by a verdict that will ring to the world, or he will be besmirched all over again. I leave to your hands the doing of full justice, and if you do that, ladies and gentlemen, you can sleep well because God will be awake. Thank you."

The moment Nizer had finished, the judge sequestered the jury but assured them that the case would be over the next day.

The jury looked confused but they were told they were not to read any newspapers or to listen to any radio or television. The next morning's newspapers carried the news of Johnson's death under such headlines as "Faulk Case Figure Dead." We learned that he had died choking on his own vomit, but the mystery was why he was in a seedy motel. Was it death by suicide or natural causes? Had he been so concerned about his loss of power, the impending verdict, or financial problems?

Nizer had his entire available staff working on the case since there was no precedent for such a situation. That afternoon we were all back in court for Judge Geller's determination and instructions to the jury. Bolan and Lang were sitting on a table, swinging their legs and laughing, seemingly happy about the new developments. The judge took his place on the bench and the jury was brought in and and told the news of the death. He then carefully explained that the verdict must be based solely on the evidence the jury had heard on the case. He then went on at length to instruct them as to the principles of law to be applied to this case. With three defendants, it would be for the jury to determine the degree of conspiracy. He discussed the two kinds of damages the jury must consider, punitive and compensatory. He clearly and gently outlined everything they should consider. Finally, he explained that a unanimous verdict was not necessary in this case, and that as soon as ten of them were in agreement they should bring their deliberation to an end. As the members of the jury filed out, I looked desperately at each face, wondering if there would be some sidelong glances, some smile, some recognition. There were none.

Nizer then suggested that a few of us go with him to a nearby Chinese restaurant to wait out the verdict while the main body of our friends went on to the usual meeting place, Gasner's, to have cocktails and dinner. I joined Nizer, his wife Mildred, Ben Bodne, and John Henry, while George Berger, who had also worked on the case from the beginning, stayed in the courtroom to convey news of the jury's return. The jury had gone out to dinner so we were sure we couldn't hear anything for a few hours. Nizer drew us a vivid picture of how a jury works. He speculated that if the jury was out a short time, it would mean a good verdict for us; if the jury got locked up in wrangling, there would be compromises and it probably would go badly for us. He made no prediction which way the jury would go. I sat, eating silently, aching for John Henry to put his arms around me, to share some of his thoughts with me, to acknowledge that I was there as a partner. He seemed completely distracted, left his dinner early, and said he would meet us back at the courthouse.

While I was musing, my reverie was broken by an excited call from Berger urging us to hurry back. The jury was coming out in an unprecedented hurry. Nizer was shocked, his predictions didn't include an extraordinarily early decision. He was worried. We all rushed back to the courtroom as the jury was being brought in. In shock, we listened as the jurors said they had a question to ask and they wanted it done in open court. I couldn't believe my ears when the foreman rose and asked, "Can the jury award more damages than the plaintiff's attorney asked?" It was as if a bombshell had exploded. Nizer collapsed in his chair, Paul Martinson and George Berger shook their heads in disbelief. Nizer had asked for three million dollars—one million in compensatory damages and one million separately against each of the defendants for punitive damages. They were asking to increase that, although Nizer had based his request on the fact that the record libel verdict in history was half-a-million dollars. In his entire legal career, a jury had never asked to give more than was asked for. The judge was astonished but explained to the jury the law on this point. It was an historic event. Nizer warned us not to celebrate before the verdict was actually in, and some of us went back to the restaurant to wait. Others wandered down to watch the drama unfolding in night court. The word finally came that the jury had reached a decision. It was twenty minutes before midnight when the clerk of the court addressed the foreman of the jury in words that I had heard on a thousand television shows. "Have you agreed upon a verdict?"

"We have," he replied.

"How do you find?"

I could hardly breathe as the foreman answered. "We, the jury, have arrived at our decision in favor of Mr. Faulk. We have awarded the plaintiff, Mr. Faulk, compensatory damages in the sum of one million dollars against Aware Inc., Mr. Vincent Hartnett, and the estate of the late Mr. Laurence Johnson. We have also awarded the plaintiff, Mr. Faulk, punitive damages to the sum of $1,250,000 against Aware Inc. and $1,250,000 against Mr. Hartnett."

I gasped when I heard the verdict, dropped my head in my hands, and whispered, "Oh, my God, thank God." For one moment I felt the relief surge through my body, the release something akin to being let out of solitary confinement after a long internment and having the stark sunlight dazzle and almost blind the vision. I couldn't fully comprehend the verdict, the size of the award. I instinctively knew that there would be problems ahead in actually collecting the award, but for the moment all I cared about was the chance to make new decisions about our lives.

Pandemonium broke loose and photographers and news people surrounded us, snapping photographs furiously. Finally, John Henry came over to me and, for the photographers, embraced me as I said, "This is our fourteenth anniversary month, the nicest present I could ever have." Then we all left for the Algonquin Hotel to have a quiet celebration. We slept well that night.

The next morning the phone didn't stop ringing. It seemed reporters from every newspaper, radio station, and television studio were calling. John Henry turned to me and asked, "What do I say to them? How do I manage to get around to all?" He was bewildered, so I slipped back easily into my role as "manager," making sure all the details were handled. I decided the next plan was to have everyone come to the Algonquin Hotel and to let them bring in their cameras and their tape machines on a schedule that would allow John Henry and me to be interviewed back to back without time out for moving from station to studio. I also felt it would give Ben Bodne some well-deserved publicity. He had been so generous with us. So I told them all when to arrive and squeezed in about ten or more interviews at once.

Before we went down for our sessions, I called our children and told them the good news. Now that the case was over, Frank Faulk was concerned that he would lose all his friends because we were "so rich," but it didn't stop him from painting his bicycle gold and pasting dollar bills all over it. His approach to the news almost matched mine. It was fantasy time, but we all knew that it would take time for the money, any money, to come to us because the defendants had given notice of appeal. We were not concerned about losing that, but there would be endless delays. Our hope was to collect a good part of the compensatory judgment from what we thought was Johnson's million-dollar estate. But that was still a long way off.

At the moment, our main concern was the press waiting for us downstairs. While we thanked them all for being so solicitous, and told them how happy we were at the verdict, we talked about what we hoped the verdict meant to all the others still fighting but without the benefit of a lawyer like Louis Nizer. I also felt it was sad that people were put under the gun and had to make compromises foisted on them by racketeers, and that while the case was important, I was also sorry we had not been able to win it by just taking the Fifth Amendment, rather than being on the defensive and having to prove "how clean we are."

The next morning the *New York Times* had an editorial headlined "The Faulk Verdict." It started out expressing hope that "the libel verdict should have a healthy effect in curbing the excesses of the superpatriots who sometimes show no more concern for the rights of the individual than the Communists they denounce." It went on to hope it would establish a judicial delineation on the lengths to which private groups, arrogating to themselves the mantle of public service against subversion, can go in blacklisting and defaming their fellow citizens. I was only sorry that it didn't make very clear that these self-styled vigilantes weren't even under the illusion they were going after Communists or Communist dupes. They knew, clearly, that they were in the business of making money and controlling thought, and the best way to do that was to denounce every activist as a possible traitor.

Although we were planning for the future, I continued to carry out my duties as co-owner of John Henry Faulk Associates and publisher of *Go Magazine*. Almost as a reflex action, I kept an appointment I had set up with the Prestige Group, which handled the magazine, to make sure all possible ads were being directed my way. I wasn't sure why I was going through this exercise, but I find it difficult to let go of one project until "the ink has dried" on another.

At the same time, Gerald Dickler was pushing me to forget the magazine now and, in fact, go bankrupt. I was horrified at his suggestion. I didn't know whether or not he had really bought Nizer's testimony or John Henry's distorted view that it was struggling. I was too angry at this assault on my "babies" to bask in the satisfaction of a job well done. I reacted angrily. "Why would I bankrupt a going concern? I am proud of what I accomplished. I have an excellent reputation, I am debt-free. Why would I cheat any of my suppliers of the money due them from my last few months of operation? Why should I have a record of bankruptcy when I have been successful?" Dickler thought it was foolish of me to worry about making payments while we needed every cent we could get our hands on until we could collect from the Johnson estate. I told him not to worry, that the agency was still paying our bills, and that when the time came I would be prepared to sell my company, that's how healthy it was. Dickler looked at me and sighed, never quite understanding why I didn't take his advice without quarreling. I realized that John Henry must have convinced him we were in trouble. He was always very good at looking for sympathy, and if it was true he was borrowing money, he would have to convince everyone that our agency was in bad shape. I couldn't believe then that he would lie so blatantly.

I began to turn my thoughts to our future and it looked as if everything might turn out all right. What more could we want? The lawsuit was over and won. We had survived and could plan ahead. I had no doubt that job offers would come pouring in for John Henry, and that there would be enough money to remove the pressure from all our daily lives. I felt exhilarated. We were going back to New York City.

CHAPTER 20

SHOWDOWN

For another week we basked in the pleasure of post-trial elation. There were parties for John Henry and Louis Nizer. John Henry started to receive offers for panel appearances on radio and television. Articles were being written about his victory. He was approached to write a book about the trial and was offered a $50,000 advance. At the same time, I was approached by book publishers and the press to write about the woman's side of the ordeal. Nizer immediately quashed any chance of that. He explained, "Lynne, you must stay in the background until we have exploited John Henry completely." I wondered why articles about me would diminish John Henry's exposure. I thought that it would magnify our case and our cause. Ours was the unusual story of a family that had stayed together through trials and tribulations. I had always questioned why Nizer hadn't shown how our family had been damaged, how our family life had been changed, forcing me to become the sole support for John Henry and the three children.

It was after the excitement died down and the round of parties petered out that John Henry began looking seriously for work. Offers weren't pouring in the way he expected. He had dreamed about being handed a national television show and was disappointed that it hadn't happened. It also looked as if it might be a long, long time before we received a check from Aware Inc., which was going to exhaust all the appeals it could. And the reality was that no matter what the court had awarded us, there just wasn't that much money in the Johnson estate. He was no multimillionaire. His estate was worth about $800,000 and $200,000 was put aside for his two sisters as an act of mercy. The remaining $600,000 was ours, except that we owed one-third of our winnings to Louis Nizer, who had taken the case on that basis.

John Henry became very moody again and began to suggest that I remain in Texas with the family while he remained in New York to decide whether we should return to Manhattan or spend the rest of our lives in Texas. He wanted me to hang on to our home, our houseboat, and our business. I was in a state of shock. We had talked of nothing else but returning to New York when the case was over. In all our time in Texas, John Henry had not been able to carve out a place for himself in his profession. There was immensely more opportunity in New York. I was concerned that he was being unrealistic about the kind of job he expected, remembering that he had made his biggest impact in radio. I was terrified at the thought of being left alone in Texas while he was away. I was certain that there would be no chance for our marriage if we didn't get together soon. I said, "I'm not going to stay. I'll go back to wind things up, and we'll start together again in New York."

About that time he was offered an excellent contract for a show sponsored by Westinghouse. It was to be a daily radio show and he was told he could be as controversial as he wished. I thought the offer and the salary were excellent. But he felt that it was only a local radio show and that it would take up too many hours of his day because the format required him to go out and do interviews. He rejected my advice and decided to return with me to Texas to do some thinking alone on the houseboat. He disappeared for a few days on the houseboat.

I took the opportunity to impress Alfredo Castaneda that that was our final meeting. I discussed my joy at the outcome of the case, told him we expected to return to New York, and explained that I wanted to make every effort for our marriage to work. I thanked him for being so supportive while I was in such need and hoped that I had also helped him through a difficult time with his separation. I tried to speak rationally about his drinking and suggested he check into a clinic. I left him to go home, only to find John Henry was trying to reach me from the lake. I called and found out that he wanted me to come up and talk. I went up to be with him and learned that he wanted to confess that he had spent the last few days on the houseboat with a young Mexican woman and was now feeling ashamed. He tried to explain, "I'm feeling my age now, and I'm worried that I'll never be able to make up all those lost years. I've been away from my profession too long. I'm not getting younger and I'm scared. I need you."

I wanted desperately to reach out to him. It was so rare for him to talk to me, even to be alone with me, but I could still feel the anger congest in my stomach. Even then he was dealing with his fears by turning to other women and then telling me about it. I felt cold and withdrawn, but was more certain than ever that we had to leave the South and talk about new guidelines for our lives together. But I knew this was not the time. I allowed John Henry to hold me in his arms. I soothed him and prayed that I could control the sadness I felt at the moment. When would it ever stop?

He finally agreed to return to New York and ask the advice of Gerald Dickler and Louis Nizer. They told him he should not waste any more time out of New York, especially when he was so hot after all the publicity from the trial. He agreed to take the Westinghouse offer. Now my job was to wind up all our affairs in Texas. I was exotically happy, as I had wanted to be back in New York City for Christmas. That gave me a few months to sell the business and the house and make arrangements to fly home. At first John Henry didn't seem too happy about our arrival at Christmas. I remember him saying stiffly, "Don't discombobulate yourself. Don't break up everything at Christmas. Have your Christmas in Texas and come up afterwards." I guessed that he had made a number of party plans and didn't want to be encumbered with settling us in. But I assured him that I was coming. "It's important that the family is together. And we can all stay in your apartment while I look for a larger one." John Henry had temporarily rented a furnished apartment and felt the two-bedroom apartment was too small. I assured him we wouldn't mind a little discomfort for a short time. The children were looking forward to Christmas with him.

I felt some pangs at leaving my business, but I began to make plans to sell the agency and the magazine. I had an excellent relationship with the advertising accounts I had left and offered my help in selecting another agency for them. I made it clear that I was also going to ask the new agency to allow me the commissions on everything I had already prepared, and they said there was no problem. They were sorry I was going to leave. I interviewed a number of agencies and was about to choose one when I heard that one on the list had gone to Earl Howell of the Austin Savings and Loan Association and told him I insisted on collecting commissions on advertising I had prepared and placed. They were very surprised to hear that I had already discussed that with Earl Howell and he approved. That bit of unnecessary underhandedness lost them the account. My agency was soon taken care of, suppliers were paid, and everybody was happy. Then I focused my attention on selling my magazine.

I had heard it whispered that it was silly to buy the magazine since everyone knew I was definitely leaving town. My managing editor saw no problem with picking it up after I left. I decided on a last-minute strategy. The latest issue of *Go* was at the printer ready to be printed. I had an excellent relationship with the printer who had always received his money on time for every issue. I told him about my problem in selling the magazine because I was leaving town. I asked him to wait until I called him before publication. If I could find a buyer, he could print it; if not, I was going to kill the latest issue. That would mean that there would be a lapse before the next issue could be put together again, and that would give the advertisers time to pull out. There is nothing worse for the image of a magazine than to skip an issue. It means that there are financial problems and it also affects the revenues of the advertisers. It is almost impossible to pull a magazine together again that unexpectedly misses an issue.

That strategy worked. Two days before I was to leave, my managing editor, Sue McBee, came to me with an offer for the magazine. It wasn't as much as I would have liked, but at least it was on record that the magazine had value, and I felt a principle was at stake. I wanted my managing editor or whoever bought it to show some integrity, some appreciation for all my work. I liked Sue McBee and was glad she decided to buy the magazine. I only hoped she would keep up the pace and be sure to have new, exciting promotions in every issue so that the magazine would continue to grow.

We then had a buyer for our house, which meant we had to find a place to stay the last few days before Christmas. The owners of the Driskill Hotel offered us a suite of rooms until our flight was ready to leave. I felt a mixture of happiness and some sadness as we packed up all our belongings, sent our furniture on ahead, and arranged for one of my nephews to transport the family in a jeep to the hotel. We had already bought a Christmas tree and had decorated it when we had to move. It was a strange sight to see us cross town hanging on tightly to the trimmed tree that we were taking to our hotel with us. It was quite festive for the next few days, as we set up housekeeping in the suite. But we were going home for Christmas, and I kept pinching myself to see if I was truly awake.

We arrived in New York City the day before Christmas, and I remember it was snowing. It had been so long since I had seen snow that I laughed out loud as I felt the snowflakes rest on my eyelids and I stuck out my tongue to taste them as they melted. We arrived at John Henry's apartment, and he had already trimmed a Christmas tree and it was waiting for us with some presents already wrapped. Money was coming in from the Westinghouse show, we were expecting the fifty-thousand dollar advance for the book, and by now the defendants had appealed the case. It had been argued before the Appellate Division of the New York Supreme Court in October, 1963. About six weeks later the court handed down its decision, and it was a resounding victory for us, except that it had differed with the jury on the amount of the damages. The judges had reduced the award to $550,000. Since we already knew that there was no chance of collecting the $3.5 million, that was of no great concern. Everything was looking good.

We found an apartment in Riverdale, twenty minutes from downtown, but the children hated the area and I sensed that John Henry wasn't happy. He seemed uncomfortable in his new radio format. He did not enjoy the research, the interviews, and the location shots. He liked sitting in a chair in front of a microphone and talking "off the top of his head." He was also struggling with the image of the saint, the hero that everyone had been talking about. Nothing that he was doing, that he could possibly do, was big enough to fit that image. He made some enemies when, on some interview shows, he talked about fighting alone, without being offered any jobs in the industry. That didn't sit well with Mark Goodson and David Susskind, who had lent a hand and were the first to offer him work after the trial. John Henry was beginning to feel sorry for himself. He really believed he was all alone.

I finally got him to listen carefully to what I had to say. "John

Henry, you are really now back on top, perhaps not in the way you expected, but I think even bigger than before in the radio field. You have a much better chance to make a real impact with your new format. I would love to make a contribution to your show, and would appreciate having a regular Friday spot. I could sum up the week's activities from a woman's point of view and I could help you with your show. I think it would have good public relations value and show the public that we are working together."

I told John Henry that I really wanted to work on our relationship. We were back on top. There was going to be at least $400,000 from the lawsuit. The Westinghouse show paid well, the advance from the book was a nice amount to start with. We had three wonderful children and our whole life ahead of us. I couldn't handle his running around. I didn't like what it did to us, and I didn't like being a part of it. I couldn't cope with the pain of having him disappear at a party or coming home at all hours without an explanation. I couldn't stomach his attitude to women. He used them and didn't really enjoy their company. And having affairs didn't satisfy me or make me feel more sophisticated. It had to stop.

In the past, when I talked about his affairs, John Henry would break down, promise he would stop or tell me to grow up or remind me that I couldn't leave him because no one else could live with me. I didn't want to be sidetracked, so I said, "I have a plan. You know how I feel. I won't bother you for a month, as we give it a trial. I won't nag about your involvement with so many people, I won't question you, but I'll assume that you will handle the woman situation. But I'm telling you, unless things change I want a divorce. I want a divorce while we still can talk to each other and handle it in a decent way. I'll accept the fact you can't give up your lifestyle, but we can be friendly about a separation. We have lived through so much together, there is no reason not to handle the rest of our lives with dignity. I'll always love you, but I won't continue to live this way."

His pattern didn't change. He began to complain about commuting from Riverdale to downtown and the time the radio show took from writing his book. I accused him of too much partying and the arguments started. I said, "It's no use. I think we better talk about a separation." He acted bewildered. "Why? I'm happy."

It was the last straw. I said, "You haven't listened to me at all. You don't even understand what I'm talking about. You say you are happy but I'm not happy." I said I didn't know how to handle my anger when he stumbled in late at night. I said that either we had to have a marriage with some commitment or that we should handle a divorce in a mature way. "After all, we are not in the middle of a crisis. I am not pregnant and we really have no money worries. You are back in harness again, and you have a new career ahead. Certainly there is enough money that we can live apart and manage very well." I thought my proposal was reasonable, and even naively expected we could stay friends, but I didn't take into account that a large sum of money might change many of John Henry's attitudes. And perhaps I half hoped that a reasonable approach would make it possible to reassess our marriage and perhaps we could come back stronger than ever.

I wasn't prepared for his announcement, out of the blue one February afternoon, in the middle of preparations for Evelyn's birthday party. He came into the kitchen where I was preparing the grape-jelly sandwiches and dropped the news on me unceremoniously. "I took an apartment downtown. I decided to give up the radio show and finish the book. I'll come back a few nights a week to see the children and we'll see what happens." Then he left. I was completely unprepared for his departure and I had no idea what to tell the children. I struggled through the rest of the afternoon trying to keep a happy face while entertaining Evelyn's friends.

Late in the afternoon the telephone rang and I jumped, eager to hear John Henry's voice. Instead it was Louis Nizer, who asked if we had received the check for $400,000. It should have arrived by now. Nizer asked, "Did you pick up the morning mail?" I told him I would look immediately. I ran downstairs and opened the mailbox. It was empty. It was only later that I realized that John Henry must have waited for the check and must have had it in his pocket when he told me he was leaving. I was unprepared for the intense flash of fear and pain that ran through my body. I realized that in the past I had always been willing to try to make our marriage work, really unwilling to be separated from John Henry. No matter how many ups and downs there were in our life, I was used to him and I really believed him when he said no one else could love me the way he did. I guess you can get used to punishment and even feel you deserve it. I felt completely vulnerable. Again I found myself helpless to obtain what were clearly my rights: reasonable support for our children, reasonable freedom to carry on my life without interference. It was only later, looking back over that painful period that, I realized that what I had lived through was in large measure a social phenomenon rather than a reflection of personal weakness.

John Henry left, but he'd show up at the house whenever he felt like it. When he was home he expected to be fed and looked after, and he usually took something with him for his apartment, the dictaphone, some books, a typewriter. There was no discussion about my need for them; after all, he was the writer. He would phone evenings to find out where I was and question the children. In the meantime nothing about our future was resolved. I went back for therapy. I had started visiting psychiatrists before doing so was the thing to do. I wanted to find some support to offset my feelings of alienation and loneliness. But even then I would go sporadically on a once-a-week basis for a year and then stop for a few years only to return at some crisis point. Although it took me a long time to assimilate the advice I was receiving, I began to make use of the information during this period. At times I would question my incessant demands for love, and I was told it was more important to focus on why I constantly became involved with men who weren't capable of giving me *any* affection. It was only when I separated from John Henry that I realized that many male psychiatrists felt that women had to be made to feel more comfortable with the role of the wife. It startled me when John Henry asked to see my psychiatrist, and then complained to him about my being out of the house when he called even though we were separated at the time. I resented the fact that he kept calling the house to check on my whereabouts or suddenly arrived at any time unannounced. The therapist said, "Why does a redhead"—I was a redhead at the time—"act like such a dizzy blonde? You should be smart enough to be there in the evening so he has nothing to complain about."

I fought with my therapist, realizing that while he approved of me on one level, as an interesting woman, he had trouble when I rebelled against the traditional role of the wife. This same psychiatrist also admired me for my strength in handling some of the trauma of my separation and divorce from John Henry. He mused, "Other people going through as much pain as you have might have turned to alcohol or drugs or had a nervous breakdown. I am amazed at how you survive." Years later I realized that people found me a paradox—a woman who could cope with the world but not with her personal problems. I never seemed to gain sympathy. I had not collapsed, only to make the long road back, as many high-profile figures had. Rehabilitation wins kudos. There is little sympathy for the thousands of people who struggle to keep their lives together in private ways or for the thousands of small daily courages of many women in our society. Yet things are gradually improving. Now there is more acceptance of the role that short-term as distinct from long-term analysis can play in a person's life. As well, patients should assess psychiatrists and therapists as they are assessed. It is quite legitimate to ask how therapists feel about politics or women's issues. Now that there are more women active in the health-care field, choices are broadened.

I finally decided to see a lawyer and get some advice. I was referred to a tough Irishman, named Mulligan, who said, "You can't allow yourself to be so vulnerable. You have to make up your mind about what you want and go after it. Do you want a legal separation? Do you want a divorce? You should be thinking of protecting your children and getting an agreement before the settlement money is dissipated or hidden." He advised me to sue for a legal separation immediately, but I wasn't ready to take that step.

The decision was taken completely out of my hands by John Henry finding some old letters from Alfredo, which I had hidden away in the bottom of a barrel in the storage room. I had no idea how John Henry even knew I had them or even knew where to look. I had stupidly kept them because I am a hopeless romantic, and I seemed to need written proof that I was lovable, and I thought that whenever I reread the letters I would feel assured that I had been loved.

The next few months were a nightmare. It was inconceivable that John Henry, who had run around so openly and had suggested that I do the same thing, would now be acting the part of the injured husband. But he evidently had a plan that I knew nothing about. I went back to my lawyer, told him what had happened, and took his advice to start legal action. I was so furious, so insulted that he would take my letters, that I decided to try and get them back. One day when he was out on a lecture I went to his apartment, told the superintendent I was Mrs. John Henry Faulk and that I needed to get into the apartment. He allowed me in. I began to look for the letters but couldn't find them. Instead, I found a diary that I recognized. I had never looked at it before, although he may have wanted me to, since it was always out in the open.

This time I began to read it, with a sense of indignation. The diary documented every affair he had ever had and how many times he had slept with each woman. A circle and an arrow represented the sexual act. There was even a description of his affair with a woman he had brought to our apartment while the family was on Fire Island. I was outraged not only at her sleeping in my bed but also that he decided to write down her negative opinion of my decorating skills. Everything was in that diary. I took it with me. He had my letters; now I had his diary. The lawyers threatened each other with evidence. There was an exchange of correspondence and diary, but each lawyer had made copies. Each side hoped that the other would negotiate. It all backfired. Instead of it being kept confidential, it exploded in the newspapers. There were scandalous headlines. John Henry had seventeen mistresses, Lynne had four lovers. It was black comedy.

John Henry sued Alfredo Castaneda for alienation of affections based on the letters. The case was thrown out because, as the judge said, "The sheer preponderance of the evidence and the weight of the letters does not prove there was an affair. Nothing in the letters talks about lovemaking." That was true.

The suit against Alfredo drew us together again. He had given up his position in Texas just to be near me. Although at first I was furious at his actions, I felt the need to stand by him through his court ordeal. I was also terrified that the community would be aware of my infidelities and tease my children. I had nothing to worry about. The amount of money we had won in the lawsuit was mentioned in all the articles about our love affairs and it far overshadowed the lurid details of our romances and our accusations. I was amazed that the only thing that was said to me was, "You must have money running out of your apartment. You must really have it stacked away." The public believed we had won over $3.5 million.

John Henry was trying to reduce his obligation to me by proving that I was an adulteress. It was an empty and vicious exercise because I wasn't even asking for alimony, only for child support. What I didn't realize then was that although John Henry had collected $400,000, none of that money was legally mine. It was money won from his lawsuit. So the amount of money for the children was based on the amount of money being earned at that moment, and he had given up his radio show to write the book. It seemed Westinghouse was unhappy with his lack of discipline in preparing material.

I was finally granted a separation and a temporary support judgment for eight hundred dollars a month. My rent was five hundred dollars, so we had to move to a smaller apartment. Soon he even stopped sending the eight hundred dollars. I would go back to court, he would plead economic problems, the amount would be reduced, a few months would pass, and he would again stop sending money. Going to court again and again was taking its toll. Besides, I had no way to budget, never knowing what money I could count on. Then my lawyer dropped the case-because he was on a contingency basis. Finally I was taken on by a huge firm, Greenbaum, Wolff and Ernst, that felt I was being forced to suffer indignities that were completely unacceptable. A woman lawyer in the firm, Harriet Pilpel, was sympathetic to my plight and assigned a young lawyer, Roger Bunting, to help me.

I tried everything with John Henry, begging him to make some settlement, pointing out that the fighting was only helping the lawyers. I asked him how much he would offer and he said, "No matter what you ask, it's too much. I don't like being told what to do. You are the one that left me, called in the lawyers. I'll do what I think is right." He went on to say, "If you could get on your knees and beg forgiveness, I might take you back." I looked at him incredulously.

John Henry demanded unquestioning loyalty. If anyone dared suggest he might be more reasonable, he would cut him off. He could not countenance anyone being friendly to me. The price was his friendship, and he began to weave a series of lies to justify his anger. His anger was also fueled because Alfredo was back in the picture. Although I made it clear to him I would never marry him, he made it his business to show up to take me out, to be a-round to make love, to beg me to consider marriage. John Henry, to harass me, would call our house and pretend it was long distance for Alfredo, hoping to catch him in the house, although his presence meant nothing legally. There were nights that I would wake up to hear someone moaning and realize it was me crying in my sleep, my pillow wet with tears.

I found some comfort in going back to work. I joined the Lynn Farnol public relations firm and handled the shoe-industry account. My responsibility was writing editorials and columns for newspapers, preparing a public-relations newspaper, and dreaming up new promotions for the shoe industry. Work went well but in my personal life I was being torn between John Henry and Alfredo, who never left me alone. I was so desperate one day that I begged a doctor to commit me to a hospital. I wanted to run away from the constant pressure. He questioned me, smiled, and said I was just overreacting. In his opinion I could handle the situation and he dismissed me.

John Henry went back to Texas and served me with divorce papers, which called me an unfit mother and asked for custody of the children. My father suggested that I turn over the children. "Call his bluff, Lynne. He'll never take them."

I was furious. "What do you mean? Even if I did, my children wouldn't know it was a bluff, and he might take them out of spite and ship them off to Texas to be raised by his sister. I don't intend to play with my children's emotions."

My lawyer, Roger Bunting, tried to soothe me by assuring me, "He is just trying to remove himself from any financial responsibility, and he is sure you would do anything to keep custody of your children." Then Bunting suggested arbitration. He told me that he had met John Henry at a cocktail party. Roger was willing to act as our arbitrator if John Henry was willing and didn't consider it a conflict of interest. I was so happy at the thought of arbitration I said I would even accept Louis Nizer if John Henry would agree. So it happened. The agreement stated that the children would remain in my custody, that I was a fit mother, and that five hundred dollars monthly in child support would be paid. Roger made sure that John Henry agreed to the amount and that he would promise never to reduce the amount without arbitration. One of the strange things that John Henry kept asking for was my library, insisting they were his books. In truth, he had not owned one book when I met him. Most of my library consisted of books I had collected over the years. I had an intense emotional attachment to books and carried them everywhere. I felt protected by my books. For some unknown reason, John Henry was obsessed with the books. Roger made a bargain that John Henry could have the books if he paid an outstanding debt from the month before of two thousand dollars. John Henry agreed but a month later reneged and also arbitrarily reduced the amount of the settlement. When he was called to task by Roger, he immediately went to court to have Roger removed, accusing him of a conflict of interest because he was my lawyer and therefore biased. That was the end of the arbitration. Roger was in a state of shock, and I remember him shaking his head and saying, "How could he do that to me?" After that Roger said there was nothing more his firm could do. Evidently John Henry was willing to spend all his money to be vindictive because there was no doubt his lawyers cost a fortune.

At that point I fell apart. I thought John Henry and I were on speaking terms and that we had worked out an agreement. I discovered that the legal system was no protection for my children if a man really didn't want to pay. He could spend thousands of dollars on legal costs and the legal system was powerless. That's an experience a lot of women have and it is unbelievably isolating and demoralizing. The saddest thing is that the children became pawns in our fight. They would visit their father and he would tell them I had hidden away a lot of money and was trying to force him to pay more. I would counter-attack by saying he was lying. I was not proud of that period. I was a nervous wreck, afraid he would turn my children against me with his lies. Sometimes they would come back, sullen and withdrawn. I would defend myself. Other times he would attack them and they would beg me not to make them visit him. I am still haunted by that period, one of the worst I had ever known.

In the meantime, Alfredo would call every night, trying to find ways to ingratiate himself with my children. He preyed on my weakness, kept telling me he wanted to take care of me, to protect me from John Henry, to be a father to my children. I knew it was all wrong. I said to him, "Look, you can't take care of my children. I'm the one who has to look after them. I can't handle any more emotional stress at this time." Alfredo promised he would give up drinking "except on special social occasions," which I later found out meant all the time. He promised he wouldn't drink on our wedding day.

It was finally after three years of being separated from John Henry that I ran, or rather collapsed, into Alfredo's arms. He had been a part of my life when I was lonely. He had supplied an escape into a never-never land in the darkness of the night. It was almost as if I was addicted to him. It was like being on dope or on tranquilizers. You know it's wrong, you know you are hooked, but you can't give it up. There were also friends who assured me that once my divorce was final and I was really free, Alfredo would run away. He wouldn't want to marry a divorcée with three children.

CHAPTER 21

REBIRTH IN CANADA

In the long run, the fact that Alfredo did not run away was flattering to my wounded ego. I had little sense of my own self-worth. I was still ashamed of myself for having the affair with him in the first place, even though such things had been a way of life for John Henry. I also felt stupid for leaving myself open to him. I was a product of social conditioning, and in spite of a liberated attitude in other areas, and my intense desire for independence, I could not shake my own personal feelings of guilt. Alfredo worked on that. He waged a campaign for me to marry him. Wasn't that the ultimate sign of love a man could give? After many fights and elaborate farewells, I finally agreed, thinking it would give my children a male figure to relate to, since their father wasn't around very much. It was a tragic mistake.

In my usual fashion, once I decided to marry Alfredo, I began planning our future wholeheartedly, fantasy and all. He came to dinner and we talked to the children about getting married. They tried to understand, but I could sense they were disturbed. Alfredo certainly was a strange man, and his drinking made him act erratically. My children regarded him with suspicion, but I involved them in our wedding plans, encouraging them to invite their friends to the Sunday wedding brunch. I put an announcement in the *New York Times* and decided I would walk down the aisle of my apartment by myself to Mexican music.

Alfredo helped me pick out my wedding suit, silk beige with a beige veil. There was champagne, and my mother and stepfather and aunts and uncles were there, and we had a beautiful catered brunch of eggs and croissants, Nova Scotia salmon, leek and potato soups. Everyone wished me happiness . . . again. I never thought there would be another divorce—that is how out of touch I was with my own feelings. That evening we went to the Plaza Hotel on Fifth Avenue to spend our honeymoon night. Our relationship degenerated almost immediately after that. Alfredo began drinking more heavily and then insisted that our bedroom was off-limits to the children. If they wanted to speak to their mother, they had to call on the telephone. I was a prisoner in my own home.

By some strange and eerie coincidence, John Henry also married the same day. Neither of us knew that independently we had asked our children to refrain from mentioning it until it was over, but when John Henry saw the announcement, he went berserk, immediately phoning his lawyer, pointing out that I had been married secretly, completely ignoring the fact that he had also married secretly. His idea was to cut off immediately the three hundred dollars he was now sending me monthly, but he was told he was responsible for his children until age sixteen.

At that time I was not only working as a fashion editor for a catalogue company but I was going to Columbia University at night, taking a writing workshop. One night in early November, 1965, I was taking a cab from my office in New Jersey to Columbia. As I crossed the bridge to Manhattan, I noticed that there were no street lights, and then I realized that all of Manhattan had plunged into darkness. It was the year of the big power blackout. Obviously there weren't going to be classes that night, so I thought I would go and meet Alfredo, who always spent my class night at his friend Eliud's house. I never thought to telephone but had the cab drop me in front of the apartment. I rang the bell and was let in by a surprised Eliud, who welcomed me loudly in order to warn Alfredo, who was deep in a loving embrace with a strange woman. It was like déjà vu. Everything in my body reacted. I stormed out of the apartment, screaming at him not to follow me.

I had spent fifteen years trying to live with John Henry's infidelities. I was not prepared for Alfredo's. In fact, I was in a state of shock. I had been so concerned with his drinking that I never dreamed he had the time or the energy to fool around. Transportation was cut off because of the blackout. In anger, I found the strength to walk the many miles to my apartment. I was in a cold fury. I had spoken to my children and knew that a neighbor was taking care of them, so I had time to collect my thoughts before I picked them up. When Alfredo finally arrived, I banished him to the couch. The next morning I awakened him and told him to get out of the apartment. I gave him a week to collect his things and I went to a lawyer to start divorce proceedings immediately. Nothing he said could convince me to forgive him.

He moved out and moved in with the woman, who was also an alcoholic. Then he started calling me in the middle of the night. He asked me to understand. He was only seeing that woman because they were fighting their alcoholism together. There was nothing between them. In fact, she wanted to meet me, so we could all gather our forces and help each other. I refused, but the calls in the middle of the night were too frequent. Finally I agreed to meet him downtown to talk. He arranged a hotel room for us to meet in and I found myself in bed making love. It was macabre. Here was "my man" calling me to tell me he needed me. The other woman wanted him but he wanted me to meet him, almost like his mistress. I began to meet him downtown for a few hours at a time. I plugged into my old habit of escaping, living on the edge of danger.

I told my lawyer that he was begging me to stop the divorce proceedings. He said, "For God's sake, Lynne, get the divorce. You can always remarry him if you want, but go through with the divorce. It sounds like a very destructive relationship, and until he hits bottom I don't think there is any possibility of change." I also knew that my children were glad he was out of the house. I told Alfredo, "I'm going through with it. If you can handle your drinking, we can always remarry."

He seemed to be completely out of control and he was weeping. "I can't get to my classes. I can't make it." Up until now he had always rationalized that he was functioning. What he couldn't face was that he was almost incoherent at times in classes at Hunter College, although his graduate students were very protective of him. They enjoyed going to bars with him and spending long evenings discussing their courses. He was brilliant and colorful.

Again, I felt needed. I went into "overdrive," as Johanna used to express it. Now I could help him. I had begun doing research on alcoholism. I knew that if you loved an alcoholic, you weren't supposed to coddle him. You had to let him hit bottom, but the more I learned the more I realized that over the last few years he had deteriorated because alcoholism is a progressive disease. He begged me not to leave him, but I was firm. "The only way I'll help you is if you promise to get help. You must go to a hospital. If you go to a hospital and get help, I'll think about stopping the divorce." I was caught again. How could I leave him to die? He agreed and I took him over to the Roosevelt Hospital, which had a special alcoholic ward. The doctors examined him and said he was seriously ill but they had no bed for him. It was ten days before they would accept him and during this time I nursed him. Then the call came that a bed was available. We left immediately, and as he neared the hospital I saw stark terror in his eyes. He pleaded with me to take him to a bar for just one more drink before he was admitted. We went to a tavern, drank together, toasted his future, and then marched to the hospital as if to his execution.

They told me that a few more days and he would have been dead. That night he almost went into convulsions. He had nightmares and hallucinated, but he began the long road back. I went after work every day to visit. I would go at five or six in the evening and stay until eleven. I'd sit with him and hold his hand. He was embarrassingly grateful to me for saving his life and told me that he adored me. He promised he would never forget what I had done for him. As he was recuperating, members of Alcoholics Anonymous came and discussed a follow-up treatment at a rehabilitation camp. He was child-like as he agreed to everything suggested. He went from the hospital to the camp and I began making two-hour trips to see him every Sunday. I suddenly belonged to a group of women who visited their men every Sunday. There was a bond between us and I began to feel that I might end up with a healthy partner. He was soon assigned to give lectures at the regular meetings. He was excellent at relating to other arrested alcoholics like himself as well as to those struggling with the problem. An alcoholic is never called cured, only "arrested."

When he was released from the camp, I took him home. For a few months I tried to help him establish a private practice helping children and parents. I thought his reputation and background as a top researcher in child psychology could be transferred to the treatment of people. I rearranged my apartment so he would have an office and I became his manager, his hostess, and his receptionist. How easily I fell into the role of promoting a male, a husband.

He seemed to be excellent at counseling and I dreamed that this might solve his problems. He could have a healthy, rewarding practice and make money at the same time. What I didn't understand was that the more successful he became, the more patients he saw, the more pressure he felt. Although he was not drinking, none of his personality problems had disappeared, and he struggled with everyday routine life. Now, instead of planning his day around drinking, I found that he had a new obsession. The house had to be filled with a certain brand of soda water. His food had to be cooked exactly the same way each day. I tried to understand. Going to AA meetings with him and speaking to other wives, I began to realize that stopping the drinking was only one of the problems. We still had to deal with all the problems that existed before the drinking or because of the drinking or in spite of the drinking. I received a great deal of support from the other wives, who kept reassuring me that I was doing a wonderful job, but their main support went to Alfredo for every day that he was sober.

I'm not sure how long I could have lasted nursing Alfredo. I was trying to manage the job I had as a public relations representative for a huge food firm. About that time, Alfredo was offered a position in Canada. He was to head the Child Psychology Department as well as become a teaching professor to graduate students at the University of Waterloo, in Waterloo, Ontario, with a cross-appointment to the Ontario Institute for Studies in Education, in Toronto. But the main purpose of the appointment was to have someone who had successfully coped with alcoholism and would work with faculty members who were having drinking problems. Evidently there were many who were protected by the system. Alfredo told me it was a two-year contract and it would give our marriage a chance in a stable environment. He hoped that I would be willing to go with him, take the children, and plan a new future together. It was just the kind of work he loved.

I asked him what Canada was like. New Yorkers are so provincial, and I was so typical. I knew very little about Canada. I thought Guy Lombardo and his Royal Canadians was just a nice commercial name, that Canada Dry and Canadian Club whiskey were also just brand names. Alfredo told me he had heard that Ontario was very English, like England. I immediately had visions of thatched-roof cottages and feudal castles. I had no idea that

Canada was such a varied country, that it was a third French Canadian, or that Montreal was a city of such charm. The distance from the United States appealed to me. I would be leaving my mother and John Henry behind. I would be in a position to disengage from those destructive relationships. I had to deal with the fact that Alfredo was telling me that he didn't intend to have me work in Canada. My role was to be his wife, entertaining graduate students and colleagues and helping him with his research and writing. That was the duty of a professor's wife.

Alfredo told me that he had about fifteen thousand dollars locked away in a pension fund. It was almost impossible to get out, but if I could find a way to have it released, it would give us a cushion for the next year. I met the pension officer and discussed our past problems and the hospitalization. I described his "cure," his new attitude, his new position, and the responsibility he had undertaken. I felt our marriage would have a chance if he had the money to help with some of the new adjustments ahead of us. I convinced the head of the pension fund and he decided to make an exception and release the money. We were ecstatic. It seemed as if everything was falling into place. Alfredo turned the money over to me to handle. I was delighted that I could pay the grocery bill, buy some new linen for our new apartment, pay the outstanding rent, and leave Riverdale with no debts left behind. I think I spent all of $1,500 of the $15,000. It wasn't until we were on the plane to Canada that I mentioned paying off all the debts, and to my horror Alfredo went to pieces. How dare I use his money to pay my bills! Why did I have to pay them if we were leaving town anyway? I tried to calm him, afraid the children would hear us arguing. I felt as if I had built a future on shifting sand.

We arrived in Toronto and stayed the night at the King Edward Hotel because one of his colleagues had said, "The King Edward is the best in Toronto. Even Elizabeth Taylor and Richard Burton stayed there." This was in 1967, and our first impression of Canada was Toronto's downtown district. I tried to hide my disappointment as I looked at that staid, commercial hotel set in the business area, which was particularly quiet and cold because it was Sunday. I didn't see any signs of thatched-roof cottages or feudal castles, but rather a few tall buildings set against two-storey buildings lining the gray streets.

We had heard that there was a section of town called Yorkville that friends thought I would find similar to Greenwich Village in New York. As we drove by later in a cab, I craned my neck to see the street called Yorkville and realized that this one street was supposed to resemble all of Greenwich Village. We settled in for the night and I began to hope that Waterloo would be different.

The next morning we were picked up by a professor of the department and driven to Waterloo, where we saw a furnished apartment that had been sublet for us until we could find our own. Kitchener and Waterloo are twin cities, dominated by the new University of Waterloo, a mammoth, monolithic development. Waterloo resembled any charming town in Midwest America. I realized we had moved to a quiet country refuge. We were immediately taken on a tour of the university. We spent time searching for an apartment and accepted an invitation to a huge party to be introduced to the community. I found a beautiful apartment in a brand-new building. It was perfect because it was a duplex and my children could have separate quarters and there was enough room to make an office for Alfredo. It was quite glamorous and unexpected in a place like Waterloo. Then we attended the big party with Alfredo as guest of honor. The other guests were anxious to meet this "celebrity" from New York, the handsome, brilliant professor with the international reputation. We had only been in town a few weeks when we went to another party, and that's where I met Don Hildebrand, the owner of a local radio station, CHYM. Don was a larger-than-life, hard-drinking character who zeroed in on me. Out of the blue, he told me about his station and asked me to come down, when I had the chance, as he would like to talk to me about taking the job of women's editor and perhaps broadcasting half a dozen one-minute editorials a day.

I was in a state of shock. I had not intimated to anyone that I was interested in a job. Alfredo had made it very clear that he didn't want me working. Besides, we only planned to stay two years, if that. I wondered how Don knew about my background and why he thought I would fit into his station. It was years later that I asked him about the instant offer. He said, "I'm a gambler. I watched you. You are a great communicator. I knew you would make money for my station." But at the time I smiled pleasantly, told him we were in Canada temporarily, and that I had my work cut out as the wife of a professor. He laughed. "That will never be enough for you. The offer is open. Come any time." I presumed someone in the university department must have told him something about my background and also my connection with John Henry Faulk, who by now had international celebrity status due to the libel suit and the huge award. I felt flattered at being asked and talked to Alfredo about it. He reiterated he wasn't interested in my working.

I spent the next few weeks settling my children in school and helping Johanna adjust to the university. To do this we had to deal with the fact that Johanna lacked Grade XIII, something that didn't exist in New York. After many meetings and tests, she was allowed to enter freshman because of her excellent record at the outstanding Bronx High School of Science. Evelyn and Frank made fairly easy adjustments to their schools, but as we settled in comfortably, my relationship with Alfredo began to deteriorate. He began to withdraw from me sexually, despite the fact that our past had been built around his courting, his letters, our illicit meetings (even as a wife), and his intense lovemaking. In fact, many of our AA friends were surprised when I discussed how sexually active Alfredo had been. Usually alcohol diminishes desire and performance. Now that he wasn't drinking, he seemed more like a vegetable. He was completely absorbed in his work but went to sleep at bedtime. We even changed our double bed for twin beds. I felt punished and missed the contact and hugging, and found the situation intolerable. He became increasingly cold to the children and explained, "I have no time for my children. They don't have a father. I can't be one to yours." I did everything to make a separate space for them, trying to keep them out of each other's way.

I began to face the fact that we couldn't go on this way and I was worried about the future. John Henry was now sending me $270, deducting $30 because at that time the Canadian dollar was stronger than the American. I took time to go back to court in New York, and the woman judge lectured John Henry on his pettiness and his obligation. So the $300 came for a while and then again stopped, and I realized that I could not spend the rest of my life fighting John Henry in court, but I also realized I had no money of my own, and if my marriage to Alfredo fell apart I would actually be penniless. I began to think about taking the offer to do a radio show, but I was suspicious of the offer because it had come so suddenly.

I went to the radio station to see Don Hildebrand and ask him if he was serious. "Do you pay?" I knew that I couldn't demand the salary I had made in New York. This was another country and they could easily suggest that I did not know the Canadian scene and that in a sense I was beginning again. Hildebrand asked, "How much do you need to live on?" I immediately calculated the amount I would need for rent, food, clothing, and the like if Alfredo left. I told him the amount and he said this could come out of the program department's budget, and then suggested I could supplement that amount by doing a series of special commercials for him. I explained that I would choose some of the accounts that would suit my style. I would sell the advertising and ask for an additional talent fee for writing and broadcasting the commercial in a personalized editorial way, using my name for credibility. My thinking was based on the success of the editorials I had written for each account in *Go Magazine*. The personalized approach meant more to the advertiser than the purchased space. So I was hired at the huge sum of four hundred dollars a month plus commissions. The money for the commercials was billed to the sales department. I threw myself into the job, immediately sending out a letter announcing my appointment and requesting information from all the public relations people who were trying to promote products, talent, or events as well as theaters and concerts. I wrote four editorials a day, making comment on everything from fashion to politics, from sex and health to lifestyles. I had something to say about everything, and my name began to spread around the community. Strangely enough, though, the commercials brought me the most immediate recognition. I started each one, "Hello, I'm Lynne Gordon." I said it with such authority that people began to ask about this "Lynne Gordon" who had been parachuted into their consciousness. I investigated the product or service thoroughly and then gave my opinion in either a straight or a humorous way. It was the forerunner of my consumer show, which used all my investigative skills to advise people about rip-offs, misleading advertising, and confusing trade jargon. But that was to come later.

Alfredo finally allowed me to work because he resented paying out money for my children. For a while we made appearances at all the parties and began to drive to Toronto for weekends to take off some of the pressure he felt at home. I hoped this would give my teen-agers a chance to enjoy the house alone, without Alfredo barking out commands. The weekends helped at first. We would stay at the Park Plaza Hotel in Yorkville and roam the boutiques and little clubs, have room service and intimate dinners. But it didn't help our love life that much, although we tried. I asked Alfredo to go with me to a marriage counselor, but he refused. I decided I needed a psychiatrist to help me through this new trauma and found one in Toronto. A friend from Alanon, the organization that helps wives of alcoholics, would drive me once a week for my sessions, and we would relieve some of the pressure by dining in Toronto and talking about our problems. Finally I found a marriage counselor, Margaret Cork, who specialized in working with alcoholics and would function as his ally.

I was enjoying myself at CHYM and felt like a different person. In fact, I acquired a new identity quite by accident. When I was ready to go on the air for the first time, my name came under discussion. They said I couldn't use Castaneda, which I loved, because "people will find it too hard to pronounce." Only later did difficult-sounding names gain cachet. I wouldn't use the name Faulk because I had sworn he would never accuse me of using his name to get ahead. They wouldn't allow me to use Smith "because no one will believe you."

"Then," I said, "call me K.C. Smith." They responded, "They'll think you are a man." Then all the names I suggested, like Hailey and Evans, were refused until they went down the telephone directory and hit upon the name Gordon. "Aha," the program director said, "that's the perfect name for you. In Canada, Gordon is a Scots name and everyone loves the Scots." And so, inadvertently, Lynne Levinson, Smith, Grabois, Faulk, Castaneda, became Lynne Gordon.

I felt reborn. I used the new name all the time, as I became better known throughout the community. People began to listen to my commercials as much as my editorials because they were little anecdotes. I had a car account and told how I lost my car in a huge parking lot during a snowstorm and in trying to find it realized that one out of every two cars was a Ford. I talked about bathroom accessories and how the best retreat in the house was the bathroom and why. I started one commercial off by saying,

"Hello, I'm Lynne Gordon. Do you want to know the easiest way to get pregnant? (Pause) Give away your maternity clothes." I was promoting a new boutique featuring maternity clothes but everywhere I went for the next few weeks I was stopped by laughing men who joked, "Hey, Lynne, we can tell you the easiest way to get pregnant." That's when I realized the impact of my commercials on the community.

I began to feel a little more secure financially, and Don Hildebrand was delighted with my work. He fixed up a beautiful office for me and gave me an expense account to travel to Toronto for interviews. Then I learned that Don was going to leave CHYM because Maclean Hunter was buying him out. I met Donald G. Campbell, the executive with Maclean Hunter who was in Waterloo to have a meeting with Don to wind up the association. I took this opportunity to meet him and discuss with him the possibility of working with CKEY, the sister station in Toronto. He seemed to be impressed with me and gave me the name of the general manager of CKEY, Doug Trowell, and said he would recommend a meeting. My mind was working overtime. If I was to survive, I couldn't be out of work a day. I would have to make the transition from CHYM to CKEY without any days off, but how to do it? I decided we should take the step and move to Toronto. After all, Alfredo had a twin appointment at OISE and he had to be there at least part of the week. I was sure I wouldn't have the same freedom under the new management at CHYM as I had enjoyed under Don Hildebrand. I asked CHYM to allow me to come to the station once or twice a week to tape the full week's schedule. In the meantime I made a consistent effort to switch to CKEY. The management accepted this for the summer. Toronto would offer me a complete social life, something I lacked in Kitchener and Waterloo.

Alfredo and I found a fine apartment in a newly built complex, the Village Green. I loved the apartment. It was in an area that had a theater, a delicatessen, fruit markets, and cafés like those I enjoyed in the past. So many of my friends wondered why I didn't move into an area called Rosedale, about ten minutes away. "With the money you are spending, you could be in a more residential area with trees." I said, "I hate lots of trees. I don't mind it if they struggle through the cement. I like the sound of fire engines. I like the energy of neon lights. I like the street action." Of course, the $200 a month I was paying for the apartment seemed so reasonable to me after the high rents in New York.

Just before we were to move in, we started to meet with Margaret Cork. It was only after two sessions that she called me in to say I should leave Alfredo. I was in a state of shock. I thought a therapist's job was to see how people could be kept together. "How can you make such a decision after only two sessions?"

She said, "Do you want to be married to a vegetable? He is not capable of having a personal relationship with any human being. He may function in his job, perhaps, but he will treat you like a piece of furniture for the rest of your life. Do you want to live like that?" I told her about the apartment we had just taken. She said, "If I get him to promise to pay the rent for the two-year lease, will that help?" I thought about the money I was making. I realized that soon no money would be coming from John Henry, but if the rent was taken care of, I thought, all things being equal, I could manage. I knew that Alfredo probably wouldn't go for more than that, and I was anxious to finish off this marriage as quickly and cleanly as possible.

I was beginning to cut a lot of ties. John Henry had his lawyer send me a letter, which said John Henry would agree to take care of his children if I would drop my New York court order. According to the lawyer, John Henry said he didn't need anyone to tell him his responsibility. I thought I might as well give that a try. It certainly wasn't practical to keep fighting John Henry in court. I couldn't keep going to New York. The children were at an age when he didn't legally have to support them, and I hoped the lawyer would make sure that he stuck to his word. I dropped the court order and never received another penny from John Henry, nor did his children.

So here I was in a strange country, a single mother with three teen-agers, and absolutely nothing in the bank. It's hard to believe I didn't panic, or even realize how destitute I was. Some women, when they say they have nothing, are not including the house, the silver, the jewelry, the investments, or the fur coats they have. When I say not a penny in the bank, I mean not a penny. I was in my late forties and starting a new career. In looking back I wonder at my calm. Also, no matter how many times I started over in a career—in New York, in Texas, now in Canada—I never felt I was beginning. I always knew I had a great deal to offer, many ideas, and many talents. The only compromise I had to make was with the starting salary. I never had the luxury of building a career without interruption, which would have enabled me to build my earnings. But I also knew how to use a charge account creatively.

I moved to Toronto in June and had about three summer months to concentrate on getting a job. I didn't think CHYM would let me continue to do my show from Toronto in the fall. I was tremendously happy at living in an urban area again. It was the big city with everything at my fingertips, and taxis and walking to get around. No more driving. I checked out the entire market in Toronto—all the radio stations and the television studios—and decided to concentrate completely on 'EY for one reason. They needed me the most. The CBC was government-subsidized and I didn't think an American would have much of a chance there. CFRB was controlled by Betty Kennedy, a veteran broadcaster and part of the establishment, and I knew she wouldn't want another woman in her territory. So I went down the list and it reinforced my decision to concentrate on 'EY. I made it a practice to send in material and ideas I thought were right for their station. I had monitored it and found it bland and had told them they would fade into the scenery if they didn't begin to incorporate features into their programming. I told them I was used to preparing tight, informative, one-minute commentaries and I could spread them out easily through their format by having the individual announcers introduce me to maintain the continuity. I pointed to the success of the "Lynne Gordon commercials" in Waterloo and convinced them they would be just as effective in a big city like Toronto. I suggested they needed more information about the city, more reviews of events and plays, and more commentary about issues.

I had a number of meetings with Doug Trowell, who was like a handsome Jack Lemmon. I found him charming and delightful, and he seemed quite impressed with me. He introduced me to his sales manager, Stu Brandy, and his program director, Gene Kirby. I remember Stu asking me if I was seeing other radio stations and I replied, "No, I have checked them out and I am not interested. I think you need me the most and you have the most to offer." He said, "Do you realize we just paid a fortune to a consulting firm to tell us we need less talk and more music. Now you want us to incorporate talk." I pretended that I knew all along, but without missing a beat I shot back, "That's fine. That format may be viable for now, but I feel certain if you don't begin to co-ordinate some talk into the format, it will stagnate and become colorless. I understand how to work with those time restrictions."

I repeated my ideas on how to throw in one-minute commentaries after two or three record plays, with the announcer introducing them. He was so impressed with my single-mindedness, I later found out, that he used my approach to train his sales people in the art of selling and focusing on an account. He also liked the idea of "Lynne Gordon commercials." I already had a track record in Canada. Then I met Gene Kirby, who had come from Hell's Kitchen in New York City. We formed a bond, although he was intent on chipping away at my New York accent, which I felt was minimal because of my training in the theater. It seemed that all three men were excited about the possibility of my joining 'EY, but at the moment there was no air time. Doug Trowell offered me a job in the promotion department under its manager. "He needs someone right now, and your background would fit right in with his needs. Why don't you take that until a spot opens for you in programming." I was sorely tempted because time was passing and I knew I had to make a decision soon, but I have never failed to respond to my "gut" reaction. I met the public relations manager and found him too high-strung for me to work with him. Also, I thought he might have a problem with a strong female personality: I knew if I was good, he wouldn't want to let me go, and if we clashed it would kill my chance to do what I wanted. So, with some trepidation, I said no, I would rather wait until they could use me for what I was best at. That has been my pattern ever since I started working. I find it hard to compromise, and I do my best work when the job is something I like and am challenged by.

At almost the last moment, the end of August, I got a call from Doug Trowell. I had been bombarding him with show ideas every week. He told me they had an opening for me. I was exhilarated—everything, at last, was turning out so right. I had a job at the station of my choice and I was almost a completely free woman. I was beginning to wake up in the morning smiling. Doug Trowell told me the news, adding, "You are a great broad." I took it as a compliment from him. I felt he was referring to my earthiness, my outspoken way. I told him that I was getting a divorce, which meant that I had plans to develop my show and stay in

Canada permanently. I felt I had to tell him about the divorce because I didn't want him to find out through gossip. But I also wanted to assure him that I wasn't leaving when my husband's contract was up. So I gave my notice to CHYM and started the very next week at CKEY. An announcement was put up on the bulletin board to welcome "Lynne Gordon, broadcaster/writer/researcher/salesman."

My first responsibility was to cover all the events and happenings in Toronto, write them up for the announcers, so it seemed as if they were personally out on the town and in the community. I took it so seriously that I tried to write amusing bits in their own individual styles. But because I also wanted to be on air, I did celebrity interviews, which I reduced to one-minute cuts so that a fifteen-minute interview could be spread out over a few hours, each minute complete in itself. It gave me an opportunity to do, on a smaller scale, all the things I loved doing in New York. I went out constantly, to press parties, to the theater, to dances, to the opera, to restaurant openings. On top of that assignment, I was given special beats to cover, like the education beat and the medical beat. I also kept trying to introduce special features. I was hungry to do everything, and I loved it.

I was one of the first women in Toronto to go to press conferences, to be seen reporting on a beat. Most women were in the background as either researchers or media buyers. I would show up at a conference with fifteen or twenty men, and I was the only woman. At first they seemed to shy away from me, as if uncomfortable with a woman in their midst. But they knew that if I showed up, there was a good news story because I had no time to cover every press conference. I had such a wide variety of conferences to choose from each day, I was on my way to a new start in life. I was free of John Henry, happy that I didn't have to depend on his money any more or even be tied to him by anger. I was free of Alfredo, almost grateful that he had brought me to Canada. I was free of the daily calls to my mother. I was living in an area that I loved and starting a new career. Only later did I realize that you cannot turn your back on your past. For the moment I liked being just Lynne Gordon.

CHAPTER 22

A NEW LIFE

My life at CKEY was so happy that I was rather surprised to find I had some problems with Evelyn, Frank, and Johanna. I had painted such a rosy picture of our future life in Toronto and freedom from Alfredo that I didn't expect to hear that Frank really hated leaving Waterloo. He had many friends there and wasn't particularly happy at Jarvis Collegiate in Toronto. Frank had a very sensitive, creative mind and I hoped he would finish school. I used to tell him that no matter what happened there would always be money for him to go to university. One day he approached me and asked, "Mom, do I have to go to university? Suppose I don't want to?" I realized then that he felt an obligation to go. I explained that all I wanted was for him to know that if he wanted to go I would make sure the money was available. I guess I had been worried he might think the money wouldn't be forthcoming because his father wasn't sending any support money.

Johanna never spent much time in the Village Green. She went back to the University of Waterloo for her degree. Evelyn was having the hardest time adjusting. I wondered if it was because she was the middle child. I was so important in her life that I'm sure I got the full brunt of her anger because she needed me so much and her need also frightened her. Johanna could look to my stepfather as a male figure and got attention from my mother because she was the first-born. Frank had some tenuous connection with his father. In fact, he had once asked me if I minded if he made it his business to connect with John Henry. Would I feel hurt? I assured him that I believed love to be something that multiplies, not divides. The more people you love, the more you have to give. In fact, if he could form some relationship with his father, I would be very happy. I worried that our fighting over the years might have colored their feelings about their father. I certainly didn't want my fight to become theirs. I warned Frank that he might not find the father he wanted, but at least he could make his own decision as to what he wanted from a father.

Johanna and Evelyn were unable to talk about their father. They were so hurt by his withdrawal from them and his inability to do simple things like send a card on their birthdays or make the occasional telephone call to find out how they were. Their visits had been traumatic, as he constantly discussed me and insisted they listen. He accused me of poisoning their minds and keeping them away from him. He reiterated that I had a lot of money hidden away. As they grew up they began to know better, but it didn't ease their pain.

I had long since given up writing or calling him. He never answered my letters, and if I called he usually hung up. I never understood the depth of his anger or his need to lie. I don't think he ever realized how much I wanted to love him, how I would have done anything to re-establish a friendly relationship. He never could accept the fact that I had made the first legal move toward the separation: I had made the decision.

When Frank was seventeen he decided to leave home. I was shocked but he had his reasons. "Mom, I don't want to become the father in this household. I find that I've become the disciplinarian, the one who's worried if the house isn't cleaned and dinner started. I can't stand the arguments." I hated to see him go because, in truth, he was so comforting to have around and the easiest one to deal with, but I respected his reasons. I told him that he was always welcome to come home when he wanted. The door was always open. "Never hesitate if you need money. I'll be glad to help." He told me, "I prefer doing it on my own. If you help too much, I'll be tempted to take the easy way out and come to you, so please don't even offer me money."

I enrolled Evelyn in an experimental school called Superschool, which had a new approach to education. The students set their own paces. I hoped that it would help Evelyn, who was having a difficult time with anger and was in complete rebellion against me. I found it difficult to make any demands on Evelyn without having her explode. I tried taking the family for counseling. I wasn't sure what was happening, whether it was more difficult because there was no male head of the household or because there was an absent punishing male or because I was so busy working. Johanna seemed more in control because she had her school and friends, but I began to realize that she also needed more from me. I wanted to do everything I could.

Then my stepfather died and my mother began coming to visit me for a few months each summer, spending the rest of the time in California near my sister. By this time I was aware that I would never receive any approval from my mother, that our relationship was only possible if I was completely adoring. I unrealistically thought that, once my father died, my mother might be freer to travel and do all the things I thought my father had kept her from doing, but all my mother wanted was for her daughters to step into her husband's footsteps and take care of her completely.

It was only after she came to stay for a few months that I realized she was a "junkie." She had complained so much that her doctor had loaded her up with pills and I angrily described him as a pusher. I fully realized it when she needed to get her prescriptions filled in Toronto. The druggist looked at the fourteen different bottles and said, "I can't refill these without a doctor's prescription. It's too dangerous." She had uppers, downers, pills for pain, tranquilizers, sleeping pills, pills for "blood disease," which she would never call leukemia, pills for her blood pressure. I then realized that her irrational angers, her unrealistic demands, and her unwillingness to go out all stemmed from her drug dependency. She acted like an alcoholic. One time she took out a pill in a restaurant and I asked, "What are those?" She said, "Percodan for pain." "But, Mother, you are not in pain now." "But I don't want to wait. I want to make sure I don't have any." Her addiction kept her from enjoying anything. These experiences were the beginning of my being free of my mother. Nothing I could say would convince her that I felt happier and more fulfilled taking care of myself and that a man wasn't necessary to my happiness any more. I began to feel compassion for her, but not love.

Living in Canada was beginning to set me free. I didn't have anyone in my house who had the power to punish me any more. I began to find that people liked me. I wasn't the bitch John Henry had told me I was. I wasn't hard to handle the way my mother said

I was. I began to realize that, in marrying John Henry, I had married my mother in the sense that I still wanted the approval that only a mother can give, and mine didn't. I began to feel like a nice person.

Now I was functioning on my own. Many women go from their parents' homes to live with husbands and never develop a sense that they might be whole or likable people in their own right. When I had been at CKEY for about three months, I was asked by a secretary if I could do a favor for a friend of hers at the Ronalds-Reynolds advertising agency. She said her friend was head of the women's department at the agency and was in the process of planning an important fashion show for a client when she found out that she had to go to the hospital. Miriam asked if I could take the job over on a freelance basis. She knew that I had been a fashion co-ordinator in New York. The client made Wabasso sheets and had a promotion going using the sheets to make up fashions – to highlight the designs and the versatility of the sheets. I could have used the extra money, but at first I refused. I was still new at the radio station and I wanted to give the new job all my time and energy. "Do you mean there is no one else in Toronto she knows who can do the job?" I asked. Miriam said evidently not. I thought for a moment and said, "All right, if she can't find anyone in a week, I'll take it over as a favor."

A week went by, the woman was rushed to the hospital, and I took on the assignment. I was told that if I needed any help, the account executive, Steve Evans, could give me all the information I needed. That weekend I visited the designer who was making up the fashions and I wrote the copy and planned the show. I couldn't believe how simple it was and thought the hospitalized woman had complicated it more than necessary. The show was to travel, first to Toronto and then to the head office in Montreal. I was concerned about the lack of co-operation from the head office. So I called Steve Evans and said, "The people at the head office are not responding the way I think they should." He asked me to hop a cab and go right over to his office. I answered rather flippantly, "My work was over this weekend. If you need me some more, it will cost more." He agreed. "That's fine, you haven't charged enough for your work anyhow." I was rather taken aback at his attitude and was curious to meet the man. I took a cab over and as I walked into his office I was rather surprised to be greeted by an unaffected and charming man, not the typical advertising executive. I had memories of the plastic, hail-fellow-well-met type from New York. He had an impish glint in his eyes and short red hair. In a pleasant English accent he said, "You know, I'm very impressed with your work, but I would like to change just a few words, if you don't mind."

"You paid for it," I said. "It's yours. Change anything you want."

So we went over the copy carefully and he was very friendly and pleasant about everything. He asked me if I was going to a special press conference that night to celebrate the merger of two weekend magazines. I told him I had planned to review a film that night but was almost positive I would make the press conference afterwards. As it turned out, I did show up at the party, and I found that he had been parked at the top of the stairs looking for me. He became my escort for the evening, showing me around, explaining the promotional videos, and making sure I was taken care of. He introduced me to a number of other executives. He was most gentlemanly and sincere. He told me later how sophisticated and "New Yorkerish" I looked. Because he spent so much time with me, I thought he was unattached, but after a while a woman came up to him and he introduced me to his wife. He said, "Lynne is new in town. Why don't we have a big party and introduce her to some men?" She replied, "Why don't we have a big party and you get the men for me and she can have you?"

I felt a stab of pain for him. It was such an unnecessary remark. I didn't like her. I looked at her and said, "Thank you. I'll take him." A little later he told me that he had not invited her to the party. She had been invited through her business connections with Avon, the cosmetic firm. Then he told me he had to leave for the department store that was having the fashion show I had arranged, to make sure everything was running smoothly. I said good-bye and wandered off into the next room. Suddenly I saw him standing before me, and almost compulsively he reached out and drew me to him and kissed me on the lips. I couldn't believe how my heart started to pound. I even thought I heard bells!

It was strange for me to allow myself to be vulnerable to anyone in the same or allied business. I had a strict rule about going out with colleagues. I was most strict about dating a boss or even anyone in the same office. Part of my caution was just self-preservation. While I was at 'EY, an executive was going through problems with his marriage. He used to spend hours talking to me about them, asking for my advice. He felt that since I had been married three times I must have some insights, and he wanted to know how I had survived. During our many talks and unplanned lunches together, he became very affectionate and began to talk about loving me, wanting to know me, even traveling to Europe with me if that would make me feel safer about having an affair. He was a very interesting, spontaneous man, but I had the sense that he was quite neurotic and needy. I was afraid that if we had a relationship, I would put my career at risk, so over the years I kept our relationship at arm's length, and his declared love soon developed into a friendship.

I decided Steve Evans belonged to another category. Although he was an account executive in advertising, his professional relationship with me was far removed. We had mutual interests but our jobs were more compatible than intertwined. The next day he called me at the station and asked if he could come to my office and go over some of the finished copy with me. Since I didn't have a private office, I arranged to greet him in a colleague's office so we could have some privacy. We talked about the copy and then he asked me out for dinner. I assumed from his wife's remark that they were having problems or else enjoyed an open marriage. I agreed to go out with him. At dinner he told me that he had once separated for a year from his wife because of the affairs she was having. In fact, he had previously lived at the Village Green where I had my apartment. A few months ago, she had asked him back, promising that their lives would be different, but it turned out that she needed him back to help out financially. She had almost lost the house by running up debts, the house he loved so much in the suburbs of Scarborough. He said it looked as if the marriage was coming apart at the seams again. He wanted me to understand what he was going through so that I wouldn't be hurt. We dated for a few weeks, during which time he said little about what was happening at home. He had an Englishman's typical reserve. That's one thing I loved about Toronto so much, the English community. Walking in Toronto one could hear wonderful, cultured English accents at almost every stop. It made me feel as if I was truly in a foreign country, although there was so much else that was similar to the United States.

I found Steve very open, enthusiastic about planning our meetings. He had an insatiable curiosity and questioned everything. He was also very courtly, and I found it easy to accept his help in putting on snow boots or carrying packages. It wasn't patronizing when he did it; it was so natural for him. Then one night he came to me and said, "I'm not going to see you for a while. My wife and I are breaking up, but I don't think it's fair to see you while I'm still emotionally involved with her. Our weekends together are intense and painful. I must handle this on my own."

I admired his frankness but I was surprised that he hadn't worked out his feelings for his wife. I thought he had and that it was just a matter of time to make the necessary arrangements. I felt an unexpected pang of rejection. "Thanks for telling me. You are quite right, after all I have heard from your friends about your relationship with your wife and the agony you've lived through, I don't want to see you until you are emotionally free. I've gone through too much pain on my own. If you still want to be together with her then you are a masochist, and I want none of it."

In the meantime, I threw myself into my work at CKEY. Toronto was exploding. Restaurants, theaters, night spots were flourishing. The influx of immigrants was giving Toronto fresh color and an air of sophistication. It was the beginning of a boom and I was in at the start. My background in writing and broadcasting was needed. It was fortunate I had the Canadian experience from Kitchener-Waterloo behind me. Nationalism was beginning to flourish and fewer Americans were given jobs. I worked hard for acceptance in the world of broadcasting, which was almost all male. I was aware that men were threatened by the image of a "pushy, aggressive New York woman," as one person put it, but I had dealt with that in Texas. It was a little more subtle in Canada. The men weren't as bold and brash but they were just as determined to keep women off the executive lists and out of the boardrooms.

Even my presence in the newsroom created anxiety. In 1968 they were still complaining, "If Lynne is going to sit in the newsroom with us, how are we going to feel free to use the language we use? Do we have to worry about her? It gets pretty rough here sometimes."

I shook my head in disbelief. "Too bad you feel you have to rely on four-letter words to communicate, but just like you, I'm used to working in a newsroom where there is a lot of noise. I'm capable of shutting out sounds, conversation, and noise pollution, but I assure you, if you bug me I can use language as strong as you can if I have to." The men watched everything I did. They weren't used to expending as much energy as I did collecting news stories and providing features. When I asked for files, bookcases, and magazine racks, they began to make the same demands. Most of their stories were "rip and tear" and came off the wire, so they had no need for files, yet they felt competitive and thought I was staking out special territory.

At the time I was making a name for myself as a consumer advocate on radio, *Luncheon Date* was a popular CBC noon-hour television talk show hosted by the well-known personality Elwood Glover. One of the talented producers of this live show of conversation and music was Sandra Johnson, who not only booked the guests but had the impossible job of finding guests to pinch-hit for last-minute cancellations. She began to book me fairly regularly because she could count on me to come up with a topical feature on the spur of the moment, as I usually worked on about ten consumer items at a time to fill my own daily radio show. She would call me an hour or even twenty minutes before air time if she had to fill a spot in a hurry. We would talk on the phone and run down my list of topics, and I would hop a cab and go on the air slightly breathless. I was a guest on the show the memorable day the very proper and formal host had a pie thrown in his face by one of the guests. It was supposed to be a joke but it so shocked Elwood Glover that he walked off the set. I was the next guest but there was no host. Sonny Caulfield, the bandleader, stepped in. I whispered a question he could ask me to kick off the interview. He asked it and I just kept talking. We got through the segment without much trouble, much to the relief of Sandra and Sonny. Nothing was as much fun in those days as live television!

At that time no one knew about my previous life. I had been catapulted into Canadian broadcasting and I saw no need to bring up my background. There wasn't widespread interest in the McCarthy period or in blacklisting and I certainly wasn't interested in talking about my traumatic divorce from John Henry or even my divorce from Alfredo Castaneda, for that matter. But then, no one asked me. Canadians don't ask many questions. I found them to be very restrained, uptight. Steven Evans had been different in his boyish approach to life, but I attributed that to his Welsh father.

While Steve was away, I spent time with some of the friends I had made in my apartment building. The entire floor was peopled by very straight-looking, successful businessmen who were gay. They were wonderful friends and escorts when I first came to Toronto, and often accompanied me to the theater and events where I enjoyed having an escort. They were so handsome and attentive that, when Steve met them at my house for Sunday brunch, he told me later he thought I was surrounded by young swains. He thought they were my boyfriends.

I found the challenges at CKEY exciting as I made plans to increase my exposure on air. I always felt excited when making new plans. It was the same feeling I had in the past whenever there was a real crunch and I was faced with survival. Sometimes I thought it must be the same feeling a racing driver or a mountain climber has when facing new challenges, setting new records, cheating death, living on the edge. Then sometimes I wondered if my ability to bounce back stemmed from my childhood and the memory of abandonment . . . the need to make it alone, to prove that I was entitled to love. Whatever the reason, I was now facing the future with the firm belief in my dreams being fulfilled, more confident than ever that I was in control of my own destiny.

CHAPTER 23

STEVE

During the weeks that Steve and I stopped seeing each other, I put him out of my mind. I was enjoying my work and I was also concerned about getting into a serious relationship too soon. I was happy with my life and didn't want to drift into a commitment before I had time to think about my future. The women's movement was just beginning to surface again, and I was finding it easy to build a network of women friends. Then one evening, as I was sitting in the lounge of the Health Club at the Village Green, a call came from Steve. Without any preliminary explanations, he asked if he could see me. I didn't ask any questions and agreed. He sat down and began explaining. "It's over. Thanks for not demanding explanations first."

For the next year, we spent time learning about each other. We went dancing, picnicking, out to dinner, and on weekend vacations. Steve was in some ways very Victorian, but the wonderful thing about him was his ability to grow and learn. He had come from England after the war and a stint in the Royal Canadian Air Force had pulled him up. He first worked as a draftsman, then as a sales representative. Recently he had gone into advertising, a complete change for him. His career had suffered through his stormy marriage. He loved his first and only wife very much. He had tried for years to understand her need to go out with other men and half-believed her when she explained, "Some people love more than others. If you love me so much, you can put up with me. Don't try to control me."

I enjoyed dating Steve and going to his home for the Sunday dinners that he cooked. His two teen-agers were living with him, since their mother said she couldn't manage them and they wanted to live in the house. Although he had left her in the house the last time, in their latest arrangement Steve insisted that he keep the house and she be paid for her half-ownership.

Although I enjoyed our steady going out, I was in no hurry to be more involved with Steve on a permanent basis. I was free of Alfredo but Steve still had so many problems to solve with his own life, although his divorce finally came through. After we had been seeing each other exclusively for about a year, Steve began to make worried noises about my finances. "How can you afford to live in such an expensive apartment? When your lease is up in a few months, you should look for a less expensive one." I was confused about his concern since I had never discussed my finances with him, never asked for any help to meet my obligations, and in fact never expressed any worry about the future. I thought it was none of his business and I certainly didn't need a man to tell me what to do with my life.

I had been doing a great deal of reading about women's issues. I was one of the few journalists and broadcasters who covered all the women's events, and I had begun to understand some of my problems in dealing with male-female relationships. Although I fought it, I still dropped into role-playing almost unconsciously, so that an internal, personal war was always being waged. I accepted some of his advice and went so far as to look at other apartments, but I hated them. I explained that I had never sacrificed my living arrangements because of money, that my surroundings were vital to me, that I loved everything about the Village Green, and that I intended to re-sign the lease. At any rate, it was not his problem.

I suddenly had the feeling that he was struggling with his own decision and probably wanted to ask me to live with him in Scarborough but wasn't sure if he wanted to take on that responsibility. So he was making decisions for me as a kind of substitute. What bothered me was that I was letting him make the decision instead of telling him that I wouldn't consider living in Scarborough. I still felt confused about my reaction to being wanted . . . and still felt flattered. So I let the time pass without saying anything until the very month I was to re-sign the lease. Then, as we were walking down Yonge Street, he turned to me and said, "Don't stay at the Village Green. I want you to come and live with me."

I looked at him, somewhat amused. "How romantic! Are you asking me to live with you as a roommate to save me rent or to share your life? Actually, I'm not sure I can live with you. I need to live alone for a while. I don't even know if I could live with you without wanting something more, without being demanding. I'm not sure I understand myself yet in relation to men. I know that I want to concentrate on my career."

He replied, "Don't worry about that. I can handle it. I want you to be with me." I could feel the old conditioning fall into place—his insistence and assurance made me feel I had to respond. He sounded so certain, so sure, that for a moment I thought how wonderful it would be to have a man who seemed in control take over. The fact that I was already in control of my own life didn't seem to enter into it.

I threw up another barrier. "You live in Scarborough. I hate the suburbs. I hate commuting, and I never want to be alone out there if you go on business trips."

He shot back, "You don't have to worry about commuting. We'll go down together every day by car and come back together every night." What I did love about our relationship was his complete support of my working. He appreciated my career, understood my need for perfection, my concern about deadlines, and he was also happy about my making money. How interesting that for so many years I had the mistaken idea that the only men who could understand me, or live with my intense behavior, were "creative" men, men outside the business world. Yet every husband I had was threatened by my working and felt my time was better spent reinforcing their careers and taking care of them. At press parties Steve would always make sure that I was taken care of and then "work the room," as we all did, leaving me to make contacts, get information, and wander back only when he thought I needed him for reinforcement. He respected my schedule and in fact enjoyed going to the theater, to restaurants, to concerts, and to press events as much as I did. It dovetailed with his work and added an extra dimension of glamor.

While I was trying to make my final decision, an ardent feminist tried to dissuade me. "Why are you moving into a dependent situation with the enemy?"

I said, "Bonnie, he is not the enemy. Men may be oppressors, but they are subjected to the same conditioning we all are. I wouldn't be a man for a million dollars. Imagine being brought up from childhood to know that you had to become a breadwinner and be completely responsible for another human being, without even the luxury of sharing that responsibility, or sharing even your fears. I think it's possible to work out individual relationships with men, based on dialogue, conversation, and information. Steve is accessible, basically kind and good. If he has problems, they are all visible. He's not manipulative. He's not complicated. I know what hurts him." I knew that part of him was closed off to me, not because he didn't care a lot but because he still couldn't handle the emotional breakup with his wife. He felt that he could never use the word "love" again because he felt his marriage had made a mockery of it. I didn't know how much that would interfere with our closeness, but I was willing to accept that he could show me love, show me affection, even if he couldn't verbalize it. I felt the other would come with complete trust.

We began to talk about the move to Scarborough, and he started making some demands. "I have a house full of furniture, so it's best if you sell yours." I refused. "Why don't you sell yours? If our living arrangement doesn't work, I don't want to leave empty-handed." We then decided to rearrange the furniture to accommodate two homes. I was proud of myself for not acquiescing automatically. I saw that as a sign of growth. We did make a commitment to each other that neither of us would become sexually involved with anyone else. We had both been hurt by the lies and infidelities of our previous partners. I didn't care whether I was being mature or not, but I knew I still couldn't handle infidelity. All I asked was that I have no reason to be jealous and that we show respect for each other in our community and never leave the other one vulnerable to gossip.

I finally made the decision to move, with a great deal of trepidation. For Steve and me, the business of putting our two lives together wasn't easy, and working it out taught me something about my feelings concerning the way men and women relate to each other. He was adamant about Evelyn not coming to Scarborough. She had been talking about being on her own for a year or so and now was the time for her to make the move. I knew she would hate the suburbs and I dreaded the interaction between his two children and mine. I knew they wouldn't get along. They had completely different values from my children. I told Evelyn of my plans and said, "This may be a good time for your move. I'll help you find a place to live. I'll pay your room and board until you get a job and get established." I wanted to believe this would be a healthy move for her, knowing in my heart that despite all her protestations about wanting to be on her own, she was still afraid. At any rate, I subconsciously resented Steve for forcing me to make that decision while he still had his teen-agers at home.

Then there was the house itself. It was about forty minutes by car from the downtown in an area sometimes jokingly called "Scarberia." It was the house in which he had lived with his ex-wife for fifteen years, a roomy house over a beautiful ravine, but it was still furnished in outlandish taste—red mood lights in the bathroom, glass-beaded curtains between the kitchen and the family room, and black walls in one of the bedrooms decorated with huge paper daisies. I had ideas for changing the décor but was soon told not to alter a thing. He liked it as it was. I was still operating on the theory that once you were married or "living together," each partner had a right to suggest or make changes in the decorating scheme. I was upset at first when he forbade me to change anything, but I have to admit that I might be the same way now, if someone moved into my house on the same basis. It would certainly be something to discuss.

I felt also that once I lived in the house, I should contribute my share to the mortgage and the living expenses. He refused. "I don't want you to pay for anything. Save your money. Put it away for your future." I thought that sounded generous, but I wasn't sure it was fair, especially since I was becoming more and more involved with feminist issues and believed in a partnership. It was later that I found out that he didn't want me to share the costs because he didn't want to share the house. It was really a way of still keeping some distance between us. Our living together instead of marrying allowed me to grow, mainly because I was working from a completely different frame of reference and so was Steve. I know that since he felt that he hadn't "given me his name," I was able to do more than he could have accepted if we were married. To many people, marriage seems to suggest that two people ought to operate in a certain way.

With all the problems we had to deal with, I think I was able to be more in touch with my needs than ever before, although I still had to struggle to break out of some of my knee-jerk reactions to demands made by a man. For example, Steve loved to putter around the house, paint, garden, and even polish his oak baseboard for hours. I was basically an apartment person, hated houses, and depended on maintenance staff to care for all of that. At first I tried to share that work with Steve. As a proper "helpmate," I helped him paint, wash windows, weed the garden . . . and soon found that I was spending an inordinate amount of time on tasks that could be done much faster and more efficiently by Steve or some experienced worker. Because I couldn't paint, I became the gofer and he gave me supposedly easier tasks. One day he asked me to tie up a bundle of papers for recycling, and I struggled for half an hour trying to knot the cord, which kept slipping and causing the papers to spill over. I suddenly started to cry in frustration and announced, "I don't want to do these things around the house. I'm going upstairs to work on a column or on my consumer book. I'll use the money I get for you to hire someone to take my place. I can't stand doing that work." That was the last time I painted, weeded, or did odd jobs around the house, but I willingly agreed to plant the annuals, the flowers that made an instant garden. I felt that was one big step for freedom and it didn't make me less of a wife or partner. The earth didn't fall apart. Steve accepted my decision, mainly because I was able to articulate what was bothering me at the time it was bothering me, instead of storing up the anger. He didn't abandon me or sulk or act like a parent.

We enjoyed going on vacations together. He was a great companion and a curious traveler, but he preferred going to the Caribbean Islands, where he could relax, indulge leisurely in sports, and spend wonderful lazy hours making love. I began to hunger for Europe, the Orient, and other faraway places. I agreed to go with him anywhere he wanted on his vacations, but to satisfy my need for more extensive travel, I created a radio travel show. I convinced my boss that CKEY would benefit from having some international stories. I told Stu Brandy, the vice-president of sales, that I needed to travel for my "soul." Stu laughingly asked me how to put "soul" in a contract. But after I outlined my idea, they agreed to budget for four travel shows a year. I called the feature "The Heartbeat of a Country." I was interested in talking about more than the usual tourist spots. I wanted to meet people from every walk of life in the countries we visited. I would interview economists, educators, celebrities, politicians, the kinds of people I had on my regular shows. I would never have dreamed of going off without a husband before, but this was such a perfect solution. It satisfied his needs and mine, and of course, after a while, he began to ask if he could come with me and loved the trips to Israel, England, and Ireland. I went off alone to do stories on Egypt, Italy, France, Greece, Yugoslavia, Ireland and China.

After a few years of life in Scarborough, I felt a tremendous need to live downtown again. I also thought it was unreasonable that we had to drive back to Scarborough every night when my work kept me downtown all the time covering events. I also hated hanging around his office until curtain time at the theater because it was too far to go home, shower, and change. One day I said, "Let's talk. I've figured out six alternatives to settle our problem. You can sell the house and we'll buy a new one together downtown; you can rent this house and we'll rent an apartment downtown . . . " I went on with six variations on the same theme. Steve laughed and said, "Those are not six alternatives. Those are six ways of getting me out of this house." I said, "Okay, you're right. I have no right to nag you any more. You love the house. I respect that. Now all I ask is you respect my fervent need to live downtown. But I'll compromise. I'll rent an apartment downtown and we'll split our time between your house and my apartment." His first reaction was very traditional. "You want to start dating, don't you?" I was bewildered. "You must be insane. I don't want to date. We have settled that. I want you to be fair and stay with me when the weather's bad or when we get out of the theater and it's too late to run home and then have to rise early just to come back downtown. I want to be able to leave the office early, come to the apartment to shower, and perhaps even cook you a light dinner instead of eating out every night." Steve found it difficult to swallow, and I could feel him withdraw. My reaction in the past would have been to retreat, afraid that I was being unreasonable or demanding or thoughtless, but I realized that my proposal made sense, and if he couldn't handle it then I was ready, though not happy, to take the consequences. I knew if our relationship was really good we could come through this.

It took about six months before I finally got the apartment. I tried including him in the choice. At first he refused, and then he decided to have input, but his last words were, "Okay, you pay for everything connected with the apartment. I want nothing to do with it." It was a critical point in our relationship, but after a while Steve was proud of our downtown pad and we began to do more entertaining there. And I paid all the expenses, willingly.

We had one other serious conflict. I found it difficult to handle because of my own confusion. We believed firmly in keeping our money separate, paying for our own clothes, and meeting our own children's expenses. Yet we gave each other presents and easily shared common expenses that made sense. But I was very sad when I learned he didn't intend to mention me in his will. We had been together by this time for seven or eight years, and I felt I had been his wife in every sense of the word except for the legal paper. Legally I was now his common-law wife. He had grown through the relationship, as I had. He had become very successful in the agency, becoming a vice-president and owning a great many shares in the company. His advancement and his happiness could have been attributed to his solid relationship with me. I was a favorite of everyone in his firm who had seen him go through hell and almost destroy himself in his previous marriage. Yet his reasoning was, "You are a strong woman, able to take care of yourself."

It bothered me that he felt he could leave me out of the will because I was competent. I felt I was being penalized. I retorted, "Did it ever occur to you that I'm getting older and it might make me feel more secure to know I don't have to work at such a pace all my life. Don't you want to take care of me, even for emotional reasons?" I made it clear that I expected him to take care of his children, but there was a fair formula. I also felt the house should be left to me. "Why? You'd never live here, you hate the suburbs," he said. "No," I snapped, "and neither will your children. They told you they don't want the house, but I would feel safer if anything happened to you. I would hate to be at the mercy of your ex-wife, who has such influence over your children. I could use it as income property. At any rate, if we ever broke up, you could easily change your will. I don't want anything monetarily from you if we aren't living together."

This took many years for us to sort out, and I always felt the shadow of his ex-wife, as if a little piece of me was chipped away. But it was undoubtedly the women's movement and the airing of issues and the rhetoric that was being put into place that helped us deal with our problems so successfully.

We even approached our sex life as partners. Steve was a naturally passionate man but was still reserved in his lovemaking. He so openly loved being with me that I found it easy to sit and talk with him about my feelings. I sat down with him one evening and asked him to read a book with me that described different techniques in making love. The book discussed these techniques in an academic, non-threatening way. It described all positions, including oral sex between two consenting adults, as normal. I told Steve that he should only do what was comfortable for him, but that I enjoyed all the lovemaking they talked about. Typical of Steve, once he had the information the floodgates opened. His natural passion exploded into a completely happy, enjoyable partnership. Evidently he had not found that freedom with his former wife. Our lovemaking became more spontaneous, joyful, a very important part of our life.

We loved going out together, but we also enjoyed the quiet evenings at home when we just held hands and watched television together or when he puttered and I retreated to my study to write. I liked the luxury of napping after dinner, of being silent after an intense day of interviewing, of just being cuddled, held, and kissed. I liked the process of nurturing a relationship, of our growing to enjoy each other more. He was also a wonderful dancer. Sometimes I think I married men because they danced so well. Dancing is like an aphrodisiac to me. Lately, the medical profession has explained that exercise and dancing release calming endorphins, the calming chemicals that produce a natural high. I get high on dancing—the same high doctors say you get from jogging or lovemaking.

I was ready for a more stable time, a time without excesses, a time to concentrate on my family and my career. Steve shied away from confrontation, had a good sense of his own identity, and was very straightforward. The things he couldn't handle emotionally were all out in the open. Actually, it was his ungrudging support and his actual understanding of my work that allowed me to concentrate on my career for the first time. Whatever our problems were at the time, he gave me what I needed, and I opened up another world for him. He never resented the time I spent writing, being on the air, traveling for my shows, or covering hundreds of events each month. It left me available to accept all the radio and television shows that were offered. I was lecturing, writing a syndicated column for a newspaper and a column for a national magazine, as well as completing a series of consumer books. I never had to look for work. My reputation as an investigative reporter, a flamboyant personality, and a woman with intense drive opened up all the doors in Canada. I accepted all the work offered and found ways to spin off all my talents and recycle my information and interviews. I rationalized that in that business, when you are "hot," you need to keep the momentum going. There is always the fear that tomorrow may be "dry." I also knew that I was the sole support of my teen-agers, and I convinced myself that I had to make enough money to supply them with the lifestyles and the education they deserved. It wasn't done out of guilt. I wasn't using money to substitute for love, but I'm sure I was over-compensating for the fact they did not have a father around to help either financially or emotionally. In addition, it concerned me that I might become a statistic, part of the "poor," women who were left without pensions, without nest eggs, without investments, in spite of the fact these women had made contributions to comfortable lifestyles when they were married.

At last I had enough money to take care of my needs and to feel that my children were taken care of. It had happened to me in seven years, in the seven years I had been in Canada, but maintaining my position and my high income meant constantly fighting to stay on top. To do this, a woman had to be twice as good as a man—especially a foreigner, a New Yorker.

CHAPTER 24

FINDING THE NET

While I had ungrudging support from Steve for my career, I felt I had to give almost all my energy to developing that career. I had to be very alert, as if I was walking gingerly through a minefield. Some of my male colleagues seemed concerned about the amount of air time I had, about my salary (how they found out what it was I don't know), and about my freedom to come and go. They envied my ability to write news stories, features, and entertainment reviews. To listen to them, what I did was all play and no work, a glamorous job. I had no patience with their attitudes and spent no time explaining that I came into the office earlier than necessary, sometimes at seven in the morning, just to do the research, the writing, and the planning so I would be free to go out and be seen and cover the events and openings at night that I thought important. The executives never challenged my right to do it my way, but I always heard the newsmen barking at my heels. Sometimes a manager would retreat on a promise, a larger office or a bookcase, "until the men calm down." I was also advised to be patient about being placed on the executive board "because the newsroom men couldn't handle a woman on the board." I railed at those excuses. "Since when does an executive make decisions about the company based on the fears and insecurities of the staff?" At one point another executive suggested that I might ease the situation by asking some of the men out for a beer, "getting more chummy with them." I answered, "Tell me how that will help. I don't like beer. I can't talk 'jock' language and somehow most of these men can't deal with women as friends. It always turns to sex."

In fact, when I asked the sports editor to have a drink with me to discuss some of the problems, his answer was, "I don't think it's a good idea for us to be seen together having a drink. The men will think we have an affair going." I laughed and unwittingly said, "Do you really believe they would think I'd have an affair with you? Are you trying to tell me that a man can't have a business meeting with an employee?" I was also told the men were threatened by me, and when I asked for an explanation the same executive said, "Lynne, face it, you are highly motivated, aggressive, outspoken, tough-minded, a perfectionist. You come from New York. It's a lot for them to handle. They are nervous about you."

I shook my head in disbelief. "I'm sorry, I don't understand. I have no clout. I can't fire them. I have absolutely no power in this organization, not even to getting the office that was promised to me as the head of my own small department because they might not like it. Why do I have to suffer for their low self-image?" I always thought it was a problem because I was a woman. I know now that men suffer some of the same problems and have the same hurdles to overcome in the executive offices as women. There is no doubt that the problem is magnified for women.

The difficulties were especially tough at the beginning of my career in Canada because I was one of the few women in broadcasting to be so visible on every front. In 1967, there was as yet no strong, visible women's front. Very few of the men would show me how to edit my tapes, do the mechanical cutting. I had always had an editor do my work, and now I was supposed to get the story, do the feature, write the material, and splice the tape. I struggled with it myself, working standing up in the newsroom at the tape decks with speakers blasting, praying no one would accidentally wipe my tape when I had to leave for a moment to take a telephone call. There was so much going on in the newsroom, and reporters and editors had to deal with so much information coming over the wires, that any unguarded tape could have easily been grabbed for an incoming story. I would turn in fury whenever it happened, hours of work erased. There was one reporter who laughed when I was angry and found it easy to goad me. Only once did I revert to the street fighter I was when I was ten years old. I was particularly frustrated. I grabbed that reporter by his tie and tightened my hand against his neck and, without thinking, said, "If you ever bother me again while I'm working, I am going to knock you straight through the wall." I suddenly realized that a startled male was looking warily at me while my hand was raised and my fist clenched ready to let go. There was a sudden calm in the newsroom. I let go of his tie and walked away. He never bothered me again.

I discovered then that I had to be more selective about sharing my enthusiasm for my own stories with my colleagues. I knew I couldn't change my personality and decided I didn't want to curb my excitement at tracking down stories, but I had to be aware that not everyone was as interested in my exploits as I was. I decided to concentrate more on getting my ideas into motion and give up looking for approval from everyone. But I was also aware that I could never rest with one format. I wanted to create dependence on my shows and my ideas, so that I could carve out as secure a place for myself as possible while weaving and running to my goals without bumping into too many people along the way.

Even my many ideas threatened some program managers. I would get reactions like "Don't you have enough to do without coming up with ideas for more work?" That statement came from a program manager who didn't want to carry the ball to the top. It meant fighting for an idea; it might mean confrontation with his immediate boss; it could mean rocking the boat. I had to learn how to get my ideas to top management without seeming to go above the program manager's head. Another manager snapped, "This is not a magazine. Why are you knocking yourself out doing so many features?" I tried to calm him by assuring him, "I get all the assignments done. Why are you concerned about the extra time I put in doing stories that excite me? You need the air time filled." For the first few years I covered the community and did interviews with a variety of people, from politicians and economists to educators and celebrities. Then I sensed that there was a new consumer movement taking hold. I analyzed what was happening and realized that there was little information for the consumer, that for years the only advice was *caveat emptor,* let the buyer beware, but no information. The federal and provincial governments took a bold step and set up a Consumer Protection Bureau across the country and a Consumer Department in Ontario. In fact, each province established its own counterpart of the federal model. I decided to present the executive board with an idea I had for a consumer show that was different.

I wasn't at all interested at the time in doing a consumer show based only on products. I discovered that most consumers were kept from complaining by a variety of tactics—lack of information, unfamiliar trade jargon, the labeling of complainers as neurotics and troublemakers. I knew, as well, that the consumer was used to being blamed for being cheated, a case in which the victim carried the burden. "If they weren't so greedy, they wouldn't get caught. If they didn't have larceny in their souls, they would know they were being taken." I felt that was nonsense. The cards were all stacked against the consumer at that time. The new protection bureaus would be a start. I reasoned that I would have to attack from another angle if consumers always blamed themselves for being cheated of money. Consumers were always saying, "I should have known better," or "We were afraid to make waves or get someone fired just to get our money back." I decided that I would have to broaden the whole idea of consumerism. I would prove to consumers that they were losing money not only because they lacked proper information or were subjected to misleading advertising or fraudulent schemes that were unchecked by proper legislation, but also that they were ripped off emotionally. If I could show them that every transaction had an emotional factor, and that they were being cheated of dreams, of health, of the ability to take charge of their own lives, then I could motivate them to action. So I planned to draw up a presentation that would not only talk about products but also discuss the purchase of services from professionals like doctors, lawyers, bankers, accountants, and the like. The consumer was buying their services and had the right of full disclosure.

I was excited about my plans for a consumer show and asked for two weeks from my regular duties to prepare a proper presentation. At first the program manager was wary. "Why don't you just call the Better Business Bureau and get some advice?" I retorted, "They are probably the last I would call. They are still an association of companies. They may help the consumer, but they still need to be monitored." I worked feverishly for the next two weeks, using my background in advertising, and with Steve's help I prepared a professional brief that outlined, step by step, the reason for the consumer show, the benefit to CKEY, the contacts I had already gathered, and the experts I would call upon. I then listed about two dozen subjects I thought I would tackle immediately and then requested an assistant and equipment to back up my long-term plans. I photocopied half a dozen of the briefs, prepared visuals to show samples of story ideas, and called for a board meeting.

Radio executives are not used to ideas being presented so formally. They were impressed, though somewhat bewildered by my approach, which was so extensive. At first there was some resistance to supplying an assistant and a telephone-answering number, which would take the flood of consumer calls I expected. "Why don't you wait until the show proves successful?" I answered rather brusquely, "It must be successful. I have worked it out." The program manager thought I was suggesting that it was his responsibility, but I assured him that I meant I would make it successful. I pleaded that I had to start off properly, not limp along. I reminded them that it was an old truism in the theater that you must grab your audience from the beginning and then you have them with you.

If I wasn't prepared in the best way possible, with the best product (my consumer show, in this instance), it would take longer to build an audience, and that audience might never come back. At least, statistics showed that it was harder to win back an audience than grab them right from the start. Finally there was an agreement, air time was programmed, and "The Consumer Desk with Lynne Gordon" was established. It became an almost immediate success.

I spent day and night investigating stories, going undercover, researching difficult areas, interviewing experts and people under attack. The cornerstone of my show was my intensive research not only to find out the facts but also to make sure I understood the language as well as the jargon used in the trade. You could have all your facts right but describe some product or service incorrectly and the focus would be on that mistake, immediately diminishing the effectiveness of the accurate facts. I spent hours with a group of automobile mechanics who were trying to clean up their image. The new group was called SAM, Society for Automotive Engineers. I asked if the words "grease monkey" were derogatory, foisted on them by an angry public, or if they in fact called themselves "grease monkeys" in an approving manner. Yes, they did, according to the president of SAM. I examined and explained terms like "bait and switch" and the methods used to "reel in suckers," using off-the-record remarks by willing con men. (Converted con men are an excellent source of information.)

I became a Canadian Ralph Nader, although I preferred to call myself an advocate rather than an activist. I saw myself as a liaison son between government, business and professional communities, and consumers. My thrust was to attack whole areas rather than any individual business. I felt it was important for the consumer to learn the questions to ask before making a purchase or a decision to buy a service. I wanted people to learn how to help themselves. As a result, I would examine broad issues rather than zero in on specific companies, as do the "action-line" columns. Action-line columns in newspapers have a function, but it is usually limited to helping a particular consumer with a specific problem. The writer of the action line fills the role of yet another authority figure.

My idea was that consumers have enough faith in themselves to take the responsibility for their problems, once armed with information. So my emphasis was on an industry or a profession. If a consumer wanted dance lessons, I was not interested in singling out a problem with one dance studio but in talking about the problems that could crop up in any dance studio. No matter where a consumer went for dance lessons, there were certain questions he or she should ask of any company. One major dance studio had been thrown out of the United States for fraudulent practices but opened in Canada. Consumers signed up with the Canadian studio because they trusted the individual instructor who sold them their contracts. What they didn't know was that the company—in fact, other companies, too—used shabby merchandising tactics, selling long-term package deals, and overlapping contracts hiding the costs of private lessons among group lessons and parties. Some dance studios were blinds for dating services. My practice was to interview a minimum of three people—a businessman or professional, a government representative, and a consumer activist in that field. When necessary I approached experts in related fields. I then presented the pros and cons of each feature, added my own editorial opinion, and allowed the consumer to make the decision about his or her purchase of a product or a service.

I felt the Consumer Show would have longevity if each show ended on an upbeat note: these are the facts, this is the reality, but here are the possible solutions. I gave a great deal of credit to the newly formed government consumer bureaus for the information they gathered, so they were well publicized. The Consumer Show was responsible for making me a high-profile broadcaster. I was respected for opening a new area, for my extensive research, and for my fair approach to each industry by making sure not to tarnish an entire group because of some bad members. As a result, other job offers came pouring in. I was asked by Jack McClelland of McClelland and Stewart to write a consumer book based on the research gathered for my radio shows. My first consumer book was called *99 Commercial Rip-Offs and How to Spot Them.*

I was called one day at CKEY by a brusque-sounding man who barked over the phone, "My name is Rafael Markowitz. I'm preparing a consumer show for Global Television and I want you as my host." There were no preliminaries. I was tempted to ask him for his credentials but some inner voice warned me that he might be important. I met Rafael Markowitz, who changed his first name as often as he changed his image. He had started out as Randy Dandy, host of a children's show, and became Raoul, Randy, and Rafael as his direction changed from performer to director to producer and idea person for television. He had some success with game shows and now was acting as an independent producer for Global Television, which had just acquired a license to go on the air. Markowitz lost no time in showing me his concept for the television show, which he had evidently based on my radio show. I was taken off guard by his blunt and high-pressure manner. He wanted me to look at the concept for twenty-six, half-hour shows and make a decision at once. He said he would be the producer and be responsible for getting the staff. I could have a budget for researchers and choose my own. I would write and do the major research and perform as host. He agreed to my demand that I receive assistant-producer credit as well as writer and performer credit and the corresponding salary. That was the only way I would receive anywhere near the right amount for my work. Even then I would have been smarter to have had an agent, but so much work came to me directly that I never had time to get one, or even to find one who knew my field as well as I did.

But I hadn't checked out Markowitz's track record. I might have found out that he was a true wheeler-dealer who knew how to cut corners at everyone's expense and could bring in a show at almost any budget required by the station but at great expense to the people he hired. I thought everything was clear between us when he signed me up to do a total of thirty-three shows. There would be twenty-six the first year and the rest would be back-up. I thought I could easily handle thirty-three subjects, each of which would include interviews with two or three people to give some dimension to the arguments on both sides, as well as time for people-in-the-street interviews and visuals on the subject.

I signed the contract after agreeing to the credits and the sum, and then found out much to my anger that he had decided to divide each half-hour program into three separate segments, all having the same elements we discussed for the half-hour show. Now there would be ninety-nine subjects to cover, and more than triple the interviews to fill those segments. I was furious and felt cheated. I insisted that I should have been paid more for the increased workload, but he pointed out the contract was signed. I decided to make the best of a bad situation and immediately began gathering all my consumer shows and the material and research I had done for radio, so they could be used as resource material for television. This was the only way so many shows could have been produced. In fact, I had used that material for my consumer book, so I was able to handle the variety of jobs and outlets by "spinning off" the work I had already collected.

It was quite an experience working for Rafael Markowitz. He was the combination of a Hollywood director, as epitomized in the Marx Brothers comedies, and a con man. He nervously puffed a cigar and wore a white or a black safari suit, depending on his mood. He boasted that he had a number of identical safari suits so that his image never changed. He worked his staff through the night to provide me with proper cue cards because he wouldn't pay for a teleprompter. He made sure the staff went out and shot plenty of visuals and people-in-the-street comments. He assembly-lined the shows, so that each day I was locked into one small studio, having my interviews funneled in to me, five minutes at a time. I had prepared five questions for each interviewee. Some-times only a minute or two would be used, and then the next person would be ushered in. It made no difference whether they were famous celebrities, busy doctors, rushed politicians; they all waited in an anteroom for their turn. Sometimes I did fifteen short interviews in a day. Then I would supervise the editing for hours afterwards. When it came time to package the shows, Markowitz decided to save studio time by having me do all my costume changes on the set so that the jacket I wore became important. What I wore underneath did not matter because a desk hid me from the waist down. All we changed from time to time were jackets, scarfs, and jewelry. He placed the camera in one position so that I read all the "intros" at one time for about seven shows, then the "extros," and then the middle of the features. Because I had written all the material and understood it, there was no problem in reading out of sequence. I didn't get paid properly for all this extra work, but I learned some valuable lessons in how to assembly-line, how to produce a show economically.

I began to be written about in columns; articles were written about my "rise to fame," about my drive, about my energy, and about the fact that I seemed to thrive on challenges. I was offered a syndicated column on consumerism in the *Sun* syndicate and a column in *Homemaker's Magazine.* I was asked to lecture to professional and industry groups on consumerism. I had a high profile in a number of areas, which caused Stu Brandy, sales manager at CKEY, to say proudly, "You are a multi-media person. You perform well on every level." I was delighted to hear that because I knew I had taken risks in extending myself to other media. I was successful in radio, but if I hadn't done well in television, it could have tarnished my image and reflected on my value at 'EY. I had a great need to meet all these challenges, and I was able to draw on all my experiences as a writer, actress, and researcher to accomplish what I wanted. So while I was working very hard, there wasn't a great deal of anxiety about what I was doing, although I made a great effort to juggle all my work so that no one could complain that I was neglecting the job I was being paid for. Actually, my success in television added to my prestige as a radio personality and made me an even more salable product for the radio station. They felt they benefited from my constant exposure to the community.

Through all this I insisted on keeping the weekend radio shows for my lifestyle and entertainment beats. At first the executive resisted. "Lynne, you don't need to bother with that soft area any more. You have a reputation now as a tough, authoritative consumer editor. Don't water it down with the weekend shows." I insisted. "I need those shows to keep my hand in a field where I have collected so many contacts and because I enjoy doing the shows so much. The entertainment industry is vital to every community. Trust me to keep that separate, just on weekends."

Luckily, I was allowed to do so because, years later, I was able to turn, as I wished, from the heavy-duty area of consumerism to lighter work as a national entertainment editor and travel reporter. My reputation was also responsible for my being invited as a guest on many television shows to discuss my work in consumerism.

My television shows received excellent reviews from the newspaper critics, and all was going smoothly until Global ran into financial difficulties. As a result, management changed and Global found it more economical to employ a consumer person rather than produce an independent half-hour show with contract people. But I was hired by the new program manager to continue on Global with my own five- or ten-minute show each night. The format didn't allow for much time to get visuals, but I still managed to include interviews and editorial opinion. Even there my experience with Markowitz helped me manage my time productively. I talked Global into videotaping my daily consumer features in two chunks of time, twice a week, two hours a shot. This eliminated the time wasted each day in traveling to and from the studio, applying make-up, assembling lighting people and camera personnel. I proved to them that the arrangement would be much more cost-effective and I could plug in my tape recorder to get the same interviews for my daily radio show. By cutting the video and audio tapes differently, the interviews would not only sound different, they would be different. It would save me time digging up separate interviews or interviewing the same persons twice.

Sometimes I would be criticized for taking on so much work. The assumption was that I must love money. At first I felt sensitive to the criticism and resented a column written by a well-known CBC producer, Ross McLean, who said there are some new pushy broads in town and one of them is Lynne Gordon from New York City. I had never met the man, didn't know what he meant by pushy, had never taken any job that I hadn't actually created, so no one could say I pushed him or her out of a job. Then McLean saw me working the telephones for a telethon. At a party he called me over to apologize. "I'm sorry I said something unfair about you. You are not pushy. You energize a situation." I thanked him but realized I had not changed. His perception of highly motivated women had changed. He had grown up.

I was aware that enough money would come in only if I worked doubly hard, and my independence could be protected only if I didn't have to depend on any one source for my livelihood. In the business in which I found myself, I realized that you took everything offered. Tomorrow was an unknown quantity. Regularly though, I would sit down and take stock, make sure I wasn't a workaholic or someone who was "running," so that I wouldn't have to face other unresolved areas. I also wanted to make sure that I had the right amount of time for Steve. When I found that I was even cautious about holding his hand because I didn't have time for lovemaking, I knew that I had to reassess my priorities, because no matter what show I was doing, what medium I was working in, the structure of my show was such that any pressure I felt was only the pressure I imposed on myself. I was so highly motivated that I was never given any direction by any superior. Sometimes I missed the fact I wasn't part of a team, that I worked so much alone. I needed feedback, I hungered for applause, but I was also grateful that no one interfered, and I know that not getting a great deal of feedback meant there was little criticism. So I accepted that state as positive.

I certainly used Steve as a sounding board and would go non-stop at home, filling him in on all the day's activities, talking about the problems, the victories, the concerns. He would ask the right questions, lead me on to explain more, and allow me to vent all my feelings at home, always interjecting the right soothing word, the professional assessment as he saw it, and the comforting assurance that he was totally on my side. I was and am a non-stop talker, but one day I saw his eyes glaze over and I realized that he was beginning to turn off. I stopped talking and said, "I have a sneaking feeling that all your training as a good salesman, an account executive, has made you act as a willing listener, and you almost unconsciously egg me on with your well-placed questions. Do me a favor. For the sake of our relationship, either limit your questions or if I go on too long just tell me simply to shut up. I can handle that." He seemed relieved and said that it would be great if I meant it because he hated to stop me, but he could just handle so much emotion in one chunk.

I was aware that while Steve was very warm and agreeable, he was also reserved when it came to talking about his personal feelings or his work. I had begged him to include me in his day-to-day problems, but he was adamant that "a man does not bring his work home." It took me a long time to convince him that he was not less a man because he talked about things that upset him. He should allow me to share in his concerns as I did with him. While my career was rocketing ahead, I was given an unexpected tribute by the Ontario government by being chosen one of twenty-five outstanding women in the province. My obsessive concern about teaching people to care for themselves, with special emphasis on women's needs, was responsible for the honor, which was offered in 1975 to mark International Women's Year. I was pleased, and a proud Steve Evans accompanied me to the ceremony. I was somewhat concerned about my excessive joy. I guess I looked upon the award as the final stamp of approval for Lynne Gordon. I was still, in a way, trying to prove I was worthwhile.

CHAPTER 25

BEHIND THE HEADLINES

O nly my closest friends in Canada knew anything about my past life, my marriage to John Henry Faulk, the blacklisting, or the lawsuit for libel. From 1967, when I came to Canada, to the mid-1970s, I was a woman with a new identity. I hadn't made a conscious effort to hide but I had nurtured a subconscious desire to forget the anguish I suffered throughout my divorce from John Henry. Having been given the name "Gordon" for professional reasons, my anonymity was almost guaranteed.

Then I received a call from a friend in New York who told me that CBS was planning to air a documentary on John Henry and the blacklisting. They were calling it *Fear on Trial* because it was based on the book of the same name written by John Henry in 1963. My friend sent me the publicity material that was being released about the upcoming, made-for-television movie. The releases referred to the show as "the true story of the blacklist; one man's ordeal and the famous libel trial; not one word changed!" The material pointed out that the documentary (it was *not* called a docu-drama) was going to be aired by CBS in a sort of attempt to right past wrongs, an act of reparation, a *mea culpa*.

I asked my friend to check with CBS and find out if the story of the family was going to be included or whether it was just the trial. She was told that it only focused on the trial. The timing was uncanny, since it had been only a few weeks before that I had spoken to the publisher Jack McClelland about writing a book about that part of my life, thinking that my past experiences and my methods of survival might be relevant to other women. I then spoke with Anna Porter, McClelland and Stewart's editor-in-chief, who said compassionately, "Lynne, are you sure you want to dig up the past again? Can you survive the pain?" I answered that I had lived through that period once and had survived. Anna replied, "But then you had no choice, or you thought you had none." Strangely enough, even the choice of reviewing the past was taken from me when the news of the television movie plunked the past right in my lap.

I decided that this was the perfect time to tell a group of friends about my life in New York and Texas. I was very proud of my contribution to the libel suit, and the documentary would give me the perfect opportunity to talk about it without dredging up the painful details of the divorce. To celebrate the evening, I planned a small party for about thirty friends. I invited them to an evening at the Park Plaza, where I rented a private room for viewing the show. I planned a huge buffet and lots of chilled champagne. All I told my friends was that they would see an exciting evening of television, a new documentary on a very important period in recent American history, and that at the end of the evening I would have some surprise announcements to make. Most of my friends were very interested in that period and also looked forward to seeing a documentary with George C. Scott playing Louis Nizer and William Devane playing John Henry, the blacklisted performer.

I was delighted that at last the trial was going to get that kind of exposure, never expecting to be included in the film, since no one had contacted me about anything. I was also realistic enough to know that any mention of a wife might be downplayed, since John Henry and I were now divorced. I discovered that a local station was going to jump the gun and show the documentary on Wednesday, before the scheduled CBS première on Thursday. Steve and I decided to watch the early showing together, so I would be free to be an attentive hostess during the party instead of staying glued to the set. I settled down, hardly able to breathe as the story unfolded. But after a few moments, I was almost jolted out of my chair when a young woman appeared on the scene, evidently supposed to be me. I watched as the actress, Dorothy Tristan, appeared in a bedroom scene with John Henry as played by Devane. She had just returned from an outing with her children and greeted her husband warmly, throwing her arms around his neck and kissing him tenderly. For one brief second

I felt tears of joy as I thought I was going to be included more prominently after all. I had waited a long time for this recognition.

But my pleasure was short-lived. Immediately the dialogue indicated the woman was a selfish bitch who resented her husband's interest in politics. The next thirty or forty minutes were spent developing the story to show that the wife, called "Laura," was leaving her husband to fight the blacklist unemployed and alone. The next scene depicts in ten seconds seven years of our life together as a memory flashing through his mind. He sits staring into space, saying over and over again, "I'm all alone. I'm all alone." As he mouths those words, you see him driving a taxi, which he never did. The film then catapults the viewer into the actual trial. No credit is given to all the friends who helped and gave money. Nor is there any credit for the wife who supported the family for seven years. The years in Texas were erased. The film gave us two, not three children, both daughters, leaving out our son, even denying him his place in the family.

For two hours I watched the show in an almost catatonic state. What unnerved me were my feelings of vulnerability, my sense of frustration. I had hoped that this documentary would be a bridge to the past, a grand gesture settling old debts, soothing open wounds, laying ghosts to rest, a gift to my children, something they could share and be proud of. I had hoped it would pave the way for my children to find their father, somewhat more mellow, a little older, and perhaps more accessible. Believing that, when I heard about the film, I had encouraged my daughters to reach out and try to meet with their father. Perhaps by making the first gesture they could find a common ground to walk upon.

I cried in Steve's arms that night. He comforted me, hurting for me and understanding my pain. I felt under attack, betrayed again by John Henry, who had evidently been a technical adviser; by David Rintels, the screenwriter; by Lamont Johnson, the director; by Stanley Chase, the producer; and by all the executives at CBS who had found it so easy to subvert the truth to hurt me and my children. It was difficult to understand how men who were fighting the blacklist could indulge in the worst kind of blacklisting themselves. How could they rationalize reverting to the destructive, time-worn cliché of a woman leaving her man in time of need, particularly when the reverse was true? The facts about the trial were a matter of public record. How could they do such a hatchet job on me as a woman, and indirectly on all women?

My first reaction was to cancel the party. How could I face my friends? I was embarrassed at the portrayal and shuddered at the thought of having to explain the truth as I had done for so many years during the blacklisting. Do I show everybody the book *Fear on Trial,* pointing to the truth; do I dig up old magazine articles, especially one in *Look* magazine that quotes Louis Nizer talking about my bravery and about how in a libel suit it's the wife and children who suffer the most? Do I prove I was in Texas with photographs of our home and my advertising and publishing office? Do I bring in all the articles celebrating the victory, showing John Henry and me in close embrace and my reaction that the verdict and award were the best fourteenth-anniversary present we could have received?

I knew there was no turning back. I had to host the party. But I did decide to bring the book, the *Look* article, and all the newspaper accounts of the trial. By the time of the party, I was a little more in control of my emotions. I announced at the beginning of the television show that, while I didn't want to influence their opinion of the documentary, I had some facts to set straight. Then I told them that Lynne Gordon was Mrs. John Henry Faulk and that I had lived through the ordeal and the trial they were going to see on film. I pointed out that I had seen the "special" the evening before and that it had some gross distortions and lies. I suggested that those who wished could glance at some of the material I had brought, before the show started, and then make up their minds about the treatment. My announcement created a buzz of excitement. There were incredulous comments about my secret past, and then everyone settled down to watch the show with interest, now fully aware that there was a drama on and off the screen.

That evening I realized that the climate of opinion had changed a great deal in the last dozen years. Whatever happened, I was not alone and unprotected. There were twelve years between myself and the woman who had divorced John Henry. In that time I was able to form a large circle of friends, establish a career in a foreign country, and maintain a warm and rewarding relationship with my two daughters and son, now in their twenties. The outspoken remarks of my friends as they watched the film were revealing and helped to clarify my thinking. Steve sat quietly in the background. My daughter Evelyn was there for support since Johanna and Frank were out of town. I worried about their reactions most of all.

As the film unfolded, there were hoots and hollers as my family and friends heard the wife Laura say she wasn't interested in politics. I was famous in Canada for my outspoken remarks and heavily publicized stands on many social and political issues, so there was almost unanimous reaction against the portrayal of the wife. Both my male and female friends felt it was shallow, contrived, and out of touch with today's attitudes. Evidently the screenwriter felt that the role of John Henry would be diminished if the truth was shown that he was dependent on his wife for financial as well as emotional support. Some expressed the thought that the lie negated the entire documentary, since it had been extensively promoted all through the United States and Canada as "the daring truth." One article quoted George C. Scott as asking if he could change a sentence only to be told, "No, not one word." Xerox was the sponsor, and a fortune was spent on its production and promotion.

I asked one producer at the party, who personally knew David Rintels, the screenwriter, how the man could be so out of touch. Didn't he realize that the true story of a family struggling together was more dramatic than the story told? How could a screenwriter like Rintels, who was supposedly fighting to end all blacklists, blacken the reputation of another human being? The answer was simple and realistic. "Lynne, you make the mistake of many people. You think because Rintels is liberal in some attitudes that he is liberal in all his views. Sadly, many good men are all screwed up where women are concerned, and Rintels has his hangups. Besides, he's not a very conscientious writer. If he had any sensitivity, he would have contacted you. What he did was unconscionable."

I spent the next month trying to decide what action to take. It was soon common knowledge that Lynne Gordon was the former Mrs. John Henry Faulk, and I was concerned about the effect this piece of information could have on my business associates and the public. After all, I couldn't go around tugging at elbows saying, "You know, the film you saw, well the part about me is untrue." I asked for advice and was surprised by what I received. A friend who had always appreciated my flamboyance and openness re-acted with some anger at the thought that I might launch a lawsuit against the producers of the television film. "Lynne," he said, "if you hadn't told everyone who you were, it wouldn't have mattered." I was amazed, and shot back, "Are you trying to tell me that the only part of my life that counts is the few years I've been in Canada? Don't you think I have friends, family in the States? I pretended my past didn't exist when I took the name Gordon, and never confronted my past or even talked about it. That was probably a big mistake. I have a history to hand down to my children. I am not just Lynne Gordon. It's time to get in touch with myself and my past."

I went to a very powerful lawyer in town to talk about suing, and his opinion was, "Oh, Lynne, what does it matter. If you sue you'll be looked upon as a bitch trying to get publicity, a neurotic woman who has a vendetta against her ex-husband." I looked bewildered. "My God, I'm talking about an injustice. I'm talking about libel. I'm talking about all women who are made stereo-typical classic bitches. I'm talking about *my* name. Why should I be intimidated by chauvinistic men who would like to keep me powerless? No thanks. You have made me realize more than anyone else that I must sue." I was proud of the fact that my lawyer at the time, Jerry Grafstein, not only insisted that I sue to right a wrong but also offered to put me in touch with an excellent lawyer in New York, once I made up my mind.

The one other person I had to discuss the possible lawsuit with was Steve, who may have had more to lose if my suing would bring to light our live-in relationship. He was with a conservative adver-tising agency, and while they had accepted our relationship, I didn't know what would happen if it was brought out in headlines. I had no idea how it would affect his clients and his future. Steve had no problem with his advice. "You must do what is right, and it is right for you to stand up and be counted. That's the way you have behaved on every issue, and I'm proud of your track record. Don't stop now." That was all the encouragement I needed.

Just before I made the final decision, I had a call from Joyce Davidson, who was then married to the producer David Susskind and was hosting an interview show. We had been close friends throughout my marriage in New York. She was outraged at the television movie and asked if she could interview me. I was a little hesitant at first because I was trying to make up my mind about suing and I was concerned about saying anything that could prejudice the case, but Joyce had done her homework and had carefully prepared the interview. When we met she hugged me and told me she was glad to see me again and had wondered what had happened to me. The interview was a very comforting experience, as she carefully drew a picture of my past, my ideals, and my loyalty to any cause I believed in. We discussed the treatment of women in films and how easily their roles had been denigrated. She helped me set the record straight. She asked if I was going to sue and I said that was the last recourse. I would be happy if they would put a disclaimer on all future shows and make a public statement that my role was fictitious. She asked if I had spoken to Rintels or John Henry and I replied, "The damage was done. The fact is that they never called me before or since. I doubt that they would even take my calls." But I encouraged other interviewers to do their research and contact both of them. According to the researchers from other television stations, John Henry blamed Rintels and Rintels blamed John Henry, who was technical adviser. I told her that if I made a decision to sue, I would notify her immediately. I left the show with assurances of her support.

After the Joyce Davidson show was aired, a listener of mine called me at the office and what she said touched me a great deal. She called me to say she had seen the television film and accepted the fact that all women were unprincipled and would leave their husbands in times of need, but when she heard me explaining the lie on the interview show, the penny dropped and she was furious at the portrayal. Then, without realizing that she had turned her mind around full circle even as she spoke to me, she said, "Lynne, I have listened to you on your consumer show for years, and you are always fighting for the rights of people. When I heard you say that the woman portrayed on television was really you, I *knew* they lied about you, and that you could never behave like that." Then she added the most important part of her confession. "How dare they do that to *us*?" This woman so identified with me that she now became a supporter of all women. Something went click.

Reassurances came from many sources, as people became more aware of the film and my role. There were many heart-warming experiences, and one with Anne Jackson and Eli Wallach stands out in my mind. I met them in the lobby of the Royal

290

Alexandra Theatre in Toronto where they were shooting a film. At first I hesitated about striking up a conversation with them, since I had not seen them for years, although we had been neighbors in New York and shared many friends. But Anne saw me and rushed up to me. Eli Wallach came to join us and Anne reminded him who I was. I didn't know whether to bring up the film, but she went on to say, "We just saw the television show about your husband's libel suit. I'm so sorry. I know how hurt you must have been to see what they did to your role in the case. It must be terrible for you. It must have been terrible then. It was terrible for all of us." I smiled, a bit more relaxed, and thanked her for her concern and said, "I am thinking of writing a book about that period." She said eagerly, "Oh, Lynne, if you do a book, and it's made into a movie, please let me play the lead. We do look like each other. We do act the same. We are the same, aren't we . . . ?" It was the beginning of my opening up and making contact with past friends, friends I had ignored when I came to Toronto because of my bitter divorce.

All the male reviewers of the television show made bitter comments about the wife. Harry Waters of *Newsweek* wrote that John Henry Faulk's "marriage ruptures after he decided to fight back in court despite his wife's objections." He also reported that Faulk "ended up with a mere $75,000, most of which was eaten up by alimony payments." Ben Stein of the *Wall Street Journal* said, "Special credit should go to Dorothy Tristan, who plays Mr. Faulk's wife, and to David Rintels who wrote the script. Mrs. Faulk is played as an unprincipled, weak woman who tried to sabotage her husband when he needed her help. The myth that families always stand together in time of crisis deserves to be kicked around a little." *TV Guide* published an article by Louis Nizer about the drama and the real trial on which it was based. Why did he not warn the screenwriter about the lies? Since the film was billed as a documentary that rarely veered from the chilling facts, the reviewers felt they had the right to comment on the actions of a real character. How interesting that no one ever thought to check the film out against the book or that although numerous friends wrote indignant letters to all of the reviewers, including CBS, not one retraction was published.

The only concern about suing was that it would affect my children. In the final analysis the decision was mine. I promised the children that, no matter what happened, they would never be involved. I would not drag them into a court case. In fact, I had no desire to sue their father. "Whatever made your father allow the screenwriter to change my role, that is his problem, his sickness. I am more interested in all the others, who didn't know me, who had the verifiable facts at their fingertips, and who never had the courtesy or the sense to call me before production to sign a release form."

Jerry Grafstein, my lawyer, called former Federal Judge Simon Rifkind, a partner in the firm of Paul, Weiss, Rifkind, Wharton, and Garrison, one of the most respected law firms in the United States, and one of the few that wouldn't mind locking horns with Louis Nizer, if necessary. I went down to New York to meet Judge Rifkind and found him most emphatic. He assured me that my position was sound. He was ready to take it on a retainer but immediately told me that his firm was not willing to handle any phase of the matter that involved litigation. He thought it could be settled out of court and this appealed to me. After all, I still had nightmares about the seven-year-long libel trial. But it wasn't long after I hired Judge Rifkind's firm that it was evident that no one was interested in settling. It would have to go to trial.

Rifkin recommended Daniel J. Kornstein, a young lawyer who had been part of his firm and who now has his own office, Kornstein, Veisz, and Wexler. I was very impressed by that sensitive, insightful young lawyer, as he listened carefully to my appraisal of the case and my anguish of the last few months. He had the priceless ability to work easily with his colleagues. I felt I had the best team available and was completely trusting and happy in his hands. At first he suggested we go right ahead and sue, explaining that in New York they could take my case on a contingency basis, which meant they would receive one-third of the award, requiring from me only out-of-pocket expenses. If I decided to negotiate first, they would charge me a modest retainer. I asked them to negotiate, but again it wasn't long before we saw this was useless, that I would have to sue to get any response from the defendants.

And sue we did. I asked that John Henry be left out of the lawsuit unless he was absolutely necessary to my case. I felt it was important to keep it from looking like a husband-wife vendetta, and I also knew that John Henry would milk that for all it was worth. He thrived on lawsuits. It was enough that the case was Lynne Gordon vs. CBS, Inc., David Rintels, Alan Landsburg, Laurence D. Savadove and Stanley Chase. The complaint read "Plaintiff Demands a Trial by Jury." The complaint highlighted the hideousness of the lie and our planned discovery would have left no doubt that a gross act had been committed. There was no excuse for the damaging and unkind attack and there was no way that any of the defendants could explain their lack of communication with me, although they had contacted everyone else of importance to the script for permission. Perhaps they felt that a former wife who lived in another country would be unlikely to make a fuss or even care. We sued for $1.5 million on two counts of libel and one of invasion of privacy.

After the suit was launched, I slept well for the first time in months. I had been obsessed with the decision to sue. I could hardly talk about anything else. But my serenity was shattered when I received a call from Johanna, who was hysterical about a call she had just received from John Henry. It seems he had heard about my lawsuit and called Johanna. "You better tell your mother to call off her lawsuit or CBS will smear her to high heaven." I was furious at John Henry for calling Johanna and assured her, "I have no idea what your father is talking about. If he is concerned about me, he should have called me, not you. If he's trying to blackmail me into dropping the case, then his actions are unforgivable." "But mother," she sobbed, "this may ruin any chance I have of any kind of relationship with my father. He'll never talk to me again." I thought for a long time and then answered her very carefully, "Johanna, nothing I do, either good or bad, has had any effect on your relationship, or possible relationship, with your father. I have tried everything, even to pleading with him, to have him communicate with all of you as a father. Nothing helped. But more important, my darling, this action has nothing to do with you or the family. This is one decision I must make alone. I promise you that you won't be hurt. I won't be frightened by anyone, especially your father."

About the time I was planning to launch the lawsuit, I received a call from the office of William Davis, Premier of Ontario, asking me to consider taking the role of chairperson of the Ontario Status of Women Council. Laura Sabia, the first chairperson, was leaving the post in frustration at her inability to get action on women's issues. The position was considered a volunteer one. Compensation was eighty-five dollars a day for the chairperson, and sixty-five dollars a day for the council members, while sitting. The *per diem* was in sharp contrast to the two hundred and fifty dollars or more a day paid to other councils. The chairperson was supposed to operate at arm's length and not be influenced by party politics. How ironic that I should be offered a leadership appointment in the government just when I had so many decisions to make about my future. I wasn't sure that I wanted or needed to get involved politically when I had so much freedom to express my views as a journalist and broadcaster. I said I would think it over.

CHAPTER 26

THE WOMEN'S MOVEMENT

Throughout my life I have been involved in political and human rights issues, usually commenting on them as a journalist or joining forces with different groups on specific issues, but I have rarely been linked with any one political group. Over the years I have been consistent in my goals, unshakable in my beliefs, and able to move along as times changed without the restrictions imposed by a mandate. I have no quarrel with organizations, and without the concerted effort of many a tightly knit group, many gains would have been impossible.

I was very cautious about responding to the invitation to become the chairperson of the Ontario Status of Women Council. I felt I had enough freedom on my radio and television shows to discuss and fight for all the women's issues that were coming to the forefront. I was concerned that assuming the position would make me responsible to a wide variety of constituents—the many different women's groups, the different members of the political parties, and my radio and television audience.

Although many friends thought the job was prestigious and that I had been offered a plum, I saw it as adding to an already heavy workload. I was told by the government that the position would only take one day a month for meetings with the Council. Even then I knew better. If it took only one day a month, it would be a token nod at women's issues and I would want nothing to do with it. If it took more time then I was going to have to manage my time even more carefully to work this so-called volunteer position into my day. I saw it as a full-time position that was paid as a part-time or volunteer one. This was pretty typical for women, taking on work that demanded full-time attention for minimum or no pay. I wasn't even sure why I was being asked to take the position, since I had never been a card-carrying member of any party or group. I voted as I saw the issues. I also knew that Premier Davis knew of me as a scrapper, someone who had berated his own government on many issues in my role as journalist. In fact, when he was Minister of Education, I brought to his attention some of the problems in his ministry. At that time I had received a warm, congratulatory note for my work. I felt that he needed some credibility for the Council and was willing to take a chance on a strong independent voice.

I was also eligible for the position because I had recently become a Canadian citizen, much to the bewilderment of my Canadian friends. They asked, "How could you turn your back on your country? It's unusual for an American to become a Canadian. What do you have to gain?" I was shocked at the low image many Canadians have of their country and what it has to offer, but I explained, "I have not turned my back on my country. Actually my country is New York City, Manhattan. I still love New York with a passion, but I am suspicious of nationalists. I feel more international in spirit. I want to make a contribution to the country I'm living in. I want to vote. I want to become involved in issues. I have spent so much time in my broadcasts advising Canadians how to fight for their rights, how to fight the bureaucracy and the government, that I want to make sure no one can say, "If you don't like it, why don't you go back to New York!" I was also very happy in my career, and very much in love with Steve. I saw no reason why I wouldn't stay in Toronto for the rest of my life, only hoping to extend my work into New York, so I could go and visit more often.

I called the Premier's office back and said I had a lot of thinking to do before I took on such a heavy responsibility. For the next few weeks I put the problem out of my mind. Then one morning I had an urgent call from the Premier's office. I was told that the Premier was about to go into the House and wanted to present my name for approval. In fact, a political columnist, Norman Webster of the *Globe and Mail,* had just written a column suggesting that news had been "leaked" to him that I was first choice for the Council head. I felt pressured and somewhat manipulated, but I was appreciative of the fact that one should not embarrass the Premier. I asked for ten minutes to collect my thoughts. I immediately went to CKEY's executives, Doug Trowell and Stu Brandy, and repeated the story. "You have to make the final decision about my accepting the position. If you think it is prestigious and it will give me the kind of high profile that will be advantageous to the station, I will take it. But that means you will have to back me all the way. I anticipate spending a great deal of time on women's issues and time away from 'EY. I promise my work won't suffer, but I'll need the freedom to operate as I see fit to do the job properly." They encouraged me to take it and, in fact, were quite enthusiastic. I called back and accepted the position.

My name was put forward, it was accepted, and the announcement of my new role immediately brought forth headlines that questioned my credibility for the job, my lack of involvement in the women's movement. These attacks came from a small segment of the movement. "What groups has Lynne Gordon belonged to? Where does she stand on all the issues? Who is Lynne Gordon?" I guess I wanted to be valued for the contribution I had made. But to be absolutely fair, I could understand in retrospect the women's anger. I had never been able to act collectively. I had not been a formal member of any women's groups. There were certainly some excellent leaders within the groups who had worked tirelessly for the movement, and they were suspicious. A Conservative government had appointed me. Was I just being used as a buffer, someone to keep the women satisfied without kicking up too much trouble? The attacks rather surprised me. I had always thought of myself as a fighter for women's rights. I was one of the few journalistic broadcasters who attended all the press conferences on women's issues, interviewed every feminist, and covered the Council's activities. I had been nominated a Woman of the Year and had a long history of involvement in the civil rights movement. Small groups of women were banding together and holding press conferences about me. I had even heard the rumor that some of the women might be using the film *Fear on Trial* against me, not knowing that the role of the wife as portrayed was fictitious and that I was in the process of suing the producers. I was heartsick and wondered why I had not been approached by any of the attacking groups.

I was asked by the CBC to appear on a midday phone-in show to answer questions about my new role, and to be ready to answer questions on what I saw as the future of the Council. I knew that it was a set-up and that the first call to come in would be from one of my strongest opponents. But putting me on radio or television was like throwing a rabbit in the briar patch. It's my natural territory. I love the microphone, and I feel so much in tune with my audience that I honestly can "hear" the response. I was introduced as the new chairman—later I arbitrarily changed "chairman" to "chairperson"—and listeners were asked to call in and question me on policy. The first call was from one of my strongest opponents, whom I had never met. I had once tried to arrange a meeting with her but was told that, as she was part of a collective, she couldn't meet with me on her own. Now she was the first on the telephone questioning me. I immediately grabbed the microphone and said with great relief, "I'm delighted that you have finally decided to talk to me. I have never met you, never had a chance to answer all your charges, and I welcome this opportunity to tell you exactly where I stand on each and every issue you've raised." I then began listing the issues as I saw them. There was the need for child care, family-law reform, equal-pay legislation, increased pensions, remuneration for homemakers, regulations against sexual stereotyping in school texts, increased health care, and on and on. Her response was, "Well, we all agree on that." I laughed and said, "Then we have no problem," and again thanked her for at last getting in touch with me personally.

That show was so successful that I decided to go a step further and make appointments with the executives of all the diverse women's groups and take the time to state my position on all the issues, issuing a challenge that it was time for us to stand together. If I was not strong enough or knowledgeable enough on any issue, I counted on them to tell me so we could iron out our differences and consolidate. This strategy worked well because most of the groups had never had an official seek them out to make positions clear. Editorials, columns, and letters to the editor began to appear, giving me full support. Soon the negative attitude to my appointment changed and I began to receive more co-operation. June Callwood, a highly respected feminist and writer, answered some of the criticisms of me by suggesting, "It was a generational thing. Lynne's warm social style may have been seen as insincere by feminists who have a more austere image."

I think what June was referring to was also my flamboyant way of dressing and my use of make-up and jewelry. At that time women were trying to make the statement that being admired for one's physical charms puts one into a position of being treated as a sex object. Some of these political beliefs were based in opposition to Freud's theory that female narcissism is biological in origin. As a result, some women felt it was inappropriate to use makeup and added adornment. I certainly understood the political statement being made, but I felt I could make a personal choice about my own dress. I was in show business, I enjoyed theater dressing (even if some of it was based on old conditioning), and I did make my living as a television personality in a world that judges people on acceptable appearances. I felt, as a result, I could make the choice of what I would wear.

Today, there is certainly more flexibility in the women's movement and the battle in the United States for the Equal Rights Amendment has introduced many mainstream volunteer organizations into the fray, where they will stay because the economic issues have politicized them.

Without doubt, I felt like quitting every day for the first few months, because there was no much frustration involved with the job. But once I accepted the challenge, I wouldn't let go. About eighteen months later, things began to fall into place. I had a staff that began to understand my methods; I became familiar with all the women's groups and began to appreciate the roles of the different cabinet ministers. I was accessible to the press, went out many evenings to make speeches, planned conferences, and attended and ran joint council meetings all over the country. I was working the equivalent of full-time, juggling all my other work to fit. It was feasible because I had the kind of arrangement at CKEY that gave me complete freedom to organize my own time.

Taking a highly visible leadership position forced me to codify my thinking. I began to see that as much as I had done for the women's movement as a journalist, I had never been forced to do the kind of reading that was required of a leader under scrutiny all the time. I had to become familiar with the history of the women's movement, to read in depth on family law, understand why women over sixty-five were the poorest in our society, and face the fact that there were centuries of vested interests involved in keeping women at home as a cheap source of labor.

As head of the Council, I switched hats from interviewer to interviewee. I soon discovered there was so much I hadn't understood over the years. Like many women who married and then went to work and raised children alone, I thought I was independent. Yes, I was independent and I had to be, but I certainly was not liberated. While I cried out for understanding, for the right to work, for the right to share household duties as partners, that cry was an angry cry. I spent most of my time being angry, and still underneath it all feeling guilty. The reflection that came back to me from society was that I wasn't normal, that I was competitive, that I wasn't fulfilling my role as a mother should. I began to understand what women had been feeling all those years. I began to understand where John Henry and Alfredo had been coming from, the background that shaped these men. It helped channel years of anger into righteous indignation.

I realized that John Henry and I had never actually spoken to one other, for it was as if we spoke in different tongues. Not only was there a vast difference in our cultures, I had no idea how much of his personality and belief system was grounded in chauvinism. I don't think he knew how much he was the product of his conditioning, since he had spent so many years denying his upbringing. I knew that my hunger to go to work, to make use of my training, was acceptable and even applauded now, not just because I needed to make money, but because I had the right to pursue a career and to meet my own needs.

But women were still being fed the myth that there was a male protector for every woman. No one ever talked about the fact that love may bring people together but anger may drive them apart, and when they are driven apart, love flies out the window along with the rational talk about financial support payments. The women's movement wasn't pushing all women to go out to work. It was saying that rational decisions should be made jointly. If two partners decided that the woman should work inside the home, then some provision needed to be made for her contribution. Most important, women should be able to make an informed choice about working inside or outside the home. Family law should also ensure that when a woman lost a husband she didn't lose her share of the assets. Women had to be made aware that they should keep enriching and training themselves, so if they ever had to go into the labor force they were able to support themselves. Men did leave, did die, in some cases a second paycheck might be necessary, and some women might never marry. The women's movement gave me a vehicle to fight for legislation, to educate other women, to keep educating myself.

I learned to work within a group as chairperson of the Ontario Status of Women Council. I reminded the Council members that their first obligation when voting on policies was to improve the lot of women, and second, to their political party. I made that a strong statement so those on the Council who felt they had a political appointment would remember that we were supposed to be an independent body at "arm's length" from the party in power. I knew that I could be a strong leader. I had no ties with any political party. I had made no bargains, and I didn't care if I was removed from the Council by the party in power. I also knew instinctively that while I might make the politicians in power uncomfortable, they needed me to give voice to their stated aims to care about women.

I described one purpose of the Council in the 1982 annual report. "One of the most important mandates of the Council is educative—to hold public meetings, issue position papers, and discuss those issues affecting our lives as women. This educative function has been a two-way street, publicly and privately. During my terms as Chairperson of the Council, I have been afforded the rare opportunity to see, 'up close,' how the system works, to become familiar with the corridors of power, and along with the other members of the Council, have made every effort to de-mystify that system by helping women see and understand the connections that exist between seemingly disparate areas of concern." I noted, "The single most important lesson we have learned is that we can't do it alone. 'If I am not for myself, who is for me? And being for myself, what am I? If not now, when?' " I was quoting Hillel, the eminent Jewish scholar.

The Council was a place of meeting but it was also a place of action. It was extemely active putting forward practical recommendations. It issued briefs on at least twenty of the most pressing problems facing women today, specifically women and advertising, aging, battered women, change of name, child care, contract compliance, education, employment strategies, family law, health, housewives, immigrant women, non-traditional occupations, pensions, pornography, recreation, sex bias in textbooks, sports, widows' rights to family property, and women with special needs for monetary security.

The women's movement draws its members from fifty per cent of the population, which is awakening at different times. It includes an older generation of women who had battered their heads against immovable walls and had set down stern and unyielding guidelines. The old guard certainly accomplished a lot. They broke through the barrier of silence. It might be a choice not to marry or live with a man, but there are times when it makes sense to work with men to get the advances we need. There are informed men beginning to understand the need for change and willing to work with women. I saw society as the oppressor, not individual men, although I recognize some compromises are intolerable.

Steve enjoyed my new circle of friends. Although he had been traditional in his thinking, he was sensitive enough and curious enough to listen and to respond. He had no problem with strong women. He thought they were interesting, alive, and provocative. My involvement in the women's movement helped us to make use of our past experiences to explore the future. Although I had always fought in the past against injustice and considered myself a civil liberterian, like many others I lacked the perception and the rhetoric to realize that women were also an oppressed group. I had no framework for any feelings of outrage, no sense of being a member of any oppressed group and thus of needing a support system.

The position on the Council, which I took so reluctantly at first, was to last six years. I had been appointed for one three-year term but was then asked by Premier Davis to stay on for another three-year term. By now I was earning approval from the media, the government, and the opposition as well as from many women's groups. I felt stronger about myself. For me, the involvement in the women's movement was a personal triumph, a vast learning experience. I can never be grateful enough for all the positive experiences I had being close to active, concerned women. I know that nothing can stop individual women from growing, from moving on. I know that the movement itself will change, grow, and become more sophisticated as it reaches out to women all over the world.

I am very proud of the way my two daughters and my son took up women's causes and are so supportive of my work. I also find that by staying in close contact with them and having constant dialogue, I am kept in touch with all sides of the women's movement and find there doesn't have to be a generational gap. Rarely do we separate on any of the issues, sometimes only to the degree, but the excitement is in being on the same wavelength. Over the years our working together on our relationships and our sharing of common goals have helped us become so close that I revel in the absolutely sound relationships I have developed with my children. I not only feel loved by them but appreciated for myself. I often think that my children provided me with the least threatening relationships I have ever had, the most equal in give and take. It was not easy. It meant years of listening, not only with my ears but also with my heart.

Their sensitivity and interest in the world later propelled them into jobs where they could continue promoting their ideas. All three of them work with people. Evelyn went on to become an interpreter for the deaf, having paid her dues as a child-care care worker. She extended her interest to disturbed children, the handicapped, and finally the deaf community. Frank found he was ready to go back to school and hone his skills as a writer, his way of expressing his feelings and political views. His new dedication as a student, after years of continuing his education on his own, made him a star student at Ryerson Polytechnical Institute. Johanna has pursued her graduate studies and shows her concern for social issues by working in the field of adult literacy.

As I was taking charge as chairperson, my lawsuit was going full-steam ahead. It wasn't long before CBS, David Rintels, and all decided to settle out of court. I think the pre-trial questions made it clear that they had completely abused their roles as director, screenwriter, and producer. I was delighted with the outcome. It was hard to believe that at last I wasn't a victim. I had made a decision to sue, a tough decision, and my house had not come tumbling down. I wasn't punished. I had won.

I immediately set about hiring a wonderful public relations person named Richard Wiener in New York. He arranged a press conference and issued as a news release my statement that I had fought this blacklist and wanted to make a point that it was time to stop portraying women as stereotypical bitches. I had settled for an undisclosed amount of money (at their insistence) and the promise of a disclaimer at the beginning and the end of any show whenever it was reshown on television. The disclaimer was to read

"The role of the wife is fictitious." This meant that the production could no longer be touted as a documentary.

I heard later that David Rintels was censured by the Screen Actors Guild for his part in lying about my role. He was never able to accept this reprimand, after having won an Emmy from the National Academy of Television Arts and Sciences for the script of *Fear on Trial* and further awards from the Writers' Guild and the American Bar Association. He was quoted by Bill Davidson in *TV Guide* as saying it was a bitter, galling experience to be accused of falsifying facts. Then he went on to excuse himself by saying he had to condense a story that took place over seven years into little less than two hours. "As for Faulk's wife, the divorce was so messy that I made the judgment that it would be better to eliminate her from the latter stages of the story rather than dredge up painful problems for a lot of people. I stuck with the record, except in intimate scenes for which there was no record . . . and that's what writers are paid to do. I'll go to my grave believing I dealt honestly with the overall facts."

The sad thing is that once a lie is told, it gets told over and over again. Wide exposure was given Rintels' statement in Davidson's article, and his views have been given greater permanence now that the article from *TV Guide* was reprinted in three anthologies. What meanness of spirit possessed Rintels that he couldn't admit the truth? He knew that there was no divorce until two years after the lawsuit, so none of that had to appear in the television script. He knew that the book *Fear on Trial* was a complete record of my role as supporter of the family, both emotionally and financially. He chose to leave out the five important years in Texas in which I founded and ran the advertising firm, the public relations office, and the successful magazine. All these were verifiable facts. While the lawsuit itself was dramatic, the true story of the family would have made it memorable. The press party arranged by Richard Wiener brought out all the press. I was pleased with the results, as the victory was announced across the country in many newspaper columns.

While I was in New York being interviewed about the lawsuit, I received a hurried call from a Bruce Ledger, an executive with Screen Gems, a subsidiary of Columbia Pictures (Canada). He said they needed a host to take over a celebrity interview show that was shown nightly at 11:00 p.m. Ledger thought a woman would be a healthy change and would help the ratings. The eleven o'clock spot wasn't the best, but it was a syndicated show and it would give me a chance to do a different type of interview from the ones I had done on consumer issues. I was interested and said I would be in his office the next day to discuss the contract. It seemed as if all the publicity about my fight and victory had helped my image. I was excited at this new challenge.

CHAPTER 27

MORTALITY

When I returned to Toronto, I met with Bruce Ledger of Screen Gems. I was interested in his offer of a night-time television show because it would give me the opportunity to show the soft side of my personality, not the investigative reporter side. It also meant traveling more, as the show went on location.

Bruce had been impressed by my lawsuit and felt that I was the high-profile person he needed for that show. He made a great deal of the fact I was the first woman considered for the job. I liked this down-to-earth, gruff man. He had the contracts all ready and left very little room for discussion. But they were fair, I liked his stated confidence in me, and I saw no reason to bargain about the money. I just made one point to him. "Bruce, this is a show I'd love to do. It will expand my profile, but I want to make it very clear that I intend to do it differently than I did my consumer shows. I don't want to act like an investigative reporter or do confrontational-type interviews. My image has been authoritarian and tough. I want to show that I can be sensitive and even tender. I intend to conduct the interviews on a very personal level, trying to find out what makes each personality tick, getting under the skin in a caring way." He agreed. "I hired you because of your track record and your guts. I trust you to handle the interviews in the way you see fit. You are the first talent I'm interested in for international distribution. Usually I only concern myself with Canada, but I think after the show gets going, I can sell you to the United States."

It seemed like a dream. Then Bruce told me that he had chosen Dan Enright as my director. He lived in California and Bruce thought it would be a good idea if I met him on his territory and did some of the first shows from there. Then Dan would spend some time in Canada and the show would travel, eventually to London, England.

I knew the name Enright and then remembered that he had once been connected with the game show *The $64,000 Question*. The producers of the show were accused of rigging some of the questions. I felt a little apprehensive about meeting him. It turned out my fears were justified. We talked on the phone and a date was made for me to go to California and do the first show. He sounded quite agreeable and I began to relax. I was happy about making the trip because it would permit me to visit my mother, who had been living with my sister in Los Angeles. She was now in a nursing home and confined to a wheelchair. I knew she could never function as a parent, but I could function as her daughter.

I was met at the airport by Dan and taken directly to his magnificent home on top of the hills. It was everything one could imagine about a home in Hollywood, including the swimming pool. A simple lunch was prepared, and we talked about ourselves and the show. He said he knew about my fight with CBS and the blacklisting. He said he'd been blacklisted, too, just like John Henry. He explained that because the show came under attack, he had suffered by association. He couldn't get a job for a long time and many of his friends avoided him. I wasn't too sure how he could compare his problem with John Henry's. I listened to Dan and tried to feel close to him, since he was in charge of my show. I had to depend on him for the next year, at least.

It wasn't long before we got into our first heavy argument and I almost thought my show would go up in smoke. As he discussed the format, I repeated to him what I had told Bruce Ledger about how I wanted to handle the interviews. He reacted immediately with anger. "What are you talking about? You were hired because you are a tough interviewer. I want you to approach your interviews the same way you did your consumer shows." I tried to explain: "You don't understand. I've been too one-dimensional. People must see another side of me. At any rate, celebrity interviews shouldn't be handled the same way. I'm more interested in getting unusual, hidden responses out of my subjects." Dan cut me off, saying harshly, "I run this show. If you don't want to do it my way, perhaps you are not interested in doing the show."

I felt my heart pound, I wanted that show so much. But I knew that we had to have this settled or I could never perform properly. Doing a confrontational show would go against everything I believed in. Actually, I wasn't confrontational when I did my consumer shows. I was just authoritative, well-researched, and persistent. I never went for the jugular. Dan said explosively, "What do you think we hired a woman for? If you won't do it my way, we might just as well go back to using a man." I was startled. "I don't know what you are talking about. I thought you hired me not only because I was a woman but also because I am a damn good interviewer. I have a following and I will probably be better than the men you've had because your ratings need a boost. Why should a woman be tougher than a man to survive? It's the kind of in-depth interview that I do that should make the show successful. I do as much research for an interview as I do for an exposé."

Dan wasn't satisfied with my answer and suggested we call Bruce in Toronto and let him make the decision. I agreed and he dialed for Bruce. Dan got on the telephone and explained our disagreement, and then I was put on the telephone to explain my side. I reiterated my strong feelings about the method of interviewing and Bruce asked to speak to Dan again and told him, "You'll do the show Lynne's way." I won my point, but I was terrified at the constant war we would have. I didn't think Dan would ever forget that I had put him in his place and that Bruce had sided with me.

In spite of the tension between us, I proved that my method worked. The shows went well and brought out unexpected sides of my guests and another side of me. I was fascinated with the instant intimacy I had to establish with each personality. Our budget was so tight that each show had to go "live to tape," which meant it was treated as live, with no editing if possible. Editing was only a last resort because that would add to costs. They started me out doing five interviews a day, then found I could do seven comfortably, which was a tough feat for most interviewers. There was also little time for pre-interviewing by my researchers, and no time at all for me to meet them in the studio before they met me when it was time for the cameras to roll. I knew that the make-up man spent some time warming up the guests so they would know who I was. Many of the Hollywood stars knew nothing about me, let alone Canada. I had to make my impression from the moment they stepped on set. I had two minutes before the interview started to establish a relationship of trust. They had to believe that I was not being a voyeur but an interested friend. I had many wonderful moments on the "Lynne Gordon Show."

I asked my director to write to Lee Grant for an interview. Lee replied saying she rarely gave interviews but she would grant me one because I had suffered from blacklisting the way she had when she was married to writer Arnold Manoff, and she also understood how difficult it was to live with a "saint" and a public figure. The marriage had been bad but it had been difficult to talk about because she also didn't want to give comfort to the enemy. The interview was an unusual one in that we both talked about that period and ended up hugging each other.

My interview with Valerie Harper touched a similar chord. She was making some major decisions about her marriage, and my questions were so timely she wondered how I knew. I didn't know but I sensed sadness in her eyes, and when I told her that, they brimmed over with tears. At the end of the interview, off-camera, she embraced me and begged me to keep in touch with her. Before the interview with Melvin Belli, I was told not to worry—the famous lawyer was also a famous talker. I agreed he was a good talker, but that made him a potentially dangerous and uncontrollable interviewee. I prepared carefully for Belli so I could extract the information I wanted and not let him ramble, telling wonderful stories that had no end.

The interview with Desi Arnaz was almost a disaster. When he finally showed up everyone thought he was too drunk to make sense. I didn't want to waste an interview, so I told my team to send him on stage and I would see what I could do. At first he rolled his eyes around a great deal, turning his head to crack dirty jokes with the cameramen. While he talked, he fidgeted with his dark glasses and rolled a cigar around in his mouth. I suddenly reached over, putting my hand firmly on his leg. "Look at me Desi, look into my eyes. Take off your dark glasses, put them in your pocket, throw away your cigar, and stop turning your head away from the camera while I talk to you. I asked to interview you because everyone knows about Lucille Ball but I want people to know about you, the contribution you made to television, your talent, and your personality. But you must look at me. Look into my eyes." I watched as I saw Desi shake his head as if to clear it, put his glasses in his pocket, put out his cigar, and fix his eyes on me. I had won. The interview worked. If viewers knew he had been drinking, they might suspect it from the slow way he talked. But all in all it was an excellent interview.

One of the funniest was trying to bring Tammy Grimes down to earth while on camera. She was in a strange state when I interviewed her and had evidently been hounded or threatened by what she called "the mafia." I never knew what the story was all about, but while on camera she would suddenly turn her profile and whisper *sotto voce*, "I don't want them to see me." I made a joke of it and reminded her that there was no way she could escape being recognized because she was on camera! I was slightly embarrassed by Leslie Nielsen. He is a handsome man and I used my method of trying to reach him by locking my eyes with his. As he stared at me, he remarked, "What beautiful eyes you have." I was completely thrown, knowing that the remark had gone over the air, and I tried to save the situation by stupidly explaining his remark. I must say I found him charming, and never expected to since he has the kind of pretty looks I don't usually relate to. I also found him much more colorful and articulate than I had expected.

A hilarious and almost touching sequence happened with Edith Head, the famous costume designer for the movies. In all her previous interviews she had talked about the stars she had dressed and how she made it a point never to compete with them. "That," she explained, "is why I kept my job for so many years. I was not a threat to them." I heard her say that and then realized that this woman had subjugated her personality all her life. She dressed quietly and had long hair twisted into a bun. Almost spontaneously, I decided she needed her own moment of glory and without warning I said, "But you must be completely different at home. I'll bet at home you let your hair down." Then I fixed my eyes on her and ordered, "Take the pins out of your hair. Let your hair down, so the viewers can see the real you, the you that you have kept private for so long." As if mesmerized, she reached up slowly and took out the pins one by one, something she had never done before on camera. It was a magical moment.

The same kind of thing happened with the football coach Leo Cahill, who had a reputation for being abusive and tough on his players. When he came to be interviewed, I started to ask him a personal question. On air he snapped, "I thought this was about sports." I immediately answered, "I never promised you that. I asked to interview Leo Cahill, the man. When you talk about sports, you are too glib, too guarded. I want to know what makes Leo Cahill tick, what makes him sad, what makes him cry?" It was that kind of fast retort that took people off guard and provided me with some spectacular interviews.

For over a year I had a wonderful time running between Los Angeles, New York, and Toronto. In between I had to tape three weeks of radio shows while I was away as I had to be on air every day. So I was working at high speed. At the same time I had to be available for decisions at the Council. While I was in California, I saw my mother a great deal. The last time I saw her she was sitting on the patio of the nursing home, with a wide-brimmed hat protecting her face from the sun. She was seventy-six years old and had milk-white skin without a wrinkle. She had beautiful brown eyes and her black hair was still worn shoulder-length. Her energy was remarkable and she had a presence at the end. But by this time she was almost completely out of touch with reality. I felt tears well up as I waved good-bye, knowing that it would probably be the last time we would see each other.

We still weren't able to communicate, but I didn't find it any problem to keep feeding her the compliments she so desperately needed. It broke my heart to see her fondle her jewelry, jewelry she didn't realize came from the five-and-dime. Her own jewelry had been put into safekeeping because so many pieces had turned up missing in the nursing home. She was unaware. I took her out to dinner and to shop and pushed the wheelchair everywhere. One of the last times I had tried to talk about my promotions in broadcasting, she had remarked, "I'm not interested in how many jobs you have. It breaks my mother's heart that you don't have a man to take care of you and you have to work so hard." As a result, I didn't discuss my show with her. But I pretended I was going to interview her for my radio show and was able to do one last interview with her and get her voice on tape.

At the end of the year, when it came time to renew my contract, I had a message from Columbia Pictures. Bruce Ledger had died suddenly of a heart attack. I couldn't believe that that big, hearty man was gone. At the same time, the scandal about David Begelman tampering with fees came out and Columbia was going through a reorganization. This was the opportunity Dan had been waiting for. He decided not to renew my contract. Columbia also decided to explore a less expensive format, doing interviews on current issues from shopping malls. I was sorry to lose a friend and sorry to lose that show.

My world was beginning to turn upside-down and I didn't know it. CKEY was going through a period of change. Because I was gone so much, I wasn't aware of the financial troubles the station was having. I learned that they were changing from a music-and-talk format to an all-music station. I approached a senior executive and said if there were going to be changes, I should be looking quietly for another job. Certainly they wouldn't need me if the station was going all-music. He assured me those changes would take a few years. While they were cutting down on a lot of talk, they still had a place for me. I had his assurance that he would let me know in enough time if his plans changed so I could resign gracefully. I thought that I would like to shift my main work from radio to television. I wanted to make the change carefully. Then I read in a newspaper column that CKEY was dropping four of its talk shows, one of them mine, and not renewing contracts. I felt betrayed by a man I had been very close to, because he had not kept his promise to advise me of major changes. I was also concerned about my public image and felt he could have allowed me to slip away as I had suggested. In the broadcasting business you learn to accept change. What I couldn't accept were the methods used in handling talent, the complete indifference to my feelings and my public image.

In the meantime I received a call from the head of CKO All News Radio, Vern Furber, who said without fanfare, "I heard that you are now free. I would like to offer you a job at CKO. I want Lynne Gordon, not a substitute Lynne Gordon." After a brief meeting with Vern, he reiterated his need for me and told me what he could pay and the amount of air time he would give me. My format would include five daily consumer shows and the weekend would be devoted to interviews, reviews, and lifestyle shows. I liked his terms and his directness. I made the transition easily to CKO. Although I had been thinking of leaving radio, I didn't think that I should leave on a down note. So going to CKO was an excellent transition for me, and after twelve years at CKEY, it was a refreshing change.

During that time I began to worry about Steve. He often looked so tired and seemed to be getting uncharacteristically irritable at minor incidents. I tried talking to him about taking a leave of absence from the office. I painted a rosy picture of us traveling or settling in England for a while. He could open a pub and write and we wouldn't have to worry about money. I felt we could pool our resources and live well. He brushed that idea aside, so I started pushing him again about moving downtown to avoid commuting. I suggested that since he liked our apartment so much he might not mind if I rented a larger one. My hidden agenda was that the more comfortable the downtown apartment became the more willing he would be to leave the suburbs. I also felt that more space would be better when my children came to visit.

When I told my accountant that I was thinking of taking a two-bedroom apartment in the ManuLife complex, he advised me to think of investing in a townhouse. I resisted at first, because I have never liked owning a house, preferring the freedom of an apartment and the luxury of maintenance at my fingertips. I told him I would never move out of the downtown core and I doubted whether I could afford a house in the heart of the city. By accident I heard that a man I knew was just about to put a brand-new house on the market. He had bought it for speculation, had added some cosmetic touches, and was reselling. The house was on one of the prettiest downtown streets in Toronto, McGill Street, the same street that gave its name to the well-known women's club, 21 McGill. I immediately went down to see the house and walked into a four-storey townhouse. I couldn't believe how beautiful it was and how much it resembled a New York City townhouse. Although it was narrow, it had been built from scratch, so it was carefullly planned. It was an open plan except for a closed area in the downstairs part that could be shut off from the rest of the house. I fell in love with the house and decided to buy it on the spot. It was six months before the boom, when real estate shot up and the house would have been out of my reach. But I wasn't thinking of it so much as an investment as a retreat, a wonderful space, a haven for me.

About this time I knew that something was seriously wrong

with Steve. His coughing, which had worried me for a long time, was noticeably worse. I had scolded him, saying, "I almost hate to make love to you because as soon as you exert yourself you go into a coughing fit. I'm beginning to associate lovemaking with coughing." I showed him the house and said the deal was closed. He seemed quite angry. "Why did you buy a house? We have a house." I said, "No, you have a house. This is my investment. But what difference does it make whether I move into a two-bedroom apartment or into a house? You agreed we needed more room." He replied, "Why did you buy a house with so many stairs? I can't walk the stairs. I can't breathe." I looked at him and said, "Something must be terribly wrong. I can run up and down the stairs without any problem."

We were supposed to move into the house in about three months, which would be in time for Christmas. My children would "be home" for Christmas. Then one day I looked at Steve and I shook my head in disbelief. "My God, you look as if you lost about thirty pounds." He insisted that I was imagining it and refused to discuss his weight, but he did supervise moving my furniture from his house into the new house. All our children were mobilized to help, but while he supervised the move, Steve wasn't able to do much lifting. He was finding it more and more difficult to eat, to breathe. I began to notice a slightly green pallor on his face. I blew up at him and said, "What the devil is the matter with you? You must go to a doctor." He was furious at me, insisted it was none of my business, and ended lamely, "Besides, my doctor retired and I don't like the young idiot who's taken his place." I said, "Then we'll find you a new one. My God, Steve, if I didn't love you so much I wouldn't be pushing you. If you don't do something, you may die of malnutrition, before any disease catches up to you. I swear I'm going to leave you if you don't do something."

At that time I didn't know much about emphysema. "Hasn't anyone at the office ever told you that you were destroying yourself with smoking? Hasn't anyone talked about your cough?" He became very quiet and then pleaded. "I promise to go to a doctor but please, first give me my Christmas. Don't spoil the holidays." I felt chilled at his answer, and frightened. It was almost as if he knew something was desperately wrong and didn't want to face it. I prayed that a few more weeks wouldn't be fatal. "I'll agree if you promise to see a doctor right after New Year's Day, not a day later." Then I set about trying to make the holidays the best he ever had.

I never discussed his sickness over Christmas, although my heart was breaking. I pretended everything was all right. It turned out to be an intense, close time, as we put all our fears on hold. Everyone seemed to be on his or her best behavior. Just before the holidays, my sister called to say that our mother had died. "She went very peacefully in her sleep, so there is no reason for you to come out now. She donated her body to science. But please plan to come out a little later to help me settle the estate." Mother's last act had been to slip away quietly without any trouble. How sad that all I could feel was relief that she hadn't interfered with the holidays. I had done all my crying years ago. June and I had also made a pact that no matter what our mother decided about the will, we would share equally whatever was left. We would not fight about anything. In fact, we vowed to nurture our relationship and make sure we saw each other regularly, either in each other's homes or for two or three weeks in Europe every year.

I spent some time meditating on my mother's death and then gave all my attention to Steve. It was right after New Year's Day that he called the doctor who had been recommended to me. He told me that his check-up would be in three weeks' time. I was appalled. I knew he couldn't wait three weeks. I knew that he had a stubborn macho streak in him and he hated it when I tried to interfere with his business or his personal decisions. If we had been a family, we would have shared a doctor, but as live-in partners we kept doctors and financial advisers very separate, as Steve wished.

But I had found the doctor. So in spite of the fact that I knew he would be angry, I called the doctor's office and asked why he had been put off for three weeks. At first the nurse was quite brusque. "If your husband is in such a hurry for a check-up, he'd better find another doctor, we are jammed." I said, "Hold on a minute, I don't need you to be angry at me. It will be bad enough when Steve finds out that I called you without his permission. First of all, I don't know why he asked for a check-up. This is an emergency. You listen to my description of his problem, speak to the doctor, and if you don't think it's an emergency then I damn well will find another doctor." I described Steve's condition, his convulsive coughing, his rapid loss of weight, and his green pallor. She answered immediately, "Get him here tomorrow. I'll make time for him."

I then called Steve at his office. "Steve, I know you are going to be angry, but I called the doctor and described your condition and he wants you to come immediately . . . tomorrow." For a moment there was dead silence at the other end of the telephone. I could hardly breathe as I waited for his answer. Finally he said, almost relieved, "Okay, I have most of my work finished for the next month anyway. Everything is in order." Again I felt a stab of terror in my heart. It sounded as if he was getting his life in order.

We went to the doctor's office together. X-rays were taken and the doctor said, yes, there was a shadow on his lung, but it was hard to tell exactly what it was until the pneumonia was cleared up. Nothing could be done until then. The doctor suggested Steve go home to rest until the pneumonia was cleared up. I wanted Steve hospitalized but he preferred to go home. So we went home with a double dose of antibiotics and the warning that the shadows could only be diagnosed after the infection had cleared up. I clung to every bit of information, trying hard not to panic. If they used the word "shadow," wasn't that more hopeful than if they had used the word "spot"? When the infection cleared up, Steve was hospitalized for a week.

How much we had grown together over eleven stable years. How we had worked on our relationship. There was a time when my daughter Johanna had worried that again I wasn't getting enough, that I had settled for less than I deserved. I used to tell her that in spite of some shortcomings, he gave me the stability I needed, the affection, the concern, and the best part of our love was that it could grow. I thought about how much he had been enjoying life, beginning at last to indulge himself. What could I have done to get him to a doctor earlier? Should I have seen the signals? I had begged him over and over to quit smoking. I began to go over the past, and little incidents stuck out. At first he stopped playing tennis with me. "You are such a lousy player, you make me run too much." I laughed and said, "If you don't like playing with me, play with the men." But he said, "I don't care much about tennis any more." Then the hours we argued because I couldn't get him to take up cross-country skiing with me. It was too much of an exertion. Then he stopped water-skiing. I began to tease him and say he was turning into an old man. But as he was finding it harder and harder to do these things, he was retreating a little more into nights at home, sipping a glass of whiskey. He liked being alone with me, relaxed.

I had saved two other husbands' lives. I discovered a growth on John Henry's neck and got him to the hospital in time to treat it before it spread. I had saved Alfredo's life when I made him admit he was having a nervous breakdown and got him to the hospital in time before irreversible damage had been done to his brain and liver. Could I save this man, the man I loved so much? I could feel the familiar burden of guilt take over. Was there a chance it was too late? Why didn't any doctor tell him he had life-threatening emphysema, or had a doctor told him and had he ignored it? There were so many unanswered questions spinning around in my brain. Then there was at least one answer. A cheerful surgeon told me he had good news and bad news. My heart stopped. My worst fears were being realized. The bad news was they had detected cancer of the lung. The good news was that it was still operable. The tests showed it had not spread. The prognosis was good. They prepared him for surgery the next day. As I look back I can't believe how little of my own advice as a consumer advocate I took. My advice to others would be to get a second opinion. Was surgery the only route to take? What was the success rate of lung cancer? What was the recovery rate? The problem is that when you are most vulnerable, you are apt to leave life-making decisions to your surgeon. Steve seemed very optimistic, and I didn't have the heart to discuss other opinions.

The next morning I waited while they prepared him for surgery and walked down the long corridor with him as they wheeled him to the operating room. I called one of my friends to come over and sit with me. She came immediately, and I talked to her about my fears for the future and my love for Steve. Then quite suddenly the surgeon appeared, all smiles. "Well, we got it all. There may be only one tiny 'button' that we have to keep our eye on. He's going to be fine. He should be able to lead a fairly normal life, at least as normal as can be with only one lung. Why don't you go home and rest? The staff will call you back as soon as he gets out of recovery."

I went home for a few hours, called my office, and began to reach out for help. I knew that all my energy would be directed toward nursing and nurturing Steve. For the first time I allowed people into my private life. I told my associates and friends I might be acting strangely and erratically but that Steve was in critical condition. I needed help and I needed people to be ready to cover for me if necessary. I prepared to tape many of my shows so I wouldn't have to go in as often. I also asked them to be ready to do repeats. Everyone responded. I thought how nice it was to be able to count on others for help. It was a new experience for me. Johanna was visiting me at the time, and I asked if she could stay longer, I needed her support. Frank visited regularly. Evelyn was in Texas and wonderful on the telephone and made sure she was always available. Soon I had a call from the hospital advising me that Steve was out of the recovery room and in intensive care. I could come right away. Then began the long vigil.

CHAPTER 28

THE VIGIL

The next six months were a nightmare that started with my race back to the hospital. They must have called me too soon. I walked into the intensive-care unit while he was just coming out of the anesthesia. It was like watching a war victim, right off the battlefield. He was surrounded by a team of doctors and nurses trying to restrain him. He seemed to be climbing the walls in pain and they were trying to awaken him. They were hitting him and calling, "Wake up, wake up." He was unconscious but screaming. I couldn't believe this was happening to Steve. How upset he would have been, knowing that he was being observed. He was so strong, so proud. I ached to run into the area and push them away and cradle him.

Soon he was moved to a bed, where I could reach him. For the next two weeks in intensive care, he could hardly sit up. I fed him every day and he had to be strapped to the bed so he could sit up and be fed. The doctor kept saying, "He's fine." Later, Steve told me, he remembered nothing about that period. They finally moved him upstairs to the surgical floor. He was still in terrible pain, but they started giving him exercises. An oxygen mask was constantly at his side. He felt helpless and frightened. I begged him to talk about his fears, to discuss his pain. "Please, don't shut me out. Please let me help. Tell me your dreams, your nightmares, your fears, anything, and I will always answer with the truth as I know it." He said, "Do you think you can handle it?" I replied, "Yes, because we'll fight this together. Whatever it is, we'll fight it together."

It was amazing. He opened up and shared thoughts with me as he had never been able to do before. We talked a lot, the kind of talking I used to dream about. How I used to want him to share his thoughts and feelings. Now he was doing it. I felt such waves of tenderness for him, so much renewed love. I wanted to believe what the doctor was saying, he seemed so positive. Steve and I had made a point to talk to the doctor separately and together. We made it clear that we wanted the truth at all times. I pleaded with the doctor to keep us informed. I made sure the words were clear so he could never say I gave him mixed messages. I was told Steve's lungs were clear, his heart was fine, he was in stable condition. The nurses in intensive care had been excellent, but as he needed less attention, they became more distant, saving themselves for the next wave of patients.

Now Steve was more irritable, but his irritation was considered a good sign that he was getting better. There were five doctors taking care of him, including a chest specialist and a surgeon. I talked to them all the time, cornering them in the halls, making sure I heard the same diagnosis from all of them. I also insisted on calling in a psychiatrist. I approached Steve and said, "I know you have never gone for counseling. Please accept all the help you can. There is no shame in getting help through a crisis. You may be able to say things to him you can't even say to me. Perhaps he will help you open up and you will be able to say things to me you have never been able to handle."

They kept testing him to find out why he still complained of pain, but each test was an ordeal. He began to dread the tests and he would begin to panic when he knew one was scheduled. He was very thin and weak, although they were feeding him milk-shakes and malts to fatten him up. He couldn't seem to gain any weight. Still, they talked about moving him to the St. John's Convalescent Home. They convinced me that they would never think of moving him if they didn't believe he was going to get well, especially since St. John's would not admit anyone who was terminal.

I was worried about Steve, but it never occurred to me to doubt the surgeon, who was dictatorial. He had taken time to sit with me in his office and talk very frankly. The story he gave me privately was the same one he gave Steve. I trusted him at first. In fact, he advised me to leave on a business trip to Italy. "If you go, he'll believe he is getting well. It will be good for him." I refused. "There is no way I'm leaving town while he is so sick, and I certainly wouldn't consider it unless he was in the convalescent home. My God, if anything happened while I was gone I would never forgive myself, and I would definitely shoot you." The surgeon didn't appreciate that last statement, annoyed that I didn't take his advice.

Because Steve was in so much pain, I spoke to my own internist about it, and she said, "I don't know why they don't have a gastro-enterologist look at Steve. After all, all a surgeon can think of is surgery." Armed with that bit of information, I went again to the surgeon's office and asked for a stomach specialist to look at Steve. He answered brusquely, "I am a stomach man. Why do you need someone else?" Armed with the information from my internist, I retorted, "You may be a specialist on stomachs, but surgeons cut. I want a gastro-enterologist who focuses on treatment that doesn't require surgery." I asked him to tell Steve that we had discussed it together and that we had agreed. I wanted a united front. He finally said he would talk to Steve, but while we were in Steve's room, he ignored our talk and went on to tell Steve that new tests had been planned. I was furious and decided I couldn't let him get away with ignoring my demand even at the risk of getting Steve nervous over an argument. I said sweetly, "Doctor, if you remember, we agreed it might make sense to have a gastro-enterologist look at Steve before any more tests." He glowered, pressed his lips together, and answered shortly, "That's right. I'll take care of it at once." Steve looked apprehensive and I explained the reason for the stomach specialist.

No matter how much advice consumers get about asking for other opinions, there is always the possibility that the doctor in charge is territorial and will make it difficult. Patients and family and even friends have to be vigilant in a hospital, to be sure the patient is getting the best treatment. The gastro-enterologist examined him and she found an ulcer, some arthritis, and a second band of pain in the stomach area that she was quite concerned about. She was the only one who recognized that there were two bands of pain in the stomach area, not one. I think the only reason I was able to push the surgeon to deal with me so much was my high profile in the broadcasting industry as a tough consumer advocate, which included the area of patients' rights.

The doctor thought Steve would benefit from going home. I wanted him to stay in my house, which meant I could care for him almost all day and still get to the station to do some of my broadcasts. I needed the work as a kind of anesthetic, a way of getting through the pain and anxiety. I always turned to work when I needed to numb my mind. I could work easily. But Steve wanted to go to his home in Scarborough. He felt the garden would soon be pretty and he wanted to look over the ravine and watch the robins and the hummingbirds. I found out that we were eligible for a homemaker and a therapist to come to the house.

His son and daughter started to visit regularly. When I first went to live with Steve, they had been so hostile. I had worked so hard at their relationship, helping them to understand their father, and it paid off. I was just a little nervous about conversations that revolved around their mother. They seemed to bring up her need for money and the impending bankruptcy with her retail store. I cautioned them about increasing their father's anxiety. After all, their mother's business problems were not their father's problems.

I knew in my heart of hearts that Steve was very sick. He was not mending the way the doctors predicted, but I did think he was home for good. I hoped that we would have at least a few more years together, and I was going to do everything to make the time we had count. I wanted those years desperately. I cooked for him at home. We set up a hospital bed in the living room so he could look out at the ravine. One day he said, "I can't stand the pain. I can't eat. I want to go back to the hospital." I felt a cold sweat break out. I didn't want him to go back. I was afraid he would give up and never come out again. "I'll get more help here. Why do you want to go back? You are in your own home. It will be spring soon; you can look out at the ravine." Things were better for a while, but then he said, "I can't breathe. I'm afraid." The marvelous homemaker from the Red Cross, Dianne Hanson, and I took him back in her station wagon. When we got to the hospital, he had to crawl up the steps, two at a time, and then rest. We finally reached the waiting room. When the surgeon saw Steve sitting quietly, he wasn't happy about readmitting him. "This is ridiculous. He's fine. He made it up here with no problems, didn't he?" I exploded, "Doctor, what the hell are you talking about? This man crawled up the stairs. He crawled!" He looked startled at my outburst and admitted him to the hospital. As soon as he was put to bed, they gave him an oxygen mask and started therapy.

I had nightmares every night. Johanna was a lifesaver for me because she was there. When you are in pain, it's difficult to call up friends. Usually the tears come at four or five in the morning. It's the very moment when you are hysterical that you need someone, not an hour later, and Johanna was at my side. About that time some strange things began to happen. Steve's ex-wife had decided to get closer to Steve again. She didn't call me to ask if she could visit. She didn't ask me if he was strong enough to receive visitors, or even ask me to check with him if he wanted to see her. In the past we had always been able to speak civilly to each other so there was no reason for her to sidestep me. She started sending little notes that were carried to him secretly by his son. They were sentimental notes: "I still love you. I still think of you. Can we still be friends?" Along with the notes came homemade bread and bits of ribbon symbolic of love for him to wear. Then one day Steve told me she had called and wanted to come and see him. He told me he had warned her that she shouldn't visit unless she was prepared to have her eyes scratched out by me. I was unhappy. "Why did you say that? I've met her before. We are not enemies. Do you want to see her?"

I was exhausted from the months of worry and pain, and suddenly this seemed like an extra and unfair burden. I could feel old stirrings of jealousy and guilt. I didn't want to deprive Steve of any pleasure, but I felt alienated, pushed aside. I felt his children had somehow betrayed my relationship with them. I wondered how much had to do with her need for money, the only reason she had ever seemed to come back in the past.

At first, Steve told me he didn't want to see her. But she arrived unexpectedly one day, and then started making regular visits. I found the situation intolerable, but I couldn't figure out what to do about it. After all, I told myself, here's a man who is very sick. How can I tell him whom to see and whom not to see. Yet I felt the visits were like a death watch. I also felt they were keeping Steve apart from me. The turning point came when two things happened. First, I asked him, "How will this continue when you get better and go home? Will you still see her regularly? Will I never know when she'll turn up again at our house?" I think the fact I talked about the future made him think there was a future. It encouraged him to see his ex-wife's visits as other than farewell visits.

But more than that was the help Dianne Hanson gave me. I had talked openly to her about my heartache when I learned Steve's former wife had showed up. I felt my place at his side was threatened. After all, although they were divorced, I was not his legal wife. Dianne hugged me and said, "I love both of you. Since I've been taking care of Steve, I've become very close to him. He talks about you constantly and what you have meant to him. I know he loves you. I don't know if he understands how much pain he is causing you. Do you want me to try and help?" I was stunned. I can't remember anyone having offered to help me like that. I had a long history of friends withdrawing when John Henry demanded uncompromising and unquestioned loyalty when it came to making a decision about being his friend or mine. I said, "Dianne, I don't know if you can help, but if you want to try, I would love it. I don't know what you can say to Steve, and I should warn you he may get angry at your taking my side. You may lose his friendship." She said, "I don't think so, but it's important to try because what he is doing is hurting you unnecessarily."

Apparently they did have a long conversation, one that reached him. The next time I went to the hospital, he looked at me very tenderly and said, "Dianne explained things to me, and I want you to know what's bothering you is over." I said, "Good. Somehow my headaches have disappeared." From that point on our relationship took a quantum leap. It was magic. It was as if during all our years together, Steve had harbored a secret hurt about his wife, a secret he never wanted to talk about. It had been a high wall between us, and now it was gone. He finally faced her and made a conscious decision about his love and loyalty; now he was free. Steve became peaceful and our relationship deepened dramatically.

Steve made a confession. "I want to tell you something. You always used to tell me that you wanted to have dialogue with me about supposed problems. I never really knew what you meant. I was suspicious. I always thought dialogue meant confrontation, and I knew that if we did have a confrontation, for my own self-respect, I would have to win. If I didn't win, I would have to walk out. Now I realize that this didn't have to happen at all. You really just wanted to talk, to try and straighten things out. I wish I had understood and we had been able to talk more freely. I wish I wasn't so sick now. I wish I had never smoked. I don't want to die, but I don't want to be an invalid all my life either." Finally, after all these years, I felt Steve had allowed me completely into his heart, his thoughts.

After Steve was readmitted to the hospital, they discovered that he had pneumonia again. They were worried about this development. He was on intravenous and oxygen. He knew the doctors were worried and he was very upset. He became quite friendly with one of the interns, who always had time to talk to Steve. The intern couldn't hide his concern. Steve started to pick at himself with his fingers. I didn't know that some dying people do that, not knowing what to do with their hands. Steve asked me to bring some craft work that he could do with his hands, to keep them busy, even some weaving. One morning I came by just as he was awakening. His hair had grown rather long and was shot through with silver. He looked almost spiritual, so handsome. He opened his eyes and said, "Oh, how wonderful, it's you!" After breakfast was over, he said, almost child-like, "Will you be back again tonight?" I was startled. It was almost as if he didn't expect me again because I had my visit in the morning. He knew I was trying to work at the same time and that I must be exhausted. He was always so thoughtful and always aware of deadlines. I said, "Of course I'll be back tonight. I have never missed our evening together." I came every evening, and I took him to one of the lounges, where we could watch television, or I made a special production of taking him to the floor where they nursed the new babies. I had some idea that if I showed him newborn infants he would feel the energy of new lives and it would enter his body. I felt very mystical about this.

That night I came back and we played cards. His daughter dropped in. I was planning a birthday party for Steve. His birthday was just a week away, on June 17th. I whispered something to her and Steve immediately asked suspiciously, "What are you whispering about?" I realized he was afraid I was keeping from him some news about his condition, so I leaked a little information. "I can't tell you, it's a surprise for next week. That's all I'm going to say." I had, in fact, asked the doctors if he could come home for his birthday, always testing them to see their response. They wanted to keep him in the hospital because the pneumonia still worried them but he could meet a few guests. We were laughing, the radio was playing Frank Sinatra singing "I can't take my eyes off you." Steve looked at me with great warmth and started singing along.

Then he said, "My darling, I love you so." I had waited so long to hear those words. I felt very happy, but very weary. His daughter was going to stay longer, so I finally said, "If you are going to stay, will you make sure Steve is put to bed and his television is working." So many nights before I had crawled into the hospital bed with him, curled up in his arms, wanting to give him my strength. The nurses would come in and smile at our closeness. I wanted to spend the nights with him, but he always said that I needed to go home to get my rest, and that he would only keep me awake with his needs.

That night I went home and tried to sleep. The telephone rang at dawn. It was the intern, Steve's friend. I could hardly squeeze out the words, "Is anything wrong?" And without a pause, without even asking me if anyone was close by, without suggesting I sit down, without any kind of humane warning, he said tersely, "He's gone." I screamed into the phone, "You liars, you bastards, you dirty rotten bastards. What do you mean? You said he was all right. Don't touch him, don't do anything before I get there." My scream battled the silence. The word "gone" clawed at my memory, like the scream I had when Miss Funk told me my mother was gone. And now Steve was gone. How much I loved him. I had promised him he was going to be all right, the doctors had promised him, and we had all failed.

I threw a dress over my naked body. I didn't bother with underwear or stockings. I put on a pair of shoes and I ran crying down the street to the hospital. I burst onto his floor and ran without stopping to his room. His bed was flat and he lay prone. I screamed, "Roll the bed up, roll the bed up. I want to talk to him." A startled nurse came and rolled him to a sitting position. I went in alone and closed the door. In all my life I had never touched anyone who had died. I sat down by his side. He was still warm, and my hot tears fell on his body. I ran my hands all over, tracing his features with my fingers. All my tears were for him. My arms were empty. I wanted to scoop him up, let all my strength flow to him, to make him well, to take him from the hospital. We had finally found complete honesty with each other and he was gone. I bent down and put my head on his chest and sobbed his name. I didn't believe he was dead. He looked so peaceful. Suddenly I felt a hand on my shoulder. It was an orderly and he said gently, "I'm sorry, you must leave now." They wanted to roll down the bed again. His children and Johanna were waiting, as was Alan Levitt, a staunch friend and my lawyer for many years. I had asked Johanna to call him first. They took me home.

CHAPTER 29

AFTERMATH

After I left the hospital I was numb. Tears coursed down my cheeks. I stared into space, not realizing or caring that I was crying. I rarely cried in front of anyone but now my mind was racing. Why had the doctors lied? Why hadn't the surgeon called me? Why hadn't the general practitioner called, the doctor who is supposed to be ombudsman for the family? Had they known that Steve was in a more critical condition than they had let on? Didn't they know they might have cheated us of those last few months of closeness by pretending everything was all right? They might have denied us the time to talk openly about death and plans afterwards.

It was only sheer instinct and love that made it possible for Steve and me to talk so frankly about life and death. Why had they pushed me to leave him when he was in so critical a condition? "Go to Italy, prove you believe he is well." Why do doctors still play God? Who are they? What are their problems, their disappointments, their failures as human beings? Had they suspected more damage, but not known for sure? My questions made me realize that people must never allow others to make decisions for them. Questions must always be asked. But I had asked, over and over again, for the truth. But whose truth was it? It was much later that I decided to ask for an autopsy and found out that the cancer had spread throughout his body, that the pain the gastro-enterologist had discovered must have been cancer. He had no chance to get well. My heart ached for all the promises made to Steve. I was only thankful that we had taken control of his last few months and had done everything possible to face his pain, not to ignore it, to pretend it didn't exist, to indulge in inane pep talks.

As I sat in my living room, beginning to babble on about our life, the telephone started ringing, and people began calling with words of sympathy. They apologized for bothering me. They thought one of the family would be answering the phone. I begged, "Oh, no. Please talk to me. I need to talk. I need to cry. I need to remember." I took every call. How much I appreciated those calls. I was glad when my friends began to show up at all hours. For the first time in my life, I allowed myself to talk about my pain, endlessly, without censorship, without caution. All the friendships, the networking I had done over the years I was with Steve, came to fruition. About thirty-five of the women I had become close to showed up, including Margo Lane, June Callwood, Lynda Hurst, Helen Hutchinson, Isabel Bassett, Ethel Teitelbaum, Rosie Abella, Mary MacEwan, Joan Sutton, and Jane Gale. They took over in every way possible. I was surrounded with love. Johanna and Frank stayed close. Evelyn was in Texas and I mistakenly had not asked her to come, thinking I was protecting her and not wanting to disturb her school year. The house was never empty, and that's how I wanted it.

The next three days were taken up with planning the funeral, the eulogy, the reception. Steve had asked to be cremated and have his ashes strewn over the ravine in back of his home in Scarborough. I asked a woman minister, Kay Cook of the Unitarian Congregation, to perform the service. She had a reputation as a feminist and the Unitarians are non-denominational. She sat with me for a few hours, integrating all my feelings into her sermon. I wrote a special piece for Steve but wanted her to read it for me. I did not want to be on-stage at all. Because Steve loved music so much, I arranged to have a guitarist play his favorite love songs. I wanted the service to be an affirmation of life, not a closing of the books. All of Steve's friends and business colleagues came and even cabinet ministers because of my role as chairperson of the Council. All of my friends came, and I found out later that Steve's former wife had slipped in with her mother and stayed quietly in the back. Steve's son wanted to read his eulogy to his father, and I asked Hank Karpus, a close friend and colleague of Steve, to read one. That was all.

I sat in the front pew beside Steve's children, and with my daughter Johanna and my son Frank. They linked arms behind my back and I felt their strength. I listened intently to every word that was said. I wore an Irish tweed suit of soft mixed pinks and a pink blouse. I did not want to wear black and it was Steve's favorite suit. He had bought it for me in Dublin.

I had such strong memories I could almost hear Steve talk. Everything went smoothly and people felt uplifted. The caretaker told me that it was one of the most inspiring services he had ever attended. I paused as I walked out, arm in arm with the children, and waited a moment for Steve to catch up. I was so sure that he was there. When Alan Levitt drew up in his car to take us home, I stopped a moment and looked up and said, "Steve, was it the way you would have done it?"

Then we all went back to the house. I was told to sit in a comfortable chair so people could come up to me. I refused. I wanted to mingle. I wanted to talk about the beautiful ceremony. I wanted to talk about Steve and I did. That night I went to bed exhausted. I seemed to be able to get through the days and the nights, but pre-dawn was my most vulnerable time. I still couldn't make sense of Steve's death. Death seemed so meaningless. I didn't have a choice in this death. I didn't feel guilty about our life together. I knew that I had opened up a great deal for Steve. I knew that I had worked hard at our relationship. I immediately contracted pains where he had pains. If my stomach hurt, I thought it was the pain he had in his stomach. When I awakened at four or five in the morning, I'd talk to Steve. Sometimes I was terribly angry at him; there were some things he hadn't done. I resented the fact he had made me wait to hear him say "I love you" until he was dying. Such a waste of time. I was angry that he had waited so long to get things for himself that he loved. I tried going away on that trip to Italy, to see if I could forget for a few weeks. It was the worst thing I could have done. I awakened crying, I felt my heart pound as I walked the streets, I cried at all the museums, places I would have shared with Steve. I couldn't stand being around couples. I began to panic and wanted to get home to my house, to familiar ground. I was not ready to go away.

One of the women friends had suggested that I might have a love affair in Italy. Maybe that would help. How strange that women's emotional needs are still equated with being serviced by a man. The last thing I wanted or was even capable of experiencing was the intimacy of another man. I needed to grieve. I needed to be allowed to heal at my own pace. I came home, almost collapsing in my bedroom, wanting to pull the covers over my head. I didn't know if I could survive. It was ironic. I'd spent the last few years telling women that they should make full lives for themselves, and that while it was wonderful to have a healthy loving marriage or liaison, that was not the be-all and end-all. They were lucky to have the feminist movement, a support group. And here I was asking myself if I could survive. Could I live on my own for the first time in my life? I had never lived alone. I had never come back to an empty house. Even now Johanna was still visiting with me and I dreaded the day she would leave, although I knew she eventually must. I had to stop leaning on her and reach out again to my own friends.

I had always been rusty in handling friendships with women. My stepfather had warned me that having single women friends was a threat to a marriage. My mother had almost made me believe that any time I had outside of work or marriage belonged to her. John Henry had actively discouraged me from having women friends who weren't part of his own entourage. So it took me a long time to learn how to nurture female friendships. I am still a little awkward at it. When my friends first gathered around, I was grateful. Then I became angry when some of them drifted away. Friendships take time to cement.

I had taken care of myself financially, physically, and emotionally almost all my life. I had supported three husbands, either emotionally or financially. Yet the old conditioning struck again. When Steve died I awakened, crying out, "Who is going to take care of me now?" My way of filling that emptiness and that fear for the moment was to become even more involved in work. That had always been my safety valve. I had to make sure every job was secure. I signed another contract with CKO, I tied up a contract as consultant with the Ministry of Tourism, and I went back to doing television features and interviews on CFTO. I decided I wanted to act, expand my horizons. I auditioned for a part in a new sit-com with Louis Del Grande to play his Italian mother. I went to an audition for the CBC show *Seeing Things*. I had been told that it was a part for an older Italian woman. It happened Louis was doing the casting himself, and there was an immediate rapport between us. I was right for the part. He liked my New York energy, phrasing, and the way I used my hands. He asked excitedly, "Will you take the part?

It's small but you are perfect." Would I? I answered proudly, "I'm an actress, no part is too small."

Once all my contracts were safely signed, I began to examine my life and ponder what it would be like alone. All my life I had been afraid of being alone at night. I'd wake up unexpectedly, hyperventilating, stifling anxious screams, vividly enacting my death. But after Steve died, it never happened again. It was as if I had dealt with death, held it in my arms, and I was no longer as frightened as I once was. Then, gradually, I stopped thinking about being alone as loneliness and began to see that being alone could create a kind of freedom. In all my life I had never gone anywhere without the nagging thought that somewhere along the line I had to check in with someone—parents, husbands, children. It was difficult to break that habit. Almost every day I would start for a telephone to make a call and realize there was no one waiting. I didn't have to ask permission to carry on, to check to see if I was needed back home, or to make arrangements to meet someone. I thought of the things I liked to do—go for a walk, run to a movie at any hour, roam my house, turn on the lights to read, call a friend unexpectedly and meet for lunch or dinner, plan a trip—and I could just go. I found comfort in continuing my involvement with charitable organizations like those concerned with multiple sclerosis and juvenile diabetes. I also cared about making contributions to the peace movements and the perform-ing-arts organizations. I was more capable of handling Steve's crisis, as I had handled other crises in the past, by being able to concentrate on the larger problems of the world as well as by being involved in my work.

I stopped following a routine simply because that was the way I had always done things in the past. Now I was proud of me. I didn't have to say, "Please stamp me approved." I began to under-stand why my daughter Johanna had complained so much about my talking constantly about my work. "Mother, I'm not interested in Lynne Gordon. Can't you just talk to me as my mother?"

I was hurt. "But what I do is so much a part of my life. Aren't you interested?"

"Yes," she would say patiently, "but I'm more interested in what you think and feel. Lynne Gordon the broadcaster isn't all of you. I want to talk to you."

Now I began to understand. I didn't need to be Lynne Gordon the broadcaster, the journalist, the actress. That was one part of me, but I had to get in touch more with myself.

After the first shock of Steve's death passed, I began to think I had everything under control. I experienced a strange sense of euphoria, as if I were starting over with no commitments. I was in a time-warp, feeling young, dreaming again about the future. I planned trips I would take, friendships I would cement, and I was enjoying new and enlightened dialogue with Johanna, now thirty, Evelyn, twenty-nine, and Frank, twenty-eight. In one way I was in a very fortunate position. It was my job to review theater, night life, restaurants, and special events, so I didn't need an escort to go out on the town. I was welcomed everywhere and given special attention and special seating. I began to choose to take women friends with me. I assumed that every woman was liberated, or at least had some feminist goals, just because they were out in the business world. That's a mistake I used to make with men, thinking everyone was progressive just because they had some concern about oppressed people. I had to learn that many women were only concerned with their immediate problems. Unless they had the time or energy to be informed, they would focus only on the problems that affected them. Women who had been accepted in the unions became as much a part of the male union leadership as the men.

I expected that most of the women I knew were free of the conditioning that made them prisoners of role-playing. But I began to be aware that, while they might have been involved in some of the important women's issues, they still had not sorted out their personal lives. In fact, I found some of the women unconsciously taking on the dominant role with me, suggesting ways for me to dress, break out of mourning, get out and begin to date again. What I was beginning to learn was what all feminists should be aware of – that the women's movement is made up of all kinds of women at all stages of their lives. We all need to be tolerant of each other. The only way women can be helped is by increasing their understanding of how the present state of things came about and how it works, so that women who have been doing what does not suit them can understand why, and at the same time learn what alternatives are possible.

Some of this I had learned as chairperson of the Council. Now I was putting it into practice in a personal way. So many of us were still conditioned to thinking that a man is needed to help us through sorrow, to provide us with happiness. It was amazing because some of those women were considered staunch, feisty, almost man-hating, but when it came right to the crunch, they could still regress back into immature relationships.

In my vulnerable state, I was willing to try the remedies suggested by a few women who thought I would be happier if I had a male companion. They wouldn't accept my statement that I wasn't interested and that I liked being unattached. About that time, the whole area of dating services and matchmaking by computer had surfaced, and newspaper advertisements under the heading "Companions Wanted" had earned new respectability. Because of this my friend Margo Lane and I thought we would try to put together a television package based on "Companion Wanted" ads and illustrate some of the experiences of people meeting this way. We would have a panel of experts to discuss the problems of the individual people involved in making the decision to write or answer such an ad. Margo convinced me that I should write an ad so I could see first-hand how they worked. I think her hidden agenda was also to get me involved and, with a wave of the magic wand, I would find true happiness. I agreed to run the ad and meet the men who answered if she would either come along on the first meeting or lurk in the background.

Margo and I pondered the exact wording of the ad. This was important for a serious response. It must be accurate without being heavy-handed, flattering without being misleading, honest, and at least suggestive of the proper age group. Our ad was a work of art. It read: "Vivacious blonde, writer, loves dancing, theater, talks a lot, enjoys dialogue and would enjoy friendship with men 50 years up." The idea was that the wording would rule out those looking for "a discreet afternoon encounter" or, in fact, anyone desperate for marriage. I placed it in the newspaper with a box number and then waited. I was amazed that from one weekend ad I received about thirty-five responses. All but one seemed serious. Margo and I sorted them out and put them in order of interest. Answering thirty-five letters was more of a chore than I realized. I decided to call the first five and arrange suitable public places to meet, either over lunch or cocktails. I was a little concerned I might be recognized as Lynne Gordon because of my voice. I wanted anonymity.

I must say the first man was absolutely charming. He had evidently been quite active answering "Companion Wanted" ads and knew all about them and had made some good friends. He was in middle management, about fifty-five years old, and someone who definitely needed a woman companion. After his first wife died, he fortunately met another woman with whom he fell in love. They were planning to marry when she died. He discussed the heartbreak. He told me all about the things he loved, and never once asked if I was willing to give up my career and join him in his well-planned life: a condominium in Florida, a trailer for camping. He assumed I would be happy to jump at the chance. It was near Valentine's Day, and he came with a Valentine package: two candles, two aluminum candle holders, two plastic wine glasses, a bottle of Bright's wine, and a message of instant romance. I was amused he instant merchandising of feelings and devoted a broadcast to it the next day. I did not mean to hurt his feelings. I forgot he was also a listener of mine. I was really making a comment on our instant intimacy. I never heard from number-one companion again. Later I heard he met someone else and married almost at once.

I then started to go through the next would-be companions. All of them are a blur. All were middle managers, very intense, wounded, and interested in meaningful relationships. I could feel the hackles on my neck rise, as each spent hours discussing his problems and I was relegated to being a silent listener. There was nothing wrong with any of those men, especially if a woman was interested in a traditional marriage. I was amazed at how eligible these men seemed. I did not have the energy to answer the other thirty letters. I still have the letters in my drawer, and I sometimes wonder if one of them would have been fun. Although it wasn't the best experience for me, I decided that such ads served a purpose and were an excellent alternative to computer-matching services, bars, and even some singles clubs for some people. Ads were inexpensive and had been successful for years in Europe. You just had to be realistic about your expectations and enjoy having a superficial date almost every day for a month, which would have happened had I met all thirty-five of my respondents. I certainly wanted to follow up the idea for a television show, but both Margo and I became busy with other projects.

I began to find my life was filled with fascinating women. I also had to realize that women were people and I could not embrace all of them uncritically. It was a form of reverse sexism to think just because they were women they were all loving, all understanding, all patient. But aware, informed women seemed to be stretching themselves more. They are more excited about life and its possibilities. So many men, for so long, have been conditioned to be one-track-minded about their careers and their areas of competence that it left them little room for personal growth, for fun, for wonderment. I began to find I could enjoy my women friends on many levels and not expect one person to fill all my needs. At the same time I was acutely aware that we must not assume that all men harbor residual anti-feminist attitudes. Many men are capable of understanding women and becoming part of women's drive for a strong and productive feminism.

After about a year and a half of managing my life alone, enjoying it tremendously, I almost had a disastrous experience. I think it must take at least two years from the death of a partner to healing inside, no matter how well one functions externally. I was particularly off guard because I was going to be introduced by friends to a man who had expressed a desire to meet me. I heard that his wife had recently died so I was aware that he was not ready for a significant relationship. He had not had enough time to grieve. But I understood he was lonely. Understanding the parameters of our relationship, I felt quite relaxed about meeting him. I, too, would like a friend.

He phoned to introduce himself. Stan seemed very bright, had a great deal of vitality in his voice, and spoke rapidly for about five minutes, knowing I was on my way out for the evening. He talked about the problems women must have today with chauvinistic men, and told me he loved to cook. He rekindled memories about jazz and 52nd Street in New York in the forties. We were both jazz buffs. He loved New York City, where he had lived for many years. We established that we had a great deal in common. Our first meeting was delightful. He was in his mid-fifties, fit, and quite strong-looking. When he came to take me to dinner, he was immaculately turned out in navy blue with a soft pink tie and striped shirt. He came bearing a gift of excellent Mocha coffee, a special cake, and a cassette of his favorite jazz. "This," he informed me, "is for after dinner. I thought you wouldn't mind if we had coffee here, later, and listened to music." He seemed so sure of himself and so at ease that I immediately liked him. I had arranged the bar so I could give him a pre-dinner drink. He refused, saying, "No, thank you. I'm an alcoholic. I haven't had a drink in twenty-one years. I can never touch the stuff." He said it without any fanfare and the subject was dropped. The first warning bell went off in my head. I had sworn I would have no more to do with "arrested" alcoholics.

He took me to one of his favorite restaurants, was greeted graciously by the host who knew him as a regular, and then proceeded to suggest what I should order. I had on a white suit that evening and asked for a large napkin to use as a bib. He laughed at that, but seemed comfortable with that little bit of eccentricity. He was quite amusing and made it clear that I could have all the drinks I wanted. It did not affect him. I told him it was no problem as I rarely drank. I didn't enjoy drinking unless I was dancing and worked it off. "In fact," I told him, "dancing is my alcohol. I get just as much of a high dancing as I suppose some people get from drinking or exercising." The rest of the evening we talked about ourselves, and the evening went very rapidly. I told him more than I might have on a first date because a magazine article was going to appear on me in Maclean's and I thought I should warn him about my past before he read it all at once. He had a great sense of humor, and I also found out that he was used to the "good life." His wife came from a very wealthy family and everything had been provided for him. It was later that I found out what the problem was. Most of the money was hers, and when she died she evidently left the money tied up so that he could not spend it all at once. Only later could I surmise that from our conversations. After dinner we went back to the house. He prepared the coffee and we sat and talked for a while longer. He sat quite a bit apart from me and I thought he was making it very clear that this was to be only a friendship and one that did not involve lovemaking. I relaxed even more. It was a lovely evening, and I guess what I liked about it was the easy friendship, the comfort of having an intelligent, caring man about without the need of any emotional involvement. It is when I am most relaxed that I get most heavily involved.

Stan asked to see me again, and it turned out that we began seeing each other on Tuesdays. The routine was almost the same, a lovely dinner out, always a pot of fresh coffee and dessert, and home for more coffee and music. Then he started bringing specially cured slabs of bacon along with the coffee. I had never tasted bacon like that. I enjoyed these off-beat gifts, although I told him that my refrigerator and freezer were beginning to bulge with the coffee.

Then he started to come more often, and one evening, without warning, he said, "Let's go to bed for a giggle." I had never heard that expression, but assumed that it kept sex in a light vein. By this time we had begun sitting closer to each other on the couch, he had begun staying longer to talk, and we had begun to settle into a comfortable friendship. I wasn't sure it made sense to change our pattern, but I was attracted to him and was curious about his ability to restrain himself and felt fairly safe in the domestic scene we had created. It was an easy one, with no heavy demands. I never asked where he was the rest of the week, and he never asked about my day. It was just Stan and Lynne, or so I naively thought. So I led him into my bedroom, lighted the candles, and turned down the bed. We slipped into each other's arms, and for the first time I felt as if another man had moved into Steve's spot.

I was anxious because I really did not know Stan that well, and yet I was already dipping into what seemed like a serious relationship. I wasn't sure how it had happened. He was passionate at first, kissing me hungrily all over, touching me, moaning as he gave me pleasure. And when he tried to enter me, he was unable to sustain an erection. He collapsed in my arms, crying. I held him close, soothed him, and said it was nothing to worry about. He explained that he wanted me so much. We talked for hours after that. He told me that while he had always loved his wife, he had very little sex with her. In fact, he had never thought it was important. He told me that he also had diabetes and that might affect his performance. I explained, tenderly, that those problems could be sorted out, that there were many ways to make love, and that he was an excellent, loving, and satisfying man. For the next few weeks that seemed to calm him, and we spent more time seeing each other during the week. The weekends he spent the time in my home. He kept bringing the wonderful slabs of bacon, the specially blended coffee, and now English oatmeal. He made

338

breakfasts for me on the weekend and then we would go for long walks.

He told me that he was still cautious about any long-term involvement, and I readily agreed with him. I thought it was too soon after his wife's death, and I certainly had not yet stopped mourning for Steve. But I admitted that our ongoing relationship was satisfying and filled a deep need in me for tenderness, for touching. I used to tell Steve, when I was away too long on business, that I was "skin hungry." I needed touching and caressing almost more than actual intercourse. I thought my understanding of his problem would help Stan, but the more relaxed I was, the more intense he became about solidifying our relationship. I found myself ignoring a thousand warning signals. But again, being the understanding woman, I allowed him to make all the decisions. He began to tell me how much he wanted me. I never was strong enough to say, "Hey, wait a minute. I enjoyed the fantasy." He began to outline our future life together. He told me that because he was diabetic it was important for him to get plenty of rest, so he liked to go to bed about ten-thirty every night. He hated television. He was worried about the rays from the set, but I could stay up and watch it if I wished. He told me that he also liked to cook, and perhaps we could have more intimate dinners at home. Fine, anything he wanted. I watched myself in fascination, from a distance, as I fell back into role-playing the happy little woman. I knew it could not work. I knew our lifestyles were miles apart. I could not even understand why I was so acquiescent. Then he told me he knew I liked to travel, so he would plan a trip to Europe for the spring or early summer. At last, I thought, he is beginning to recognize my needs.

By this time, my women friends were dying to meet my new lover. I didn't want to introduce him as yet, because I knew in my heart of hearts that I was play-acting. Something didn't seem real about the whole affair. Where were all my stated principles that I would never compromise again, unless it was an equal compromise? Where were all my stated principles that I didn't want ever to be married again? I was even reluctant to have a man share my house. I still had so much to learn about this man. Then he told me that he had a lovely country place and he wanted me there. I could write my autobiography and he would see that nothing disturbed me on the weekends. He would cook for me and pamper me. Then we would go for long walks. That would be good for me.

Now he hit a nerve. He wanted to take care of me. John Henry was going to give me New York, my own city. Alfredo was going to protect me from my neglectful husband. Why didn't I remember that in all those cases I ended up being the protector, the one that handed over the city? What was so wrong with me that any sign of affection made me feel worthwhile? Does one never free oneself from those damaging relationships of childhood? When does that change? How many victories are necessary? How many rewarding friendships, how many assurances from loving children are required? Here I was melting because Stan was taking over and planning to direct my life, a life I was quite capable of directing, a life I wanted to direct, a life I was in complete charge of. How long before we exorcise the damaging old conditioning? A few weeks before I was to be his guest at his country farm, Stan began to talk about our moving in together. I felt the first strong waves of fear, of doubt. I questioned, "Why do you want to move in? I haven't ever seen your apartment. If we decide to live together maybe it makes more sense for us to share your condominium. Aren't you moving too fast? You said you didn't want to rush. Why don't we go along as we are and see if we can actually live together?"

Things began to change. Suddenly Stan was saying he needed some sort of closure. Perhaps we were moving too fast. Perhaps he couldn't handle his intense emotions. At the same time, I was aware that he wasn't bringing the coffee any more. He stopped bringing slabs of bacon. Were they signs he was breaking off the relationship? I couldn't understand why. It was comfortable. He had been pushing, not me. I tried to get him to talk honestly about his feelings. I felt that little hole of emptiness. It frightened me. Any potential loss frightened me. Why did I even get into a position where I could feel loss, pain?

We were still planning to go away for the weekend to his country home. He was telling me what he wanted, not what I needed. I took up reams of paper to start my book. I took up extra clothes to leave. I refused to recognize the fact that the coffee had stopped coming. In fact, all I had left were a few coffee beans in a large jar. It looked sad. We drove up to the farm. I was shocked at his quarters. They were very austere, not palatial as he had described. Two bedrooms, a small living room, and a den. He seemed to be detached. We went out for dinner and came back and lay down in front of the fire and talked for hours. He kept telling me that he cared too much, that he couldn't handle his emotions. I didn't understand. We spent our night apart, in separate bedrooms. He slept in the one his wife had used; I was in his special, private bedroom.

The next day he recounted the wonderful days of the war. He showed me his library all about the war. He told me that after the war was over he stayed on another year after volunteering for cleanup duty and partying. It was as if his best memories were of that period. I told him if I were his wife I would have come to Europe and dragged him back. I began to wonder about his ability to love a woman. That night he dug up some cedar trees for my front yard. When we arrived home, he kissed me and said he would call me after he got out of the hospital. He had to go for a minor operation that he hoped would help his sex life. He asked me not to visit because his family might be coming up, and he didn't want me to see him in the hospital. Then I didn't hear from him for two weeks.

I looked at the near-empty bottle of coffee beans. I knew our love affair was over. What I didn't understand was why it had ever begun. Logically or not, I was very hurt. Finally, he was due out of the hospital and I called him at home. I asked him to come down and see me for the last time. I was so angry at him. For years I had suppressed my anger at men but I needed to let him know how I felt. I focused my animosity on him. He came and I locked my outside gate. I have a large iron gate across my front door that I lock from the inside. No one can get out unless they have the key. Some men who visit me get very nervous when I lock that gate. It seems to take all their power away from them, their authority. I watched as Stan looked at me locking the gate. I knew I wanted to say things to him, and I didn't want him walking out on me. It was delicious revenge. I had never wanted revenge before, but his words over the last few months kept turning over in my mind, his laying down of the rules of our life, his plans for the future, my passive acceptance, and his brutal withdrawal. I then spent the next hour telling him what I thought of his method of seducing me, of promises, of pressure, and of his instant withdrawal when I didn't agree to his demands to move in. I felt used, as if he was looking for a woman to care for him. Intellectually I knew that I had allowed the situation to get out of hand, but most of all I resented the fact that he wouldn't even discuss our problems on the telephone when I first called for an explanation. I told him what I thought of his relationship with his wife, his fear of commitment, and his abuse of women. At one point he said, "I don't have to listen to this." I sat back and said, "Of course not, just leave." He stood up, realized he couldn't open the door, and sat down. Finally I had said everything I wanted to say, and I asked him to leave. He reached over to kiss me good-bye and apologized for his weakness.

After he left I sat down, feeling very relieved. Poor man, he had been the object of years of my repressed anger, anger directed at myself. It was the first time I had coldly and calculatingly blamed someone else without being told I was overreacting. My outburst made it easier for me to forget that period with Stan, and I vowed I would stop allowing myself to get in those situations again, but I had a great deal of work to do in that area.

Over the years, I was particularly grateful to one man in my life . . . who although married found time to be my constant adviser and friend. While there was no doubt that we would have liked to consummate our relationship in bed, our friendship meant more. But we met regularly at Fenton's restaurant to sit before the fire, eat leisurely, drink a few glasses of wine, and talk about everything from business to politics to love. Other times we found a secluded table at Sanssouci in Sutton Place. Sometimes we indulged ourselves by going to a late afternoon movie, feeling like teen-agers on a date. His warmth and attention helped me realize the value of male friendships.

It's hard for some feminists to understand that we do backslide, we do play games, we do forget. There were so many unanswered questions about my personal life and my relationships with men. For instance, I worried that perhaps I left my first marriage simply because I could not live with a "good man," so used was I to a violent relationship with my mother. Perhaps that was the only measurement I had for love. I worried because I still had not been able to get John Henry out of my system. I still wanted to justify myself to him, defend myself. I was still trying to get his approval, just as I had tried for years to get my mother's approval. John Henry treated me exactly as my mother had treated me. I wondered why I didn't marry Paddy Chayefsky, a good man who had the promise of becoming a great and disciplined writer even when we were going together. I wondered at how I allowed myself to get embroiled with Alfredo Castaneda. Certainly this last debacle with a man I hardly cared about made me wonder what work I still had to do in that area. I decided to go back into my past to understand some of the things I never had time to work out. I would see all those men again.

CHAPTER 30

FULL CIRCLE

O ver the years I have struggled to integrate my personal life with my creative and work life. For so many years I felt schizophrenic. I did not understand why I could be so clear-eyed about my professional goals yet entertain such a low image of myself personally. When I started to write my memoirs, it was almost as if the book had a life of its own. It kept revealing new secrets to me, secrets that I imagine many women and perhaps many men keep suppressed about themselves. I had to examine my life, my excesses as well as any contributions I had made. I didn't want to hide anything, not because I thought that every incident was vital, but because people tend to hide experiences they feel ashamed of, or that may seem self-serving. Women, in particular, do not live in a forgiving society when it comes to their excesses, so the tendency is to deny the extremes.

We do not grow in one straight line. Even as we learn about ourselves, we slip back, we hurt, we become children. But what matters most is that we go forward. Writing the book intensified each period of my life and held it up to the harsh light of reality. Many women in their thirties came to the women's movement without suffering the long-term conditioning that women of my age went through. They had less patience with mistakes, less patience with themselves. Some had no experience with other political movements, but embraced the women's movement uncritically without an historical perspective. Once they accepted the rhetoric intellectually, they found it difficult to understand those women who still hadn't learned to handle relationships with male partners. I had the advantage of entering the women's movement much later in life, after I had been through so many battles. I now had a greater appreciation for tolerance.

I found that many young women, as well as older ones, were interested in my past, how I survived, and how I used this new knowledge to carve out a future for myself. Going back into my past was a necessity for me. I had to put into perspective the important men in my life and understand how they had shaped my future. I know that experience yields self-knowledge. I decided to visit each man in turn on that search.

Over the years I had thought so much about my first husband, Buddy Grabois, that I needed to meet him again, to go back in time. The only excuse I had for calling him up after thirty years was my book. I could tell him that I was writing the chapter that dealt with our marriage and that he was very much in my thoughts. I had no idea whether he would even see me. After all, I had left him, and although I had done it as gently as I knew how, I had made him miserable at the time. I looked up his office number in the Manhattan telephone directory, and then, feeling slightly anxious and short of breath, I dialed his telephone number. I said to the person answering, "May I please speak to Mr. Bernard Grabois." The woman's voice answered, "Just a moment, please." She didn't ask for my name. There was a short pause and then a male voice, "Mr. Grabois here." I was shocked at how quickly he had come to the phone, and I rushed, afraid he might hang up. "Hello, Buddy . . . this is Lynne." Then I started to rattle off all my names. "This is Lynne Levinson, Smith, Grabois, Faulk . . . " By that time, I could sense his bewilderment as he repeated, "Lynne Levinson, Smith, Grabois," and as he came to his name, he said, "Wait a minute. Lynne, it's you! What are you doing in New York?" I told him I was in town for a few days and I was doing some research for a book I was writing. I was still confused about what had happened to our marriage. I added, "Buddy, if you have time, I'd love to see you." He replied, "What do you mean, if I have time. I'll make time. Of course I'll see you!" He said he would like to take me to lunch and asked where he could pick me up. I suggested we meet in the lobby of the Plaza Hotel, where I was staying for the weekend.

I dressed very carefully, wondering if we would recognize each other. Would he remember me? Would I remember him? It was uncomfortable for a few minutes as I looked around the lobby, catching glances from different men, all of whom seemed to be waiting for someone. I paced for a few minutes, then turned abruptly toward the desk to see if a message had been left for me. And as I turned, my eyes met the eyes of a man standing there. Our eyes locked, and he smiled, "I knew the most beautiful woman here would be you." It was Buddy, almost as I had remembered him, but his face had been settled by time. He stood very straight, as always, but his bearing was almost rigid, repressed. My heart went out to him, and I reached impulsively for his hand, as I had done years ago when we were dating.

We went out to lunch, and we talked very cheerfully, very warmly about the past. I said, "Buddy, you were such a good human being. I always wondered, worried, about you. In fact, whenever I've been in trouble or miserable, I remembered your loving attention. At times my own children would ask me to call you up, suggesting that you might be a good father and that I should get in touch with you. I hope I didn't hurt you too much. I never understood why I left you."

He answered simply. "I know why you left me. You see, I always remember you as bubbly and warm, and I was so passive. I haven't done half the things I've heard you've done. I don't have any children, although I make up for it by becoming an uncle to all our friends' children and by donating time to the little leagues. Don't spend too much time on me in your book. Just say that I always loved you."

My heart stopped. I thought how generous of him to give me that gift of himself, to help me get rid of the confusion and guilt I felt over the years. I liked him so much and realized that he had played a very important part in my life. I will always remember our young love, and hope that other young people will make sure they are not pushed into marriage just because parents and friends think "it's time." I told him he was a wonderful man and he said, "Thank you for making me feel so good." I gave him my latest consumer book, wrote my address down, and we waved good-bye to each other. Just as in a slow-motion commercial, we watched each other go, promising that if we ever needed the other we would call.

I started thinking about the other men who had had an impact on my life. I heard that Paddy Chayefsky was in Toronto filming his movie *Network* at television studios at CFTO. Paddy Chayefsky, who had turned into one of the most successful and respected playwrights and screenwriters . . . Paddy who had warned me to stay away from John Henry . . . Paddy, the man who had wanted to marry me. I was a little reluctant to call him off the set, but I had no idea how to get in touch with him otherwise. I had a strong urge to see him again and discuss the times we shared together and to rehash those wonderful naive days when we were so involved in changing the world. I felt stupid, but I dialed the set at CFTO and asked to speak to him. I was surprised when he came to the phone. I started to introduce myself. "Paddy, I don't know if you'll remember me, but I was once married to John Henry Faulk, and before that we used to date. . . ." Without missing a beat he answered, laughing, "Of course, it's Tuesday, I'm in Toronto . . . it must be Lynne." It was as if we had never stopped seeing each other. We talked a little to bring things up to date. He gave me his number in New York and agreed we should get together. Sadly, the next time I called Paddy in New York he had just been rushed to the hospital and soon after he died, a tragic death for so young a man. So little has been known about Paddy's private life. He had lived very simply and seemed to keep his business and private lives quite separate. Now he was gone.

My next encounter with my past came when I was visiting Johanna in San Francisco. She was getting settled at Stanford, getting ready to take her Master's degree in education. One of the attractions at Stanford was that Alfredo Castaneda was a professor there and she admired his intellectual capacity. He had offered to help her get oriented and his home was hers until she found a place of her own. I was in the hotel room when he called to say he was waiting for her in the lobby. We spoke briefly, but pleasantly, for a few minutes.

I thanked him for extending his hospitality to Johanna, and we made some pretense at getting together for a drink in the future. Then he laughed, and added, "For tea, that is!" I had no desire to see Alfredo. My brief time with him was nightmare enough. I was mainly grateful to him for bringing us to Canada. Then I learned that he was involved in the same destructive behavior with his present wife, setting down rules about when her children could and could not spend time with her. Later he turned from drinking to drugs, then back to drinking again, and then he died.

I continued on my journey into the past, trying to codify my life, to put everything into place. How many people have a chance for a second look? The person I most wanted to see, and was the most troubled about, was John Henry. I had a great need to see him again, to try once more for his approval, to slay some of the dragons that still stalked me. He was able to keep my memories alive in direct proportion to the pain my children felt at his rejection. Part of the problem was that in spite of every effort they made to reach out, he still could not stop talking about our break-up and all the things I had done to him. I told my children not to defend me in his presence but to try and get him to deal with their personal and individual problems. I had tried over the years to reach John Henry and ask for some kind of truce, wishing to impress on him the importance to his children of his role as a father. Nothing I said appeased him; he seemed determined to keep up the battle. I began to believe that if he ever doubted for a minute his position, he would have to examine himself and crumble. His only protection after all his lies was to draw a wall around himself, an impenetrable wall which sadly kept him apart from his children.

An opportunity came for me to see John Henry, if I could arrange it. My daughter Evelyn was living in Austin, Texas. She had gone down a few years before to visit her father, the first specific request he had made to see her in years. She found her visit so painful she left his house after a few weeks. But once in Texas, she decided there were enough memories from our past to keep her in Austin. She also felt it was time to break some of the strong dependency ties she had with me. She felt the separation might do her good. She had made up her mind to enroll in the University of Texas and took a position as house mother for deaf and disturbed children. I was concerned about her decision to stay in Texas, afraid her proximity to John Henry would end up being painful. But she needed that time alone. By now she had been there a few years and asked me to visit. I thought it would be a good opportunity to visit, do a radio feature on Texas, and try to arrange to see John Henry.

I thought of a way to approach him. Recently, in the news, Ed Asner had complained that he had lost his television series because of supposed left-wing activities. He said he was being black-listed. I thought what better person is there to interview than

John Henry? He could talk about his own experience and philosophy and his fear that blacklisting could happen again. I reasoned that he would agree to see me if I appealed to his vanity. I could tell him, truthfully, that he was a legendary figure and that his opinions were valued. I had to convince him that I had no ulterior motive, that this was strictly a business proposition, a non-threatening meeting.

My children were upset, thinking I was putting myself in a position to be hurt again. I promised them that I would not raise any personal matters with their father, I would make no demands on him, I would not even try to straighten out some of our past, and I certainly would not talk about them and their feelings. "Then," they asked, "why are you doing this?" I tried to convince them that it was a last effort to meet him on neutral ground, that perhaps if he enjoyed the interview, saw me looking so well and together, he would stop badgering them about me. The children were skeptical, and I had to admit to myself that part of my hidden agenda was to encourage John Henry to see me as a successful and reasonable woman.

I called his sister, Mary Koock, to tell her I was coming down to do a story and was interested in seeing the family. Her voice was a little guarded as she warned me, "The whole family is visiting here right now." I picked up on her cue immediately and said, "Oh, is John Henry there? I would like to talk to him. I want to set up an interview with him." She turned and called, "John Henry, it's Lynne on the phone. She wants to talk to you." He came to the phone and said, "Why, hello, honey. Where are you?" For a minute I thought he had forgotten my name. I knew that he always used the appellation "honey" for woman friends, especially for women whose names he had forgotten. I told him I was in Canada but was planning to go to Texas. "I'm doing a story on Austin for my radio show and combining it with a reason to visit Evelyn. I would love to interview you while I'm there because you have so many stories to tell about Texas, what it was, and where it's going. You can give me an overview of the blacklisting situation, whether it's happening again as it did in the fifties. If you are happy with the idea, I'll be willing to provide you with some of the questions ahead of time, so you'll feel completely comfortable."

He accepted. "Well, that's just fine, honey. Write and tell me when you are coming and I'll arrange to be in town." I immediately wrote out my questions and sent them with my consumer book so he could check my credentials. He wrote back a formal letter in reply and set a date.

When I arrived in Texas, I was immediately escorted around to all the family. Parties and suppers had been set up to welcome me. It was wonderful seeing the family again and being so accepted.

After visiting with Evelyn and meeting her friends, I began to wonder if John Henry would change his mind at the last minute. I set up the interview at my hotel, the grand old Driskill, and I waited for him to show up. At the scheduled time, I heard him walking along the hall to my room. I opened the door and we looked at each other. We both felt awkward. I invited him in and sat him down at the table, where I had my recorder and questions waiting. I said, "Would you like to sit and talk a little, or shall we do the interview first? How is your time?" He said, "I'm all right for a couple of hours." I didn't want to be a hypocrite but I knew for John Henry to perform well, he needed constant approval. So I gave him just that. Usually I need no more than half an hour at the most for a good fifteen-minute interview. But I decided to let the tape run as long as necessary. He was not comfortable in front of a microphone when there was a time limit. He was best when he could ramble, play records, or perform on the lecture platform, where he could manage the time. At first John Henry would answer a question by saying formally, "Well, Miss Gordon . . . " I put a stop to that at once by framing the next question, "John Henry, do you remember when we were courting, just before we got married . . . ?" Then he knew it was a personal interview. I questioned him on topics dear and familiar to his heart, blacklisting, the environment, and big business. I asked him to perform his best monologues, and I let the tape run until I saw that he was tired. He didn't seem to want to stop. But since we had spoken for almost an hour, I told him I had enough for a series of shows.

He was so pleased with the interview he called Cactus Pryor and said, "Guess who I'm with? Little ol' Lynne. We just did a mighty fine interview. You ought to talk to the girl. She's dynamite." I said hello to Cactus and set up a time to meet him for lunch and also do an interview. Then John Henry began listing all the friends who would be good subjects for interviews. For me this was another step to freedom. I was able to observe John Henry without all the emotional trappings. I saw that he still was not

capable of saying that a wrong had been done me in the film *Fear on Trial.* He found it hard to discuss it at all, only making slight references to the fact that he wasn't speaking to the producers. I didn't ask why at the time because I was afraid to get into any kind of discussion with him that could break off the meeting.

I probably went to Texas with the fantasy that he would see me and say, "Darling, I'm so sorry for everything that's happened. Let's see if we can be friends for our children's sake." He didn't say anything like that at all, but I realized that I could have no expectations of him, and that my children were already dealing with their own feelings about their father. I hoped I could now accept my past and let go of my own anger.

In looking over my life, I know that I have had to deal with my deep-seated need for approval, my fears of abandonment, and my feelings of low self-esteem. Letting go of my anger also made me realize that I was strong enough to distance myself from destructive relationships. It was a lesson for me on how to be selective about partners and friendships, how to face the fact that some relationships never did work or never will work again. When I understood that I acquired the power to change old patterns.

The past cannot be changed and I have few regrets, for I lived every day fully. I'm more concerned about today—not yesterday, not tomorrow, but today. I have always been aware of the future, but I am reluctant to give up one day's experiences for its distant promises. I will not put my life on hold, because I have watched too many people put off living until they are retired, until they have more money, until they establish their businesses, or until their children are grown up. In many cases they have waited too long. Growing more aware over the years, I can even let go of some of the anger I felt at past personal injustices. Becoming stronger makes forgiving easier.

It's fortunate that my life paralleled the emergence of the women's movement. It has given me the leverage to fight for what concerns me. For me, survival isn't enough. Life is more—it is learning how to reach out and give love as well as to want it. It is balancing the need for love and work and the desire to help others. Life is learning how to depend on other people for support, both women and men.

I have a whole set of new decisions to make about my future. It's time to move on. I have new dreams. I need new challenges. I am ready to take new risks. Risk-taking never stops at any age if you are truly alive. I have to reassess my present career. Do I want to continue in full-time radio, a safe and secure and lucrative job? Do I want to explore even further the medium of television and produce my own TV shows? Do I want to spend more time traveling, as a journalist or as a consultant to a ministry of tourism or culture? Do I want to become more active in the political arena, in public life? Do I want to comment on political life as a humorist and satirist? And outside my work, is there room in my life for yet another "ongoing" relationship?

There are so many options to consider. I'm sure I will experience some anxiety, some depression, some panic before a decision is made. But I have less to fear because I now have a net . . . a safety net.